O-Parts HUNTER™

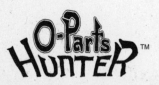

[redacted]

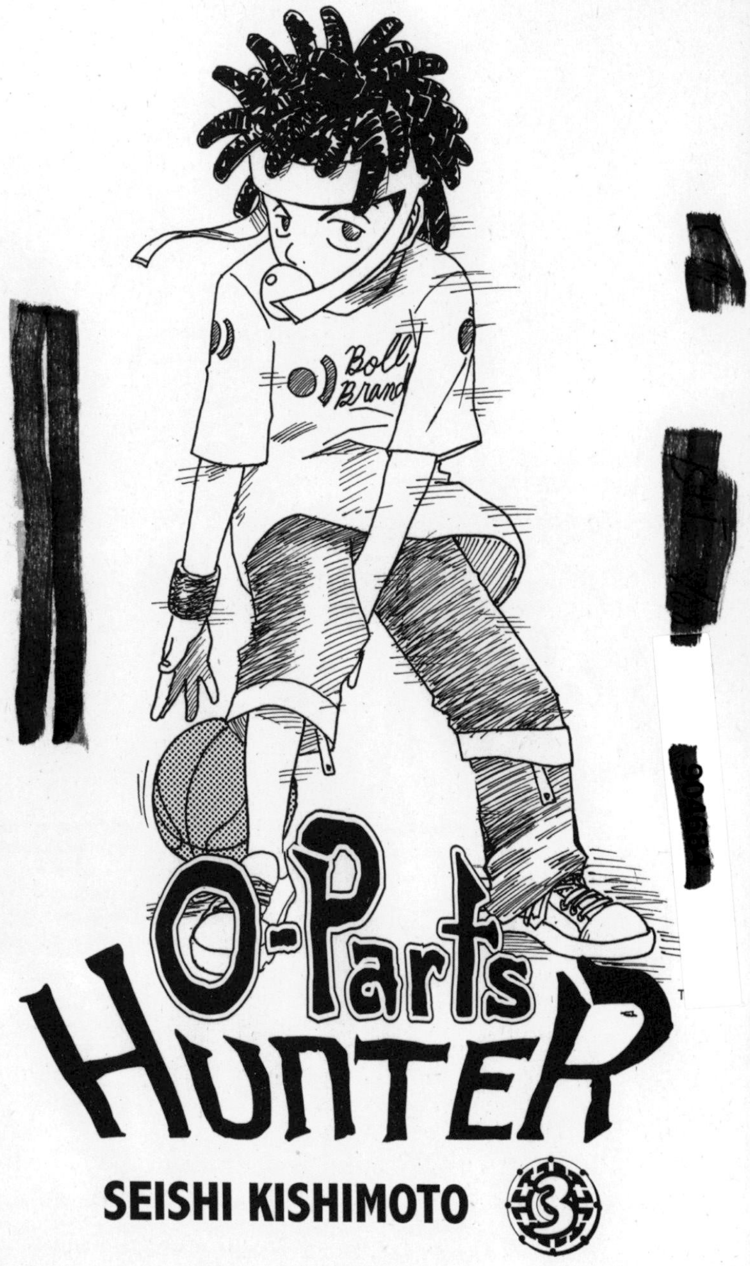
Boll Brand

O-Parts HUNTER

SEISHI KISHIMOTO

3

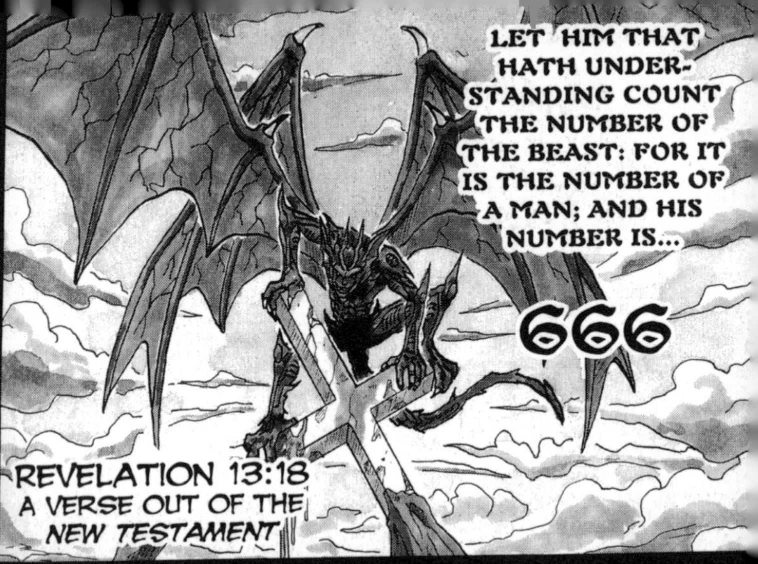
LET HIM THAT HATH UNDER-STANDING COUNT THE NUMBER OF THE BEAST: FOR IT IS THE NUMBER OF A MAN; AND HIS NUMBER IS...
666
REVELATION 13:18
A VERSE OUT OF THE *NEW TESTAMENT*

O-Parts Hunter

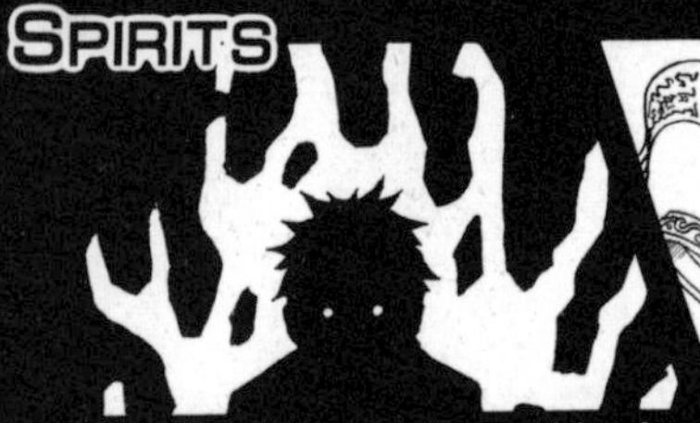
SPIRITS

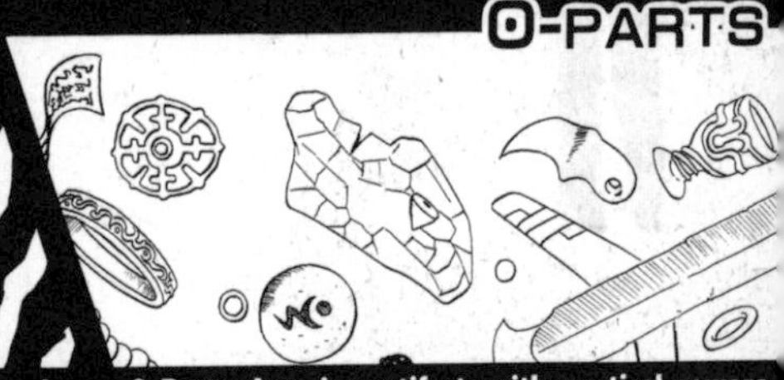
O-PARTS

Spirit: A special energy force which only the O.P.T.s have. The amount of Spirit an O.P.T. has within himself determines how strong of an O.P.T. he is.

O-Parts: Amazing artifacts with mystical powers left from an ancient civilization. They have been excavated from various ruins around the world. Depending on its Effect, O-Parts are given a rank from E to SS within a seven-tiered system.

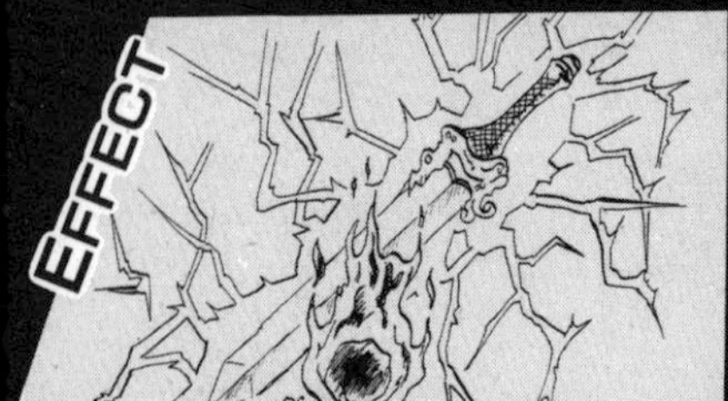
EFFECT

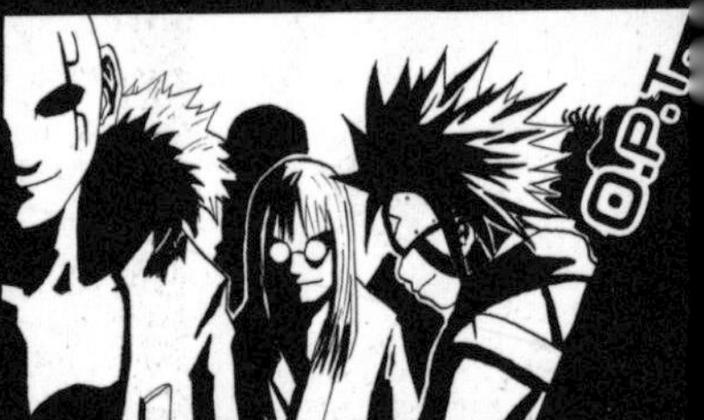
O.P.T.

Effect: The special energy (power) the O-Parts possess. It can only be used when an O.P.T. sends his Spirit into an O-Part.

O.P.T.: Those who have the ability to release and use the powers of the O-Parts. The name O.P.T. is an abbreviated form of O-Part Tactician.

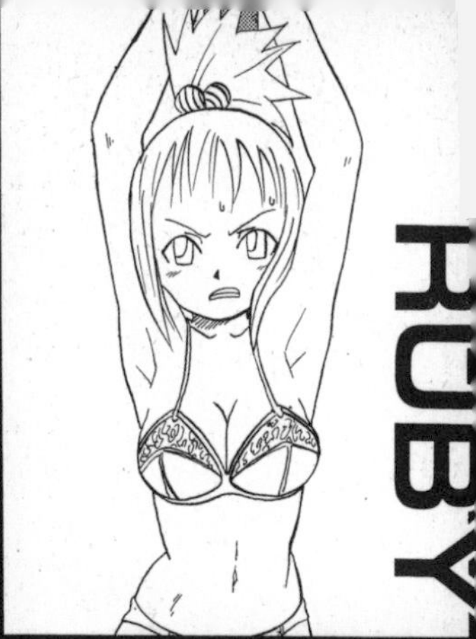
RUBY

Ruby
A treasure hunter who can decipher ancient texts. She meets Jio during her search for a legendary O-Part.

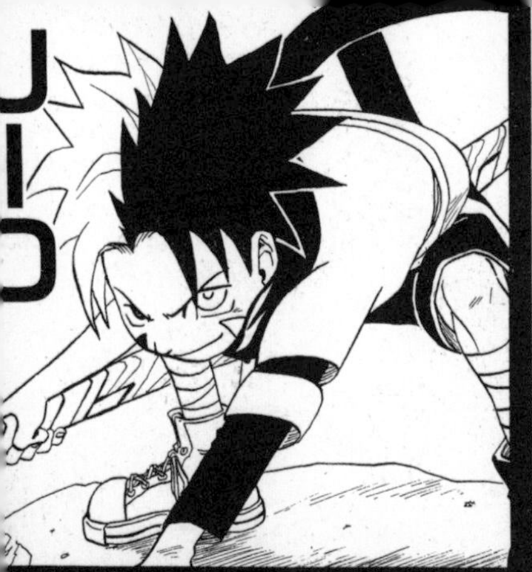
JIO

ïio Freed
wild O.P.T. boy whose dream is world lomination! He has been emotionally damaged rom his experiences in the past, but is still gung-ho about his new adventures! O-Part: Zero-shiki Rank C) Effect: Double (Increasing Power)

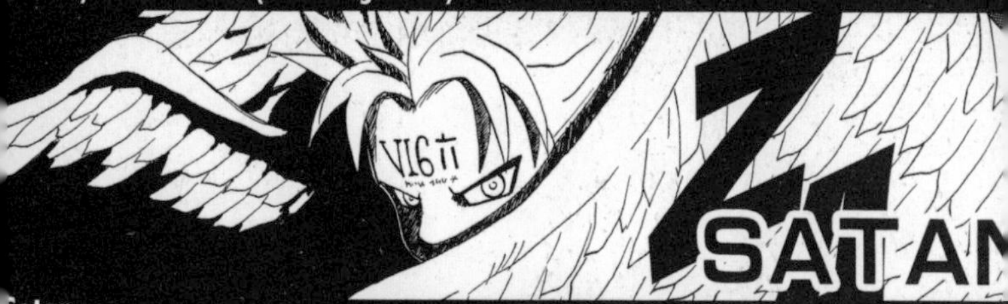
SATAN

Satan
This demon is thought to be a mutated form of Jio. It is a creature shrouded in mystery with earth-shattering powers.

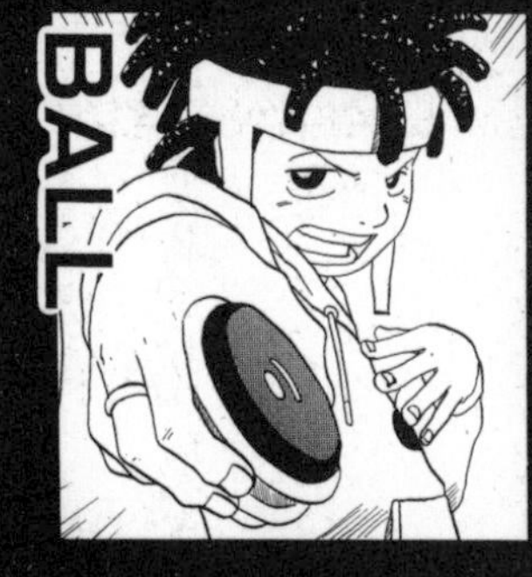
BALL

Ball
A young member of the resistance movement in Entotsu City. He is a happy-go-lucky kid who yearns to become an O.P.T.

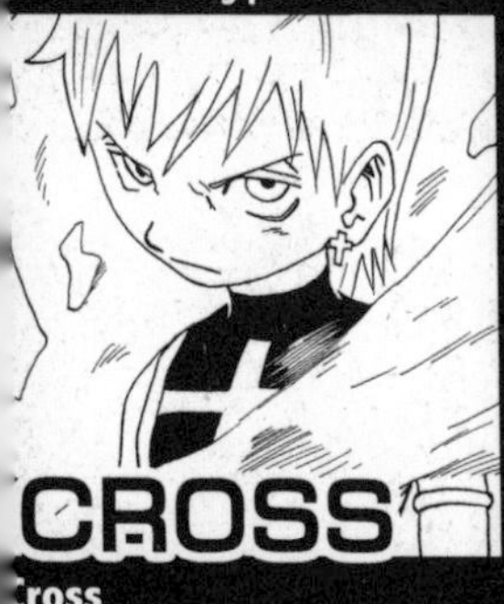
CROSS

Cross
An O.P.T. boy who worships God and is also the Commander in Chief of the Stea Government's flying fortress. His aim is to find Satan and bring it to justice. O-Part: Justice (Rank C)

O-Parts Hunter™

3

Table of Contents

Chapter 9: The Crimson Magician......7

Chapter 10: Escape!!......43

Chapter 11: The Powers of the
                      Ancient Civilization.......79

Chapter 12: The Three Ordeals.......115

Chapter 13: Kirin?!......151

CHAPTER 9: THE CRIMSON MAGICIAN

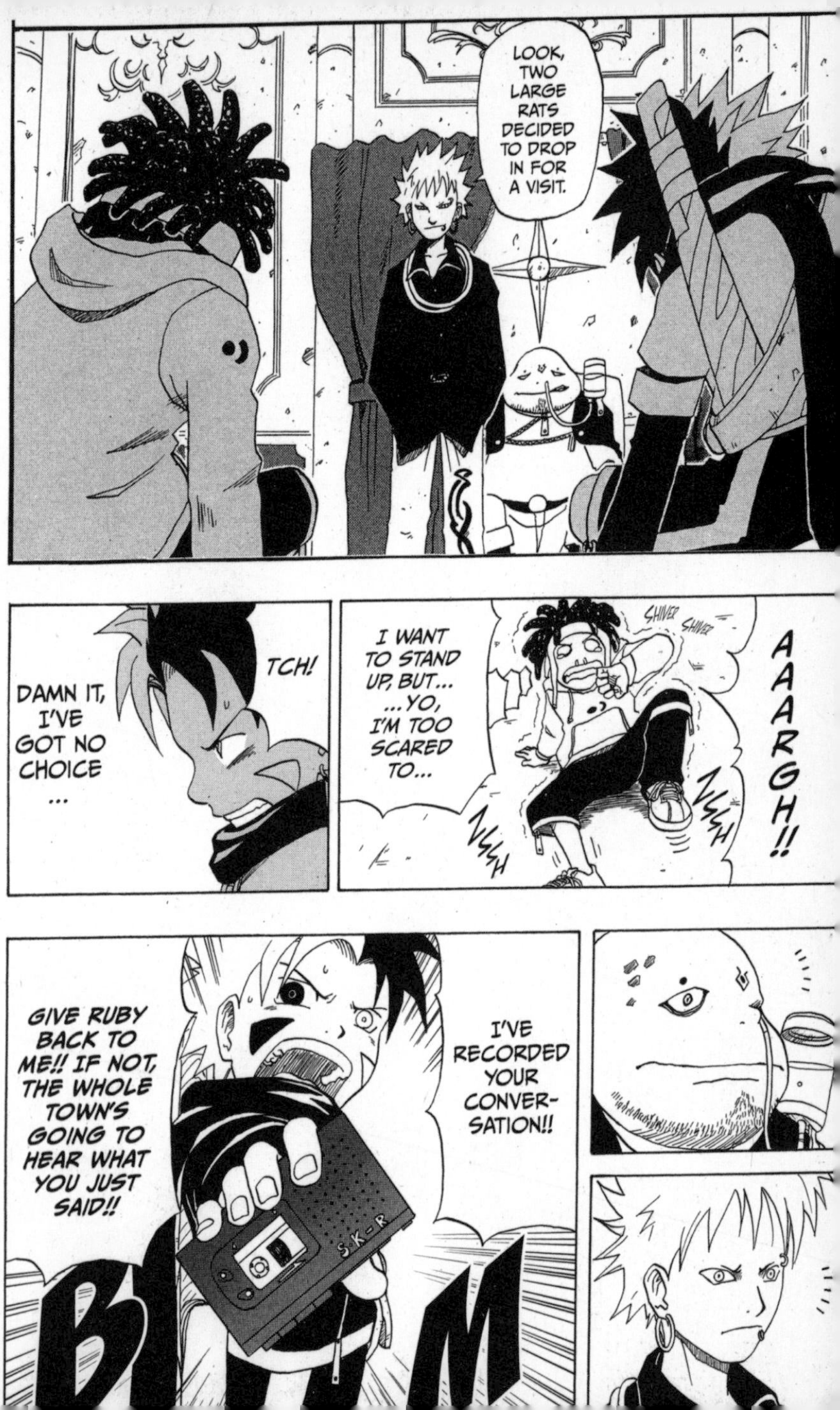
LOOK, TWO LARGE RATS DECIDED TO DROP IN FOR A VISIT.
SHIVER SHIVER
AAAARGH!!
I WANT TO STAND UP, BUT... ...YO, I'M TOO SCARED TO...
TCH!
DAMN IT, I'VE GOT NO CHOICE ...
I'VE RECORDED YOUR CONVER-SATION!!
GIVE RUBY BACK TO ME!! IF NOT, THE WHOLE TOWN'S GOING TO HEAR WHAT YOU JUST SAID!!
S-K-R

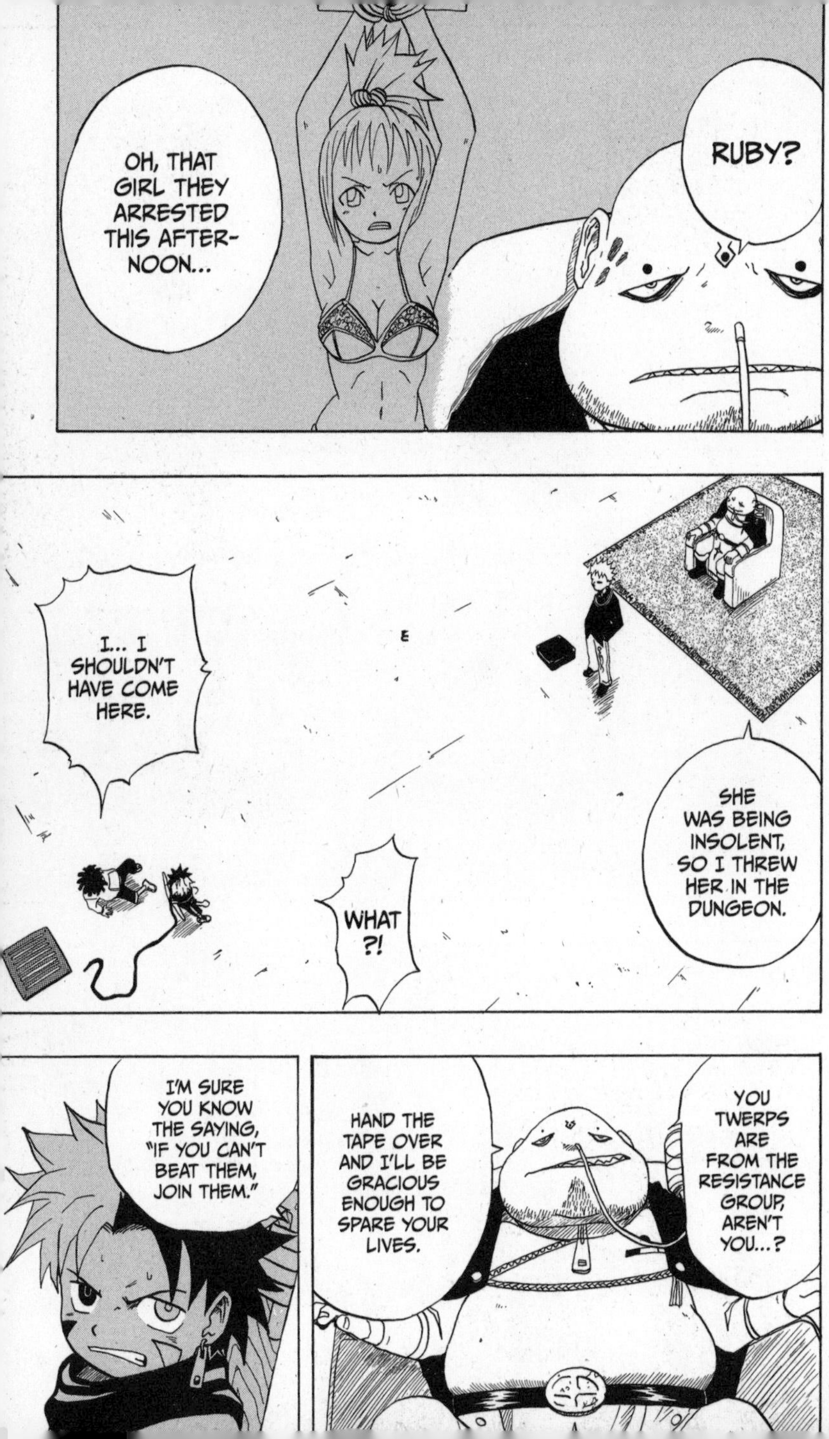
RUBY?
OH, THAT GIRL THEY ARRESTED THIS AFTER-NOON...
SHE WAS BEING INSOLENT, SO I THREW HER IN THE DUNGEON.
WHAT?!
I... I SHOULDN'T HAVE COME HERE.
YOU TWERPS ARE FROM THE RESISTANCE GROUP, AREN'T YOU...?
HAND THE TAPE OVER AND I'LL BE GRACIOUS ENOUGH TO SPARE YOUR LIVES.
I'M SURE YOU KNOW THE SAYING, "IF YOU CAN'T BEAT THEM, JOIN THEM."

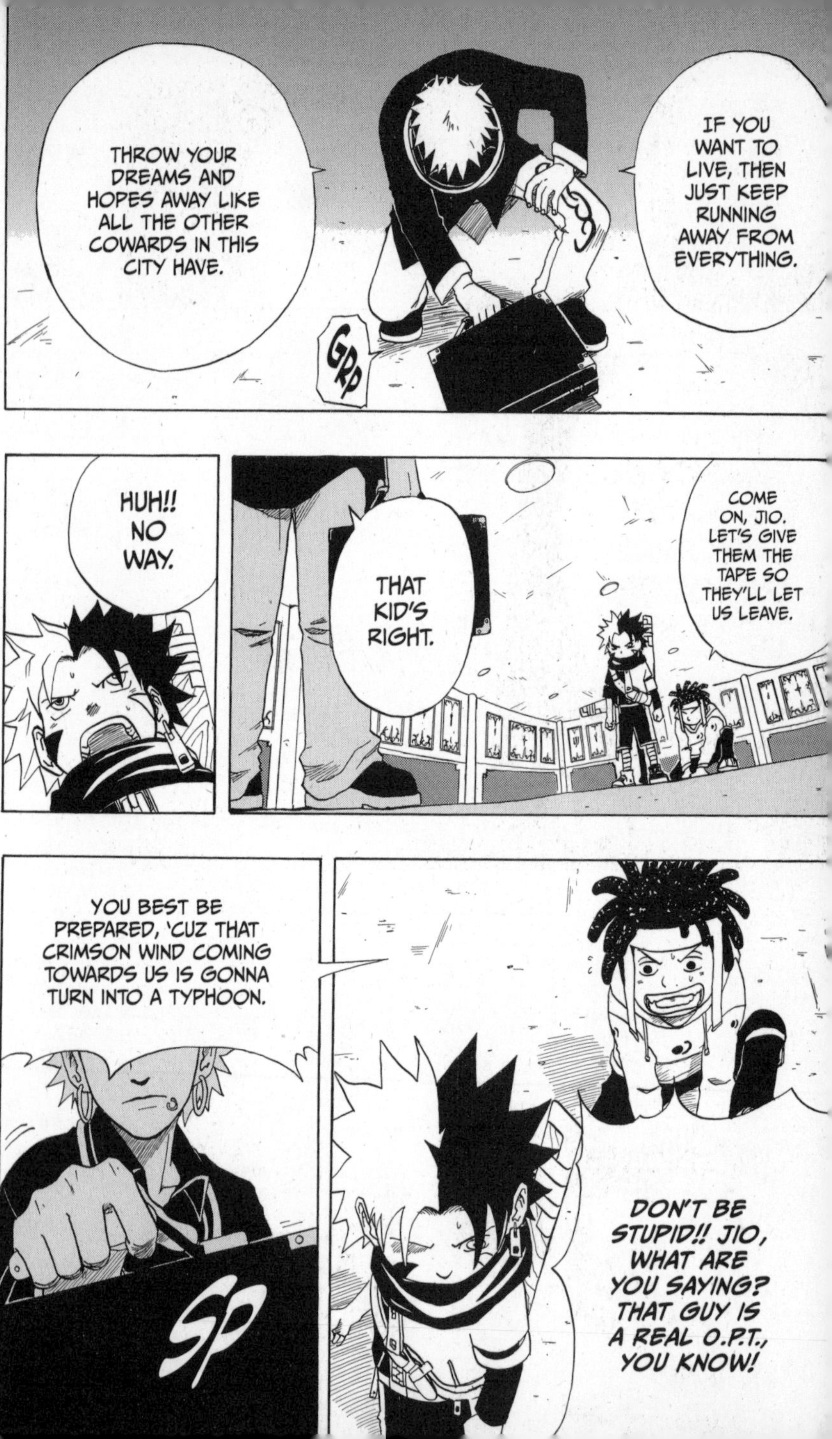
IF YOU WANT TO LIVE, THEN JUST KEEP RUNNING AWAY FROM EVERYTHING.
THROW YOUR DREAMS AND HOPES AWAY LIKE ALL THE OTHER COWARDS IN THIS CITY HAVE.
GRP
COME ON, JIO. LET'S GIVE THEM THE TAPE SO THEY'LL LET US LEAVE.
THAT KID'S RIGHT.
HUH!! NO WAY.
DON'T BE STUPID!! JIO, WHAT ARE YOU SAYING? THAT GUY IS A REAL O.P.T., YOU KNOW!
YOU BEST BE PREPARED, 'CUZ THAT CRIMSON WIND COMING TOWARDS US IS GONNA TURN INTO A TYPHOON.
SP

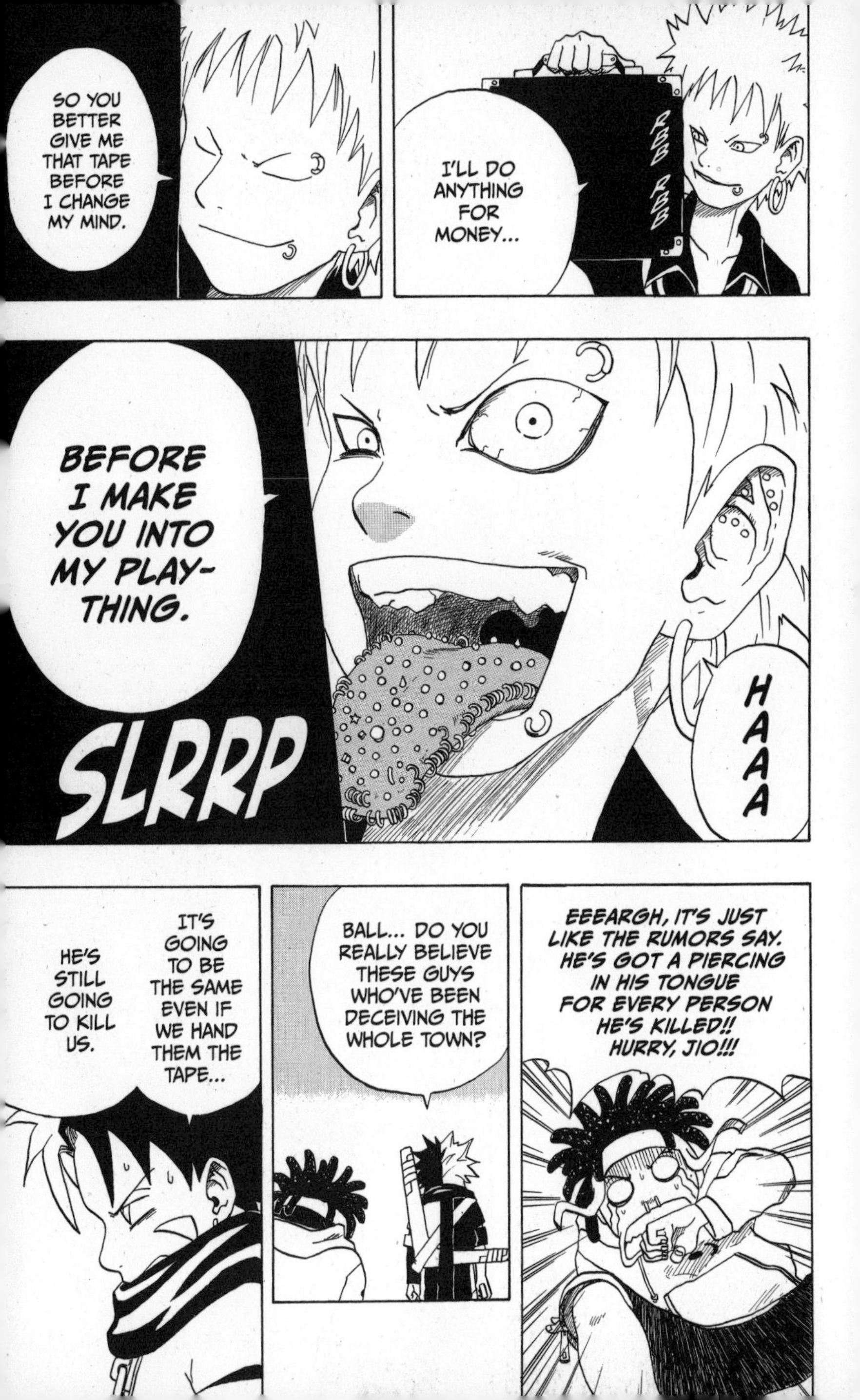
RBB RBB
I'LL DO ANYTHING FOR MONEY...
SO YOU BETTER GIVE ME THAT TAPE BEFORE I CHANGE MY MIND.
BEFORE I MAKE YOU INTO MY PLAY-THING.
HAAAA
SLRRP
EEEARGH, IT'S JUST LIKE THE RUMORS SAY. HE'S GOT A PIERCING IN HIS TONGUE FOR EVERY PERSON HE'S KILLED!! HURRY, JIO!!!
BALL... DO YOU REALLY BELIEVE THESE GUYS WHO'VE BEEN DECEIVING THE WHOLE TOWN?
IT'S GOING TO BE THE SAME EVEN IF WE HAND THEM THE TAPE...
HE'S STILL GOING TO KILL US.

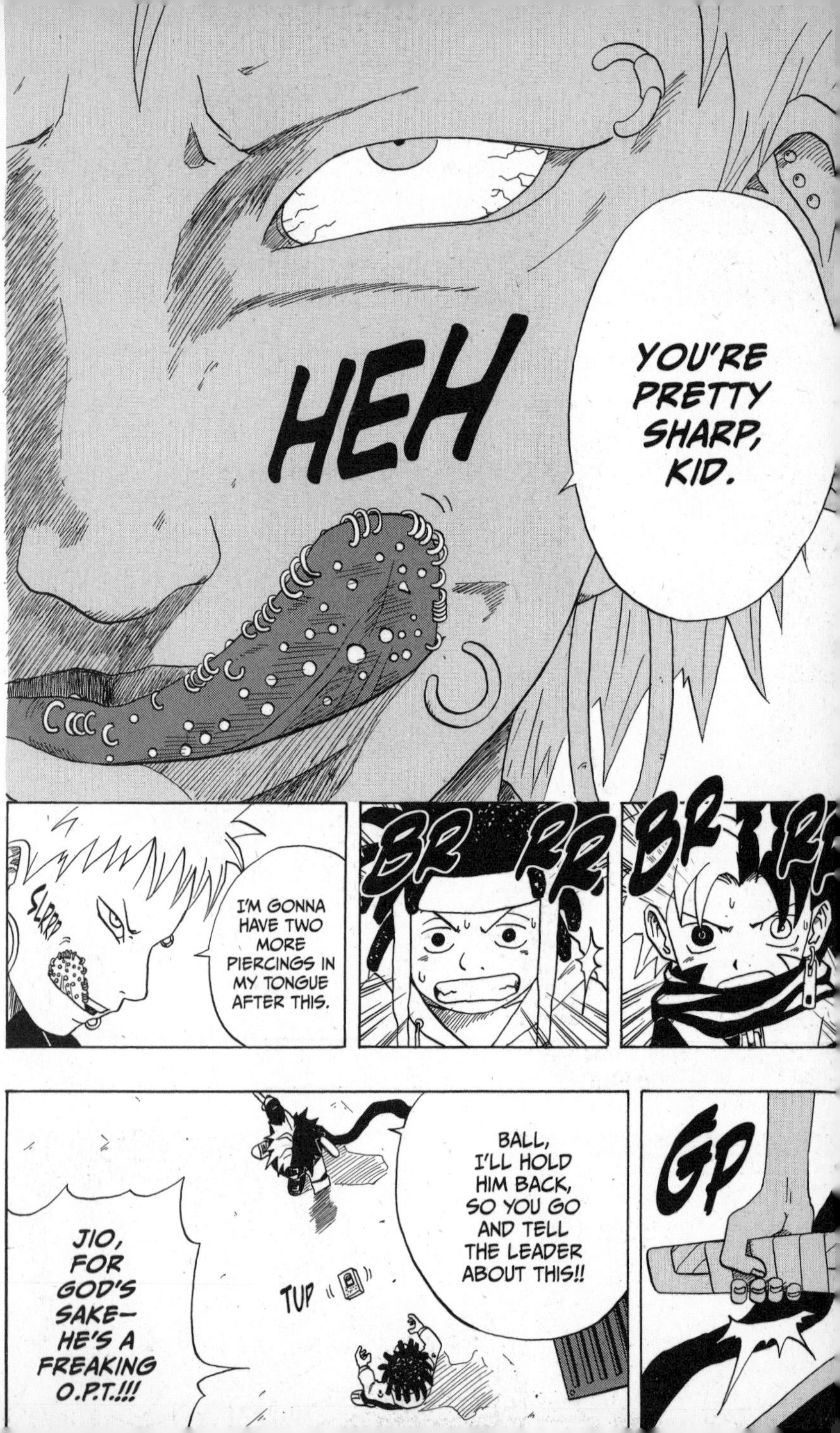
YOU'RE PRETTY SHARP, KID.
HEH
BR
BR
RR
SLRRP
I'M GONNA HAVE TWO MORE PIERCINGS IN MY TONGUE AFTER THIS.
GP
BALL, I'LL HOLD HIM BACK, SO YOU GO AND TELL THE LEADER ABOUT THIS!!
TUP
JIO, FOR GOD'S SAKE— HE'S A FREAKING O.P.T.!!!

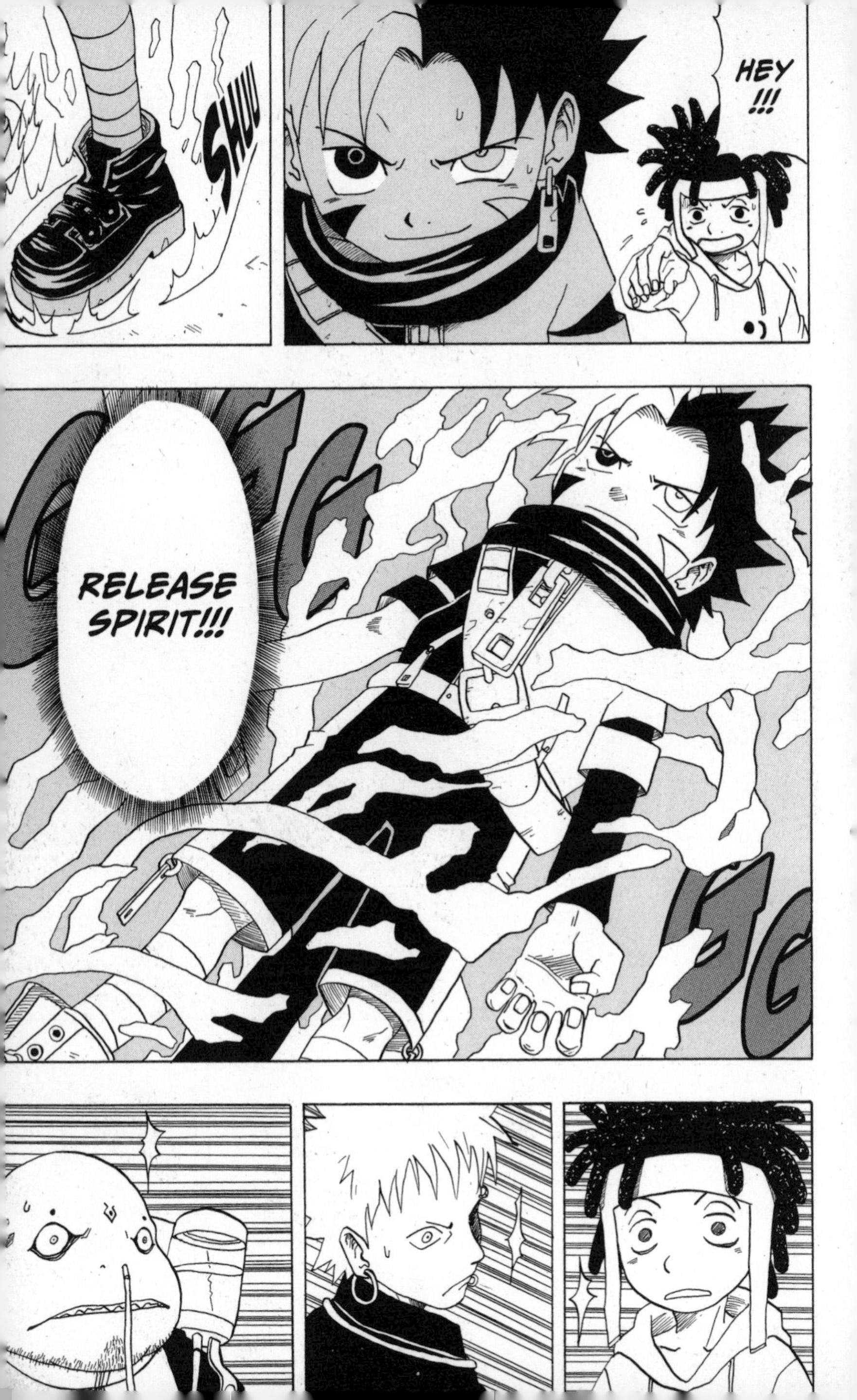
HEY !!!
SHUU
RELEASE SPIRIT!!!

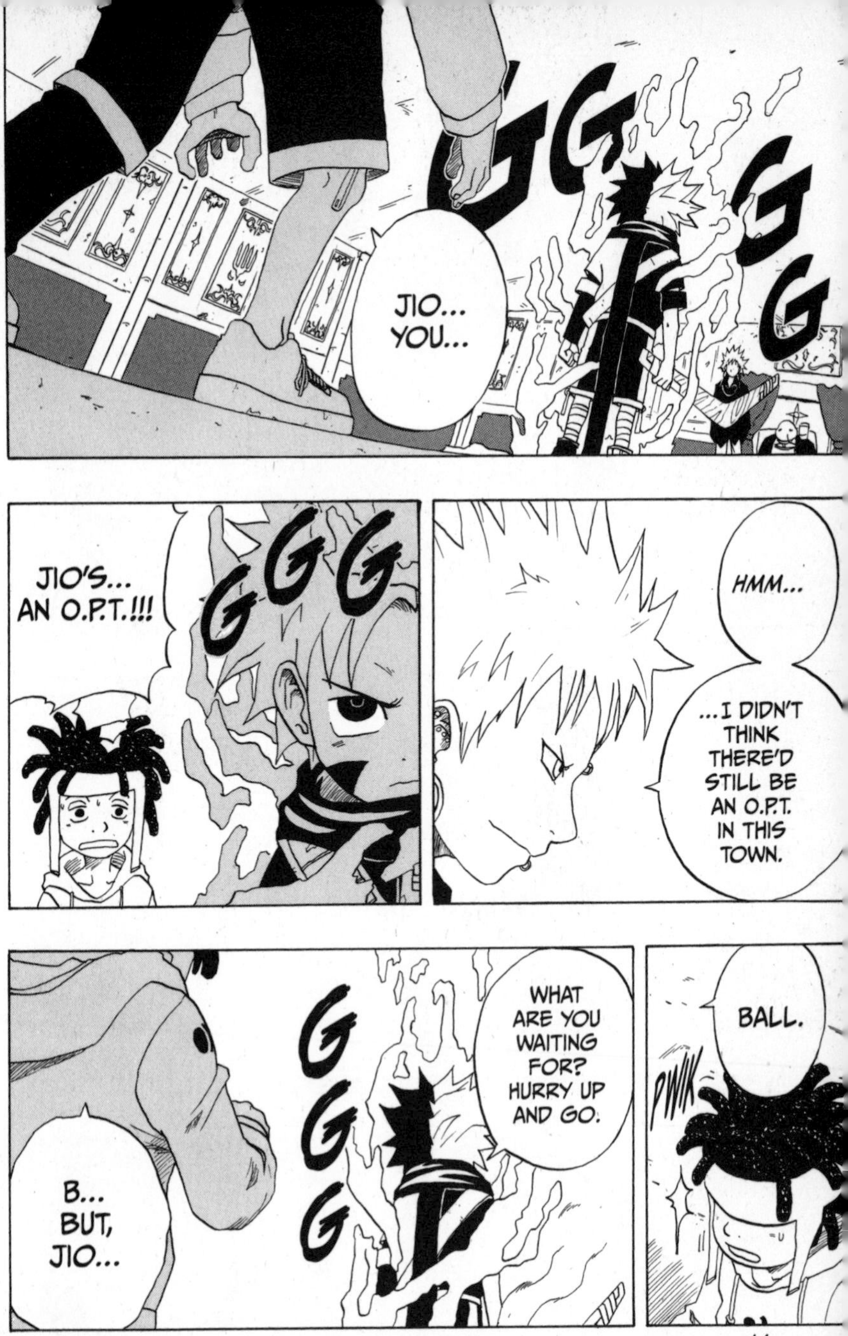
GGGGG
JIO... YOU...
HMM...
...I DIDN'T THINK THERE'D STILL BE AN O.P.T. IN THIS TOWN.
GGG
JIO'S... AN O.P.T.!!!
BALL.
PWIK
WHAT ARE YOU WAITING FOR? HURRY UP AND GO.
GGG
B... BUT, JIO...

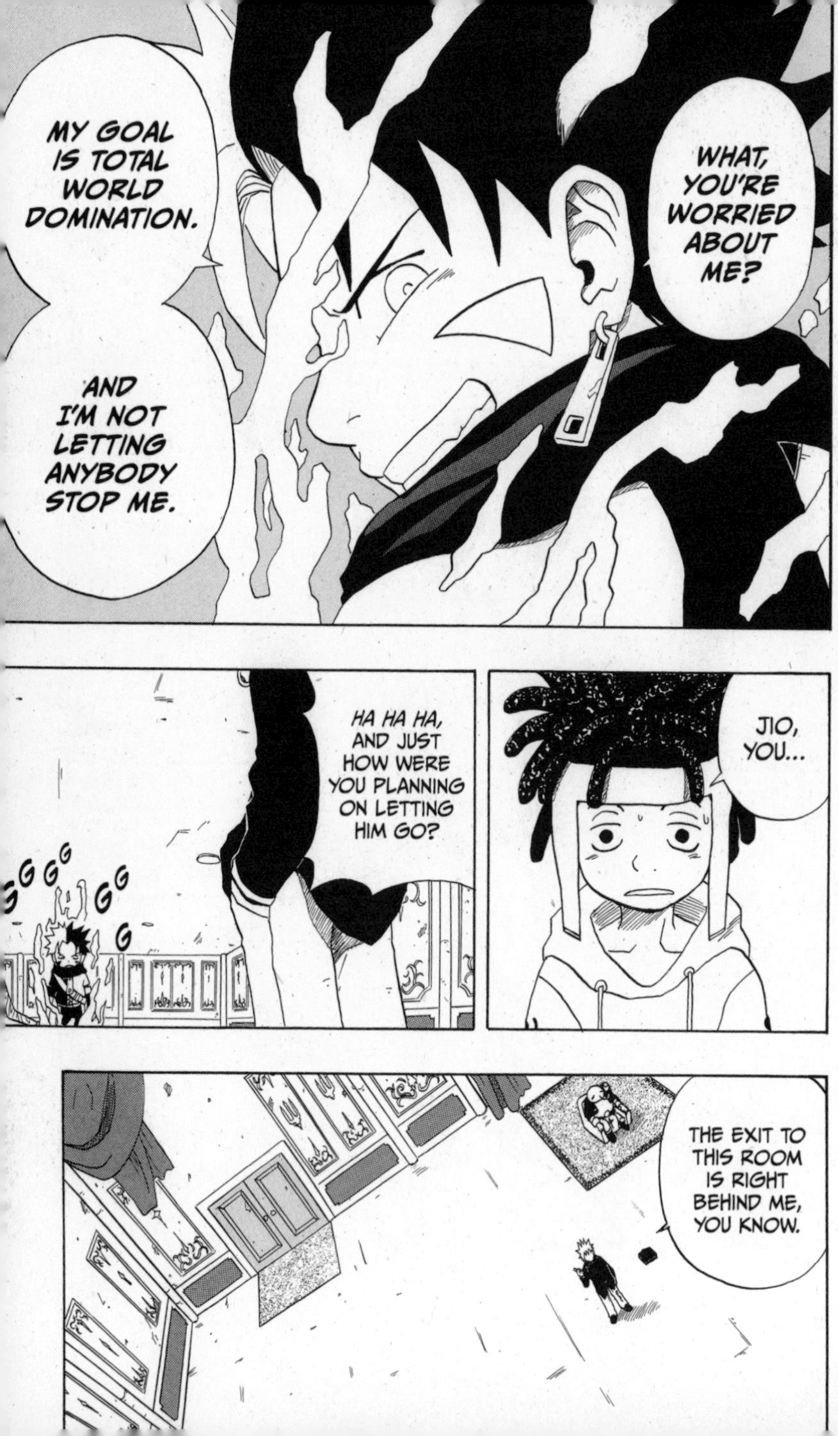
WHAT, YOU'RE WORRIED ABOUT ME?
MY GOAL IS TOTAL WORLD DOMINATION.
AND I'M NOT LETTING ANYBODY STOP ME.
JIO, YOU...
HA HA HA, AND JUST HOW WERE YOU PLANNING ON LETTING HIM GO?
THE EXIT TO THIS ROOM IS RIGHT BEHIND ME, YOU KNOW.

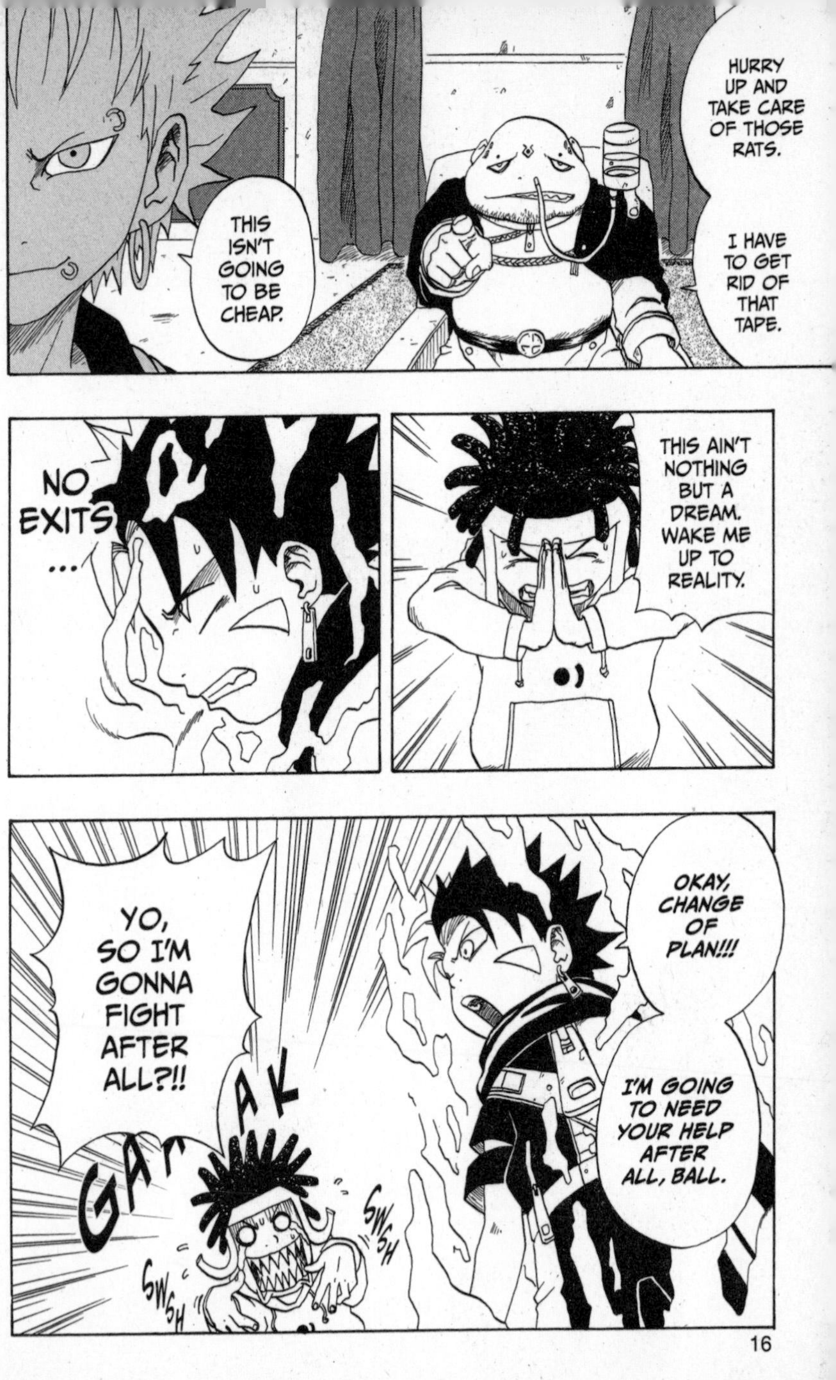
HURRY UP AND TAKE CARE OF THOSE RATS.
I HAVE TO GET RID OF THAT TAPE.
THIS ISN'T GOING TO BE CHEAP.
THIS AIN'T NOTHING BUT A DREAM. WAKE ME UP TO REALITY.
NO EXITS ...
OKAY, CHANGE OF PLAN!!!
I'M GOING TO NEED YOUR HELP AFTER ALL, BALL.
YO, SO I'M GONNA FIGHT AFTER ALL?!!
SWSH
SWSH

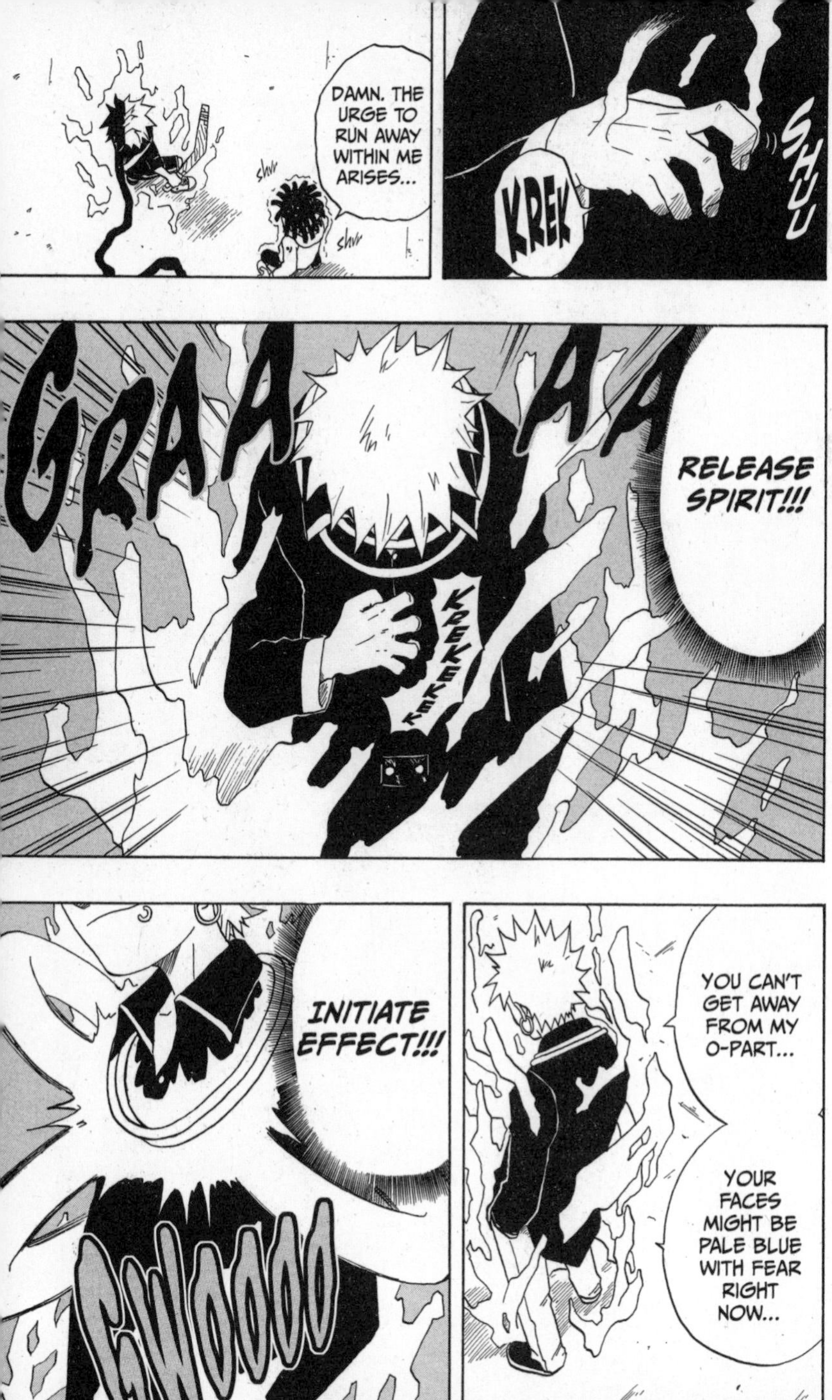
SHUU
KREK
DAMN. THE URGE TO RUN AWAY WITHIN ME ARISES...
shvr
shvr
GRAAAAA
RELEASE SPIRIT!!!
KREKEKEKEK
YOU CAN'T GET AWAY FROM MY O-PART...
YOUR FACES MIGHT BE PALE BLUE WITH FEAR RIGHT NOW...
INITIATE EFFECT!!!
GWOOOO

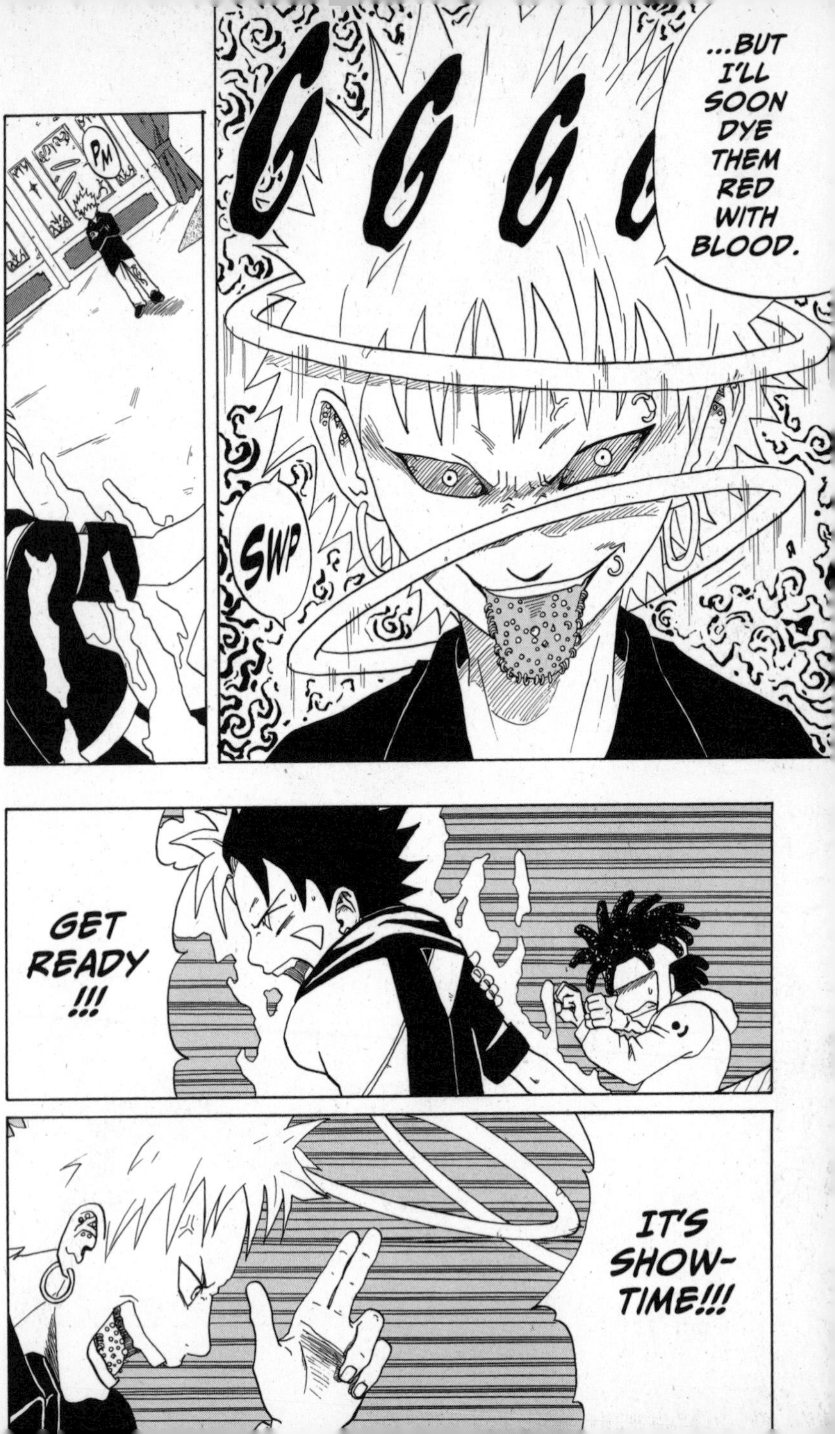
...BUT I'LL SOON DYE THEM RED WITH BLOOD.
GGGG
SWP
PM
GET READY!!!
IT'S SHOW-TIME!!!

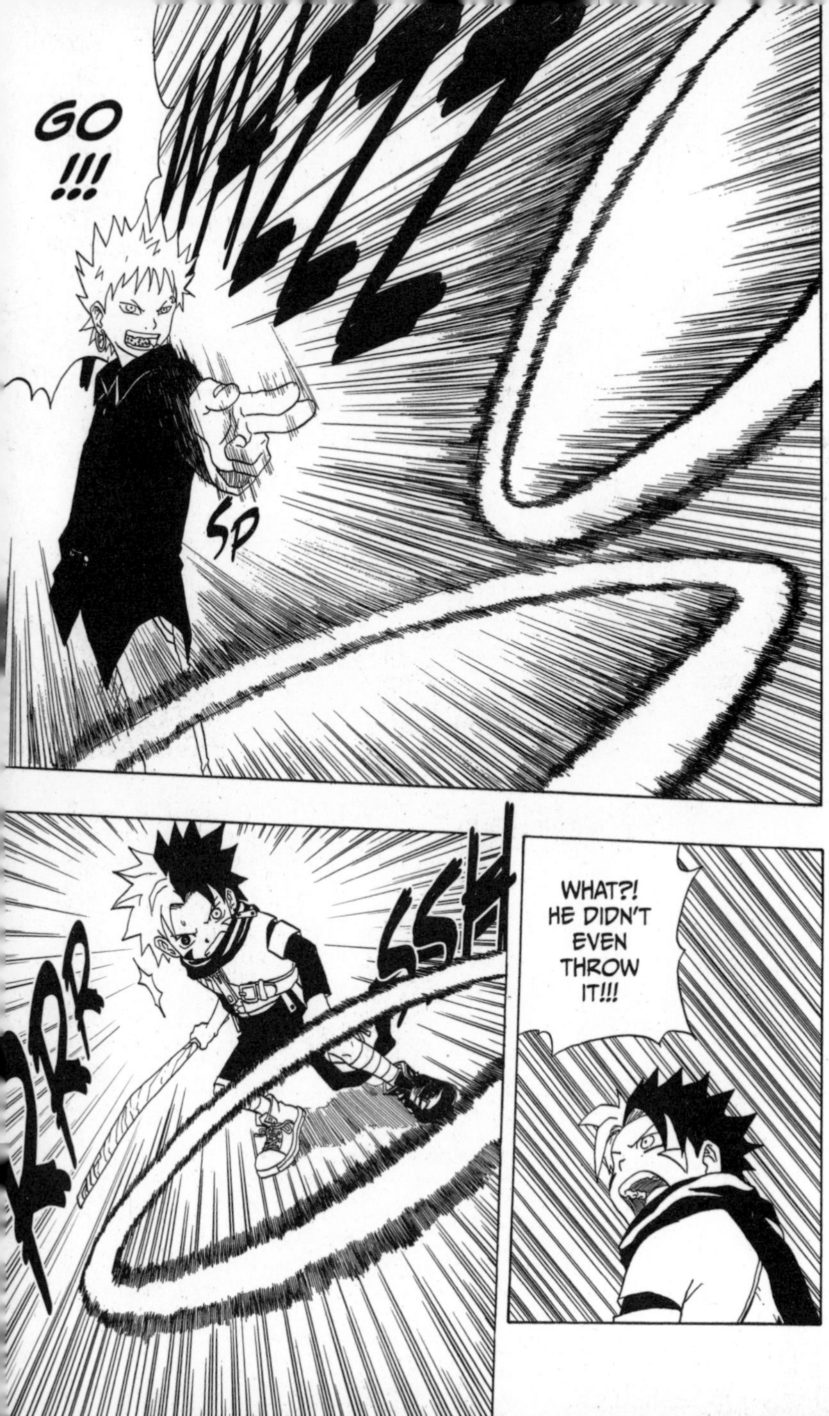
GO!!!
SP
WHAT?! HE DIDN'T EVEN THROW IT!!!

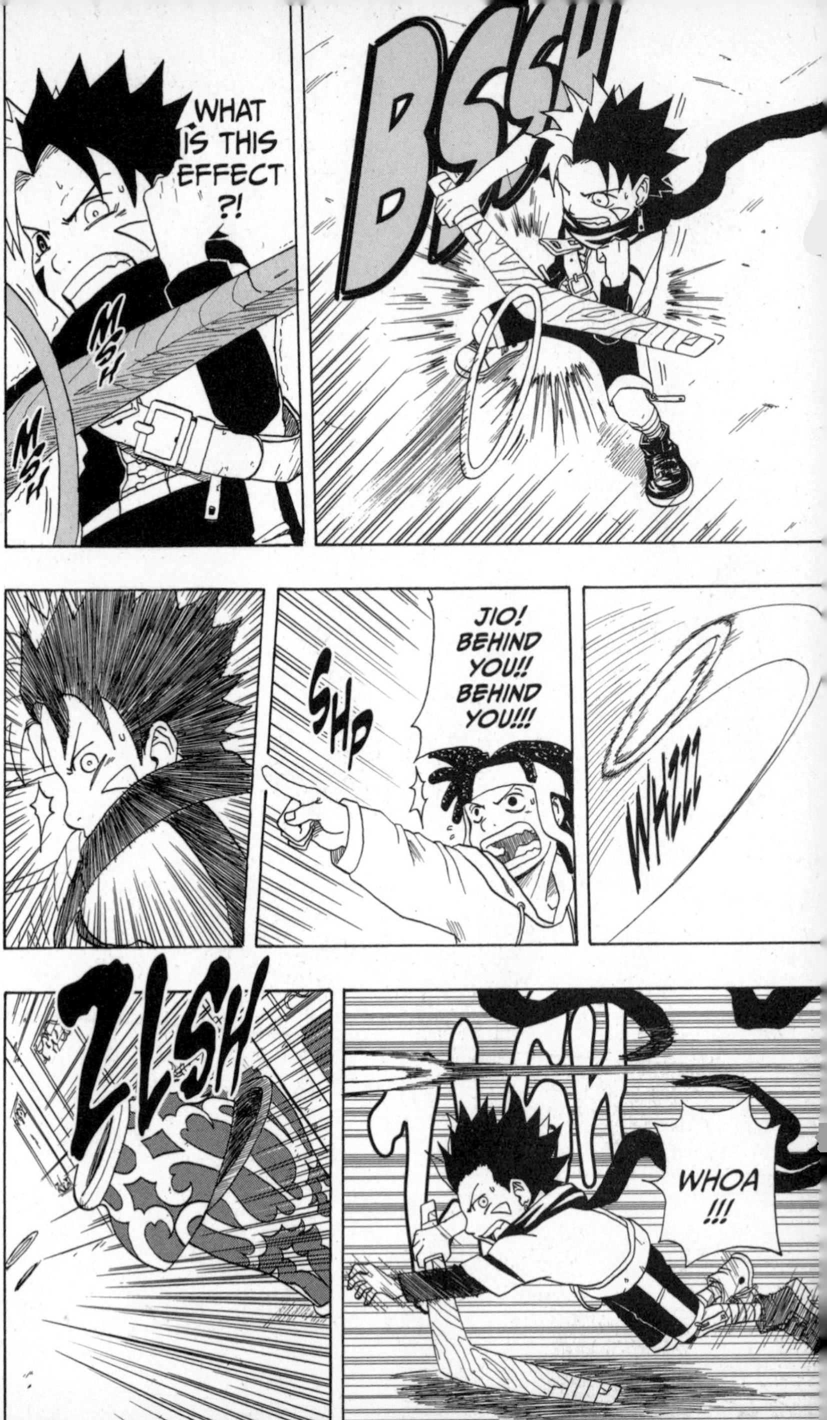
BSSH
WHAT IS THIS EFFECT ?!
MSH
MSH
WHZZZ
JIO! BEHIND YOU!! BEHIND YOU!!!
SHP
WHOA !!!
ZLSH

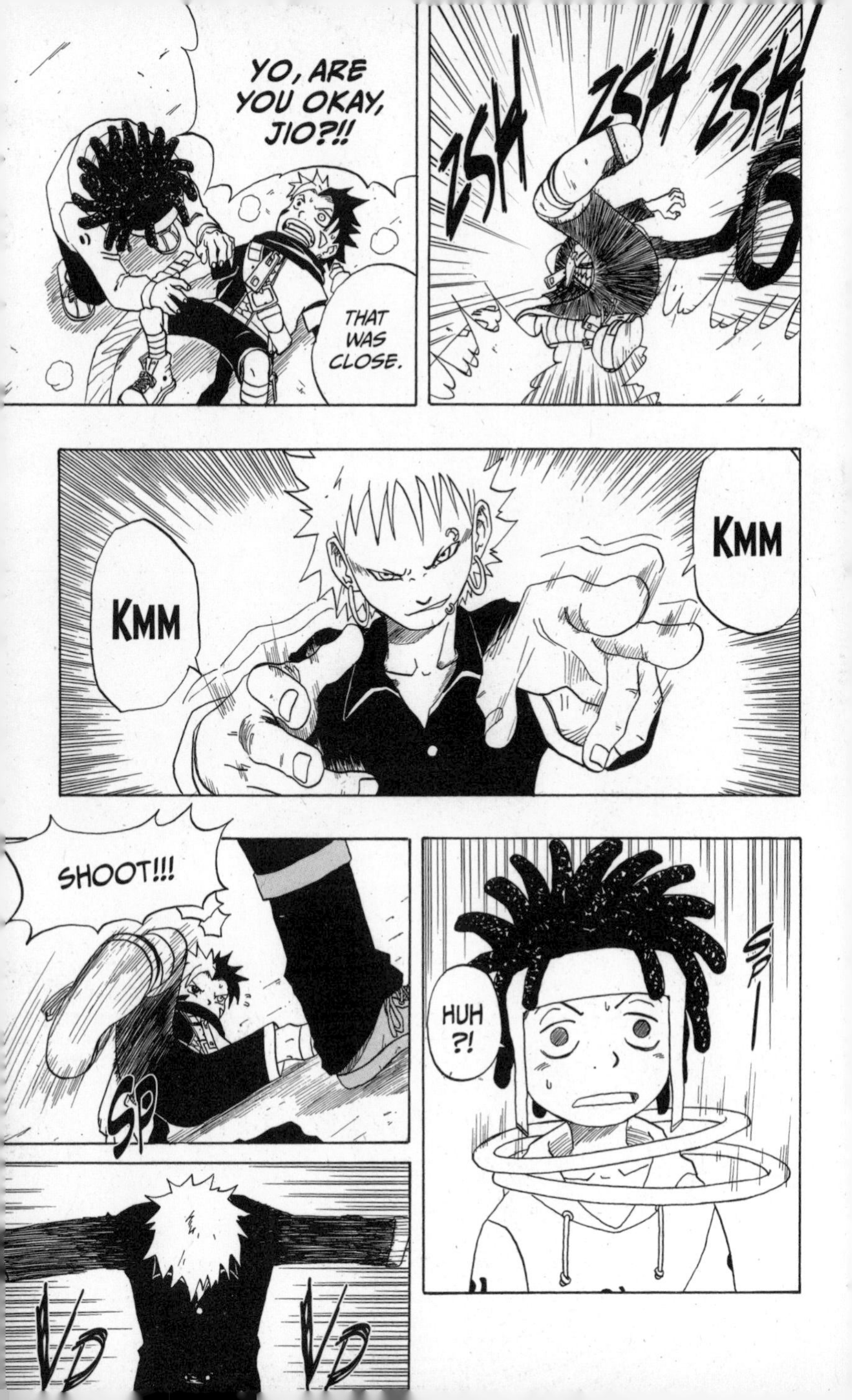
ZSH ZSH ZSH
YO, ARE YOU OKAY, JIO?!!
THAT WAS CLOSE.
KMM
KMM
SP
HUH ?!
SHOOT!!!
SP
VD
VD

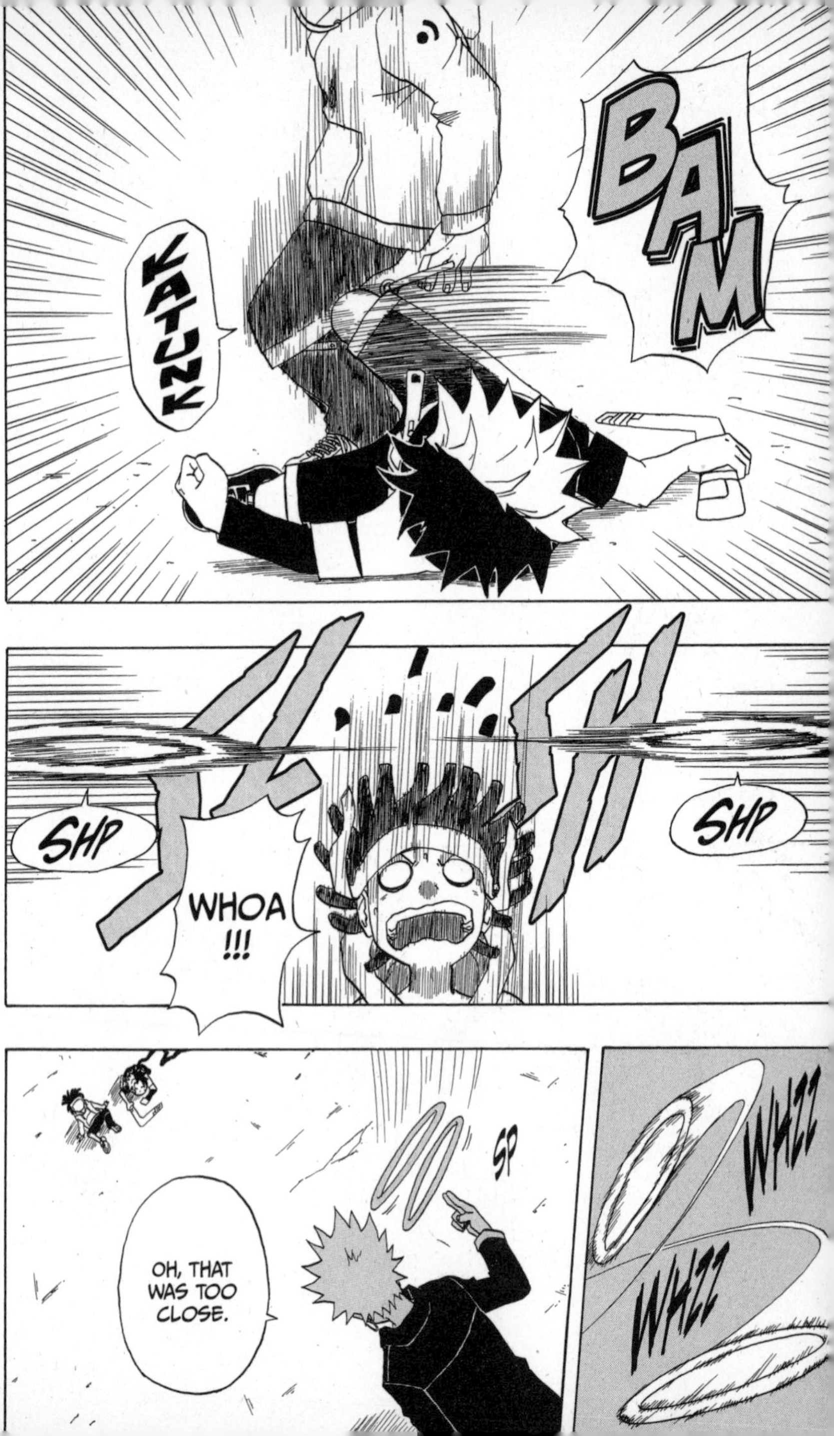
BAM
KATUNK
SHP
SHP
WHOA!!!
WHZZ
WHZZ
SP
OH, THAT WAS TOO CLOSE.

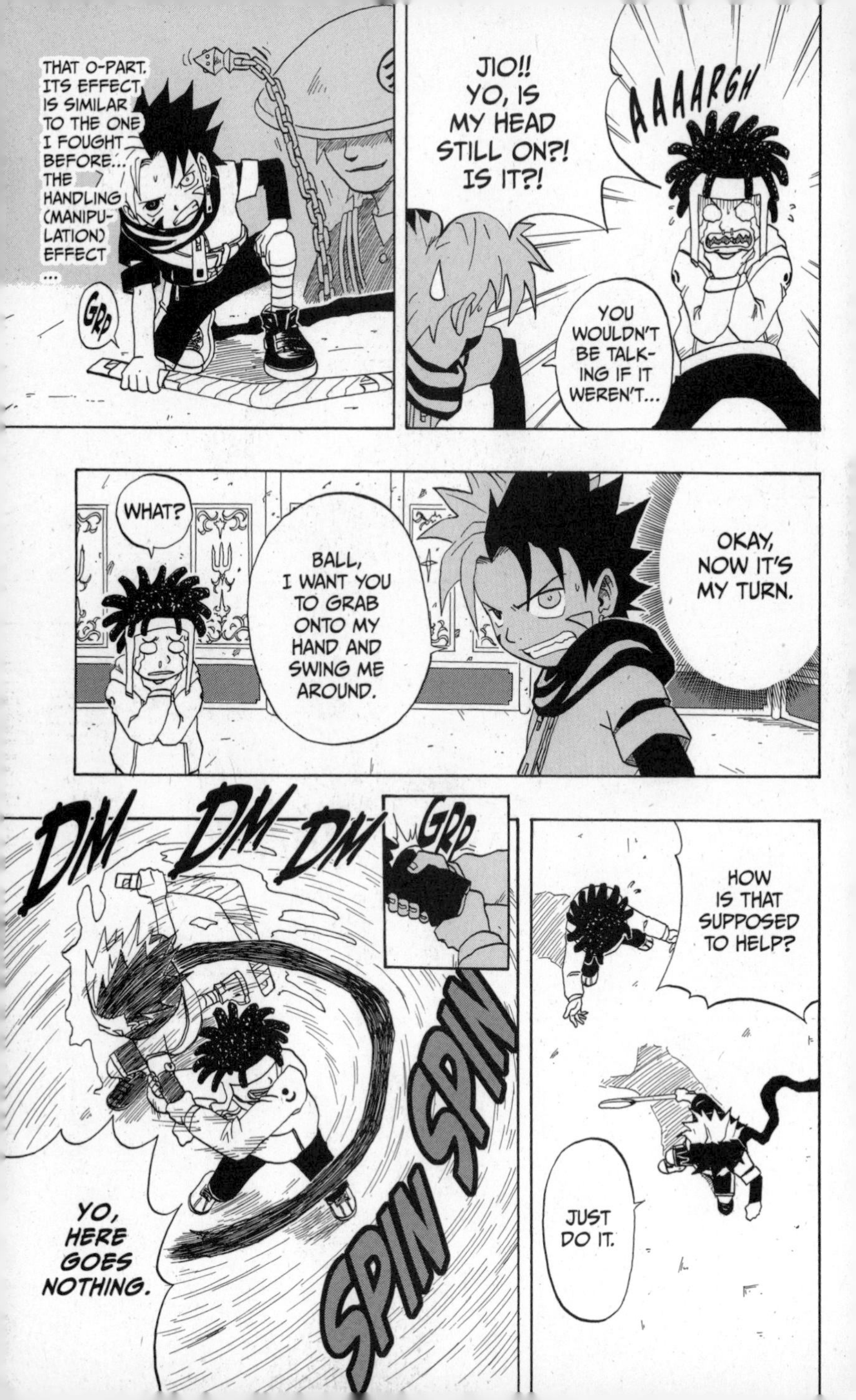
AAAARGH
JIO!! YO, IS MY HEAD STILL ON?! IS IT?!
YOU WOULDN'T BE TALKING IF IT WEREN'T...
THAT O-PART. ITS EFFECT IS SIMILAR TO THE ONE I FOUGHT BEFORE... THE HANDLING (MANIPULATION) EFFECT ...
GRP
OKAY, NOW IT'S MY TURN.
BALL, I WANT YOU TO GRAB ONTO MY HAND AND SWING ME AROUND.
WHAT?
HOW IS THAT SUPPOSED TO HELP?
JUST DO IT.
GRP
DM DM DM
SPIN SPIN
YO, HERE GOES NOTHING.

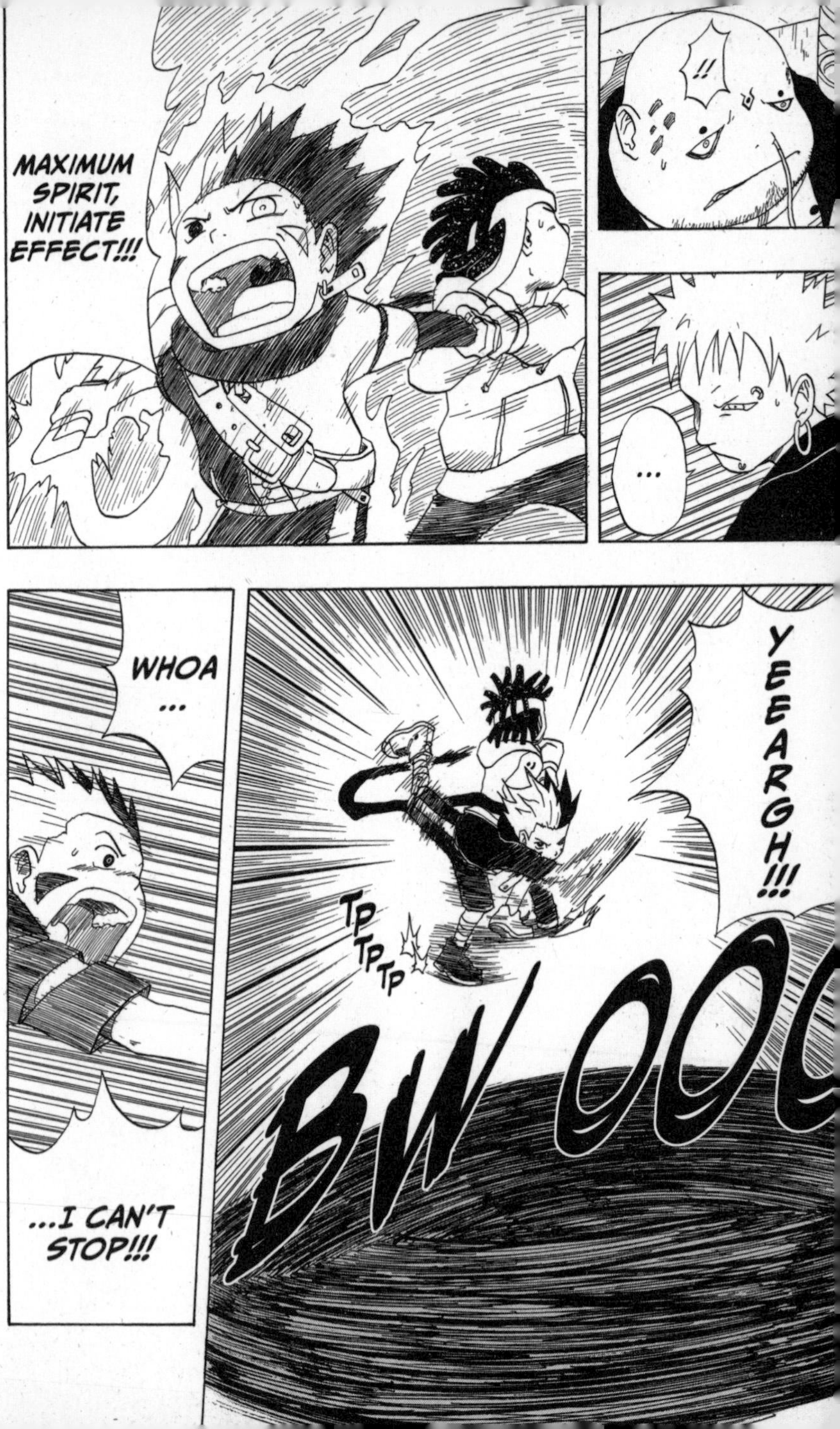
!!
...
MAXIMUM SPIRIT, INITIATE EFFECT!!!
YEEARGH!!!
TPTPTPTP
BWOOO
WHOA ...
...I CAN'T STOP!!!

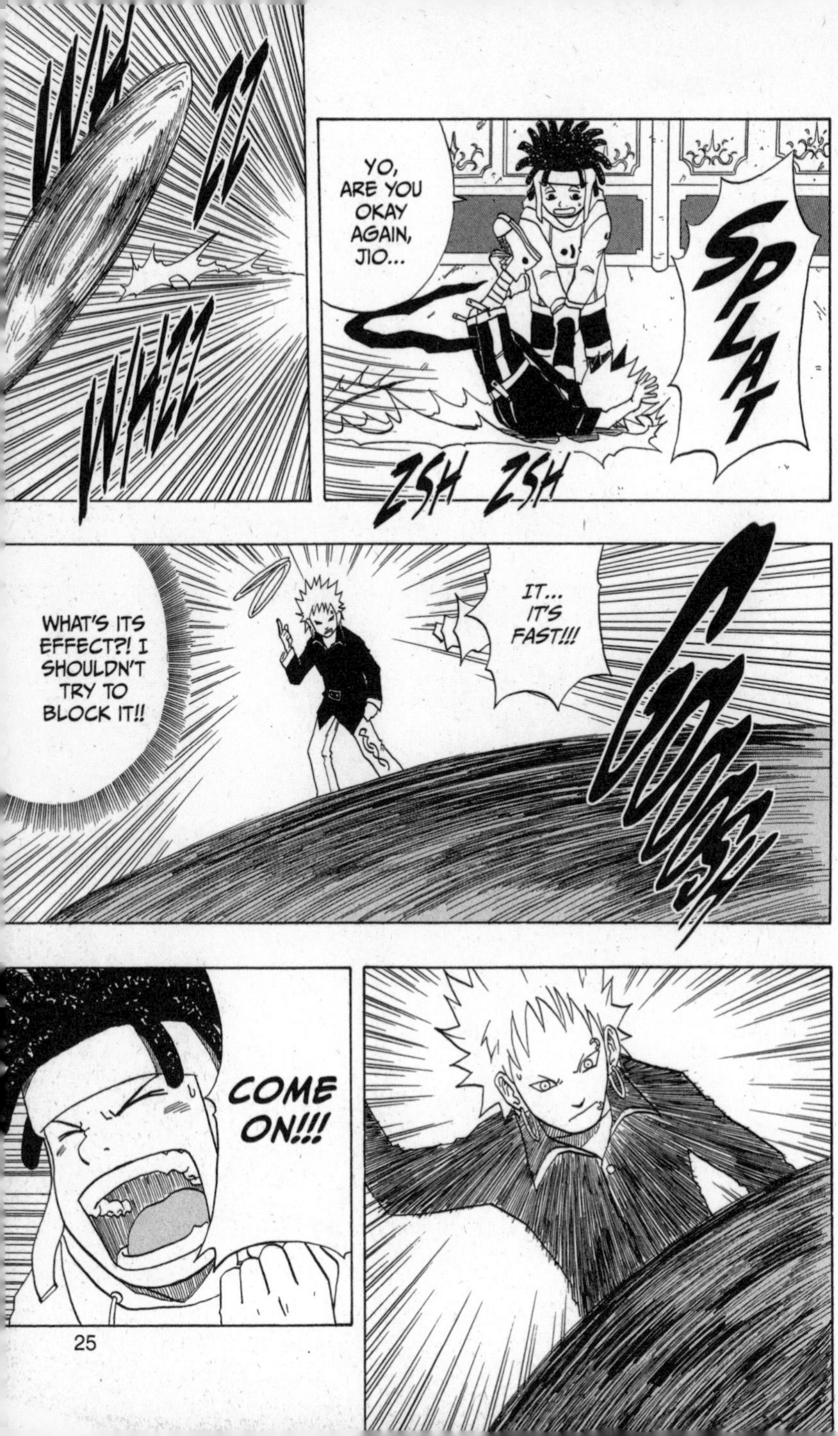
YO, ARE YOU OKAY AGAIN, JIO...
SPLAT
ZSH ZSH
WHAZZ
WHAZZ
GOOOSH
IT... IT'S FAST!!!
WHAT'S ITS EFFECT?! I SHOULDN'T TRY TO BLOCK IT!!
COME ON!!!

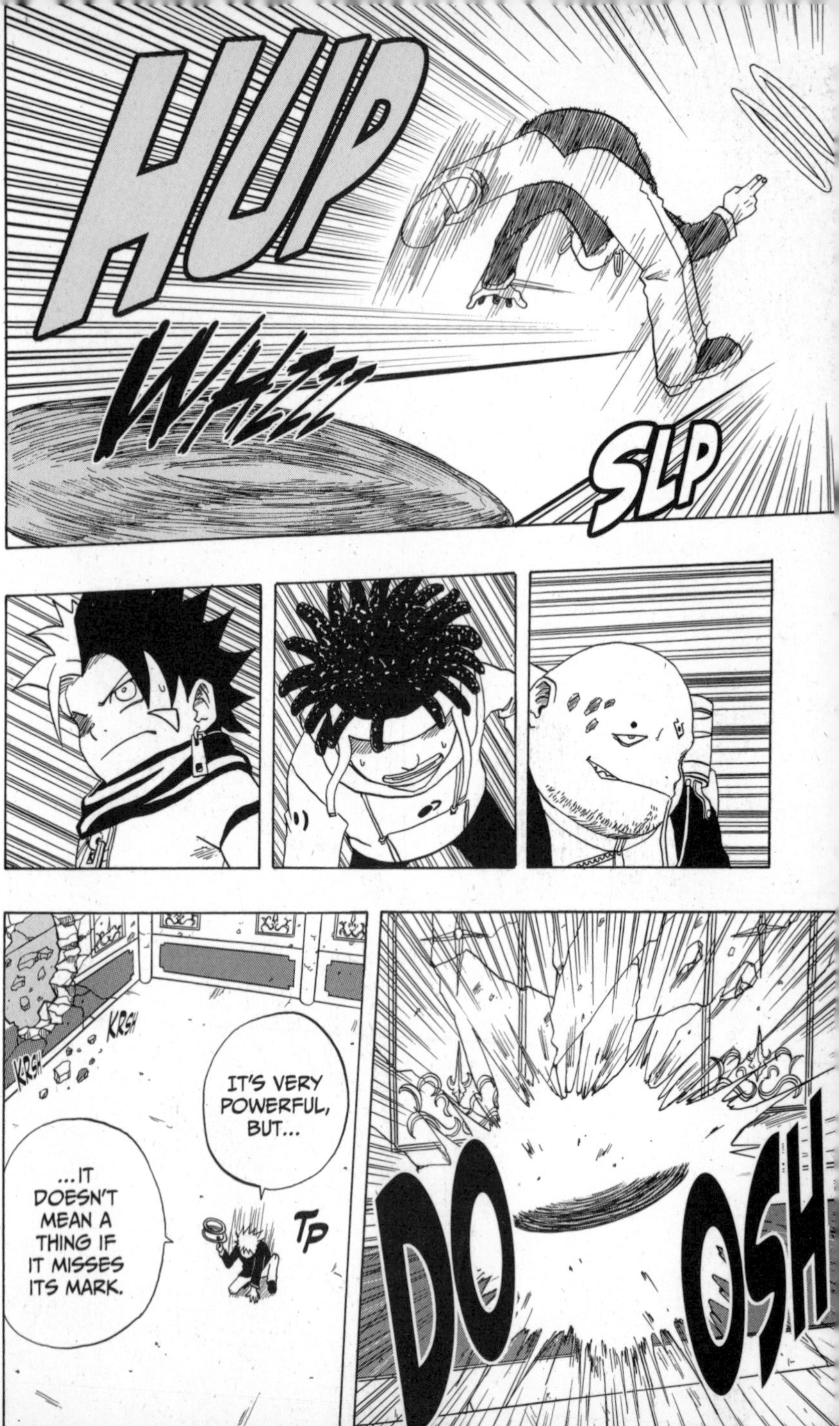
HUP
WHZZZ
SLP
DO—OSH
KRSH
KRSH
IT'S VERY POWERFUL, BUT...
...IT DOESN'T MEAN A THING IF IT MISSES ITS MARK.
TP

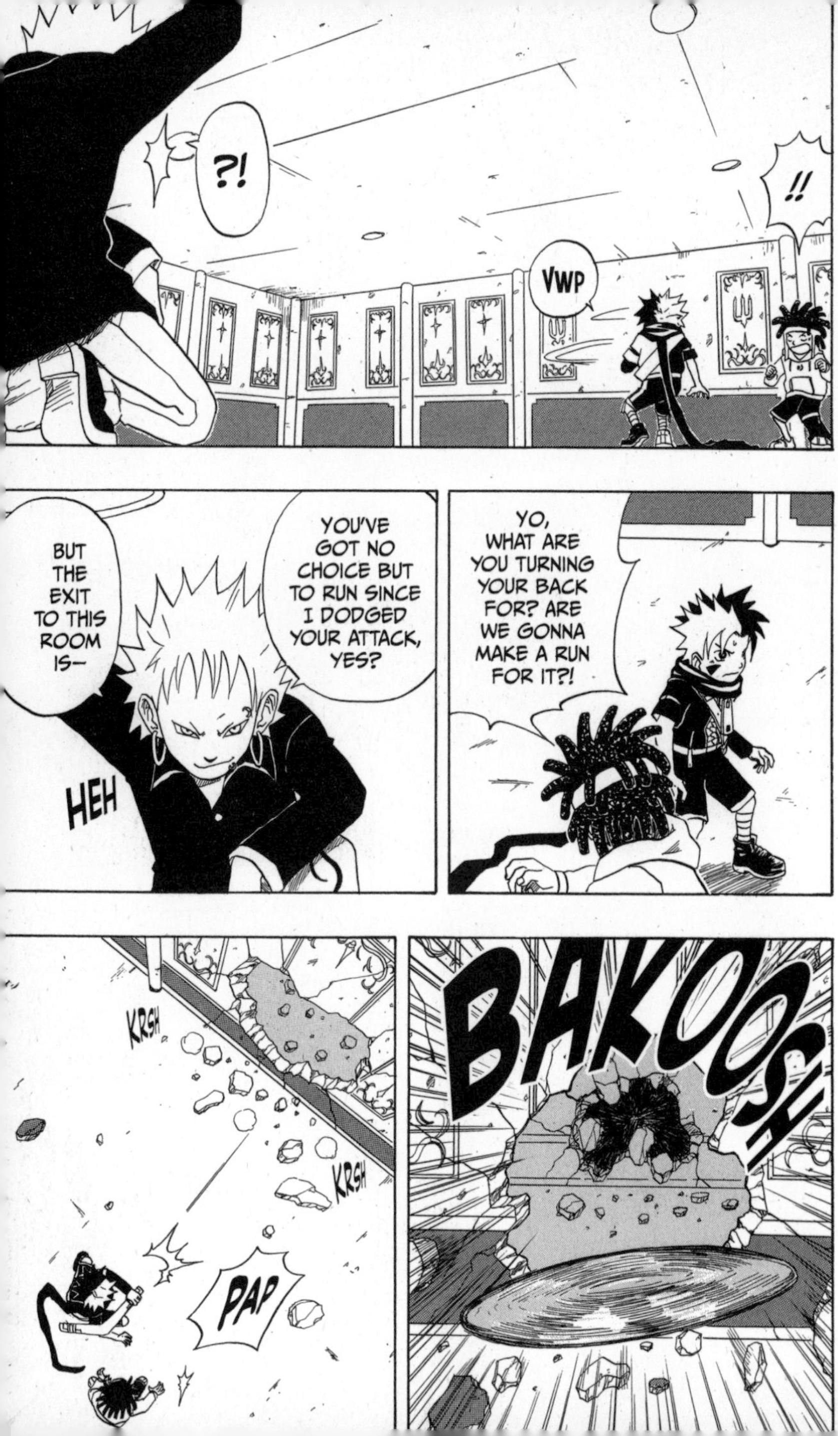
!!
VWP
?!
YO, WHAT ARE YOU TURNING YOUR BACK FOR? ARE WE GONNA MAKE A RUN FOR IT?!
YOU'VE GOT NO CHOICE BUT TO RUN SINCE I DODGED YOUR ATTACK, YES?
BUT THE EXIT TO THIS ROOM IS—
HEH
BAKOOSH
KRSH
KRSH
PAP

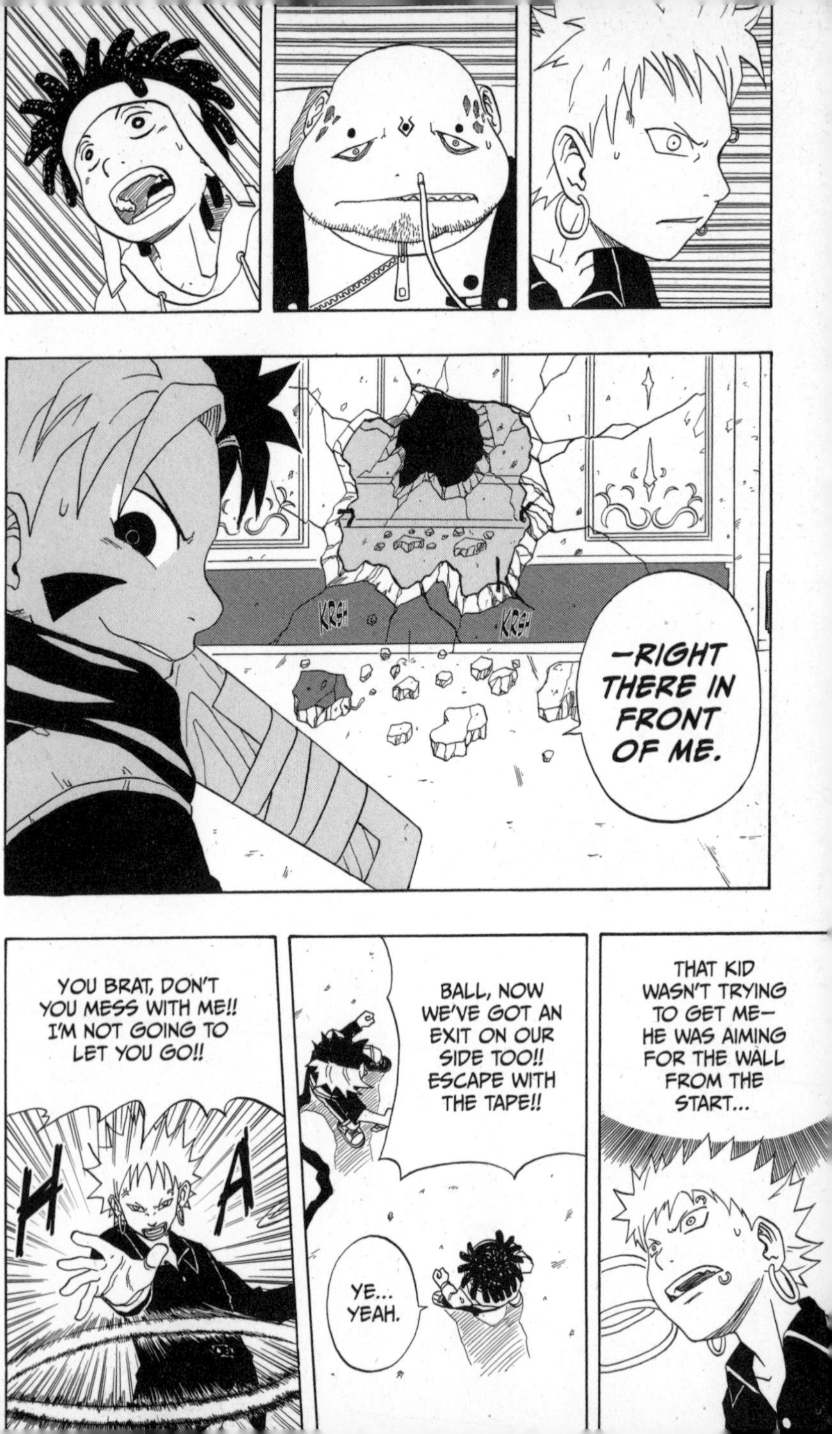
KRSH
KRSH
—RIGHT THERE IN FRONT OF ME.
THAT KID WASN'T TRYING TO GET ME— HE WAS AIMING FOR THE WALL FROM THE START...
BALL, NOW WE'VE GOT AN EXIT ON OUR SIDE TOO!! ESCAPE WITH THE TAPE!!
YE... YEAH.
YOU BRAT, DON'T YOU MESS WITH ME!! I'M NOT GOING TO LET YOU GO!!
HA

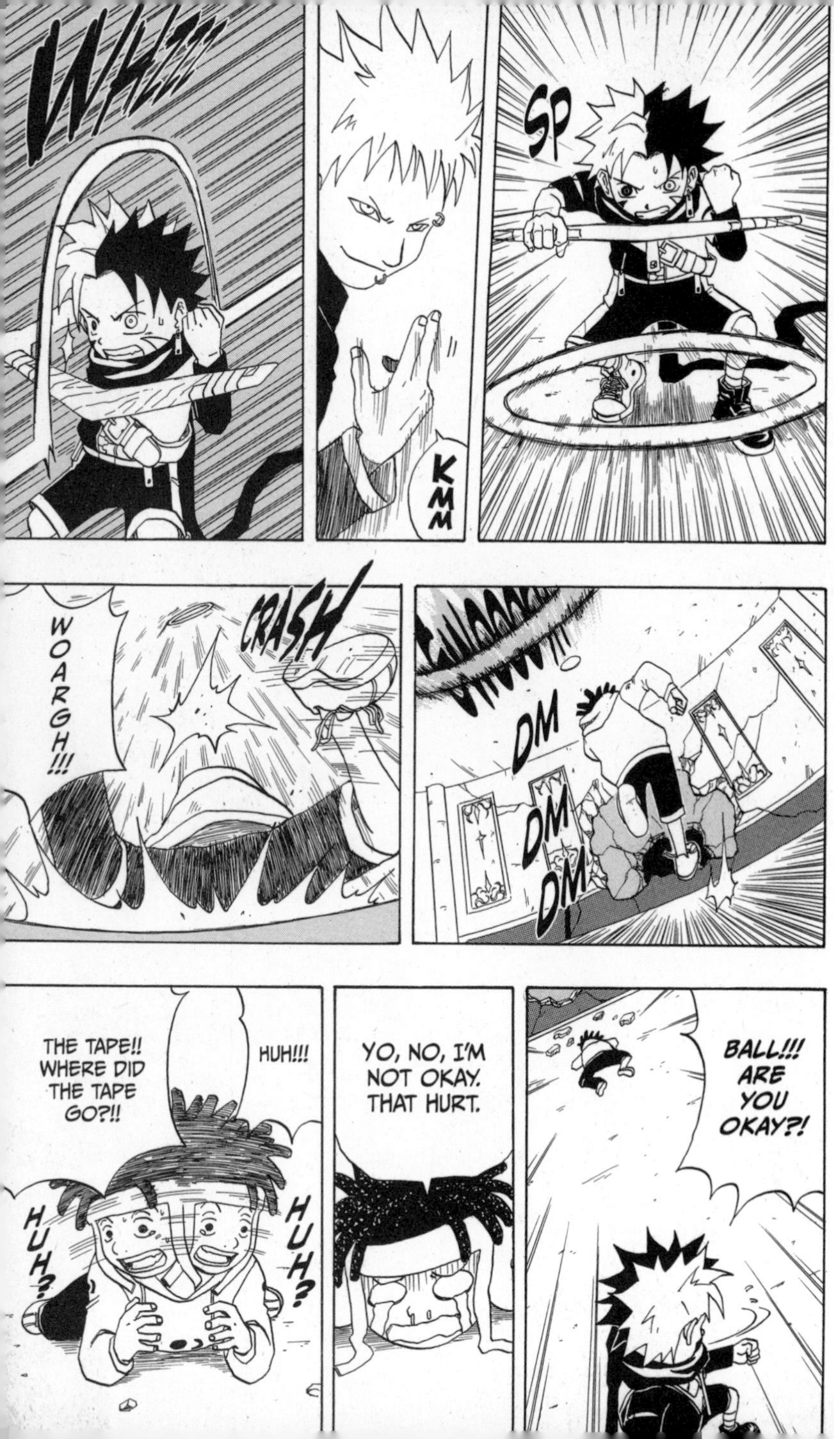
SP
KMM
WHZZ
DM
DM
DM
CRASH
WOARGH!!!
BALL!!! ARE YOU OKAY?!
YO, NO, I'M NOT OKAY. THAT HURT.
HUH!!!
THE TAPE!! WHERE DID THE TAPE GO?!!
HUH?
HUH?

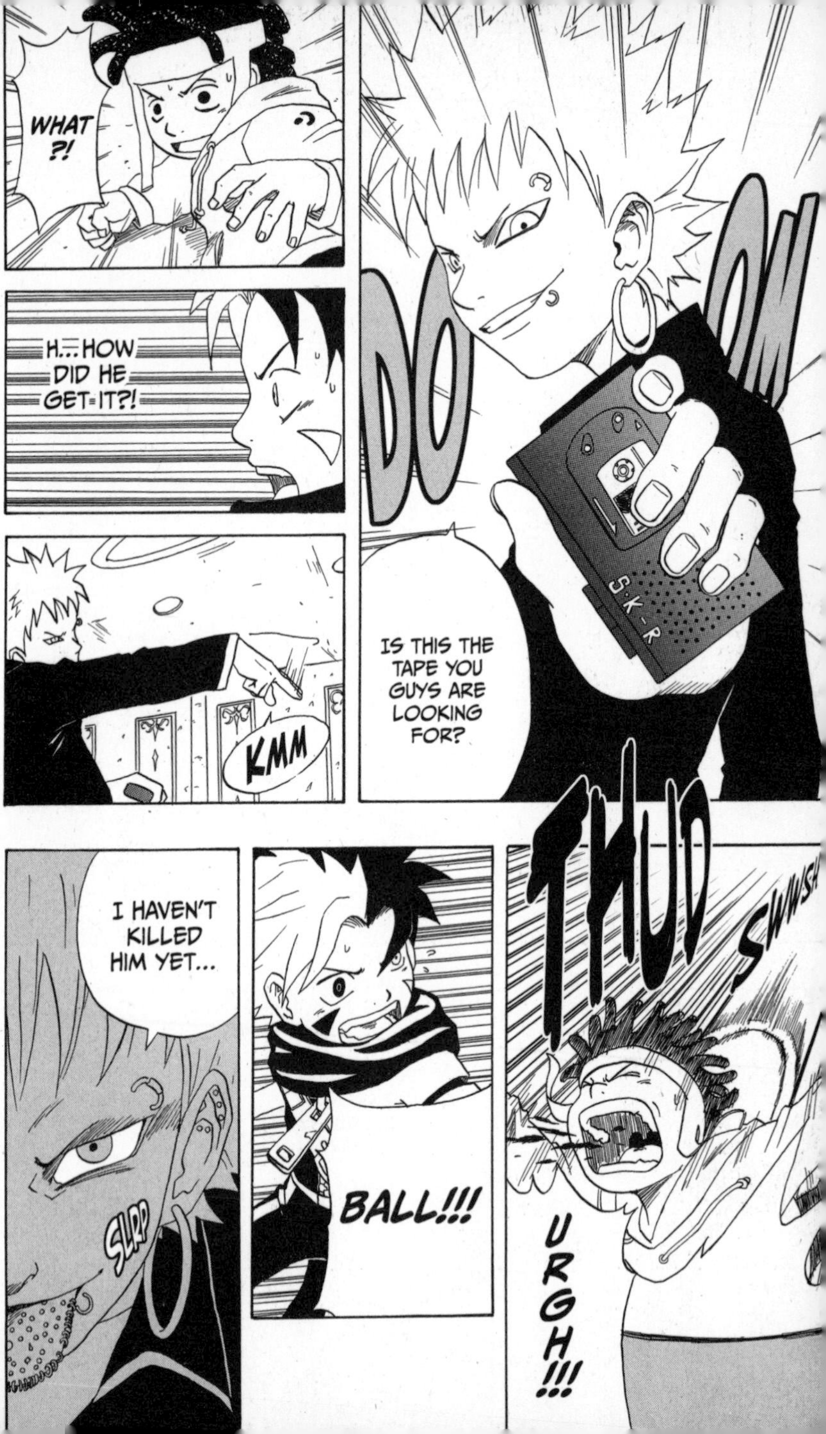
DO
OM
IS THIS THE TAPE YOU GUYS ARE LOOKING FOR?
S.K.-R
WHAT ?!
H...HOW DID HE GET IT?!
KMM
THUD
URGH!!!
BALL!!!
I HAVEN'T KILLED HIM YET...
SLRP

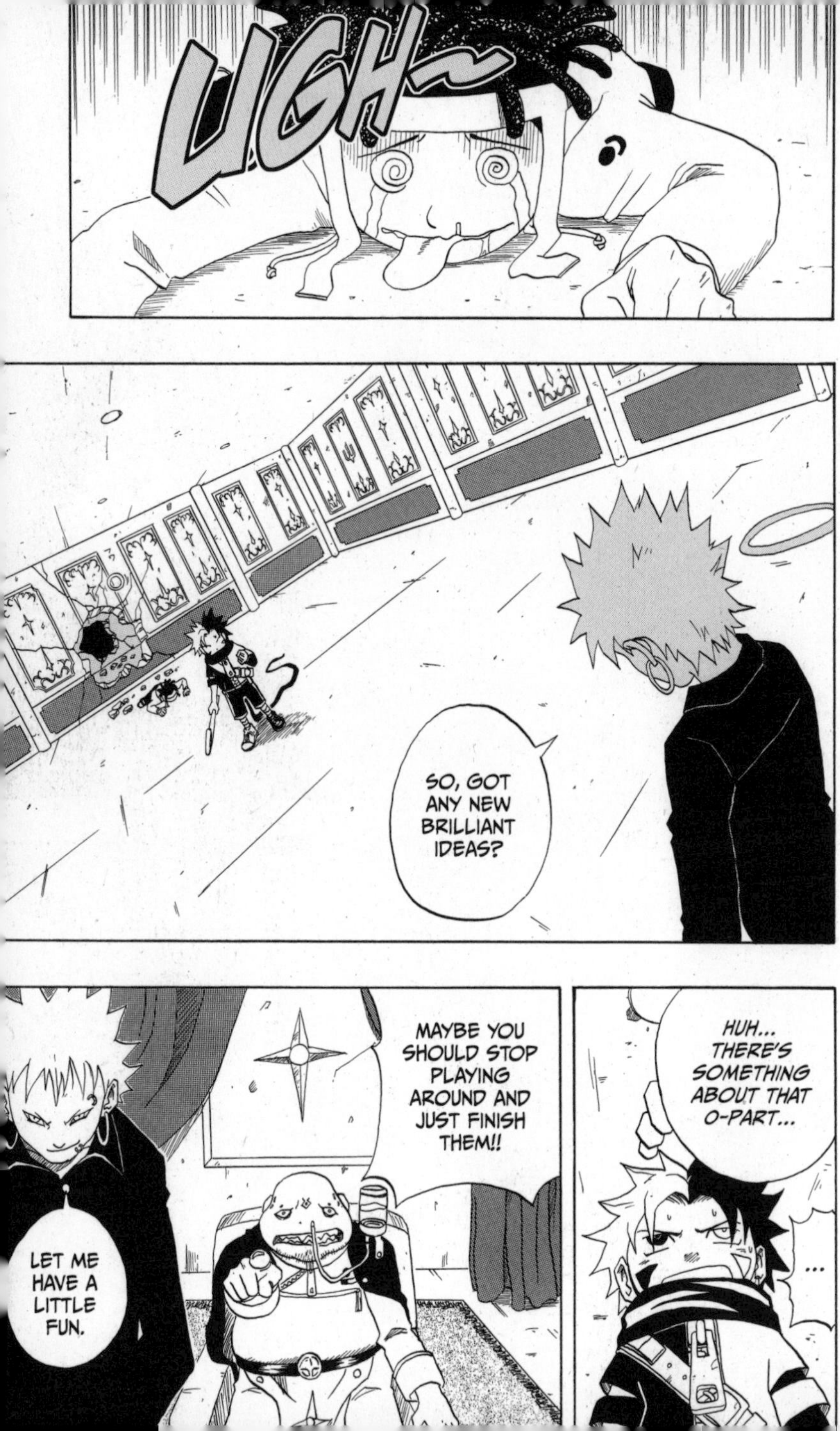
UGH~
SO, GOT ANY NEW BRILLIANT IDEAS?
HUH... THERE'S SOMETHING ABOUT THAT O-PART...
...
MAYBE YOU SHOULD STOP PLAYING AROUND AND JUST FINISH THEM!!
LET ME HAVE A LITTLE FUN.

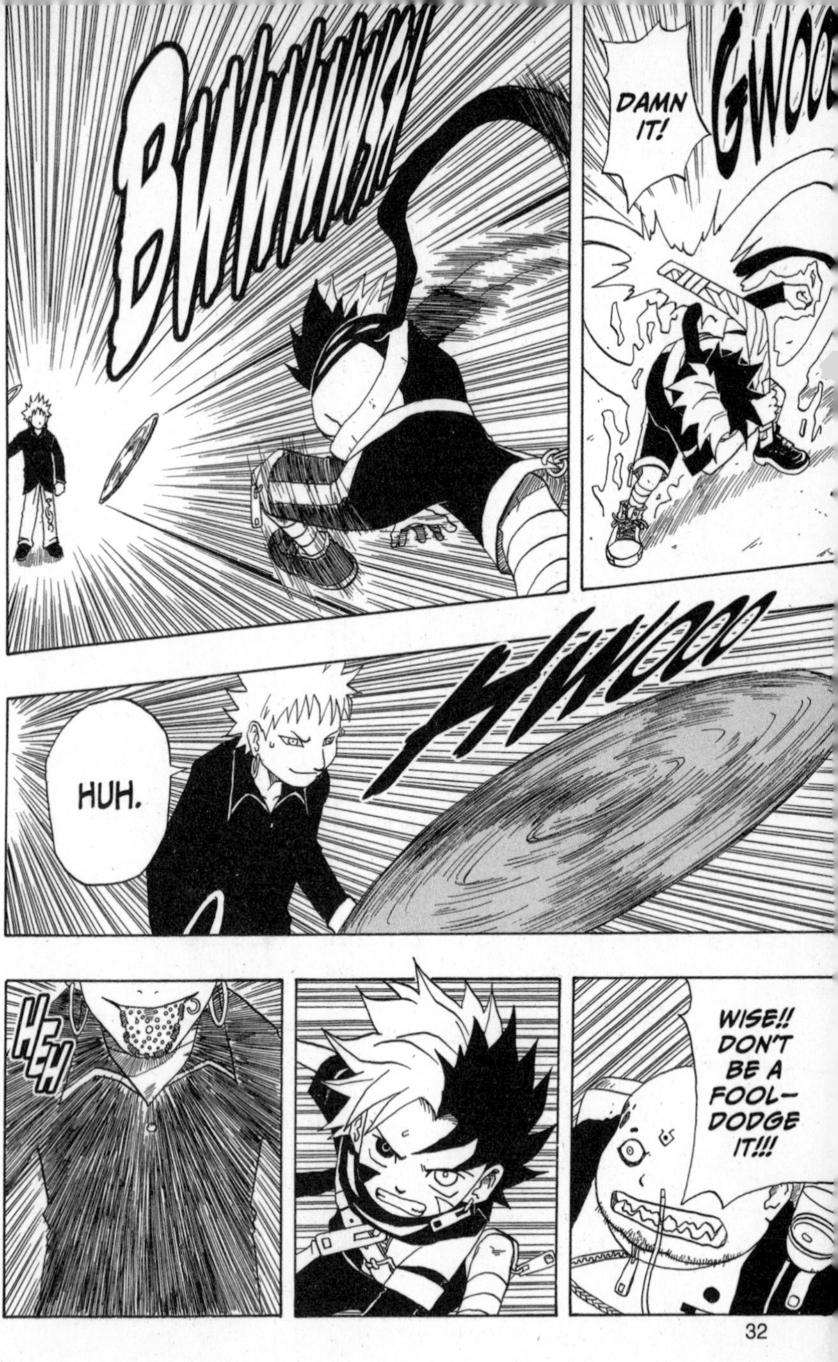
DAMN IT!
HUH.
WISE!! DON'T BE A FOOL—DODGE IT!!!
HEH

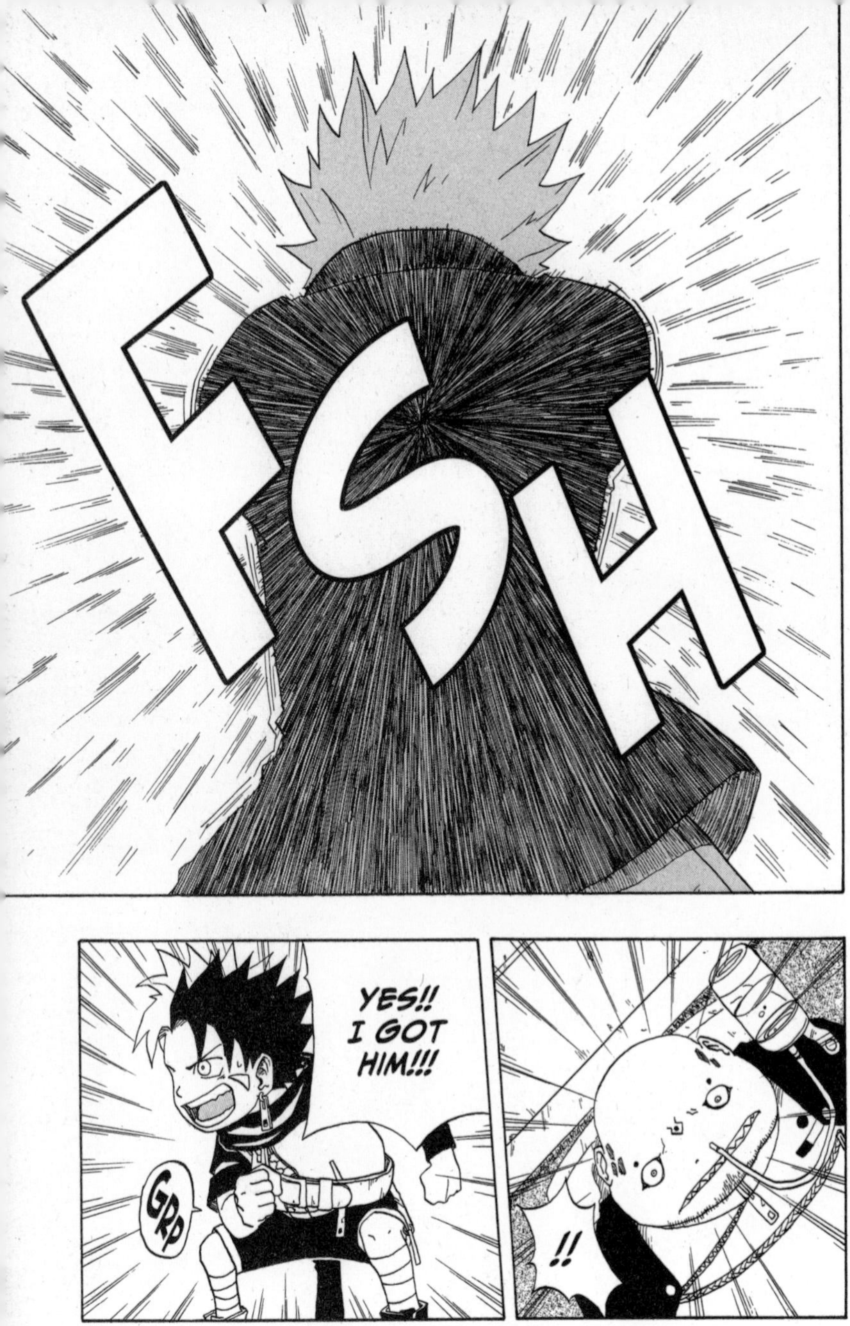
FSH
!!
YES!! I GOT HIM!!!
GRP

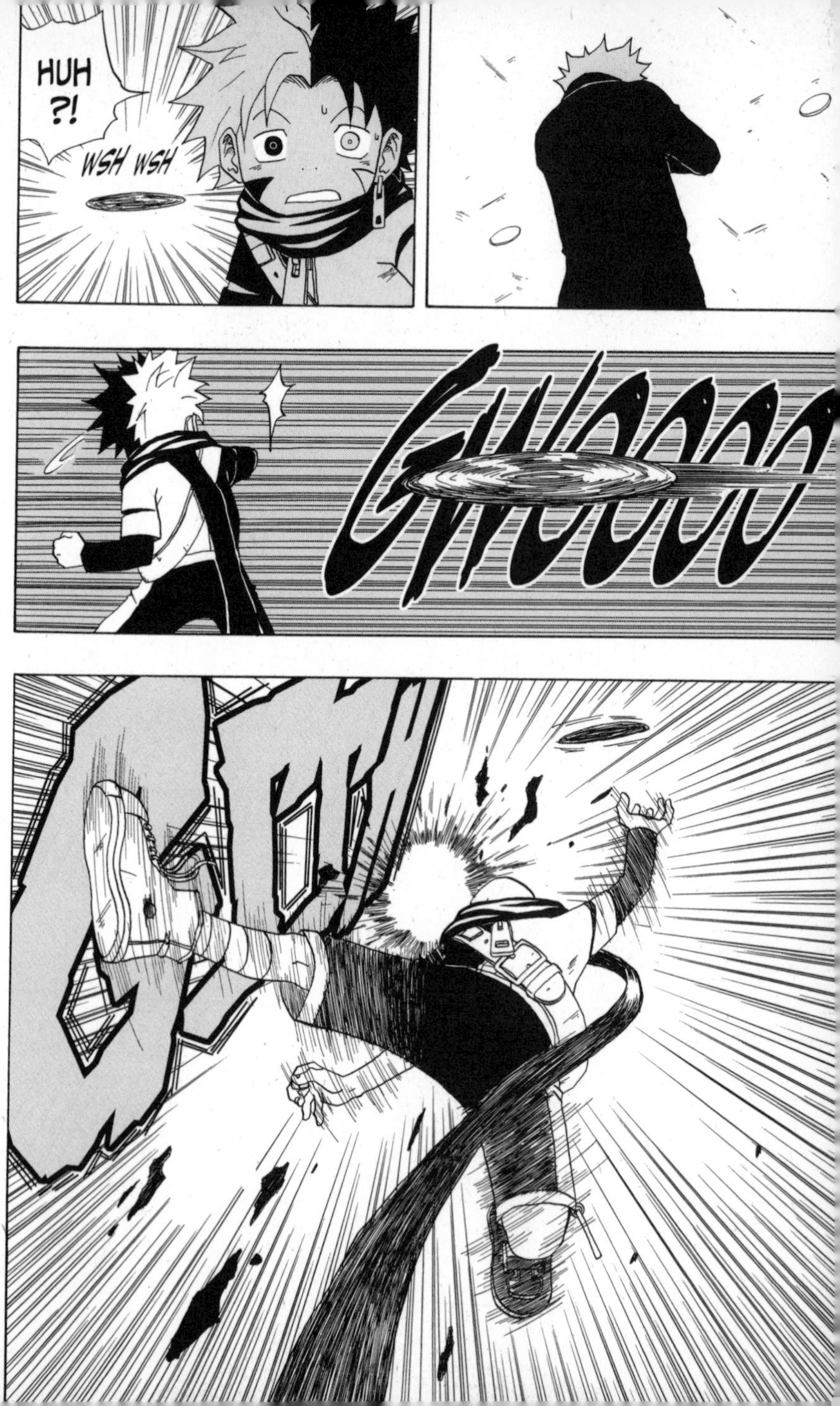
HUH ?!
WSH WSH
GWOOOO

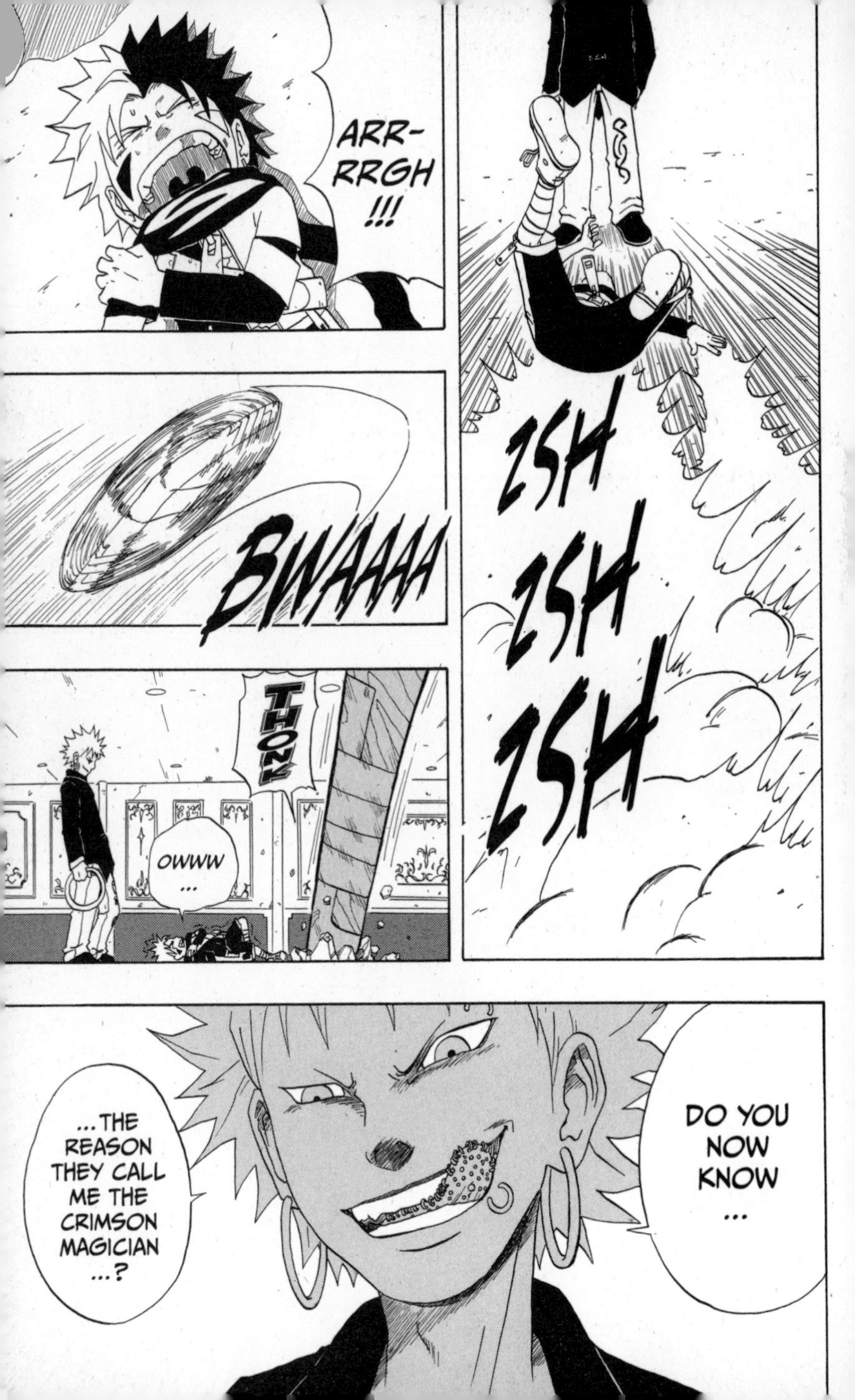
ZSH
ZSH
ZSH
ARR-RRGH!!!
BWAAAA
THONK
OWWW...
DO YOU NOW KNOW...
...THE REASON THEY CALL ME THE CRIMSON MAGICIAN...?

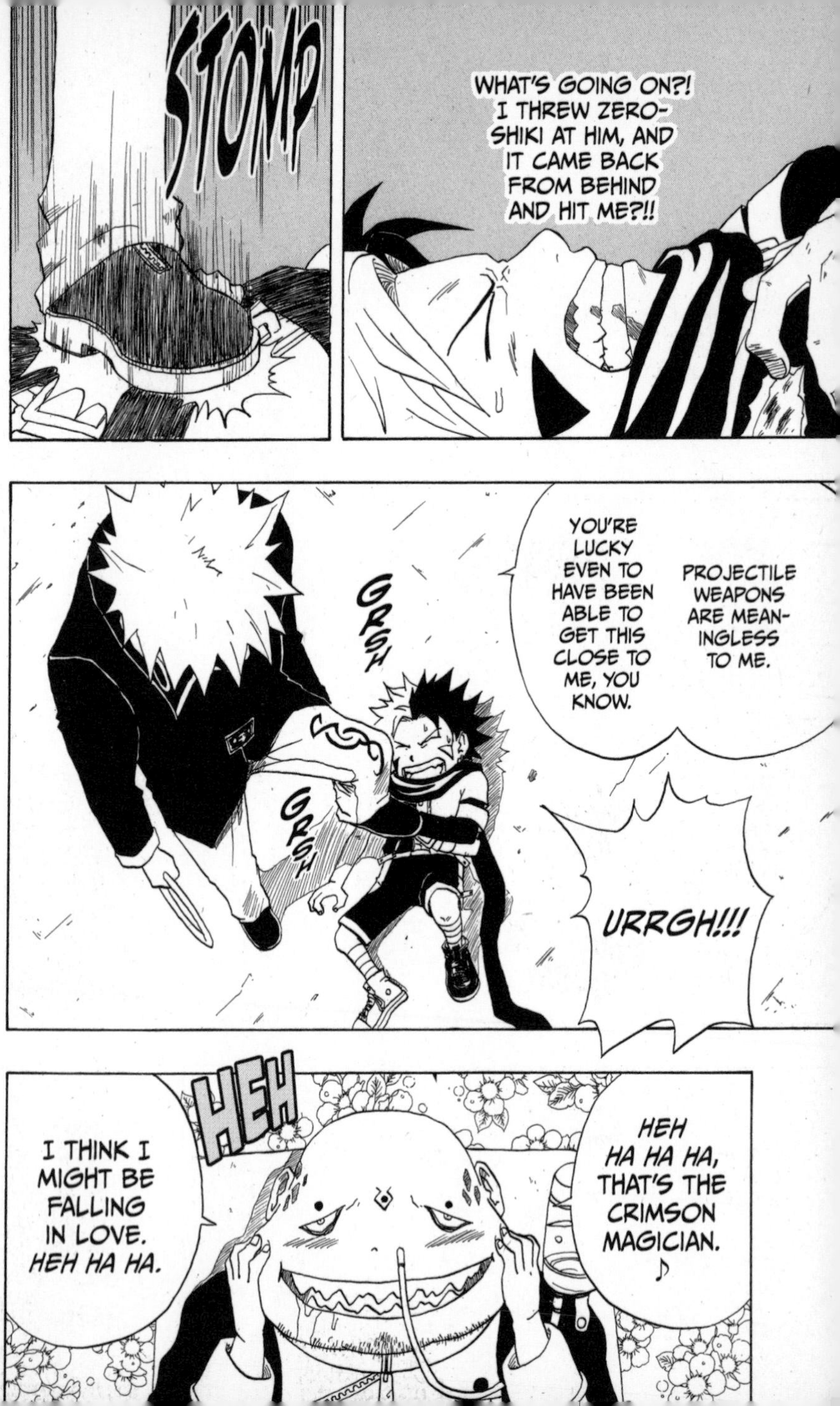

WHAT'S GOING ON?! I THREW ZERO-SHIKI AT HIM, AND IT CAME BACK FROM BEHIND AND HIT ME?!!
STOMP
PROJECTILE WEAPONS ARE MEANINGLESS TO ME.
YOU'RE LUCKY EVEN TO HAVE BEEN ABLE TO GET THIS CLOSE TO ME, YOU KNOW.
URRGH!!!
GRGH
GRGH
HEH HA HA HA, THAT'S THE CRIMSON MAGICIAN. ♪
HEH
I THINK I MIGHT BE FALLING IN LOVE. HEH HA HA.

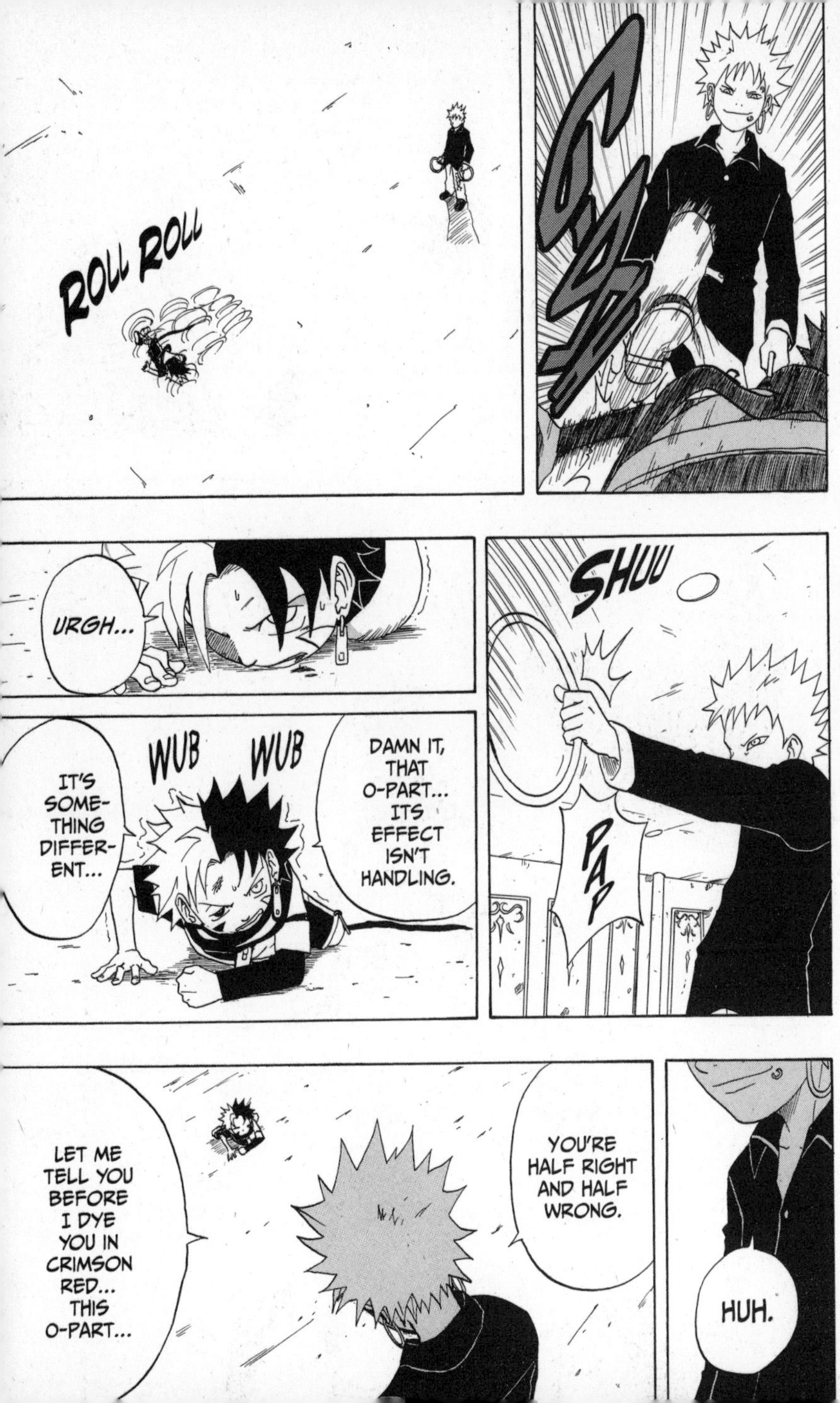
ROLL ROLL
SHUU
PAP
URGH...
WUB WUB
DAMN IT, THAT O-PART... ITS EFFECT ISN'T HANDLING.
IT'S SOMETHING DIFFERENT...
HUH.
YOU'RE HALF RIGHT AND HALF WRONG.
LET ME TELL YOU BEFORE I DYE YOU IN CRIMSON RED... THIS O-PART...

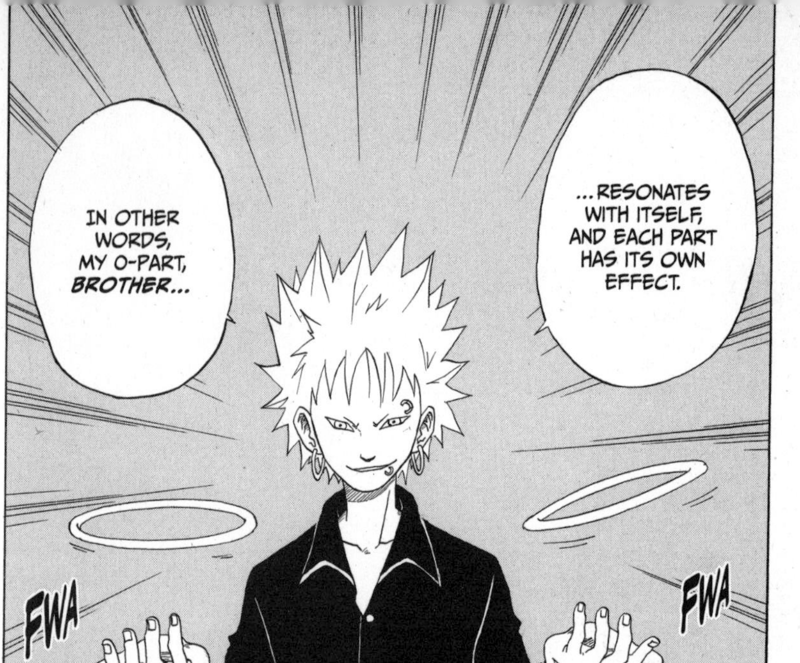
IN OTHER WORDS, MY O-PART, BROTHER...
...RESONATES WITH ITSELF, AND EACH PART HAS ITS OWN EFFECT.
FWA
FWA

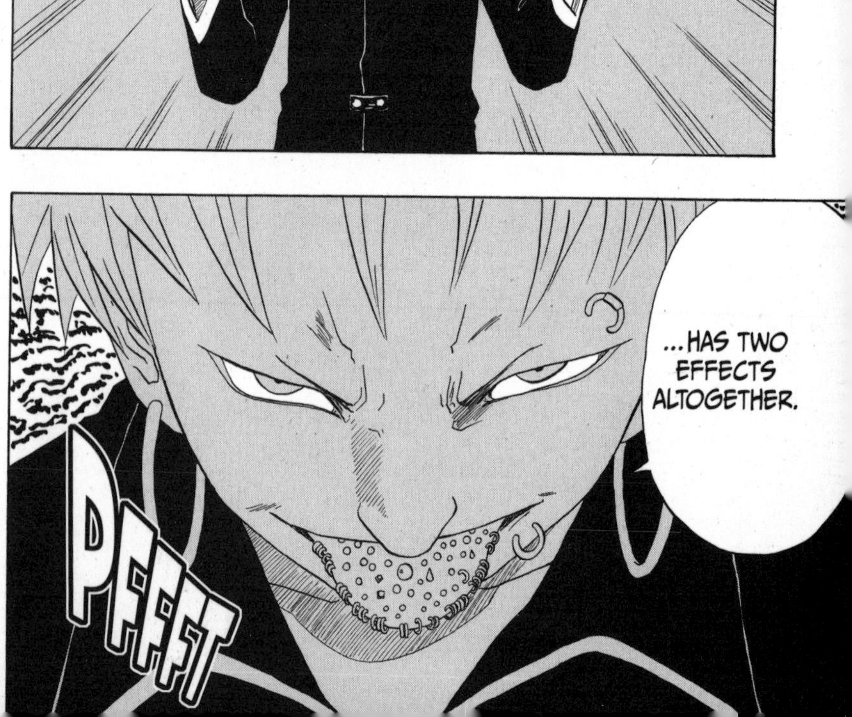
...HAS TWO EFFECTS ALTOGETHER.
PFFFT

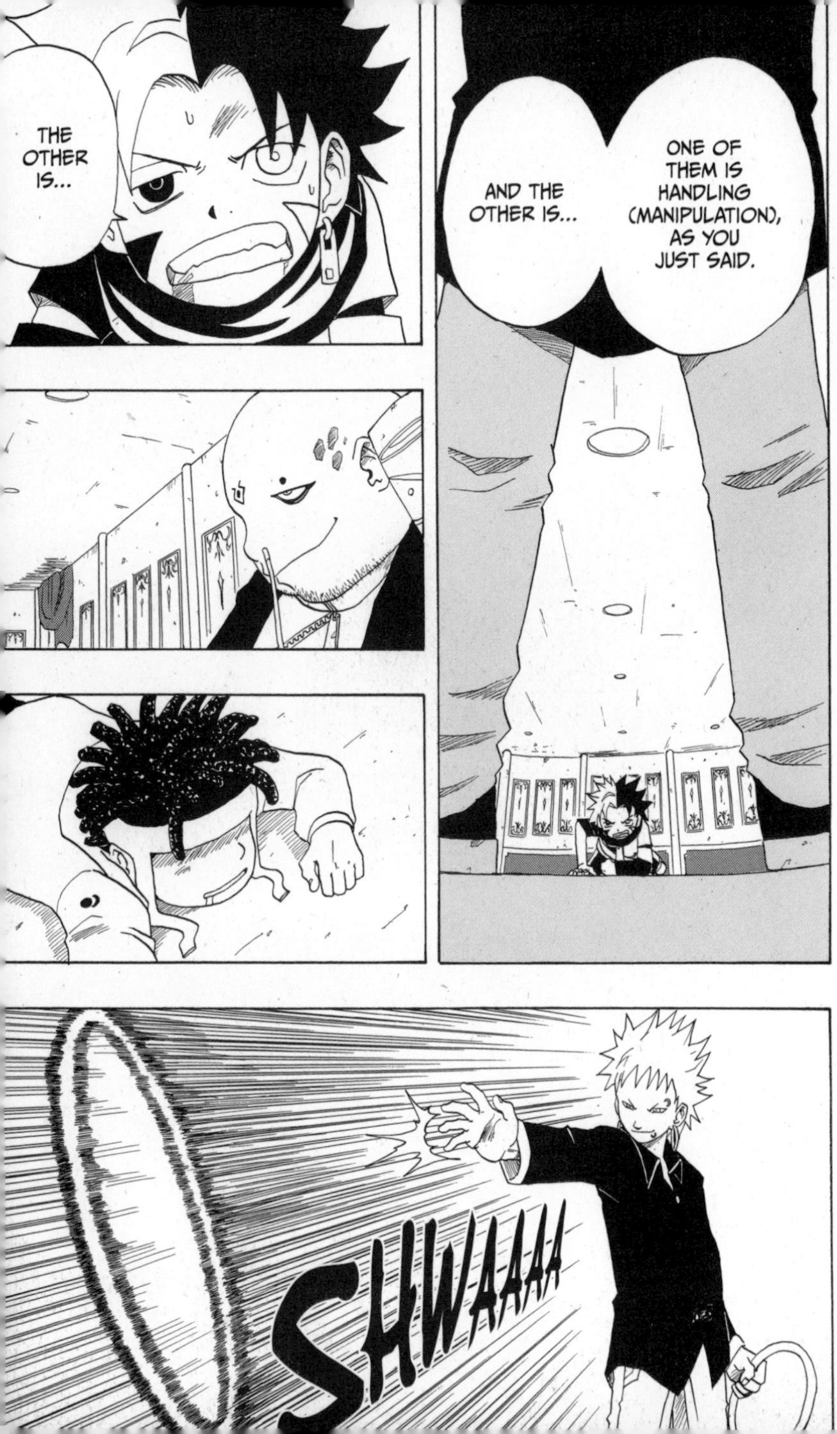
ONE OF THEM IS HANDLING (MANIPULATION), AS YOU JUST SAID.
AND THE OTHER IS...
THE OTHER IS...
SHWAAAA

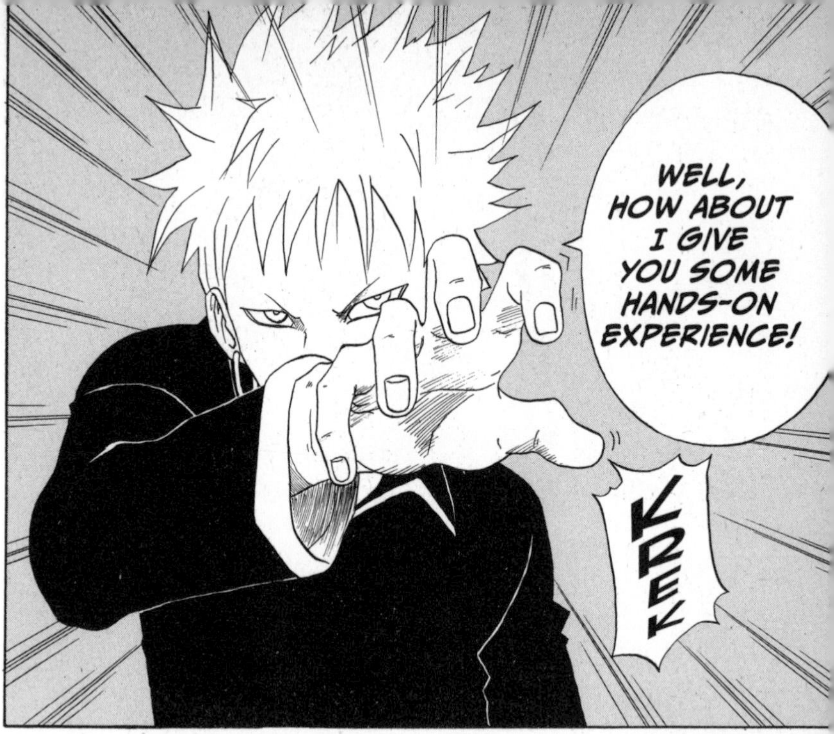
WELL, HOW ABOUT I GIVE YOU SOME HANDS-ON EXPERIENCE!
KREK

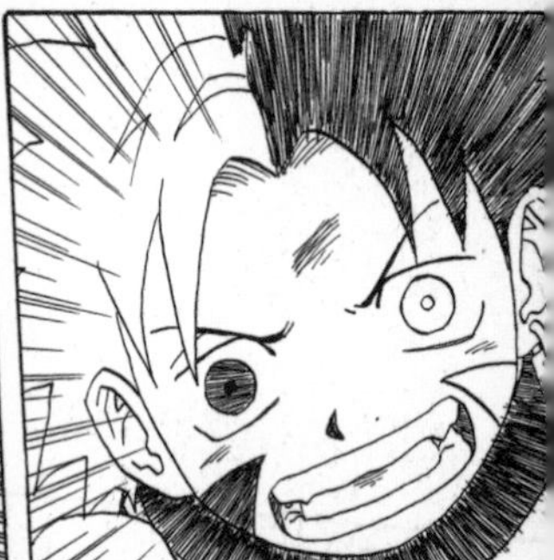
!!!

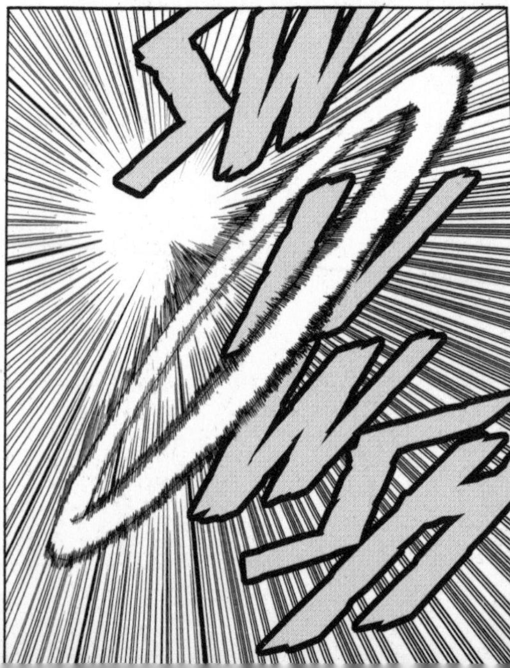

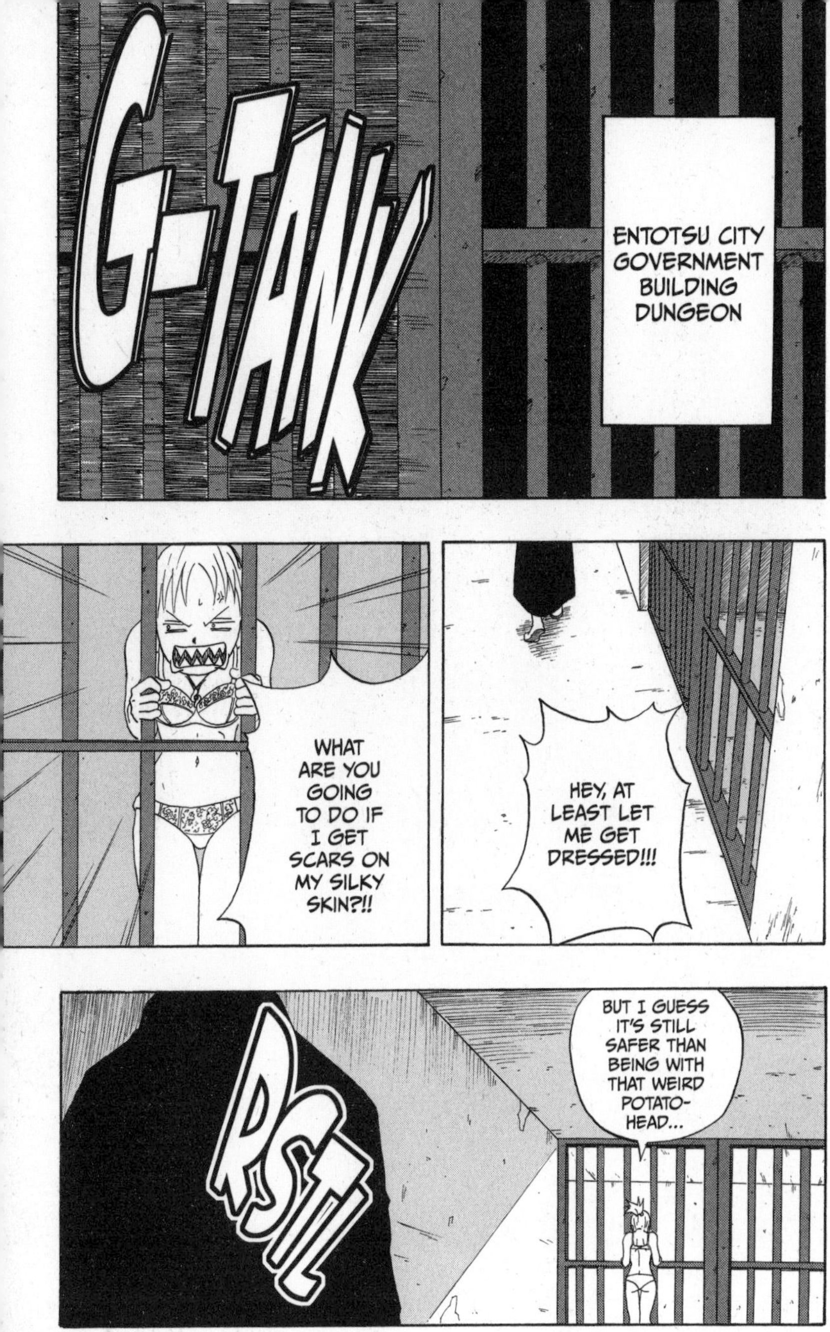

ENTOTSU CITY GOVERNMENT BUILDING DUNGEON
G-TANK
HEY, AT LEAST LET ME GET DRESSED!!!
WHAT ARE YOU GOING TO DO IF I GET SCARS ON MY SILKY SKIN?!!
BUT I GUESS IT'S STILL SAFER THAN BEING WITH THAT WEIRD POTATO-HEAD...
RSTL

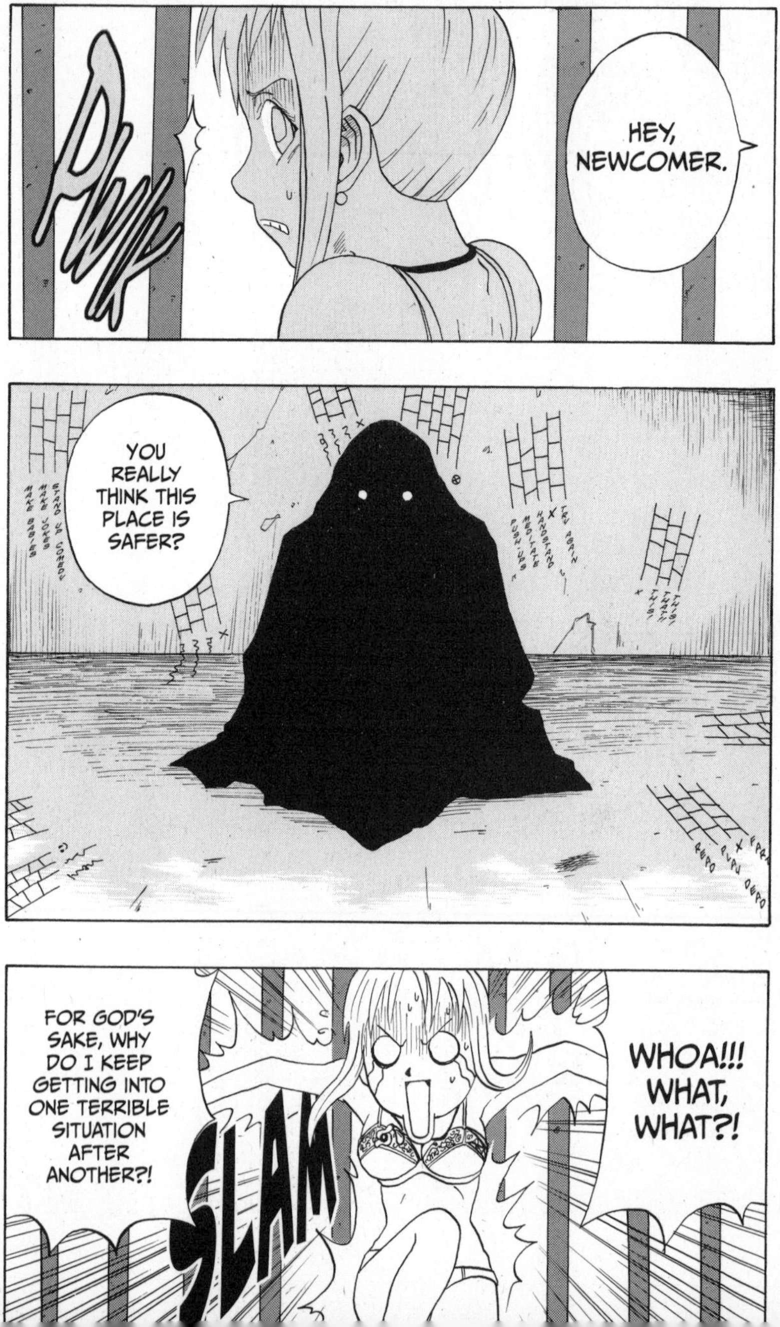
HEY, NEWCOMER.
PWK
THIS! THAT! THIS!
TRY AGAIN
HANDSTAND
MEDITATE
PUSH-UPS
YOU REALLY THINK THIS PLACE IS SAFER?
STAND UP COMEDY
MAKE JOKES
MAKE BABIES
WHOA!!! WHAT, WHAT?!
SLAM
FOR GOD'S SAKE, WHY DO I KEEP GETTING INTO ONE TERRIBLE SITUATION AFTER ANOTHER?!

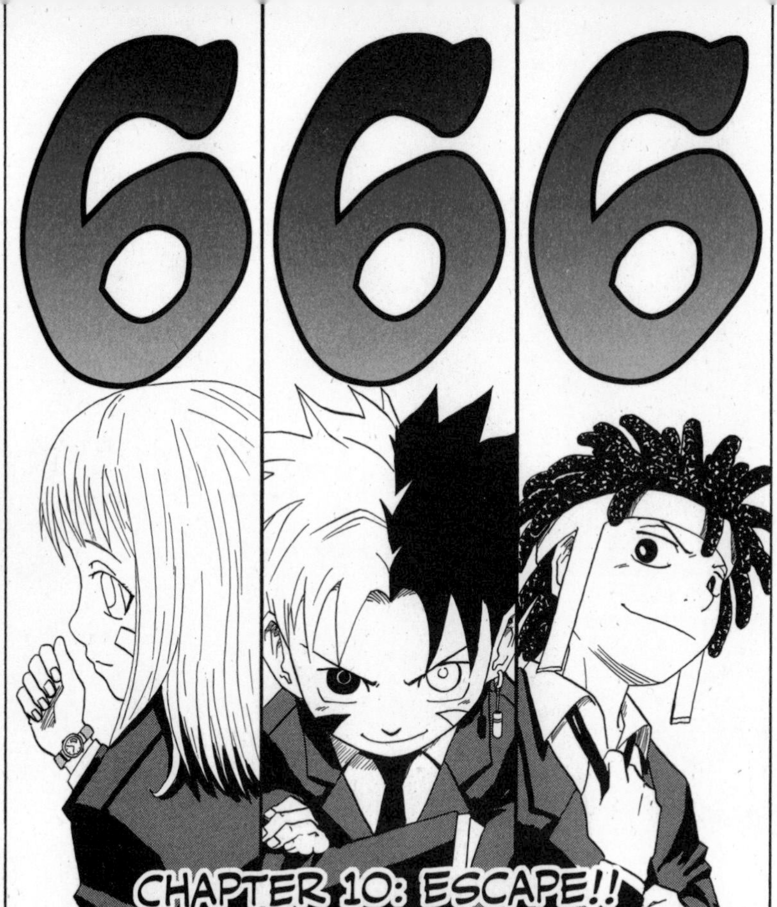
666
CHAPTER 10: ESCAPE!!

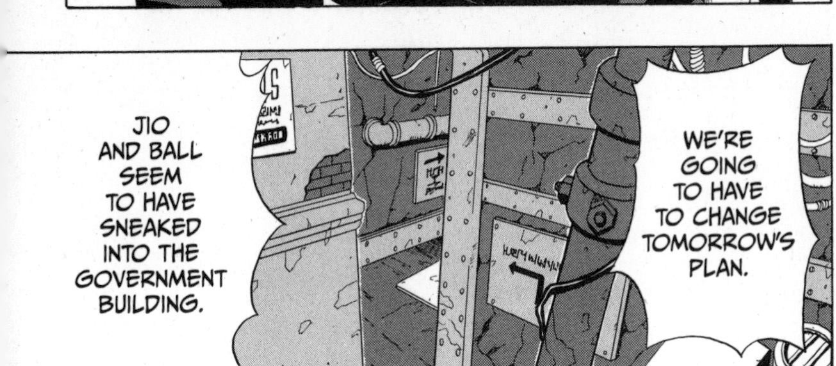
WE'RE GOING TO HAVE TO CHANGE TOMORROW'S PLAN.
JIO AND BALL SEEM TO HAVE SNEAKED INTO THE GOVERNMENT BUILDING.

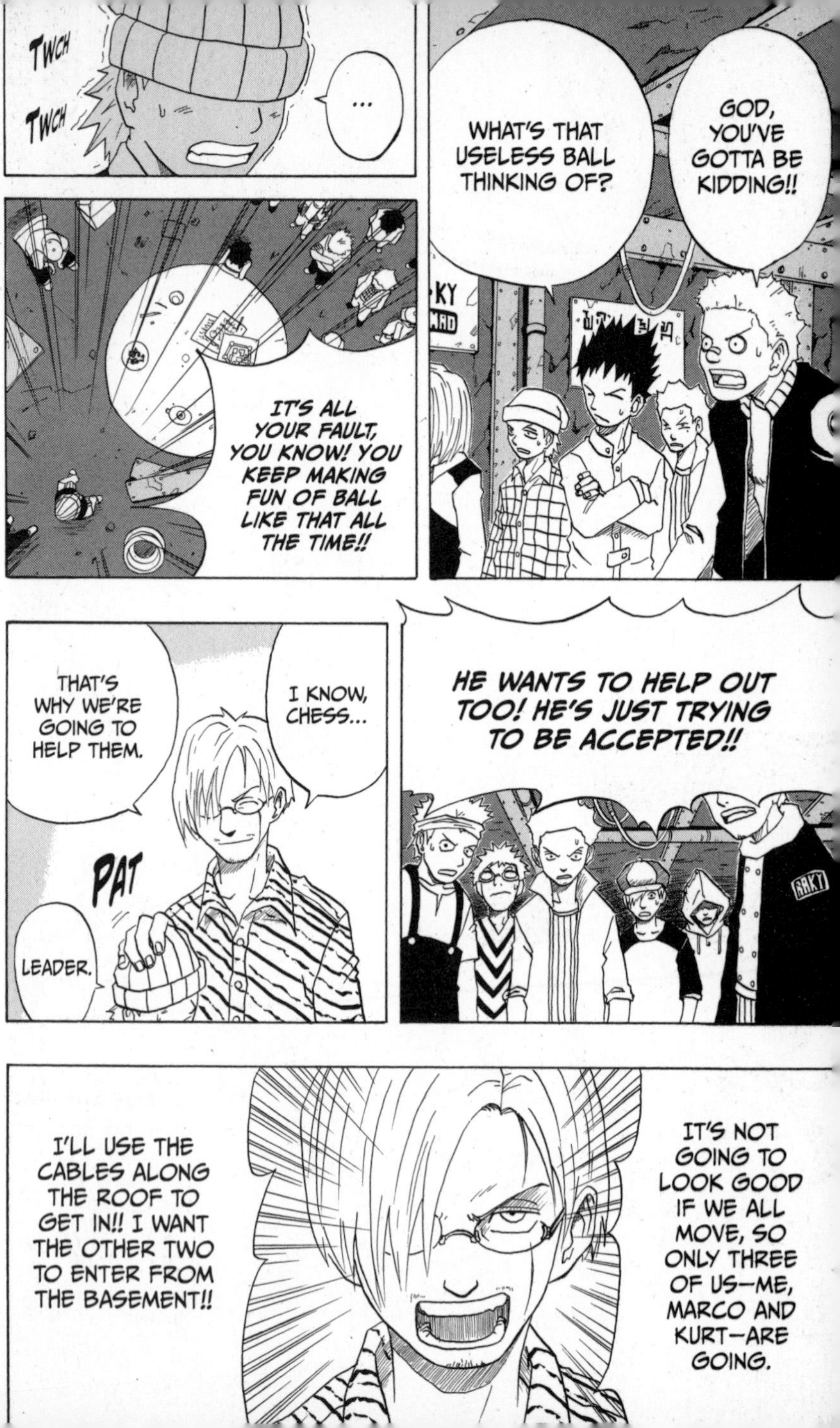
GOD, YOU'VE GOTTA BE KIDDING!!
WHAT'S THAT USELESS BALL THINKING OF?
TWCH
TWCH
...
IT'S ALL YOUR FAULT, YOU KNOW! YOU KEEP MAKING FUN OF BALL LIKE THAT ALL THE TIME!!
HE WANTS TO HELP OUT TOO! HE'S JUST TRYING TO BE ACCEPTED!!
I KNOW, CHESS...
THAT'S WHY WE'RE GOING TO HELP THEM.
PAT
LEADER.
IT'S NOT GOING TO LOOK GOOD IF WE ALL MOVE, SO ONLY THREE OF US—ME, MARCO AND KURT—ARE GOING.
I'LL USE THE CABLES ALONG THE ROOF TO GET IN!! I WANT THE OTHER TWO TO ENTER FROM THE BASEMENT!!

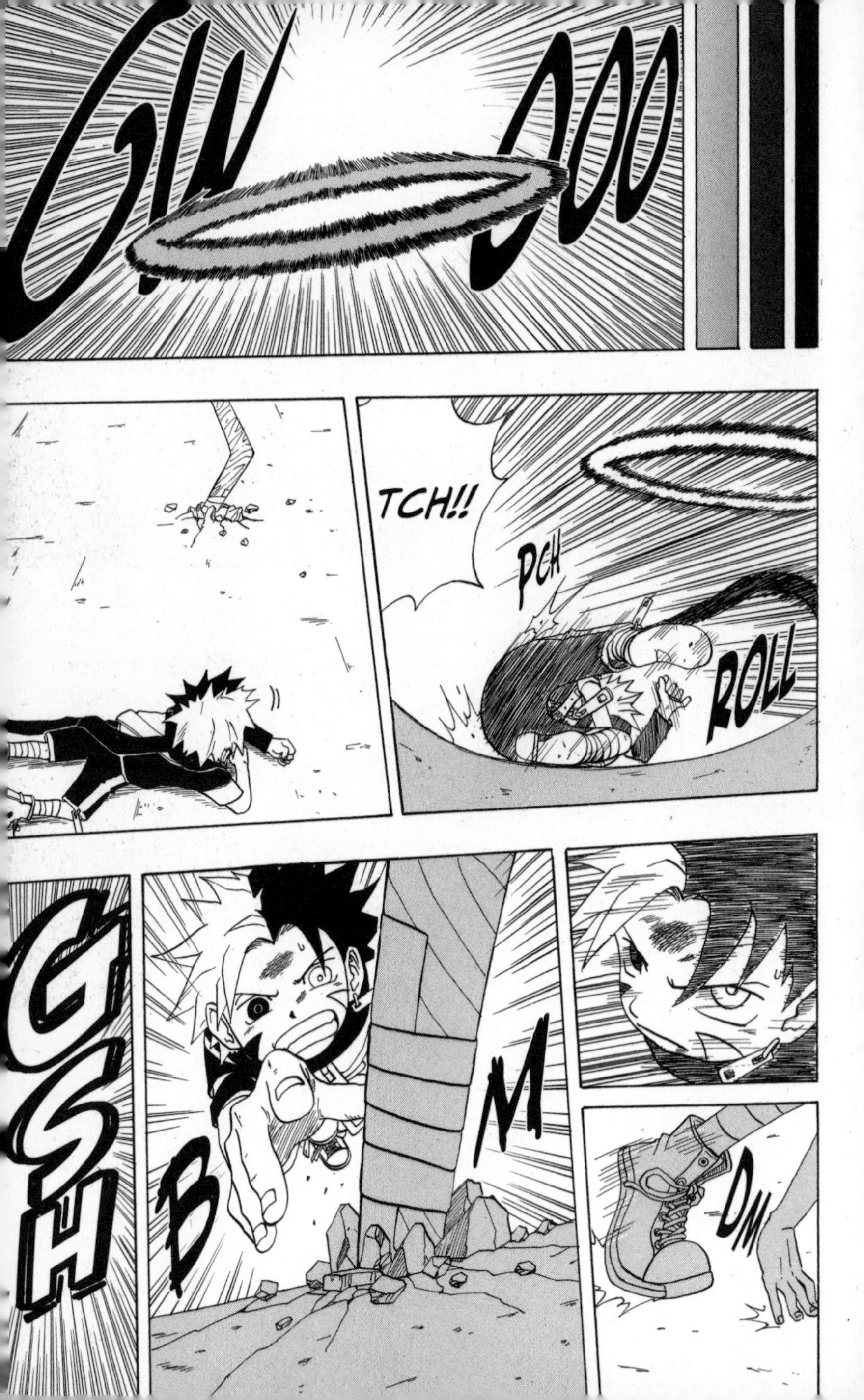
GWOOO
TCH!!
PCH
ROLL
DM
BM
GUSH

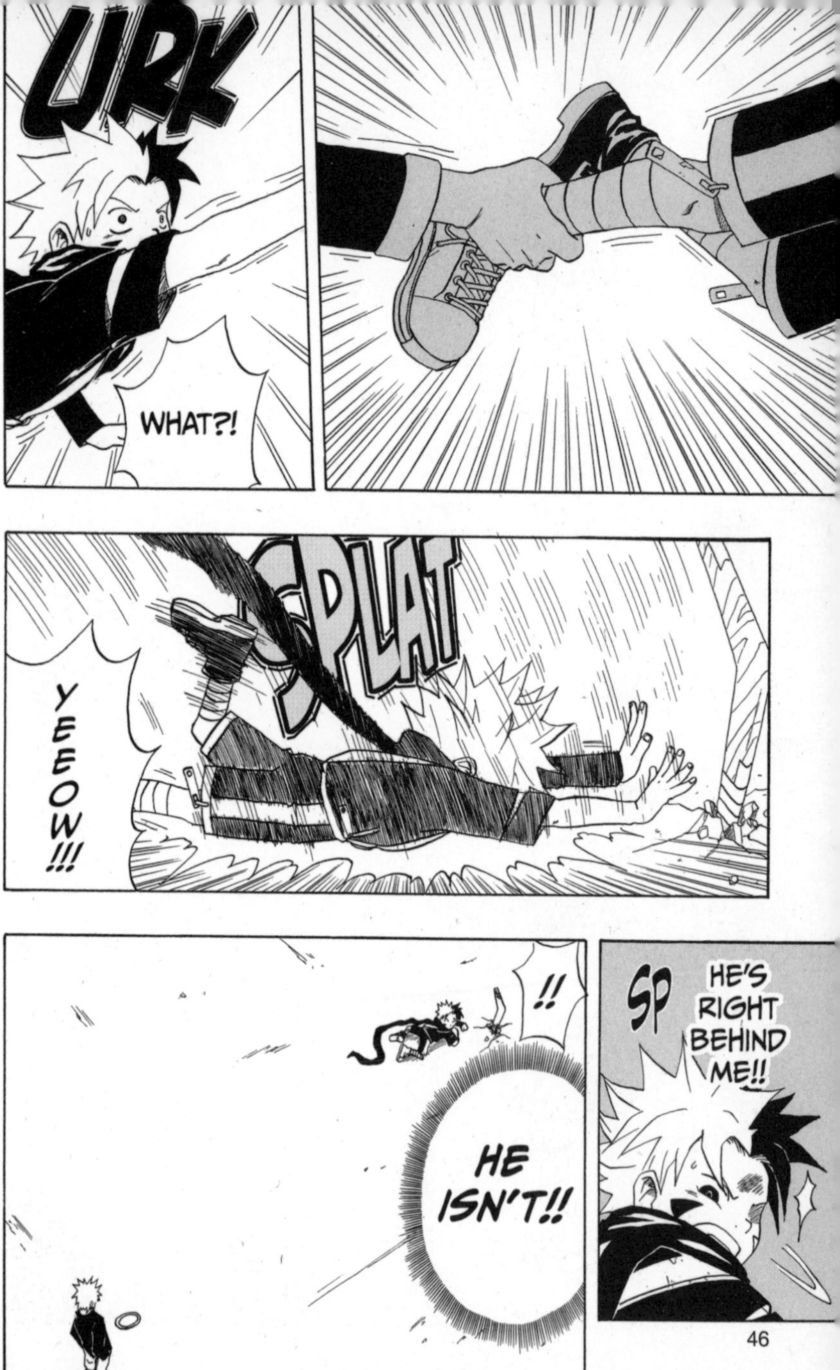
URK
WHAT?!
SPLAT
YEEOW!!!
SP
HE'S RIGHT BEHIND ME!!
!!
HE ISN'T!!

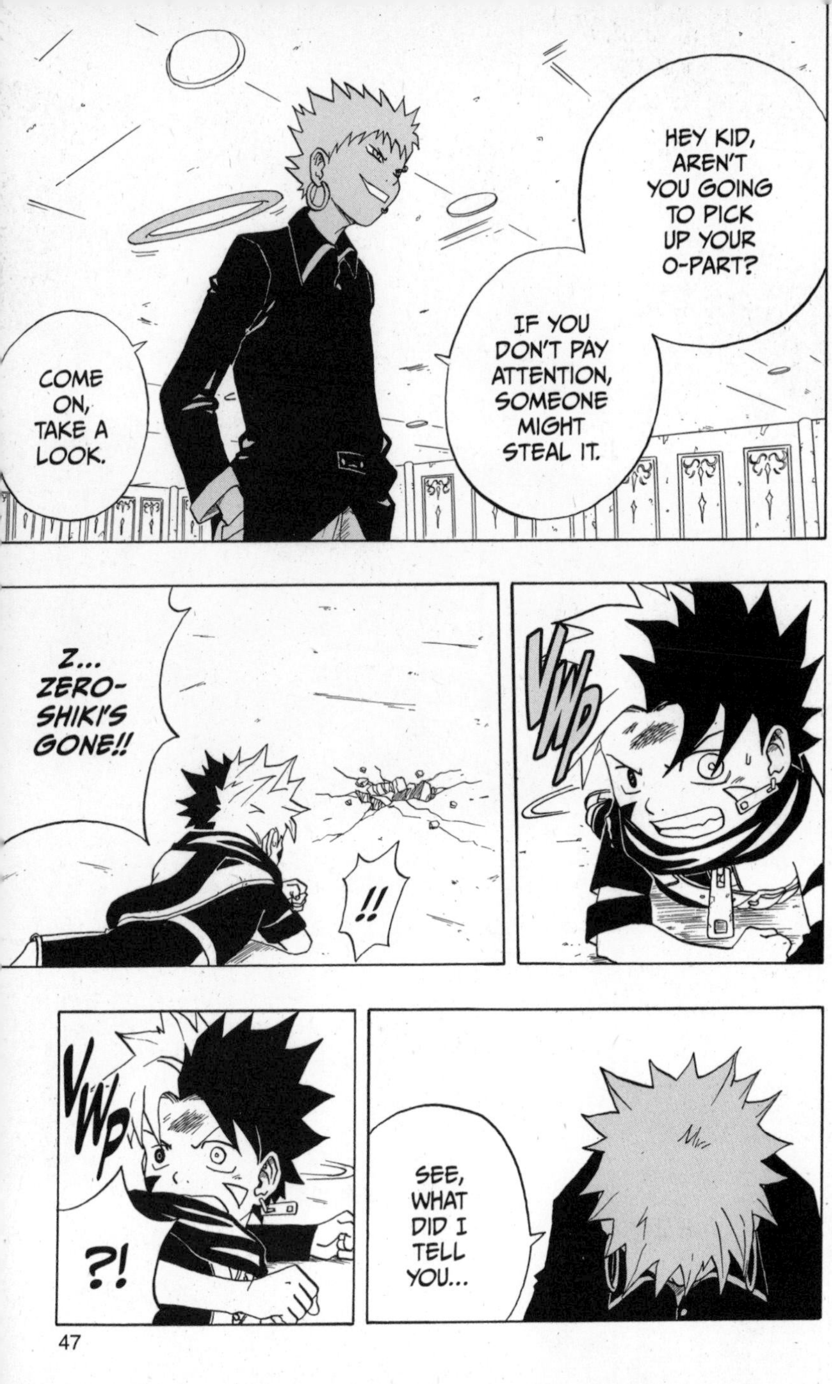
HEY KID, AREN'T YOU GOING TO PICK UP YOUR O-PART?
IF YOU DON'T PAY ATTENTION, SOMEONE MIGHT STEAL IT.
COME ON, TAKE A LOOK.
VWP
Z... ZERO-SHIKI'S GONE!!
!!
SEE, WHAT DID I TELL YOU...
VWP
?!

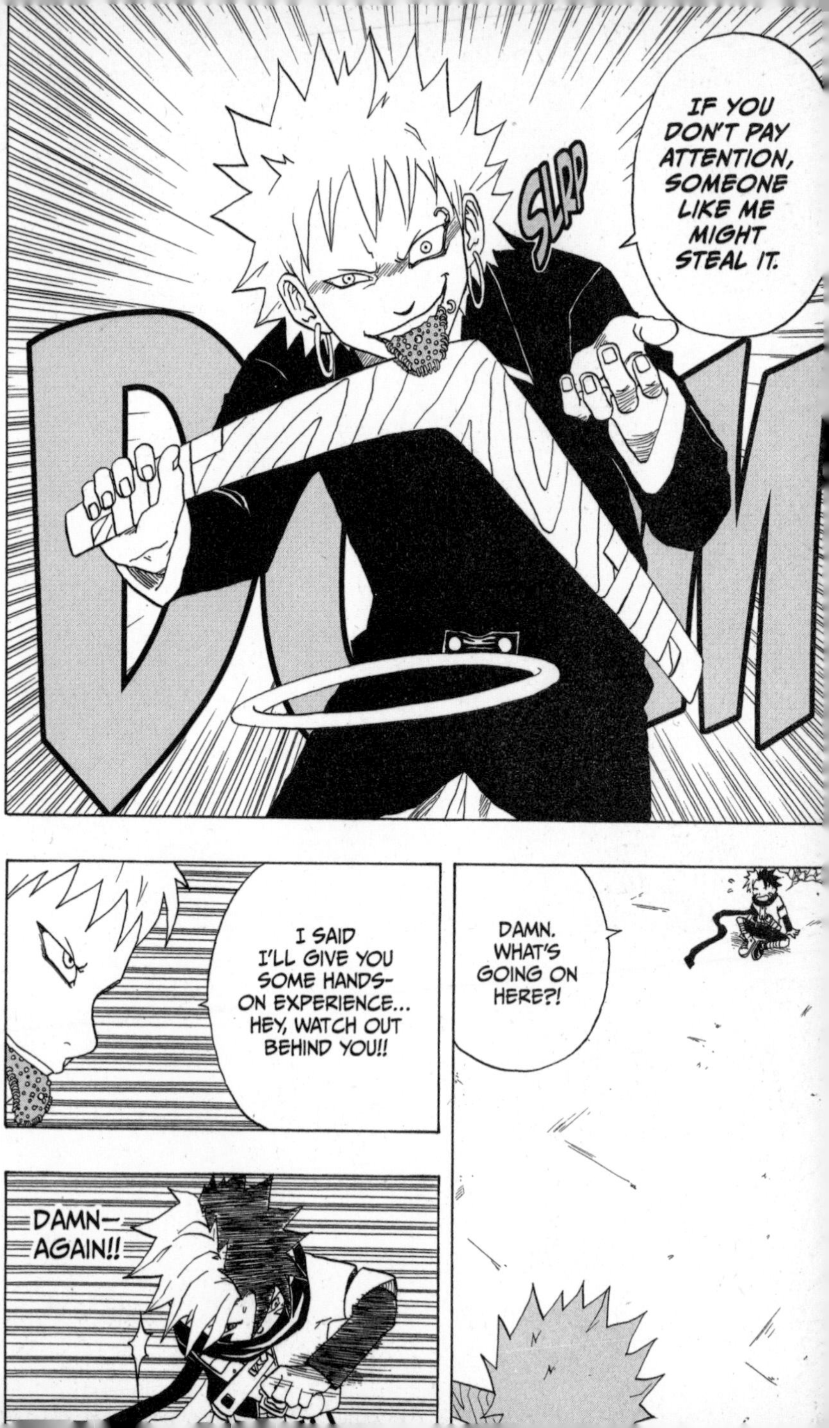
IF YOU DON'T PAY ATTENTION, SOMEONE LIKE ME MIGHT STEAL IT.
SLRP
DAMN. WHAT'S GOING ON HERE?!
I SAID I'LL GIVE YOU SOME HANDS-ON EXPERIENCE... HEY, WATCH OUT BEHIND YOU!!
DAMN— AGAIN!!

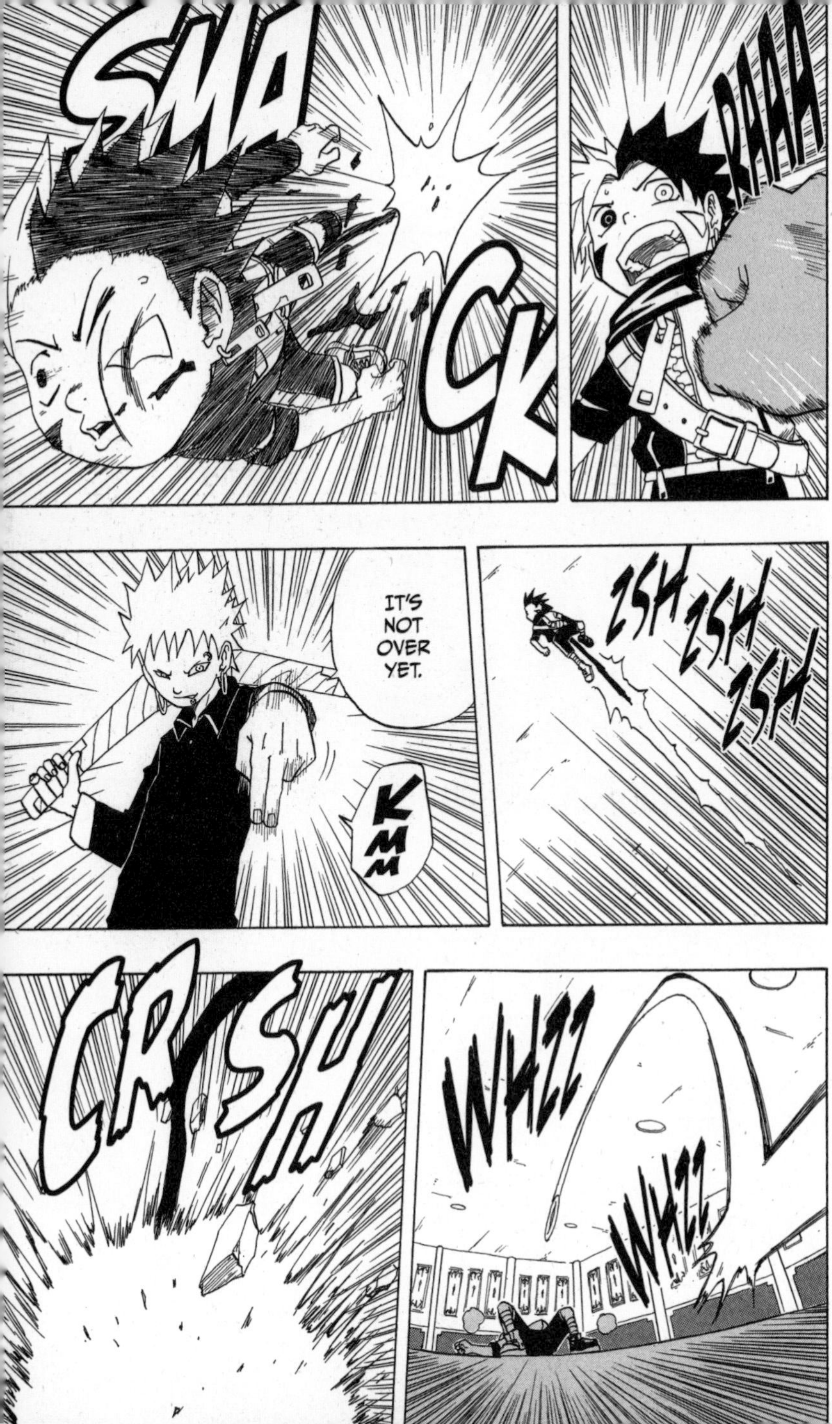
RAAA
SMACK
ZSH ZSH ZSH
IT'S NOT OVER YET.
KMM
WHZZ
WHZZ
CRASH

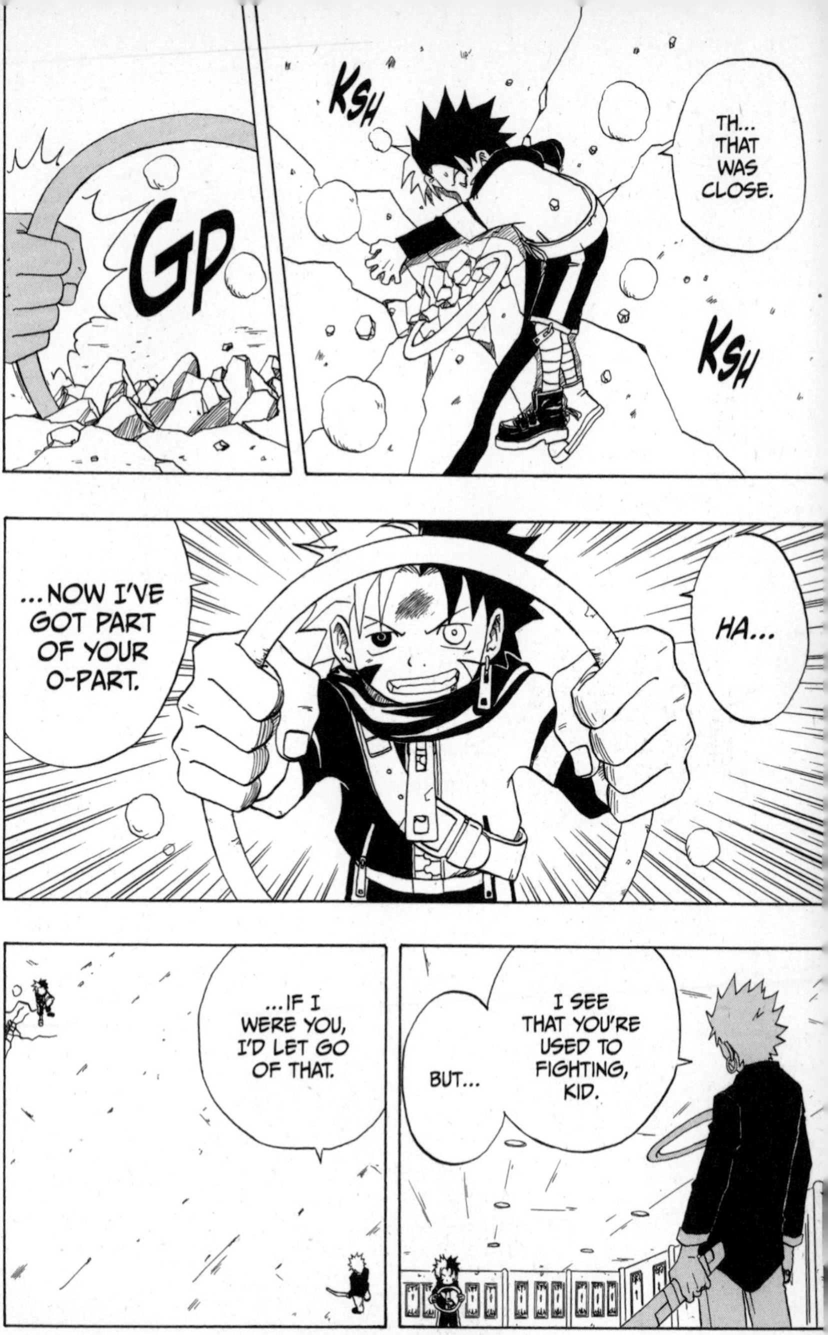
KSH
TH... THAT WAS CLOSE.
KSH
GP
HA...
...NOW I'VE GOT PART OF YOUR O-PART.
I SEE THAT YOU'RE USED TO FIGHTING, KID.
BUT...
...IF I WERE YOU, I'D LET GO OF THAT.

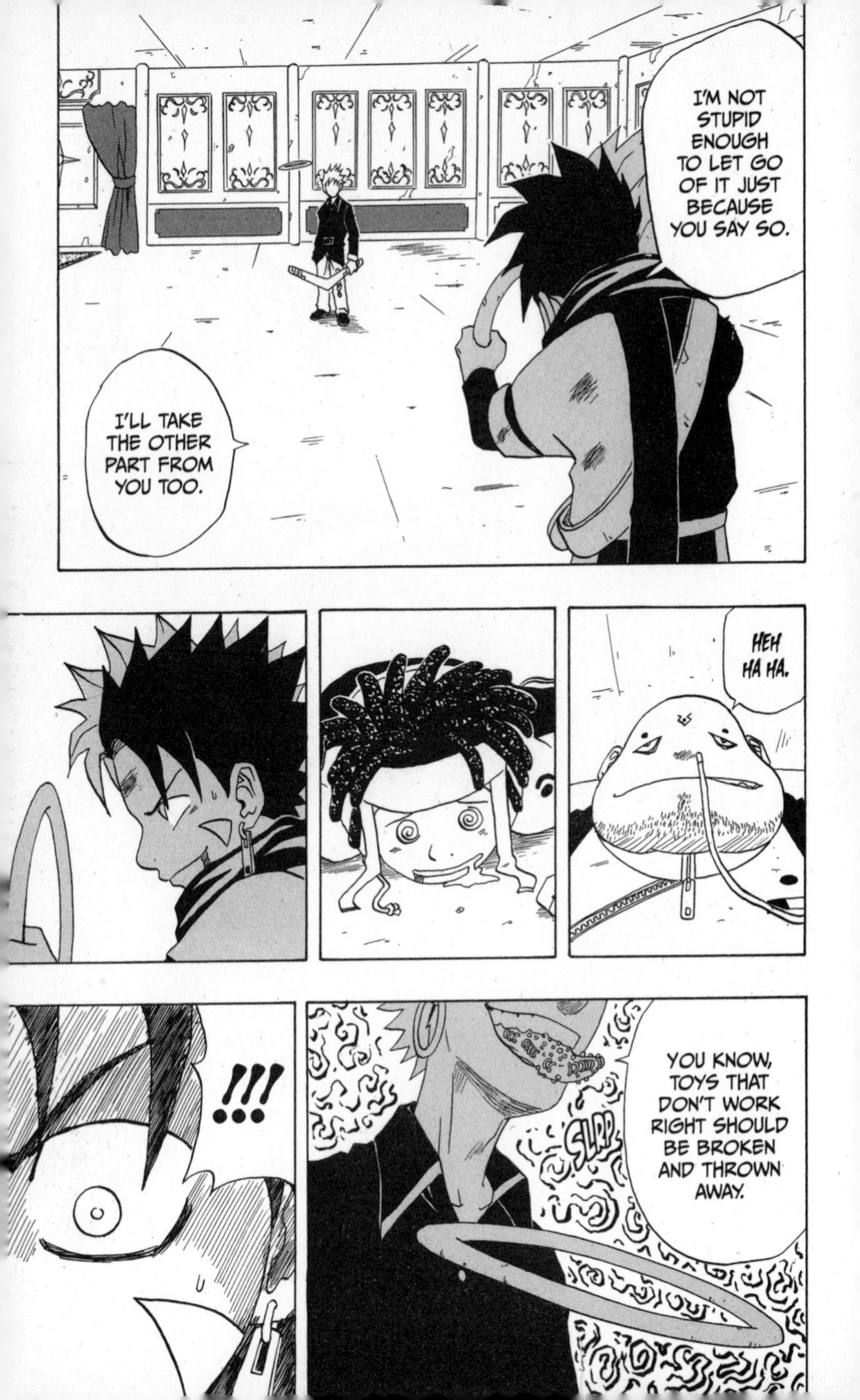
I'M NOT STUPID ENOUGH TO LET GO OF IT JUST BECAUSE YOU SAY SO.
I'LL TAKE THE OTHER PART FROM YOU TOO.
HEH HA HA.
YOU KNOW, TOYS THAT DON'T WORK RIGHT SHOULD BE BROKEN AND THROWN AWAY.
SLRP
!!!

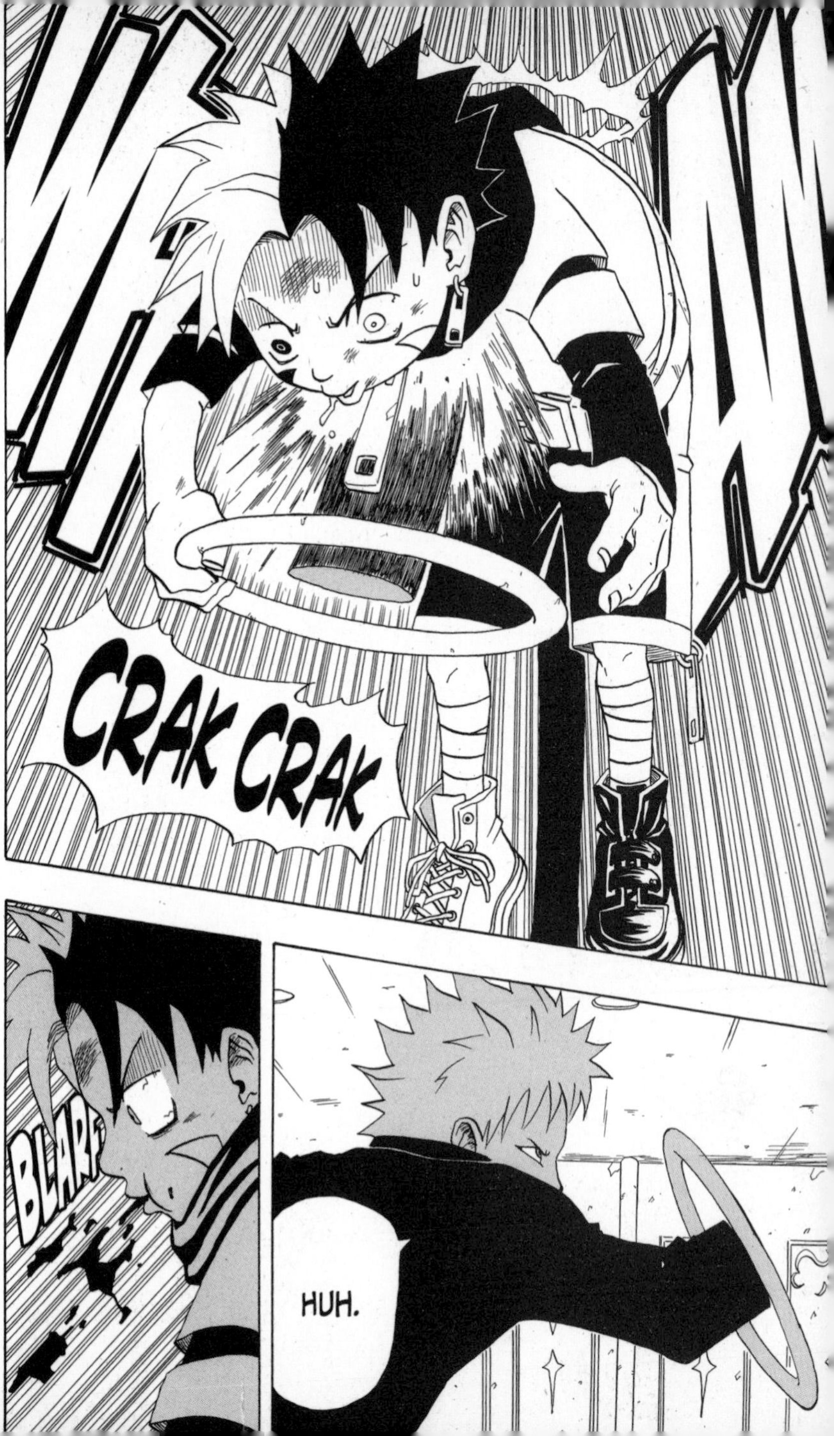
CRAK CRAK
HUH.
BLARF

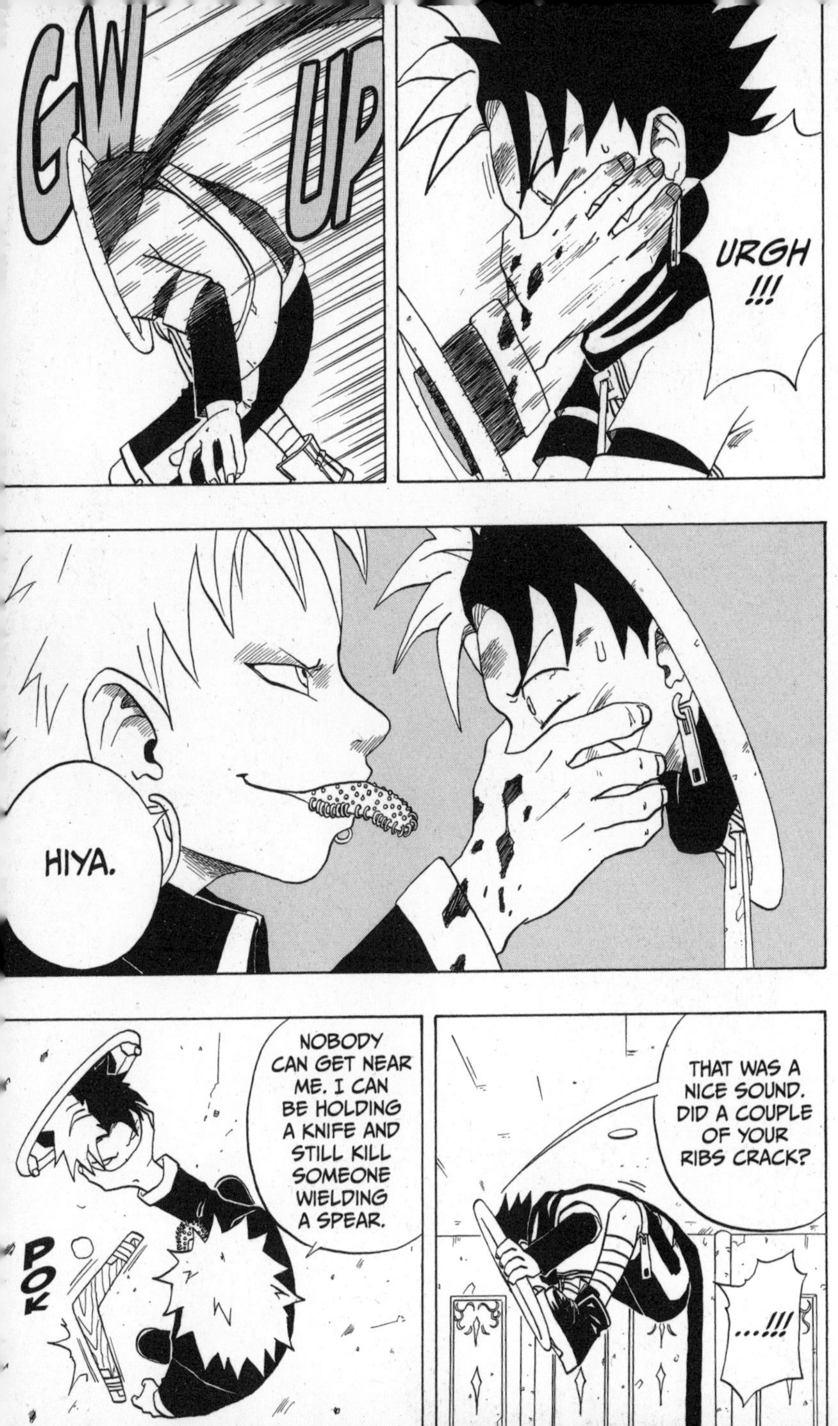
URGH !!!
GWUP
HIYA.
THAT WAS A NICE SOUND. DID A COUPLE OF YOUR RIBS CRACK?
...!!!
NOBODY CAN GET NEAR ME. I CAN BE HOLDING A KNIFE AND STILL KILL SOMEONE WIELDING A SPEAR.
POK

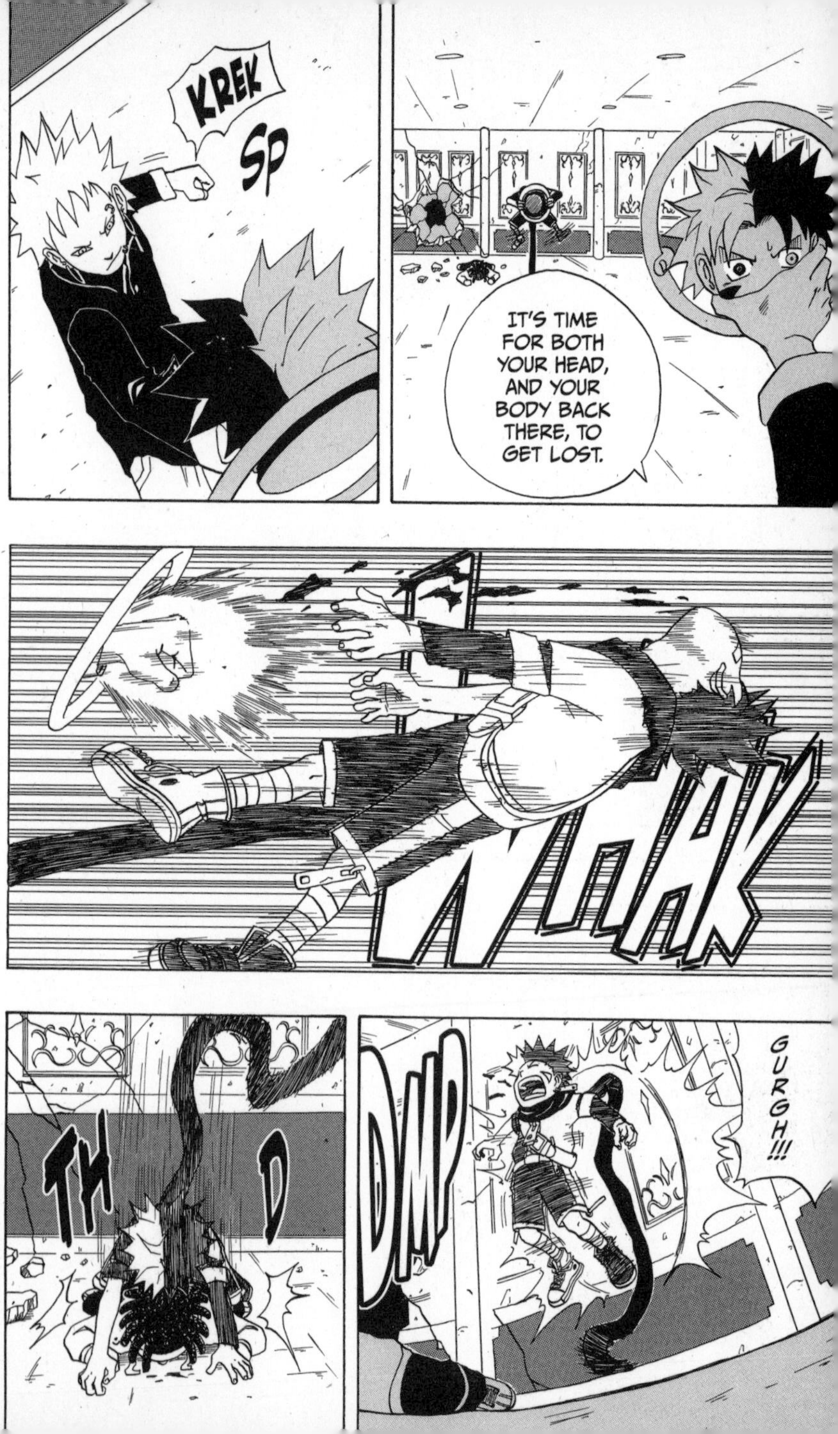
IT'S TIME FOR BOTH YOUR HEAD, AND YOUR BODY BACK THERE, TO GET LOST.
KREK
SP
WHAK
GURGH!!!
DMP
TH
D

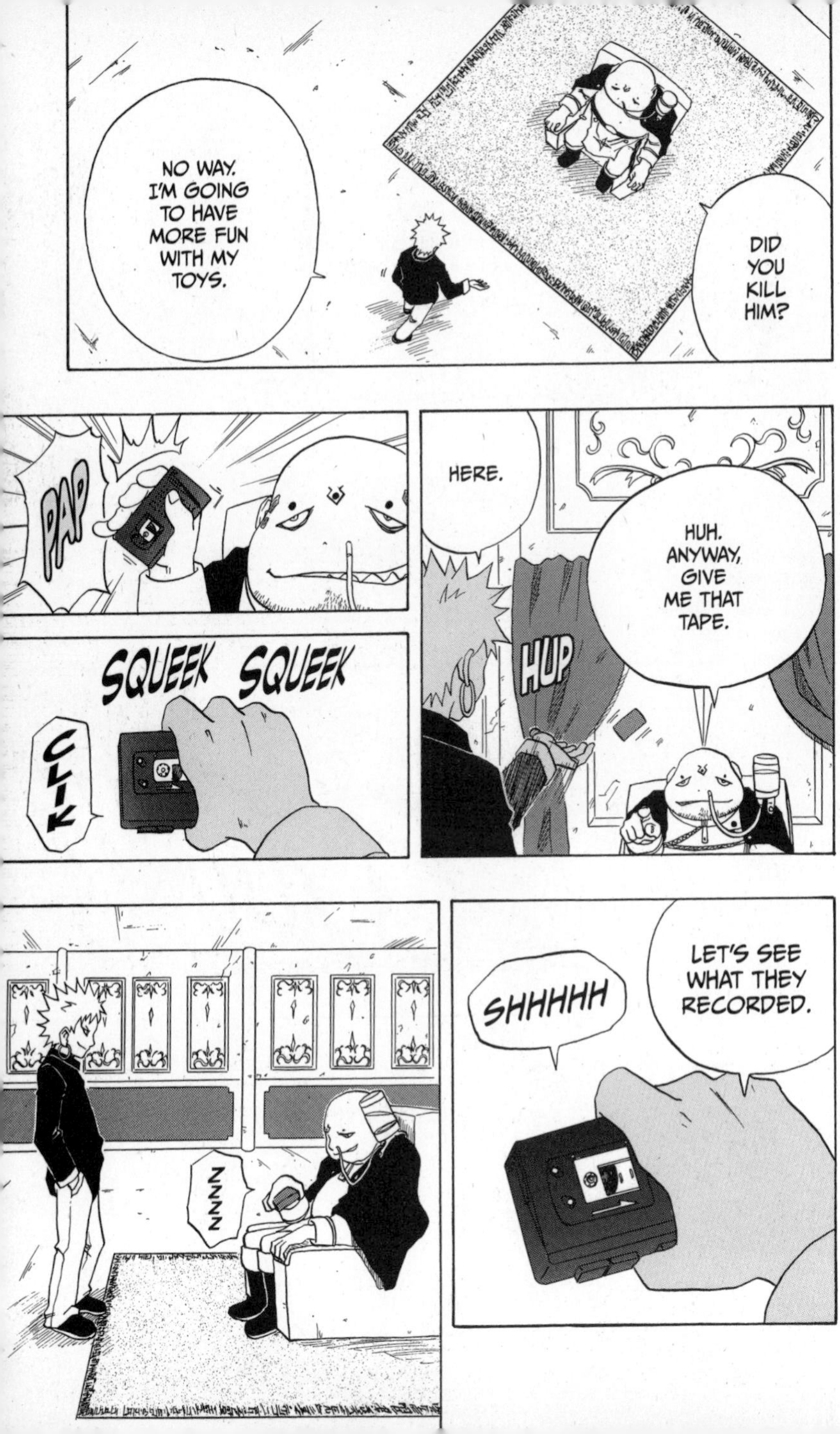
DID YOU KILL HIM?
NO WAY. I'M GOING TO HAVE MORE FUN WITH MY TOYS.
HUH. ANYWAY, GIVE ME THAT TAPE.
HERE.
HUP
PAP
SQUEEK SQUEEK
CLIK
LET'S SEE WHAT THEY RECORDED.
SHHHHH
ZZZZ

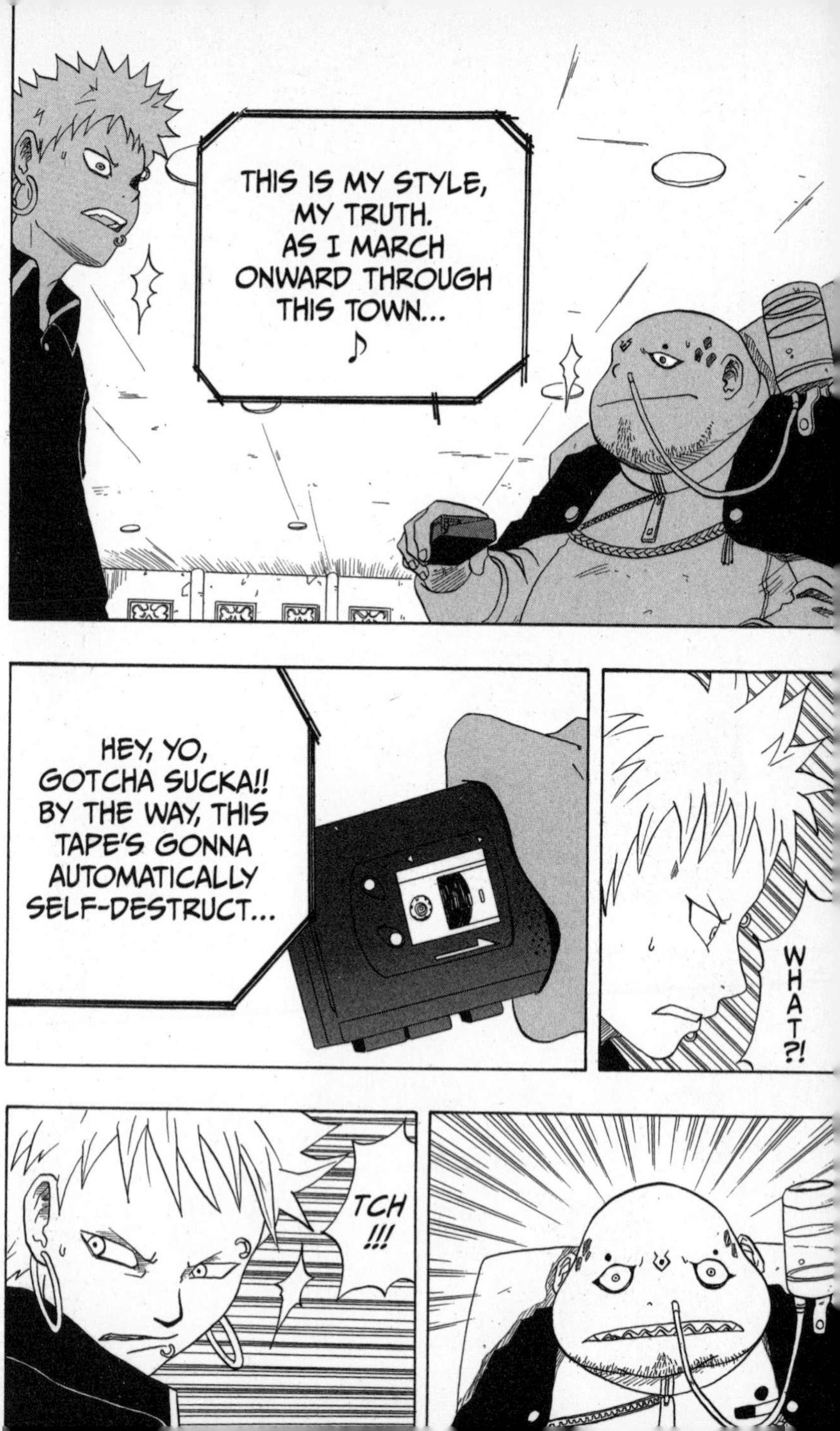
THIS IS MY STYLE, MY TRUTH. AS I MARCH ONWARD THROUGH THIS TOWN... ♪
HEY, YO, GOTCHA SUCKA!! BY THE WAY, THIS TAPE'S GONNA AUTOMATICALLY SELF-DESTRUCT...
WHAT?!
TCH !!!

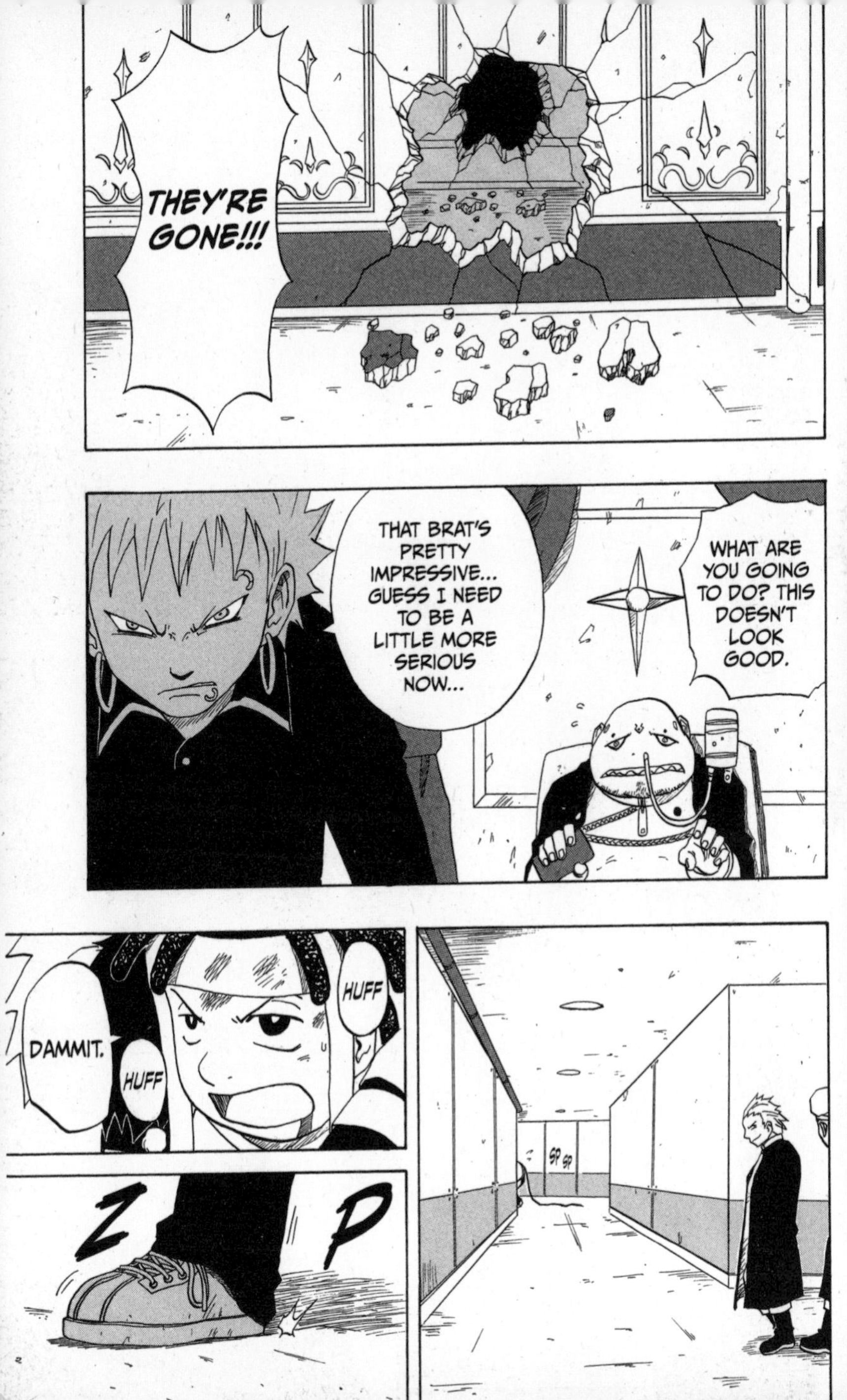
THEY'RE GONE!!!
WHAT ARE YOU GOING TO DO? THIS DOESN'T LOOK GOOD.
THAT BRAT'S PRETTY IMPRESSIVE... GUESS I NEED TO BE A LITTLE MORE SERIOUS NOW...
SP SP
HUFF
DAMMIT.
HUFF
ZP

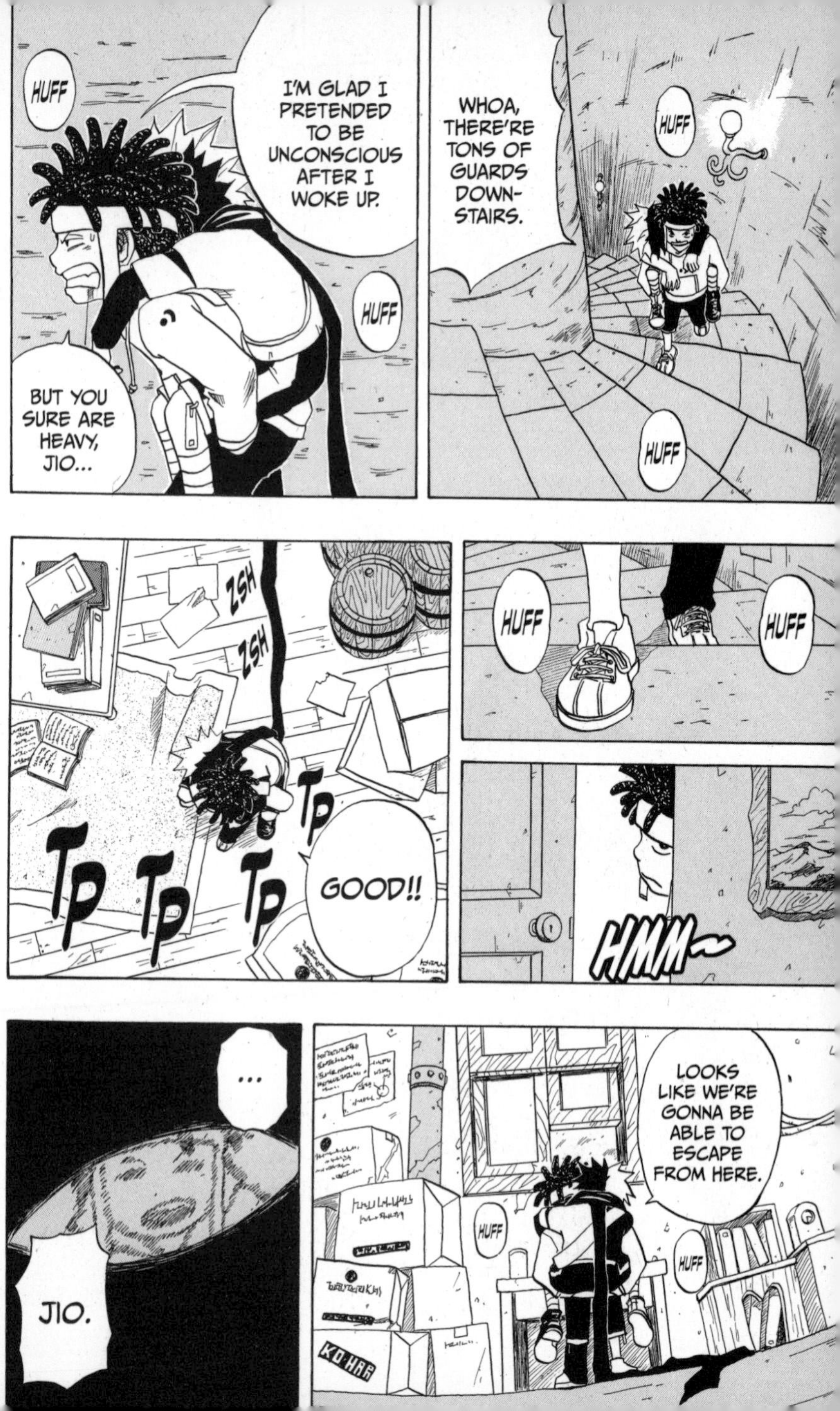
HUFF
WHOA, THERE'RE TONS OF GUARDS DOWN-STAIRS.
HUFF
I'M GLAD I PRETENDED TO BE UNCONSCIOUS AFTER I WOKE UP.
HUFF
HUFF
BUT YOU SURE ARE HEAVY, JIO...
HUFF
HUFF
HMM~
ZSH
ZSH
Tp
GOOD!!
Tp
Tp
Tp
LOOKS LIKE WE'RE GONNA BE ABLE TO ESCAPE FROM HERE.
HUFF
HUFF
...
JIO.

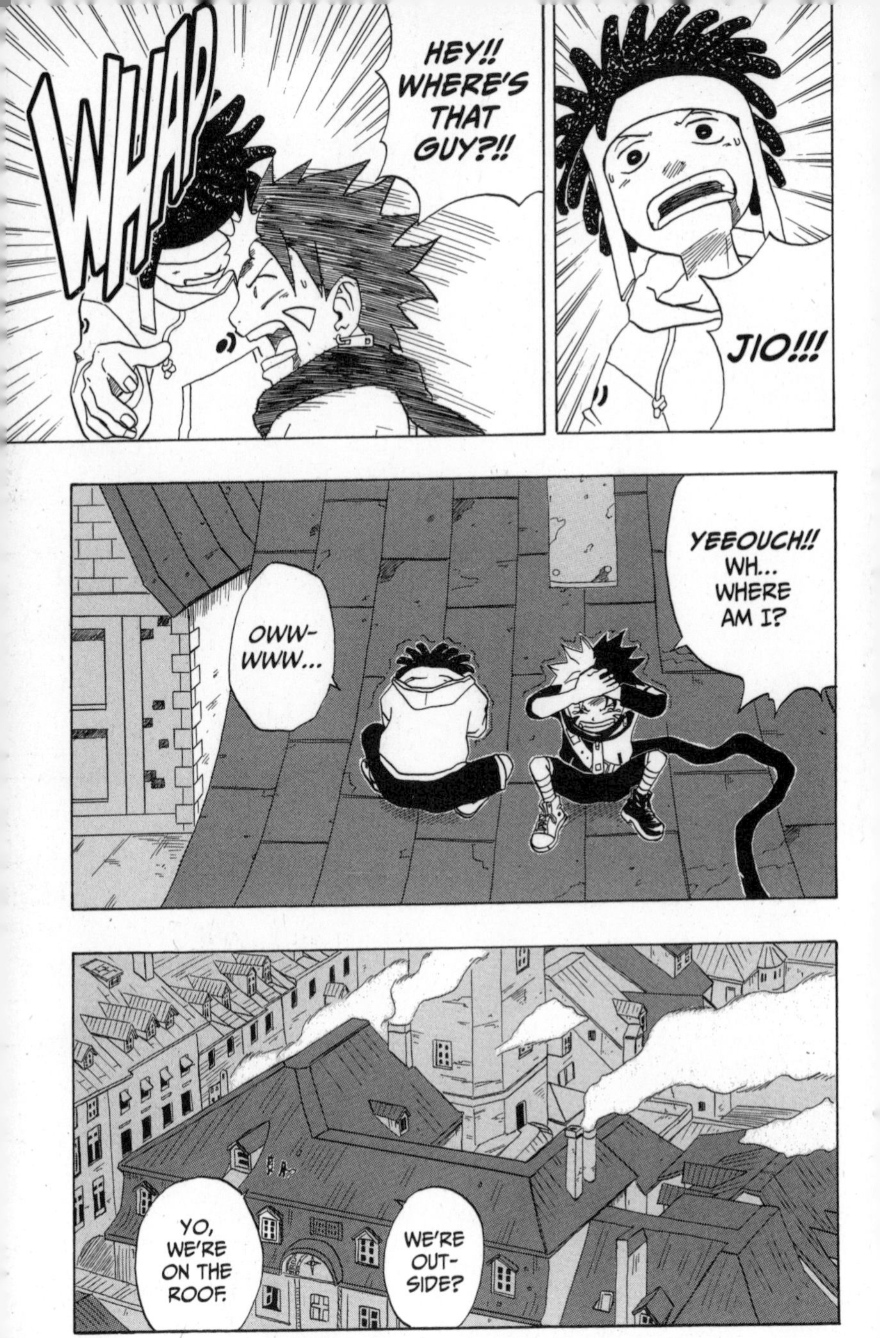
JIO!!!
WHAP
HEY!! WHERE'S THAT GUY?!!
YEEOUCH!! WH... WHERE AM I?
OWW-WWW...
WE'RE OUT-SIDE?
YO, WE'RE ON THE ROOF.

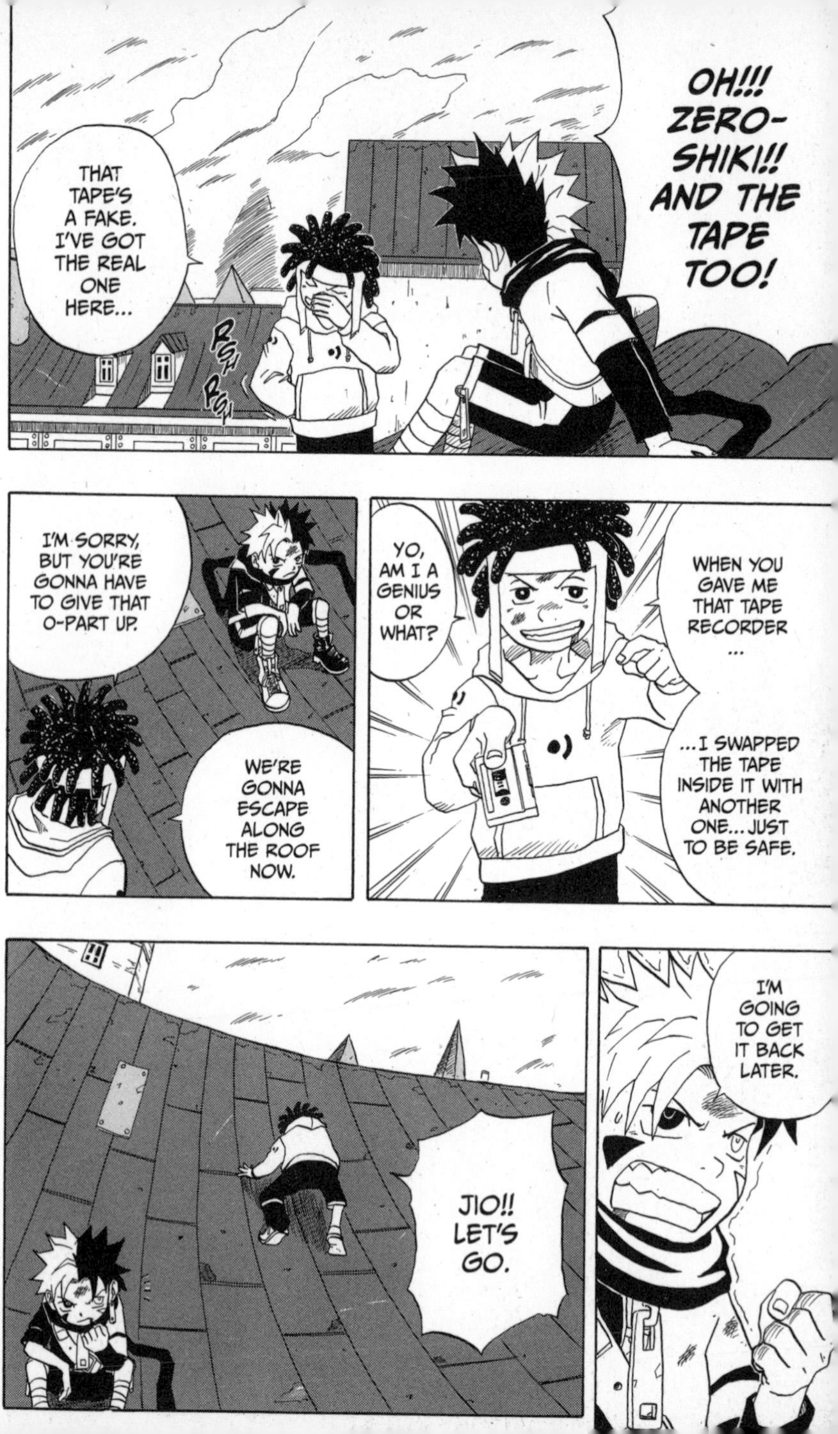
OH!!! ZERO-SHIKI!! AND THE TAPE TOO!
THAT TAPE'S A FAKE. I'VE GOT THE REAL ONE HERE...
RSH RSH
WHEN YOU GAVE ME THAT TAPE RECORDER ...
...I SWAPPED THE TAPE INSIDE IT WITH ANOTHER ONE... JUST TO BE SAFE.
YO, AM I A GENIUS OR WHAT?
I'M SORRY, BUT YOU'RE GONNA HAVE TO GIVE THAT O-PART UP.
WE'RE GONNA ESCAPE ALONG THE ROOF NOW.
I'M GOING TO GET IT BACK LATER.
JIO!! LET'S GO.

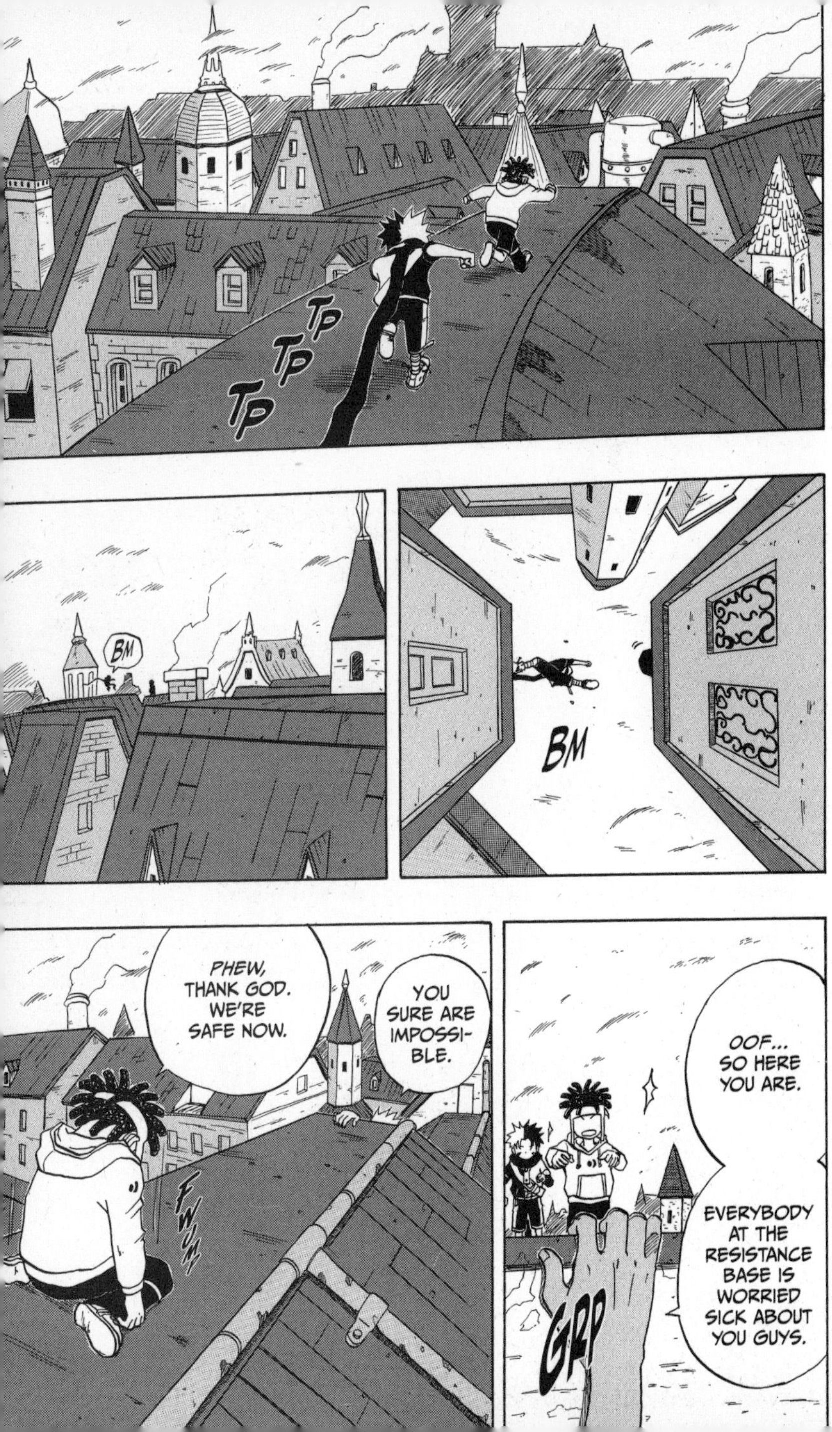
TP
TP
TP
BM
BM
OOF... SO HERE YOU ARE.
EVERYBODY AT THE RESISTANCE BASE IS WORRIED SICK ABOUT YOU GUYS.
GRP
PHEW, THANK GOD. WE'RE SAFE NOW.
YOU SURE ARE IMPOSSI-BLE.
FWUM

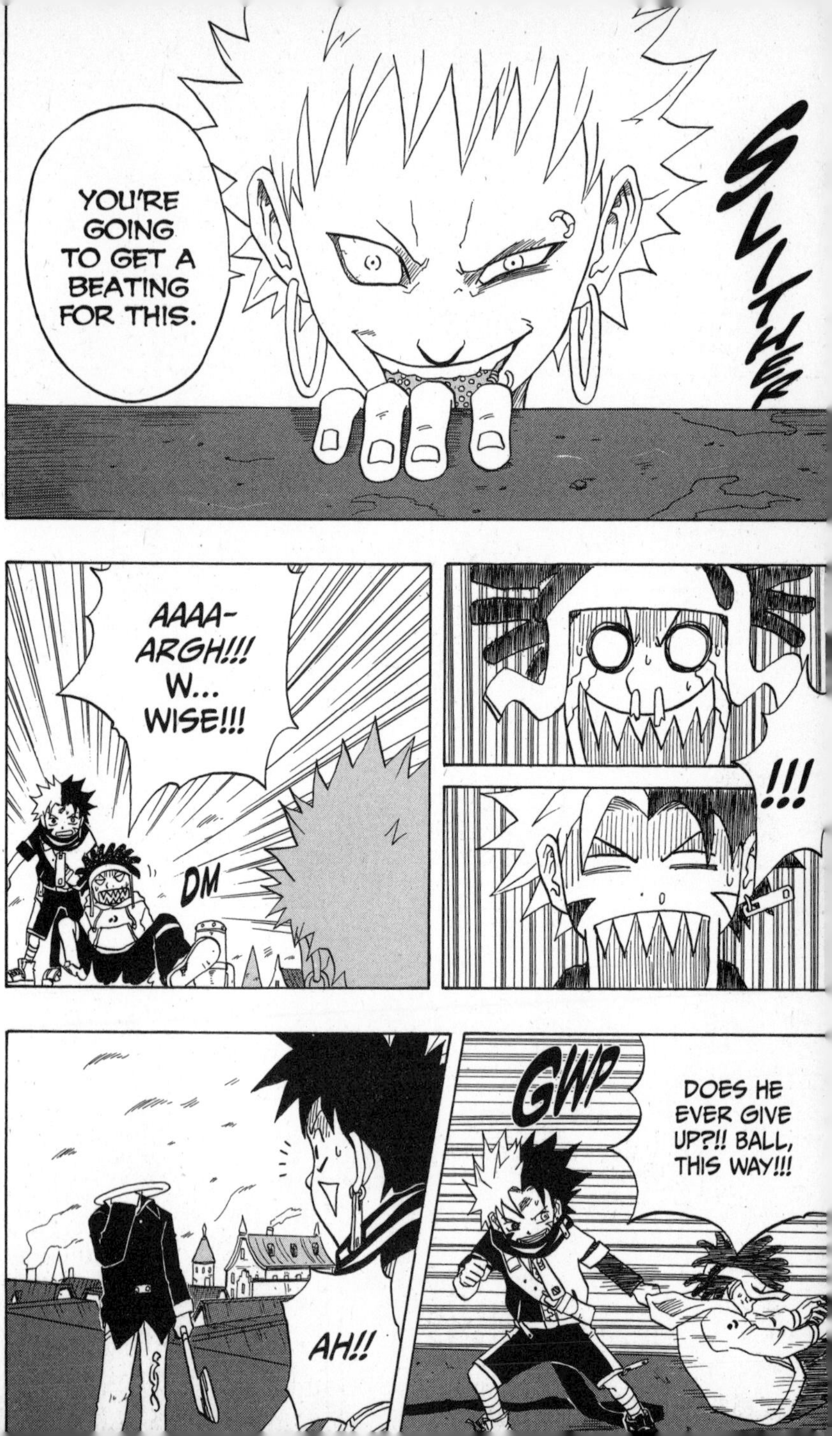
SLITHER
YOU'RE GOING TO GET A BEATING FOR THIS.
AAAA-ARGH!!! W... WISE!!!
DM
!!!
DOES HE EVER GIVE UP?!! BALL, THIS WAY!!!
GWP
AH!!

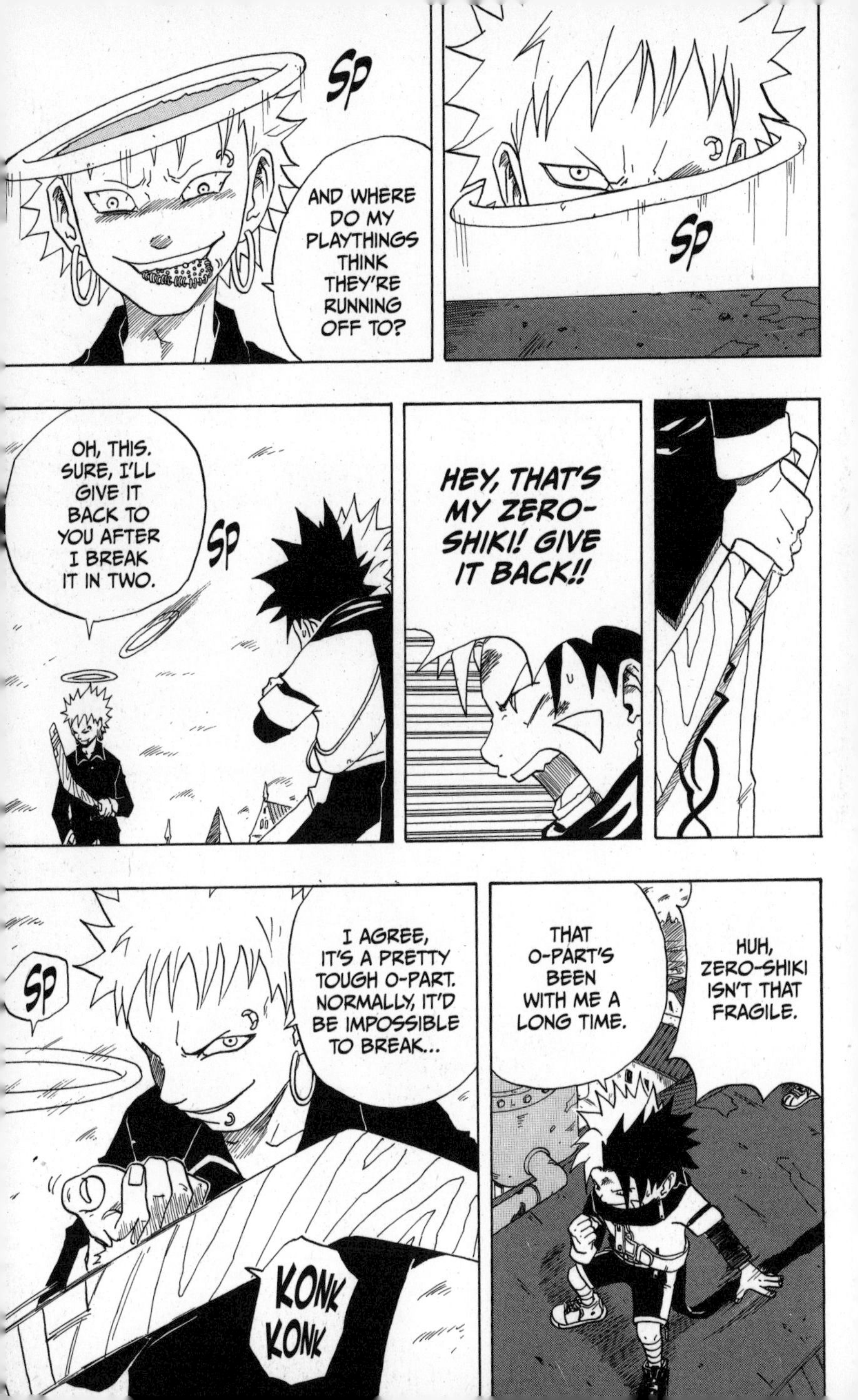
SP
SP
AND WHERE DO MY PLAYTHINGS THINK THEY'RE RUNNING OFF TO?
HEY, THAT'S MY ZERO-SHIKI! GIVE IT BACK!!
OH, THIS. SURE, I'LL GIVE IT BACK TO YOU AFTER I BREAK IT IN TWO.
SP
HUH, ZERO-SHIKI ISN'T THAT FRAGILE.
THAT O-PART'S BEEN WITH ME A LONG TIME.
I AGREE, IT'S A PRETTY TOUGH O-PART. NORMALLY, IT'D BE IMPOSSIBLE TO BREAK...
SP
KONK KONK

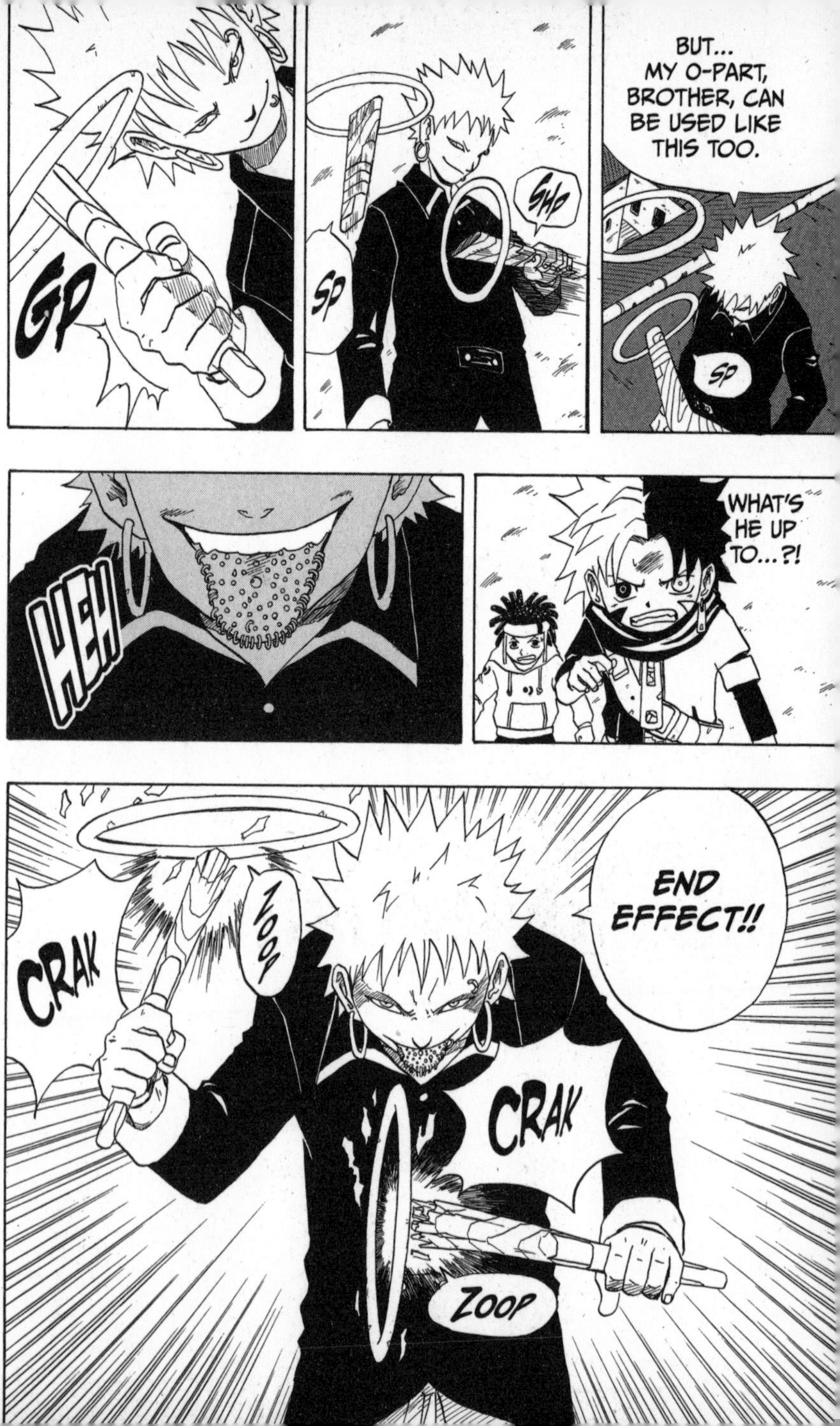
BUT... MY O-PART, BROTHER, CAN BE USED LIKE THIS TOO.
SP
SHP
SP
GD
WHAT'S HE UP TO...?!
HEH
END EFFECT!!
ZOOP
CRAK
CRAK
ZOOP

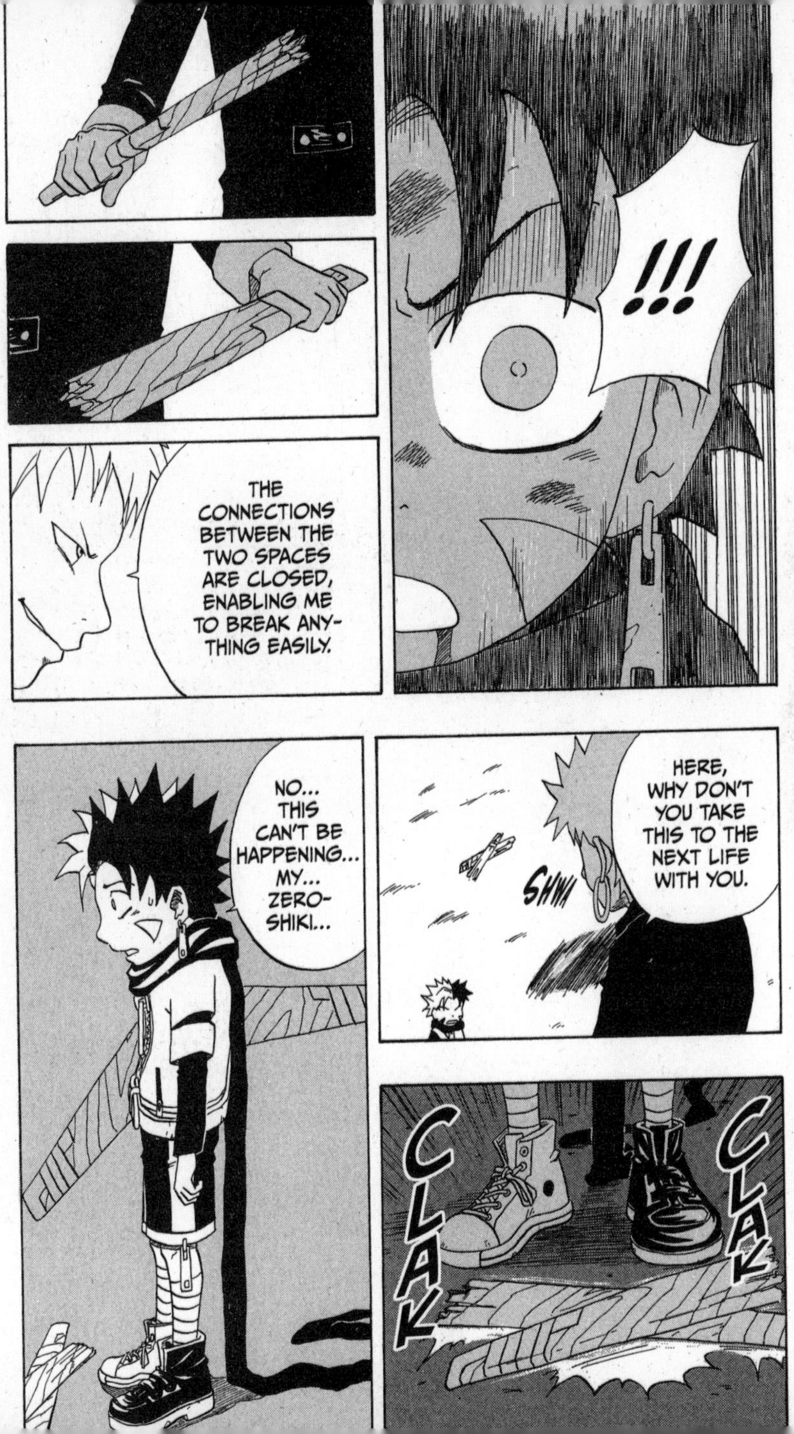
!!!
THE CONNECTIONS BETWEEN THE TWO SPACES ARE CLOSED, ENABLING ME TO BREAK ANY-THING EASILY.
HERE, WHY DON'T YOU TAKE THIS TO THE NEXT LIFE WITH YOU.
SHWA
CLAK
CLAK
NO... THIS CAN'T BE HAPPENING... MY... ZERO-SHIKI...

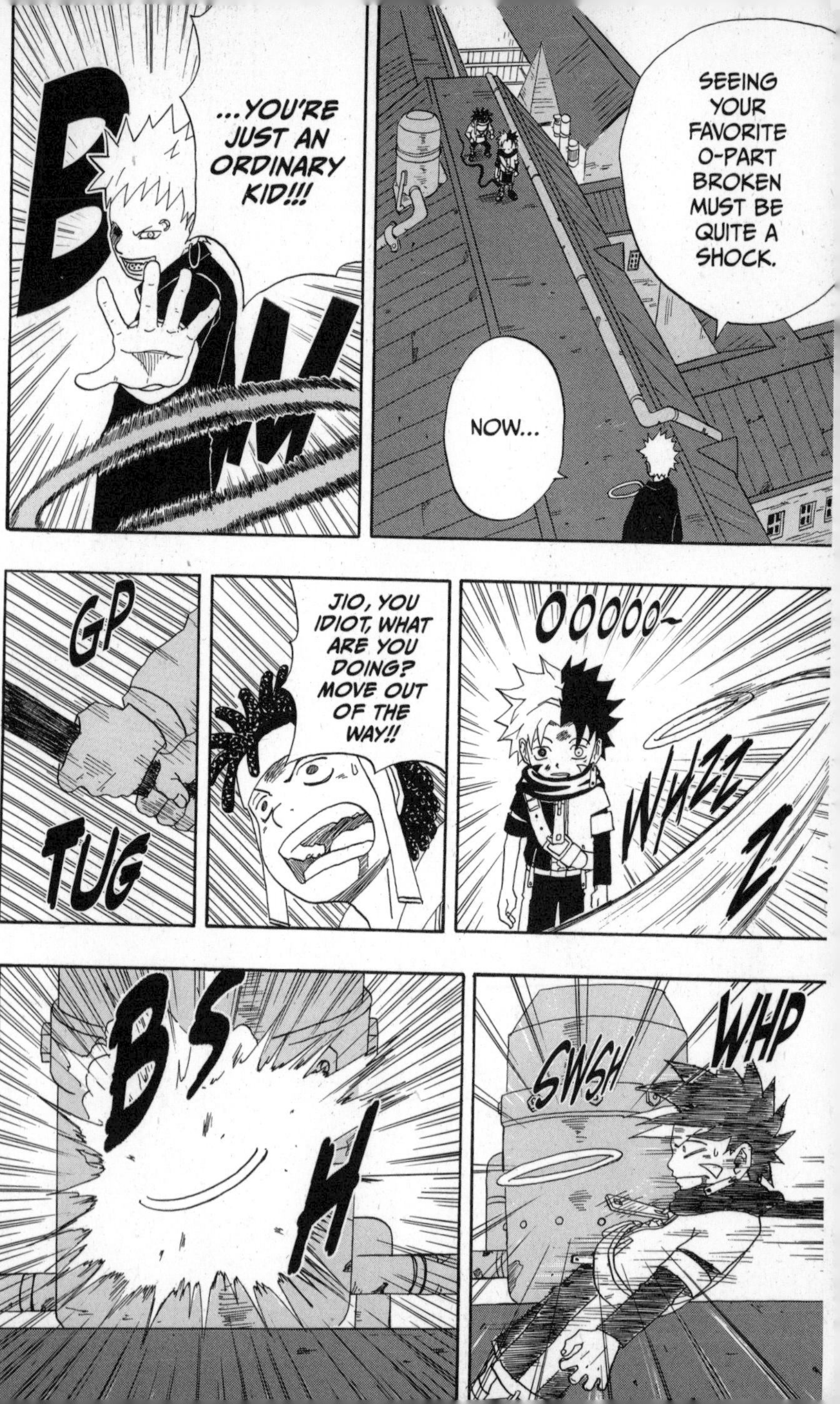
BAM
...YOU'RE JUST AN ORDINARY KID!!!
SEEING YOUR FAVORITE O-PART BROKEN MUST BE QUITE A SHOCK.
NOW...
GP
TUG
JIO, YOU IDIOT, WHAT ARE YOU DOING? MOVE OUT OF THE WAY!!
OOOOO~
WHZZZ
BSH
SWSH
WHP

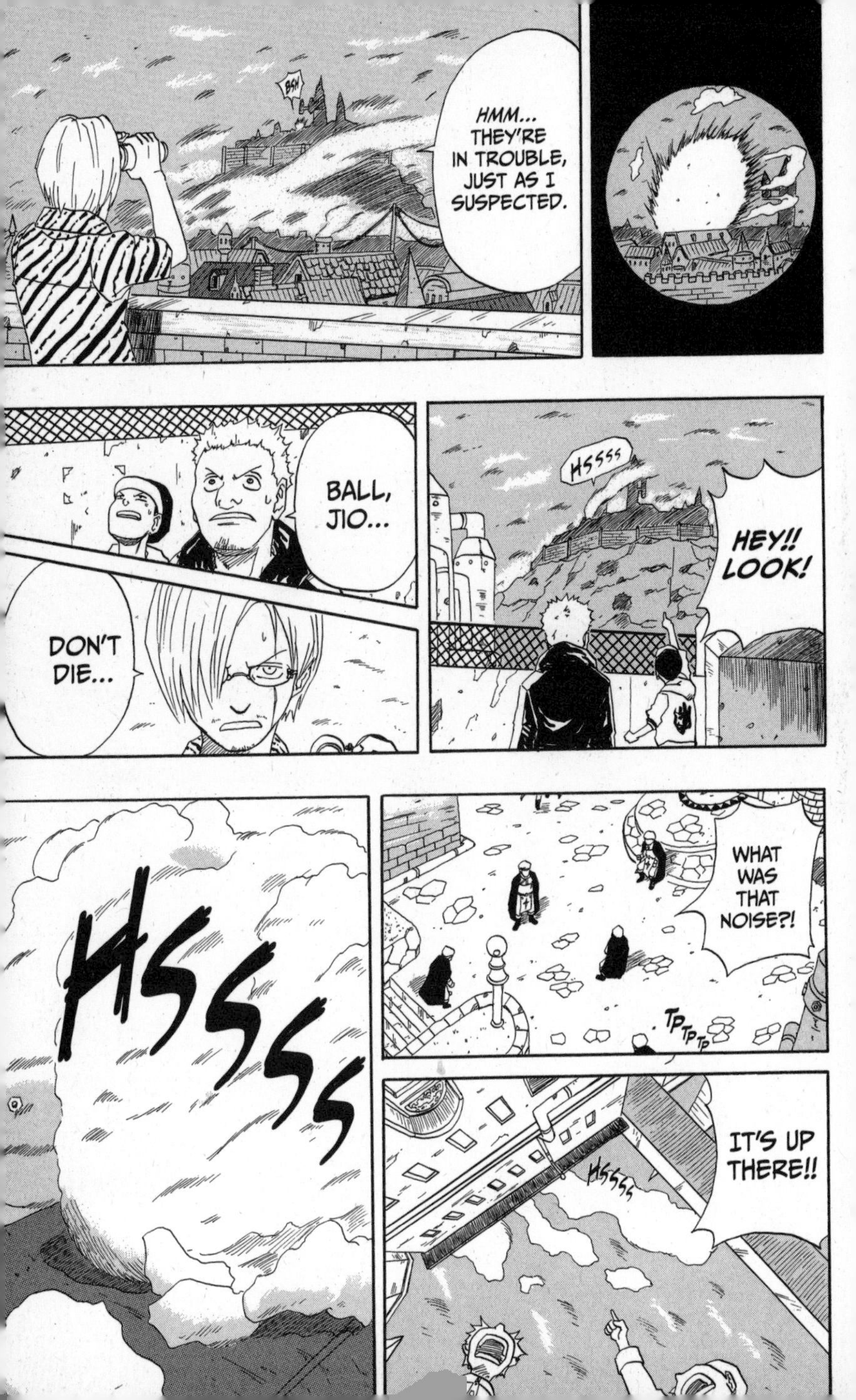
BSH
HMM... THEY'RE IN TROUBLE, JUST AS I SUSPECTED.
HSSSS
HEY!! LOOK!
BALL, JIO...
DON'T DIE...
WHAT WAS THAT NOISE?!
TPTPTP
IT'S UP THERE!!
HSSSS
HSSSS

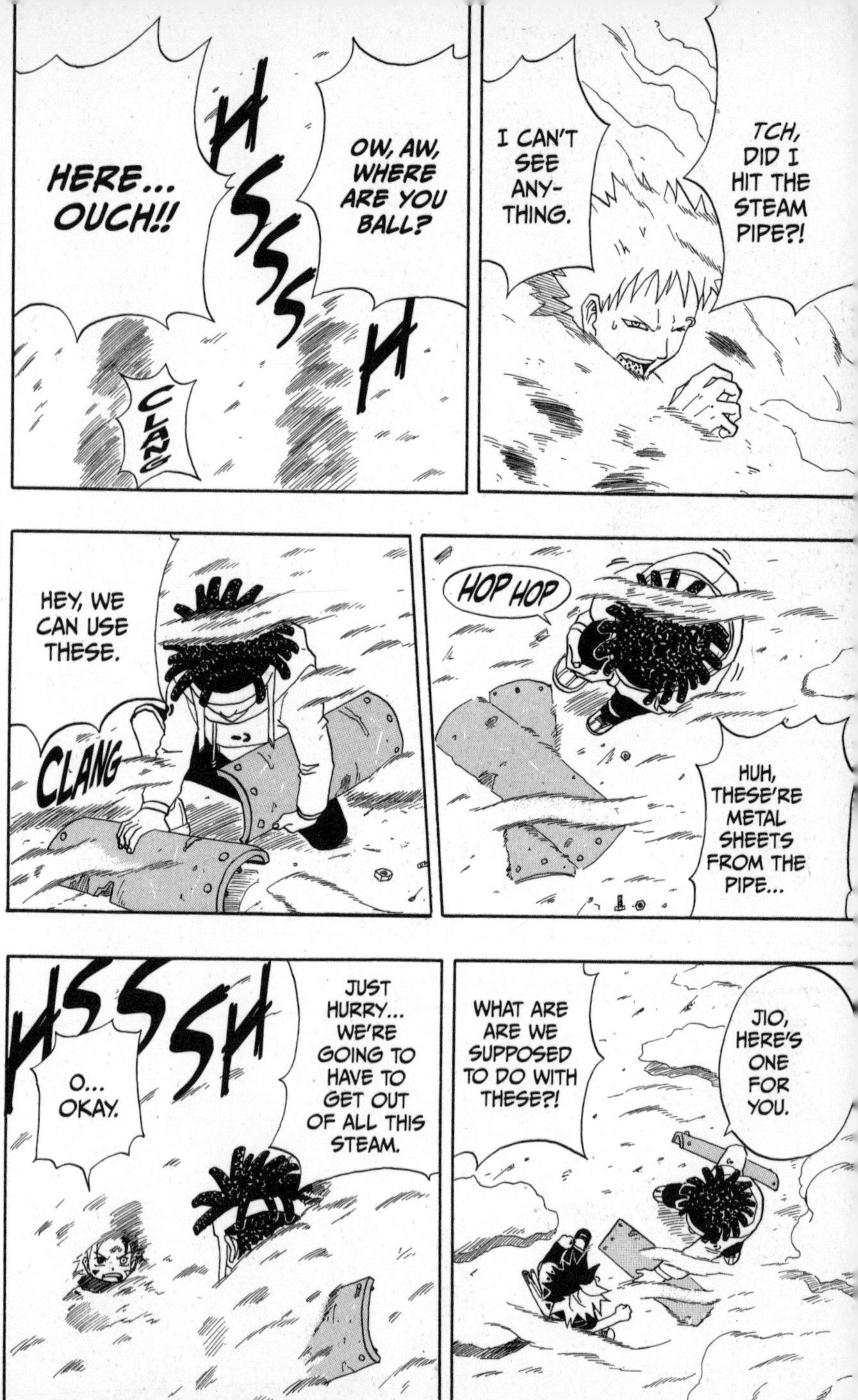
TCH, DID I HIT THE STEAM PIPE?!
I CAN'T SEE ANYTHING.
OW, AW, WHERE ARE YOU BALL?
HISSSH
HERE... OUCH!!
CLANG
HOP HOP
HUH, THESE'RE METAL SHEETS FROM THE PIPE...
HEY, WE CAN USE THESE.
CLANG
JIO, HERE'S ONE FOR YOU.
WHAT ARE ARE WE SUPPOSED TO DO WITH THESE?!
JUST HURRY... WE'RE GOING TO HAVE TO GET OUT OF ALL THIS STEAM.
HSSSH
O... OKAY.

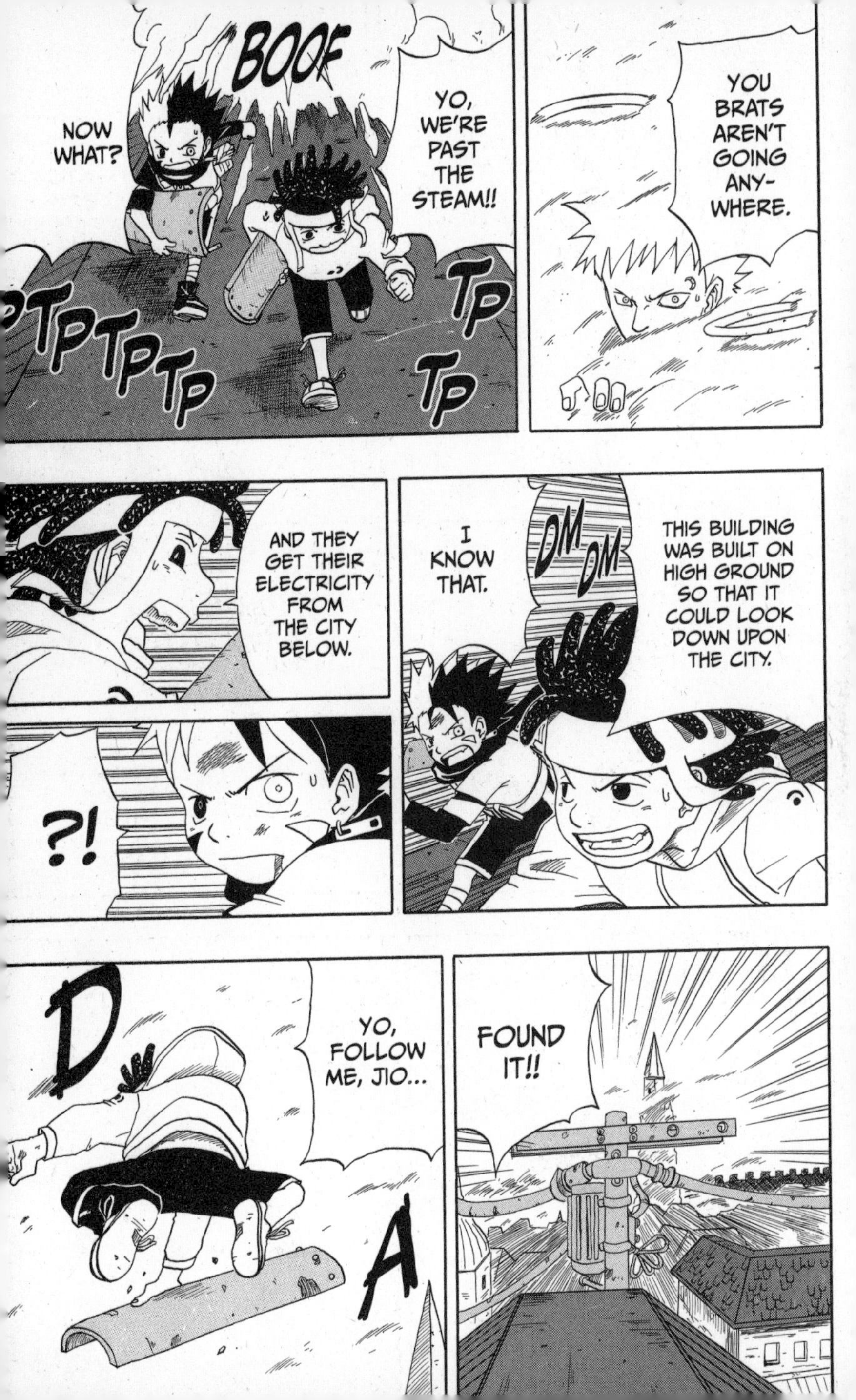
YOU BRATS AREN'T GOING ANY-WHERE.
BOOF
YO, WE'RE PAST THE STEAM!!
NOW WHAT?
TP TP
TPTPTPTP
THIS BUILDING WAS BUILT ON HIGH GROUND SO THAT IT COULD LOOK DOWN UPON THE CITY.
DM DM
I KNOW THAT.
AND THEY GET THEIR ELECTRICITY FROM THE CITY BELOW.
?!
FOUND IT!!
YO, FOLLOW ME, JIO...
D
A

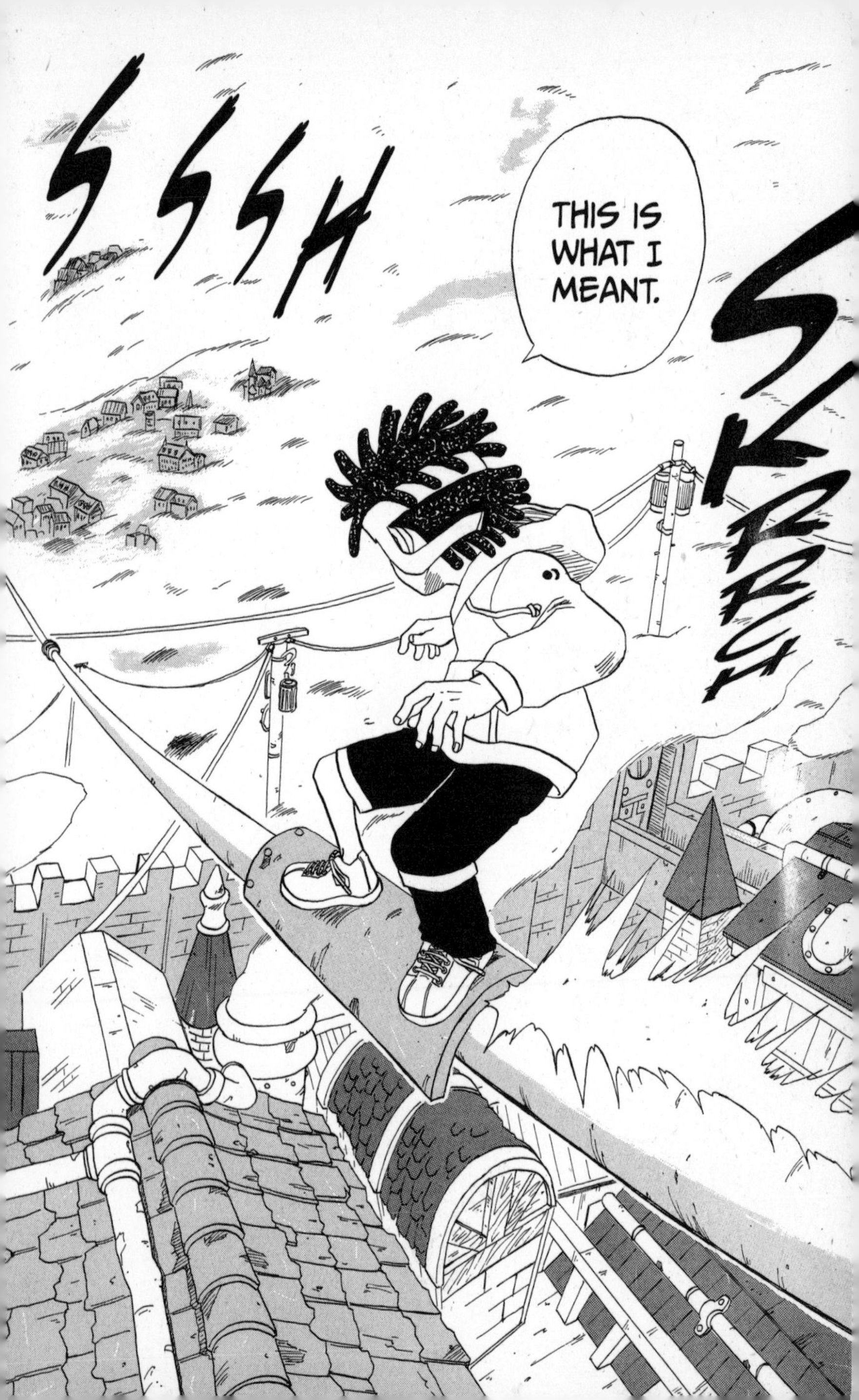
SKRRUT
THIS IS WHAT I MEANT.
SSSH

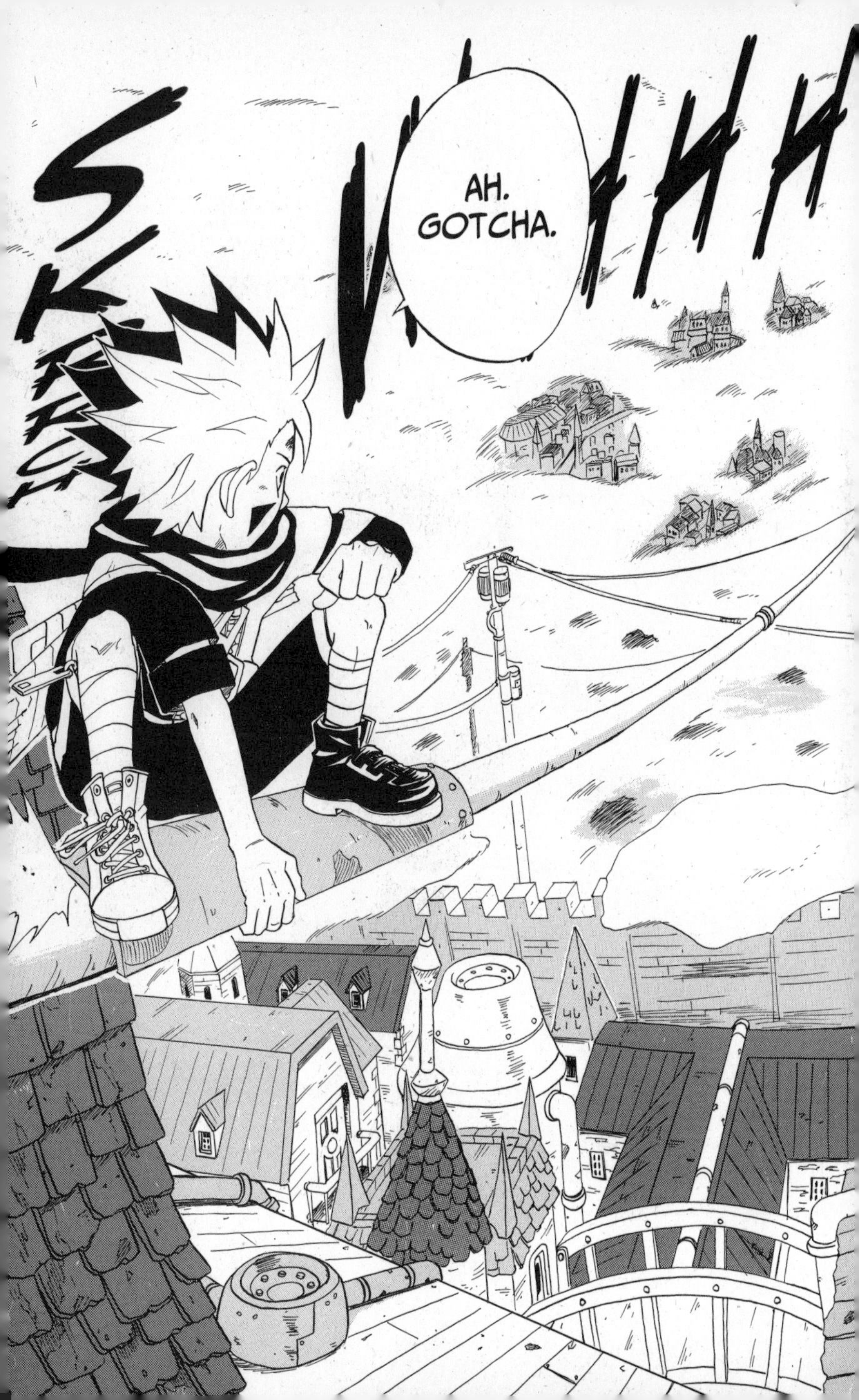
AH. GOTCHA.

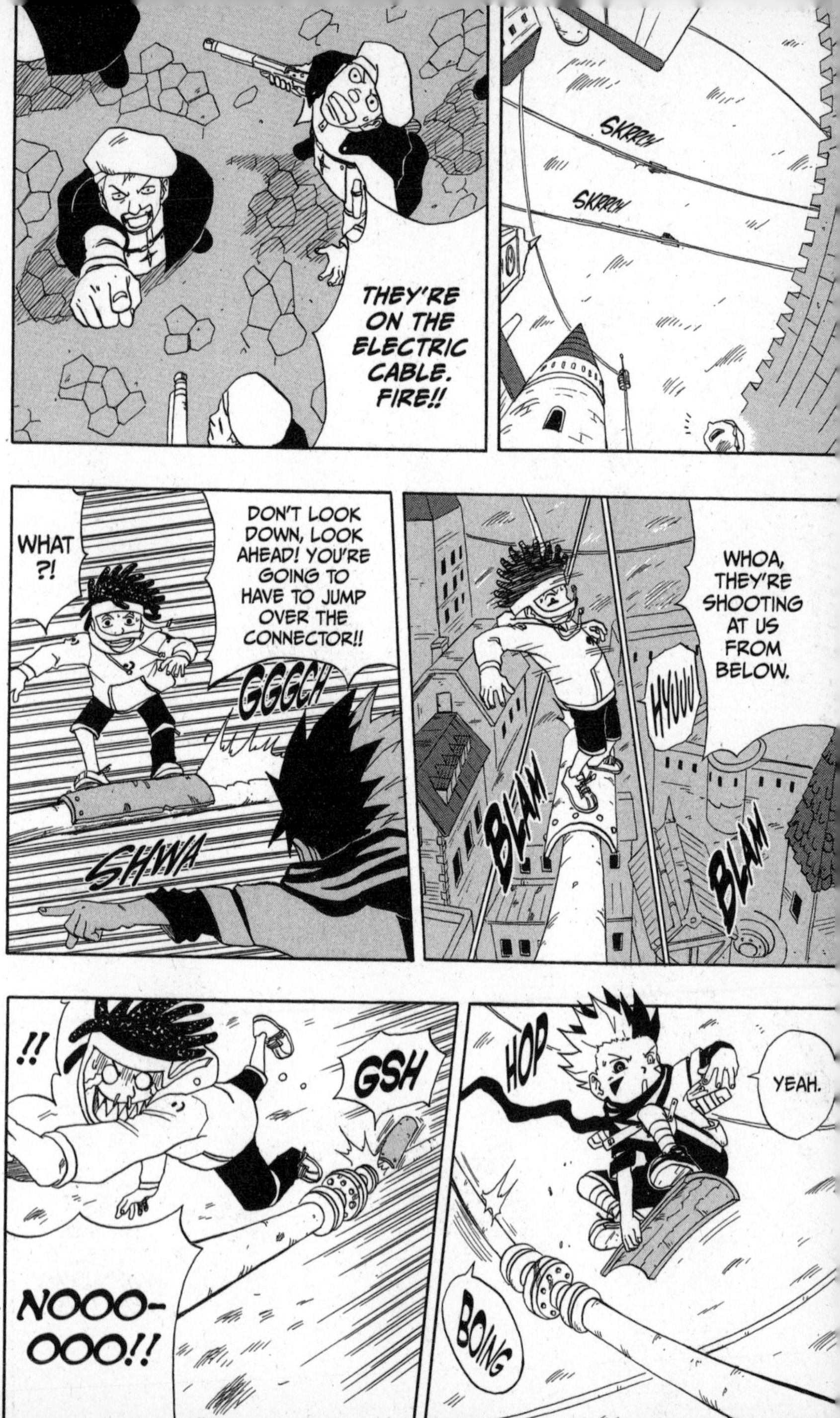
SKRRCH
SKRRCH
THEY'RE ON THE ELECTRIC CABLE. FIRE!!
WHOA, THEY'RE SHOOTING AT US FROM BELOW.
HYUUU
BLAM
BLAM
DON'T LOOK DOWN, LOOK AHEAD! YOU'RE GOING TO HAVE TO JUMP OVER THE CONNECTOR!!
WHAT ?!
GGGCH
SHWA
YEAH.
HOP
BOING
GSH
!!
NOOO-OOO!!

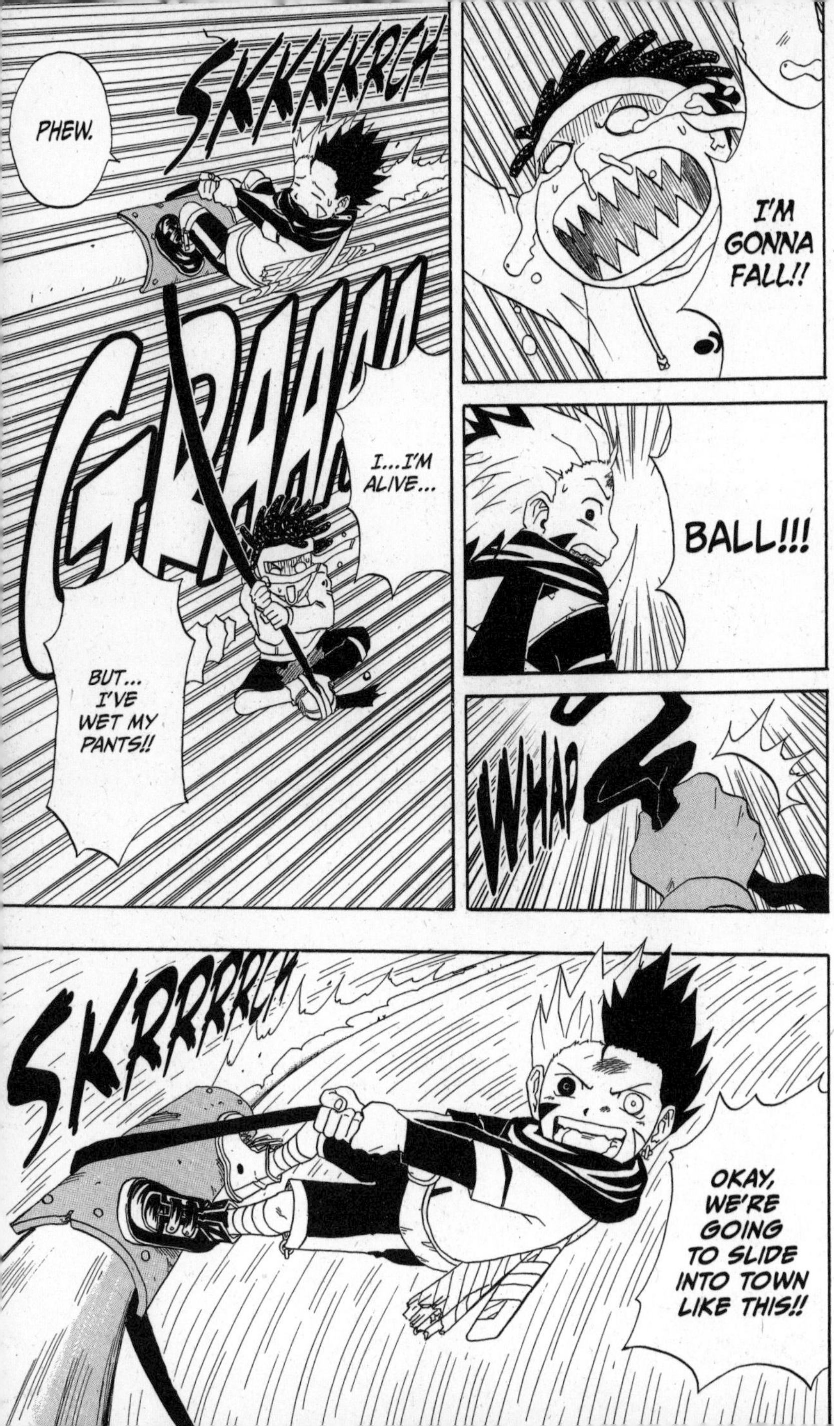
I'M GONNA FALL!!
BALL!!!
WHAP
SKKKKRCH
PHEW.
I...I'M ALIVE...
BUT... I'VE WET MY PANTS!!
SKRRRRCH
OKAY, WE'RE GOING TO SLIDE INTO TOWN LIKE THIS!!

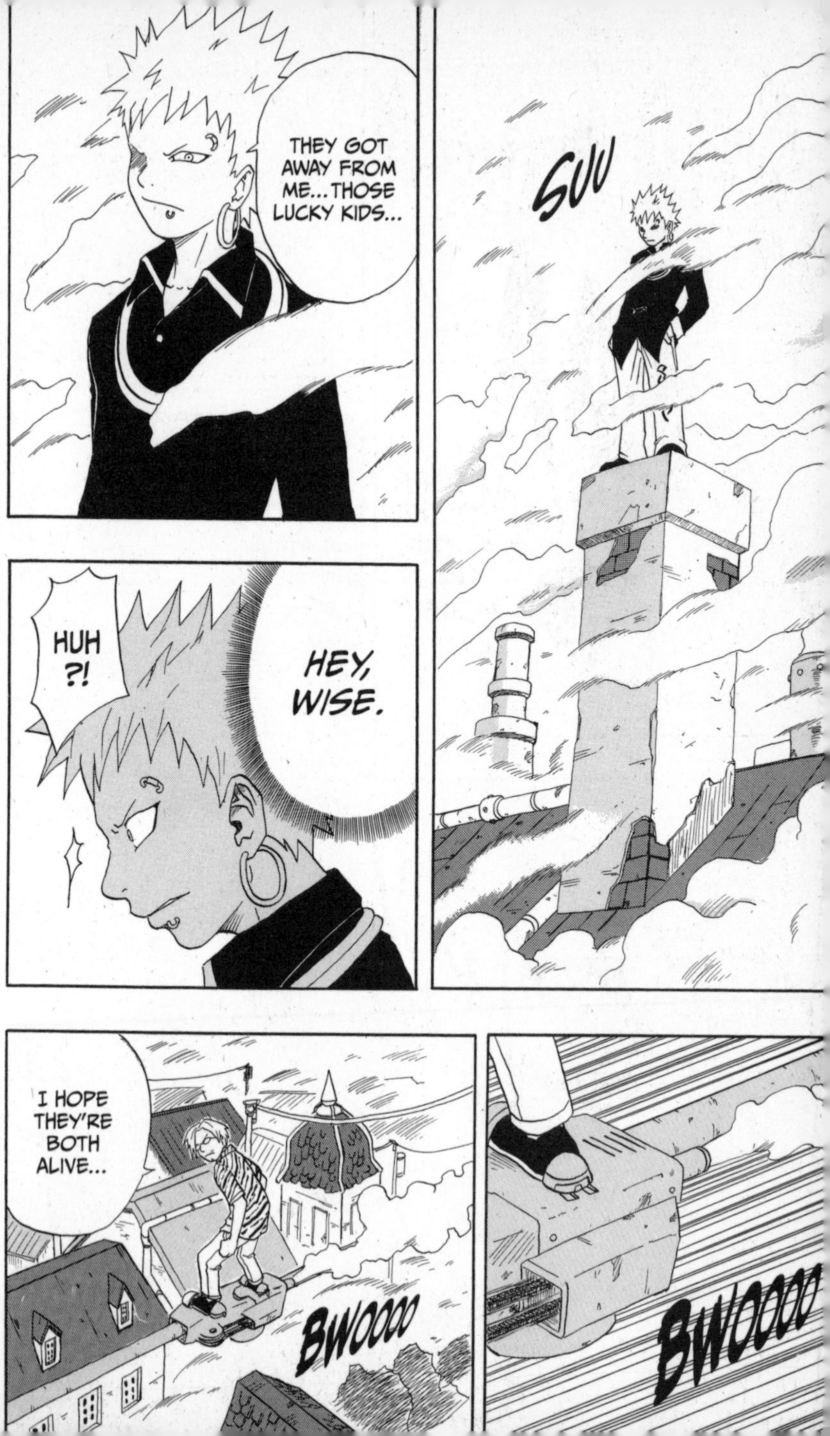
SUU
THEY GOT AWAY FROM ME...THOSE LUCKY KIDS...
HEY, WISE.
HUH ?!
BWOOOO
I HOPE THEY'RE BOTH ALIVE...
BWOOOO

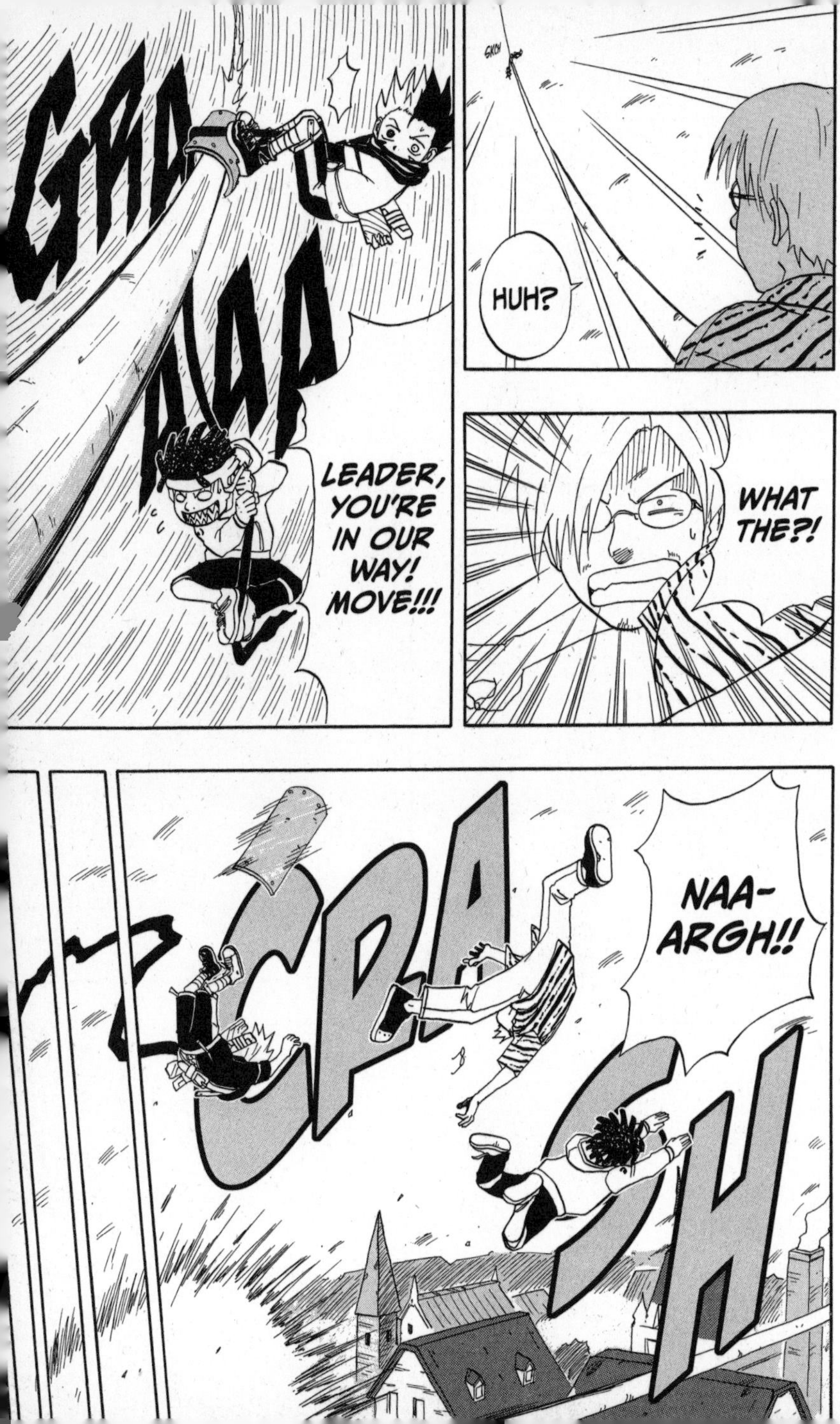
HUH?
WHAT THE?!
GRAAAP
LEADER, YOU'RE IN OUR WAY! MOVE!!!
NAA-ARGH!!
CRASH

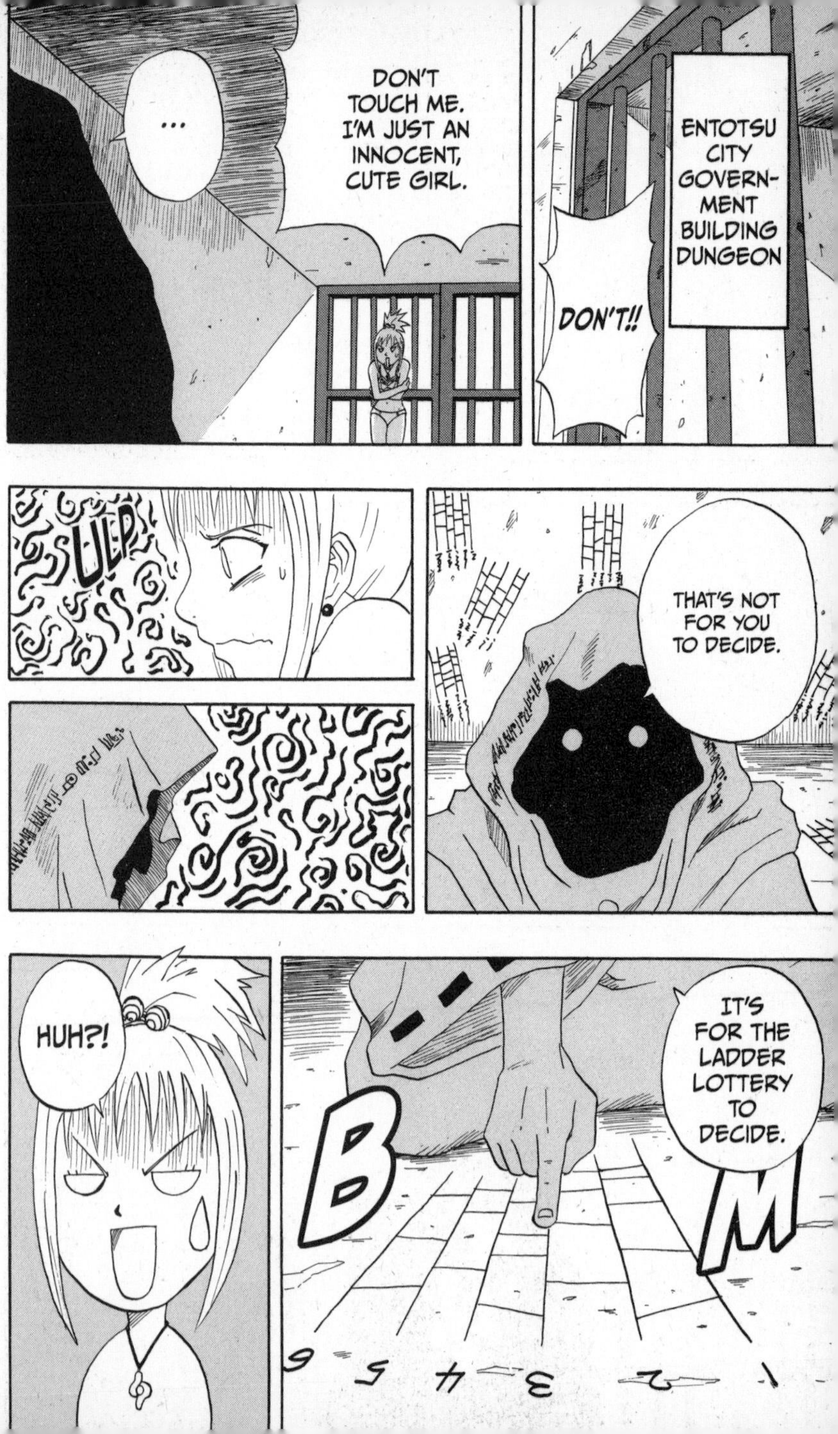
ENTOTSU CITY GOVERNMENT BUILDING DUNGEON
DON'T!!
DON'T TOUCH ME. I'M JUST AN INNOCENT, CUTE GIRL.
...
THAT'S NOT FOR YOU TO DECIDE.
ULP
IT'S FOR THE LADDER LOTTERY TO DECIDE.
BM
1 2 3 4 5 6
HUH?!

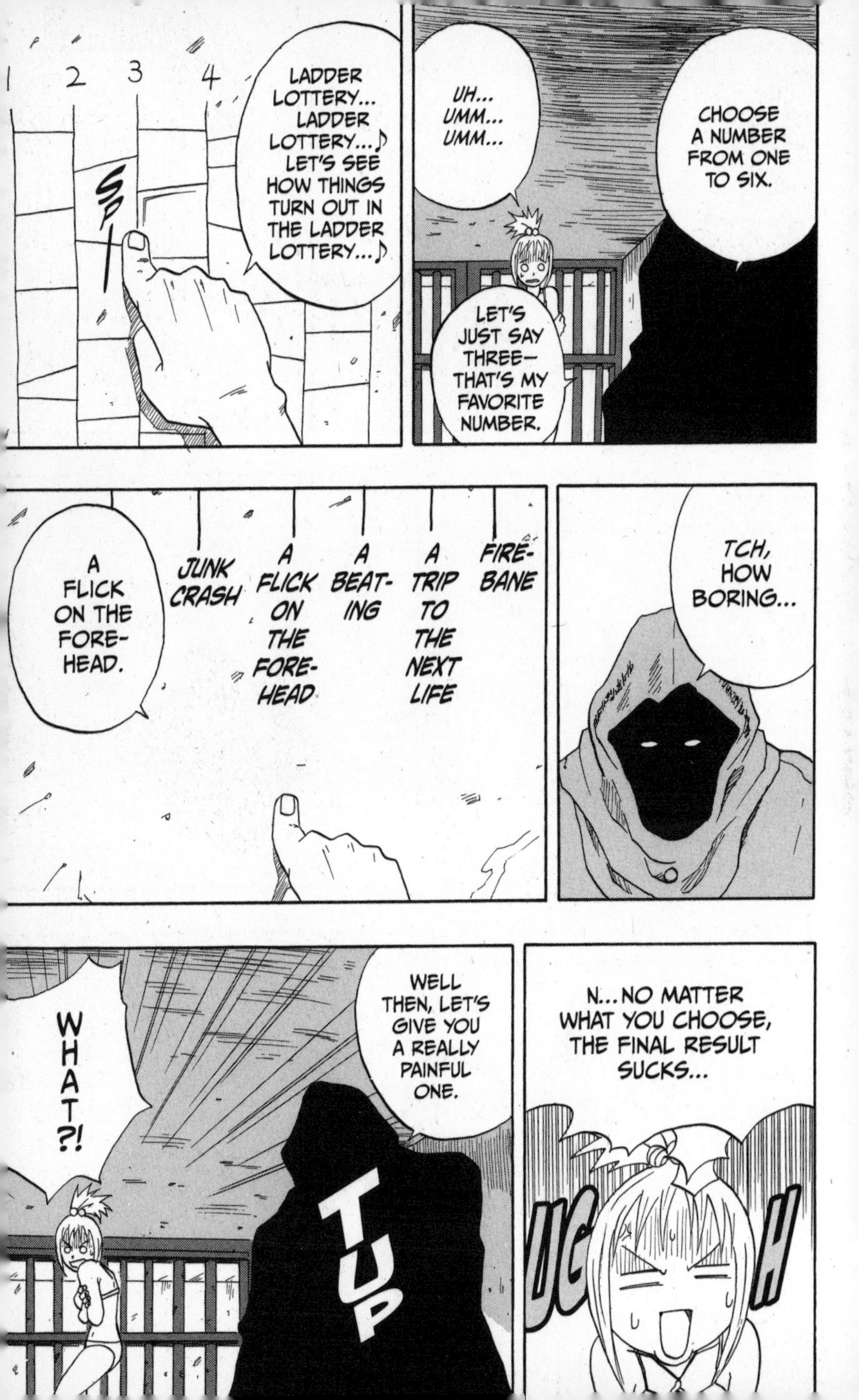
CHOOSE A NUMBER FROM ONE TO SIX.
UH... UMM... UMM...
LET'S JUST SAY THREE—THAT'S MY FAVORITE NUMBER.
LADDER LOTTERY... LADDER LOTTERY...♪ LET'S SEE HOW THINGS TURN OUT IN THE LADDER LOTTERY...♪
1 2 3 4
SP!
TCH, HOW BORING...
FIRE-BANE
A TRIP TO THE NEXT LIFE
A BEAT-ING
A FLICK ON THE FORE-HEAD
JUNK CRASH
A FLICK ON THE FORE-HEAD.
N...NO MATTER WHAT YOU CHOOSE, THE FINAL RESULT SUCKS...
UGH
WELL THEN, LET'S GIVE YOU A REALLY PAINFUL ONE.
TUP
WHAT?!

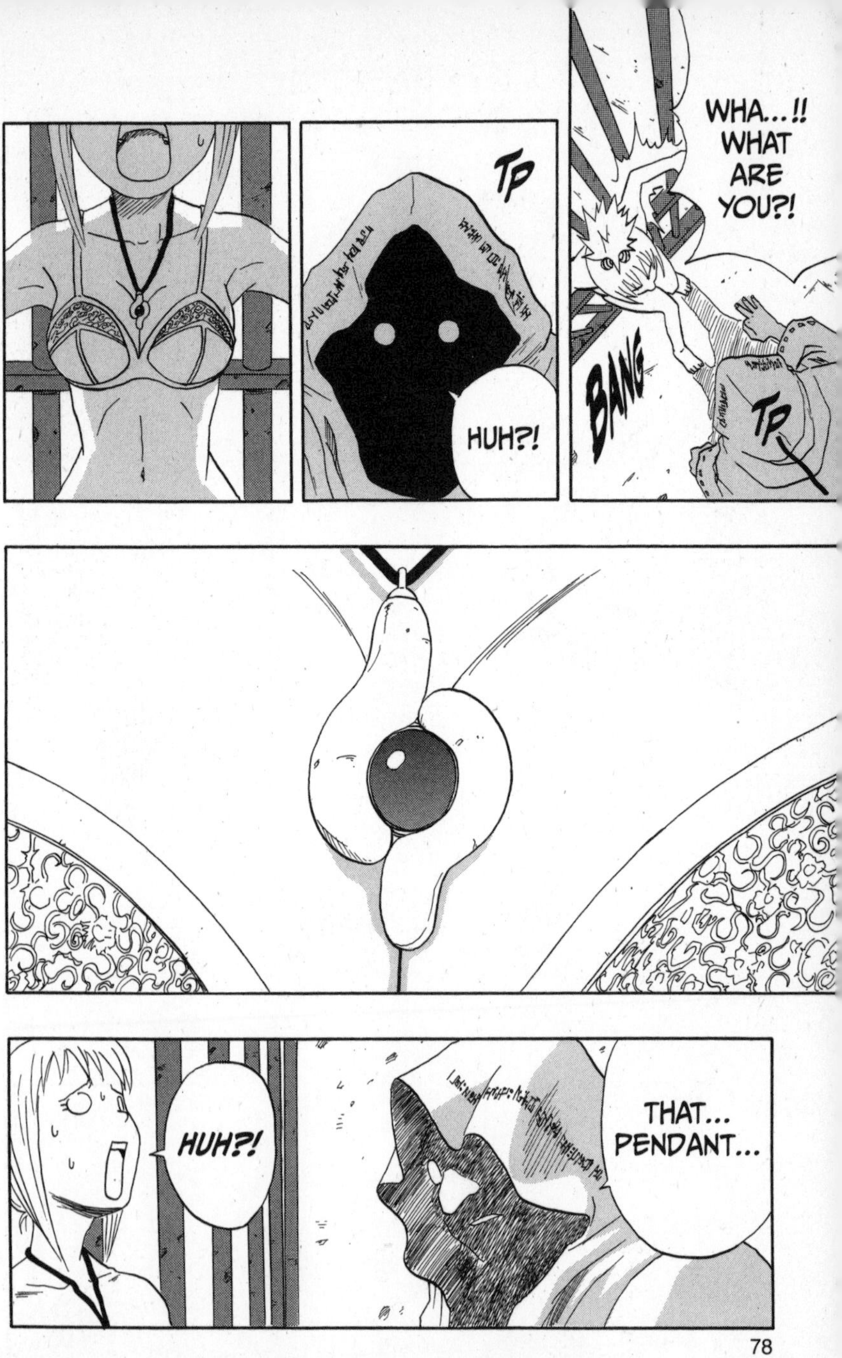
WHA...!! WHAT ARE YOU?!
BANG
TP
TP
HUH?!
THAT... PENDANT...
HUH?!

CHAPTER 11:
THE POWERS OF THE ANCIENT CIVILIZATION

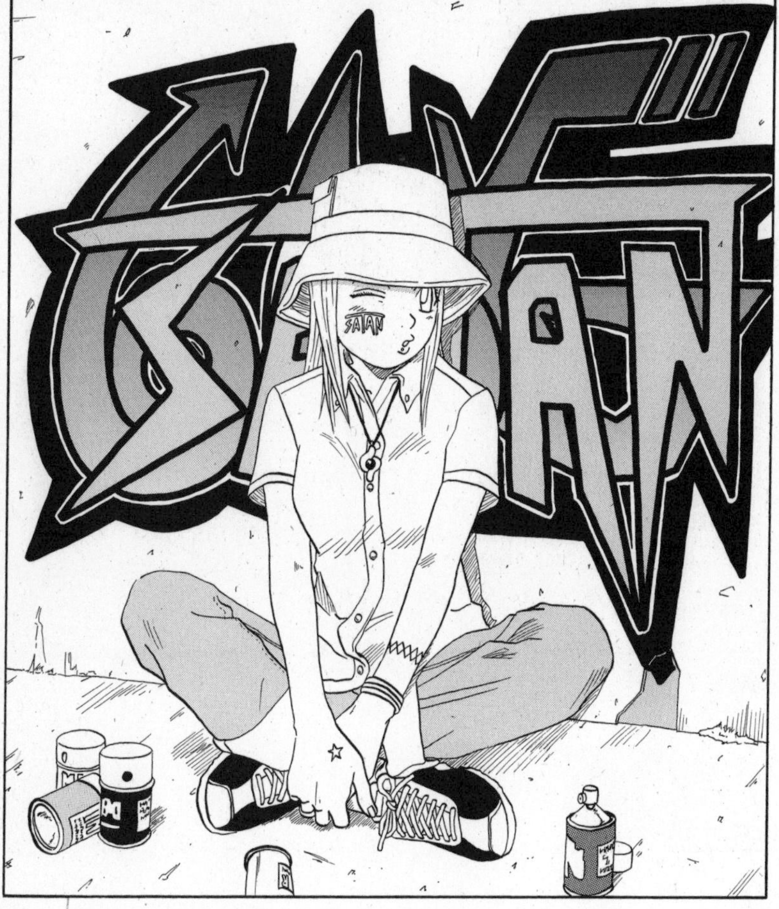
SATAN

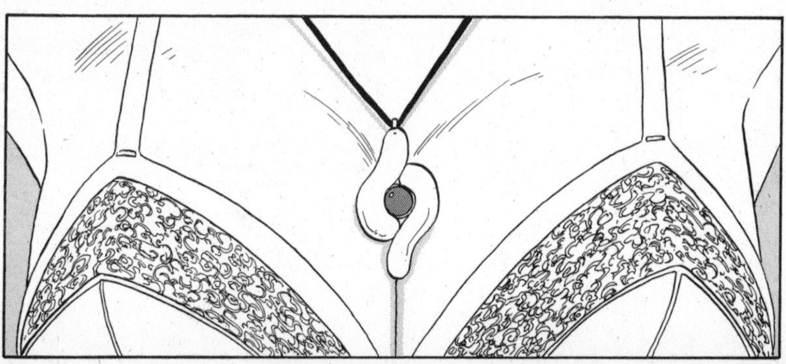

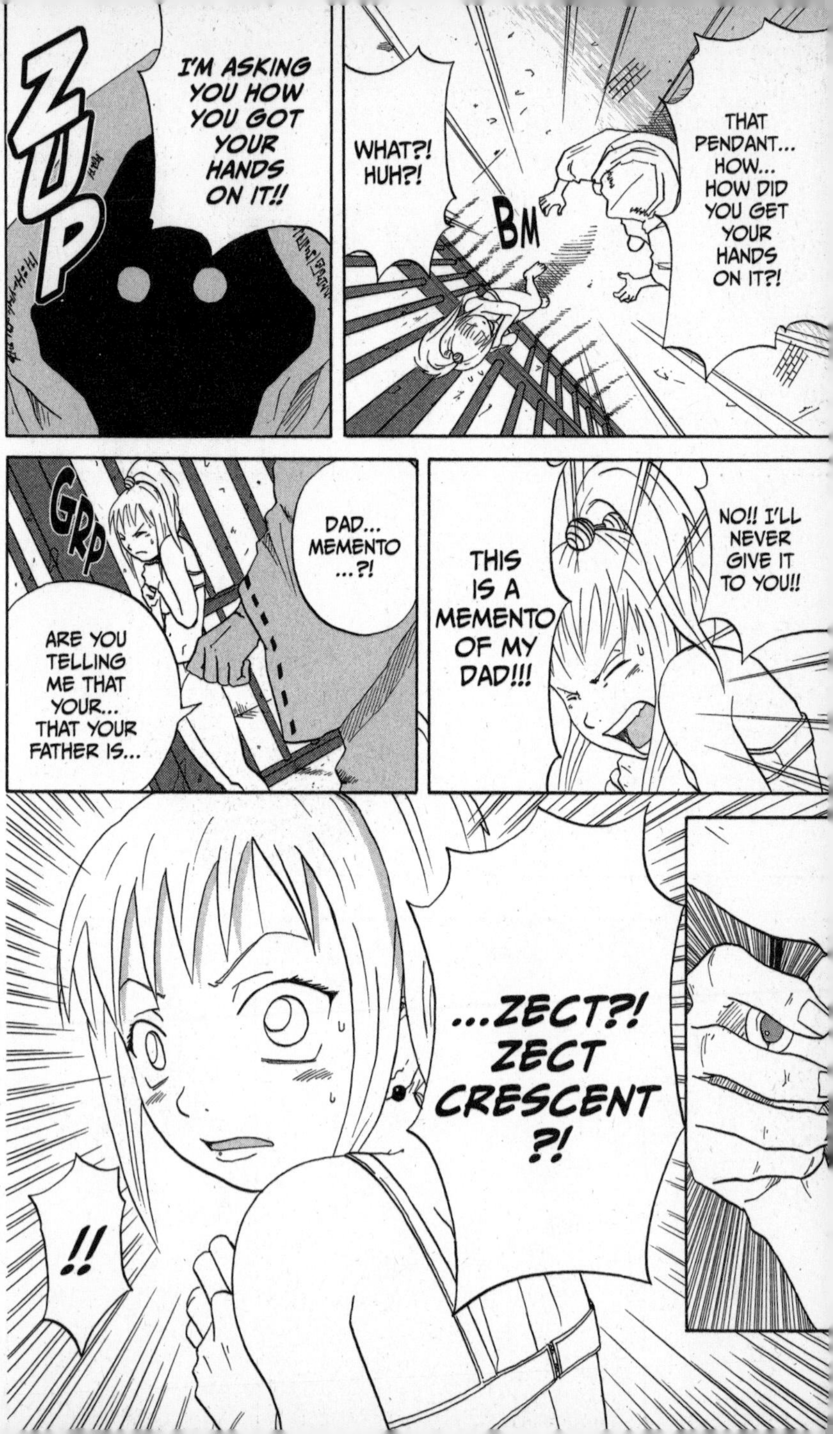
THAT PENDANT... HOW... HOW DID YOU GET YOUR HANDS ON IT?!
BM
WHAT?! HUH?!
I'M ASKING YOU HOW YOU GOT YOUR HANDS ON IT!!
ZUP
NO!! I'LL NEVER GIVE IT TO YOU!!
THIS IS A MEMENTO OF MY DAD!!!
DAD... MEMENTO ...?!
GRP
ARE YOU TELLING ME THAT YOUR... THAT YOUR FATHER IS...
...ZECT?! ZECT CRESCENT ?!
!!

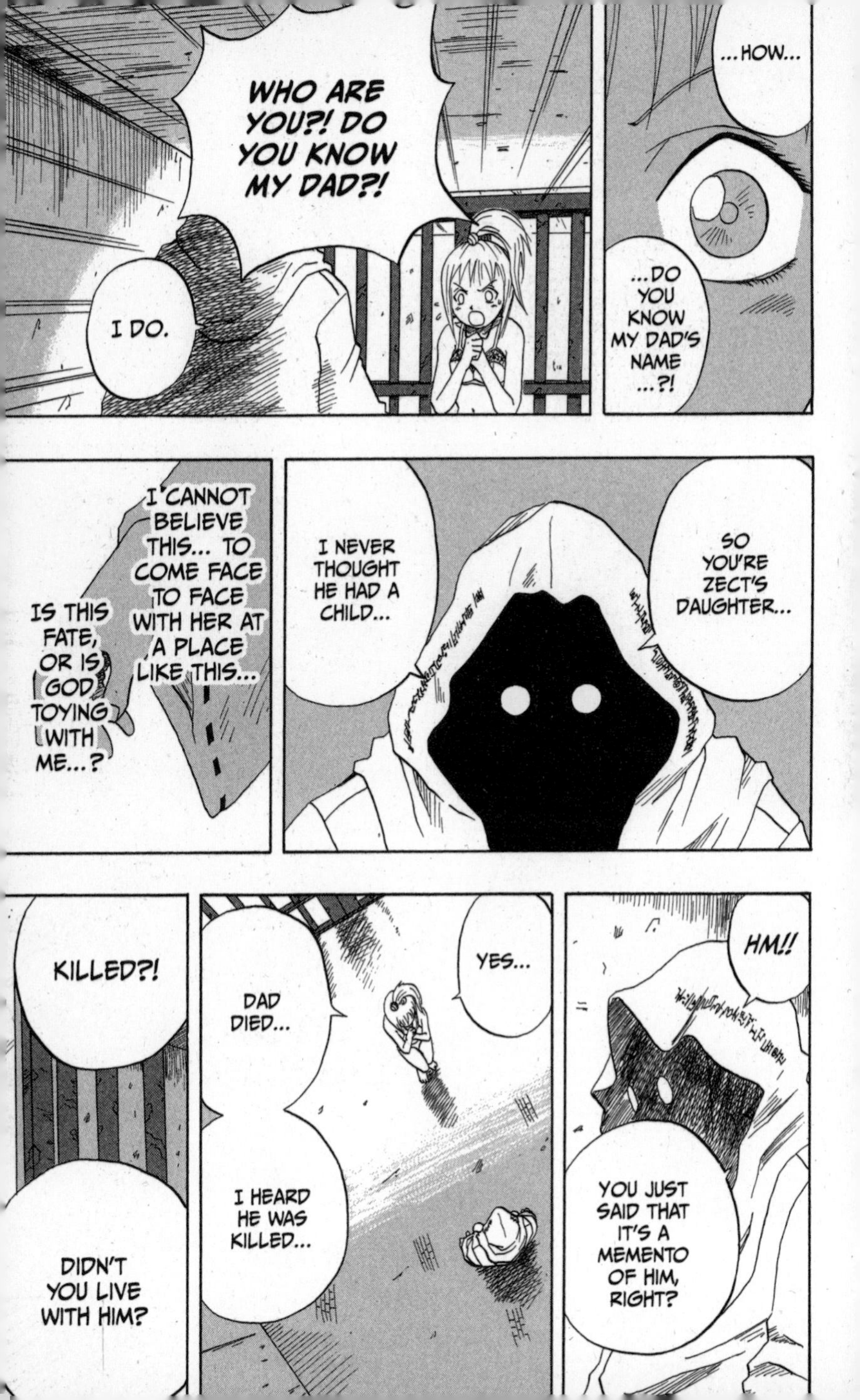
...HOW...
...DO YOU KNOW MY DAD'S NAME ...?!
WHO ARE YOU?! DO YOU KNOW MY DAD?!
I DO.
SO YOU'RE ZECT'S DAUGHTER...
I NEVER THOUGHT HE HAD A CHILD...
I CANNOT BELIEVE THIS... TO COME FACE TO FACE WITH HER AT A PLACE LIKE THIS...
IS THIS FATE, OR IS GOD TOYING WITH ME...?
HM!!
YOU JUST SAID THAT IT'S A MEMENTO OF HIM, RIGHT?
YES...
DAD DIED...
I HEARD HE WAS KILLED...
KILLED?!
DIDN'T YOU LIVE WITH HIM?

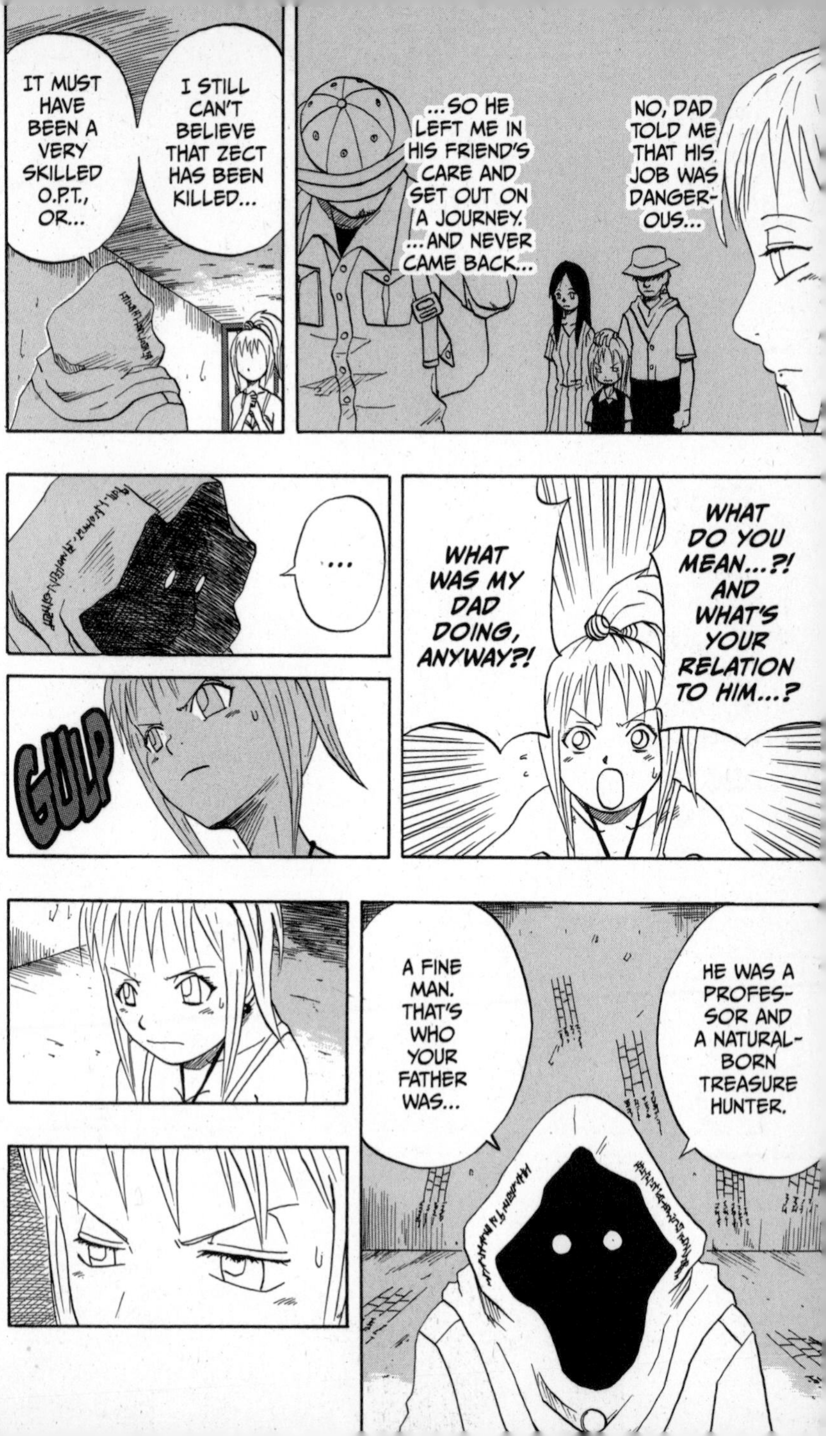
NO, DAD TOLD ME THAT HIS JOB WAS DANGEROUS...
...SO HE LEFT ME IN HIS FRIEND'S CARE AND SET OUT ON A JOURNEY. ...AND NEVER CAME BACK...
I STILL CAN'T BELIEVE THAT ZECT HAS BEEN KILLED...
IT MUST HAVE BEEN A VERY SKILLED O.P.T., OR...
WHAT DO YOU MEAN...?! AND WHAT'S YOUR RELATION TO HIM...?
WHAT WAS MY DAD DOING, ANYWAY?!
...
GULP
HE WAS A PROFESSOR AND A NATURAL-BORN TREASURE HUNTER.
A FINE MAN. THAT'S WHO YOUR FATHER WAS...

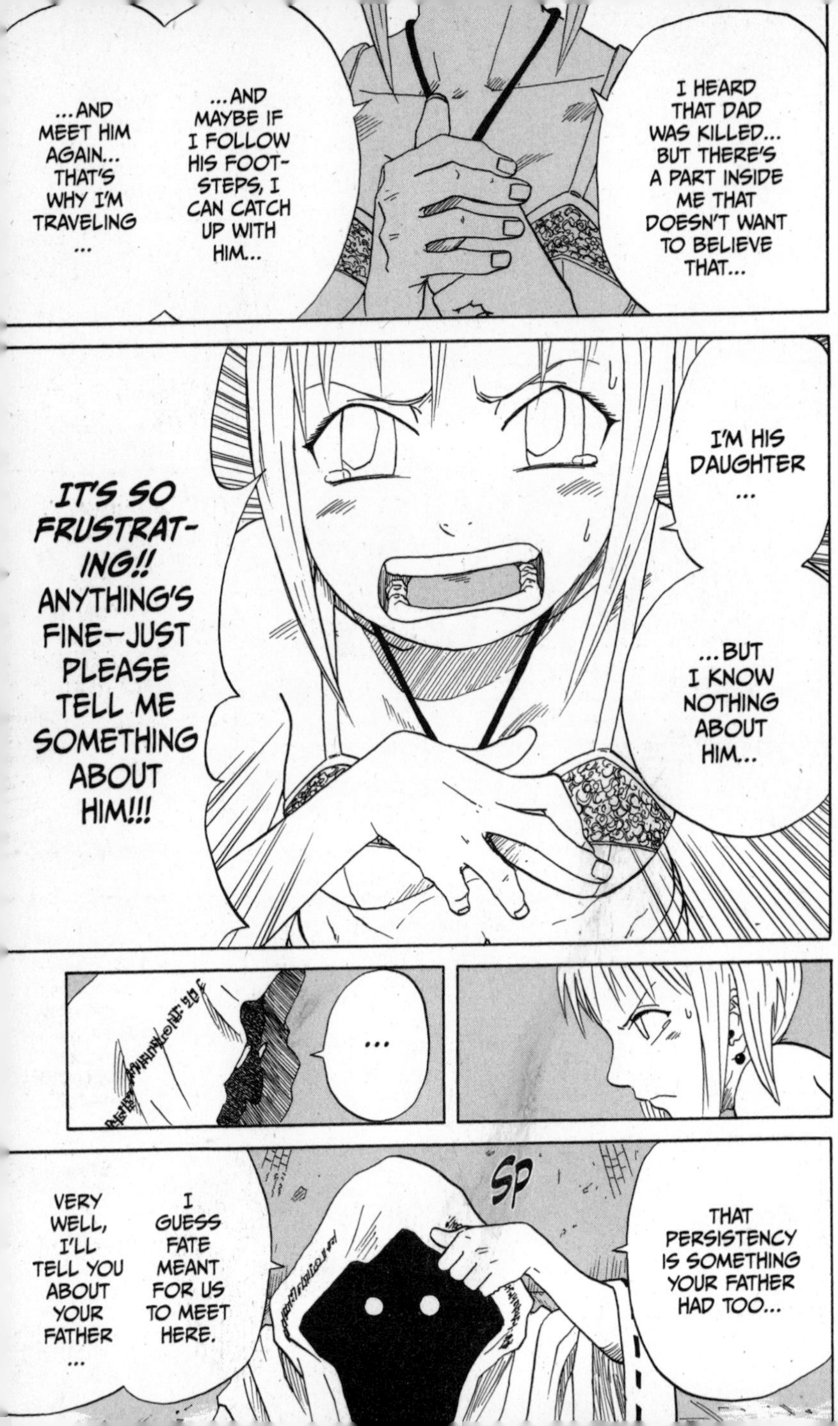
I HEARD THAT DAD WAS KILLED... BUT THERE'S A PART INSIDE ME THAT DOESN'T WANT TO BELIEVE THAT...
...AND MAYBE IF I FOLLOW HIS FOOT-STEPS, I CAN CATCH UP WITH HIM...
...AND MEET HIM AGAIN... THAT'S WHY I'M TRAVELING ...
I'M HIS DAUGHTER ...
...BUT I KNOW NOTHING ABOUT HIM...
IT'S SO FRUSTRAT-ING!! ANYTHING'S FINE—JUST PLEASE TELL ME SOMETHING ABOUT HIM!!!
...
THAT PERSISTENCY IS SOMETHING YOUR FATHER HAD TOO...
SP
I GUESS FATE MEANT FOR US TO MEET HERE.
VERY WELL, I'LL TELL YOU ABOUT YOUR FATHER ...

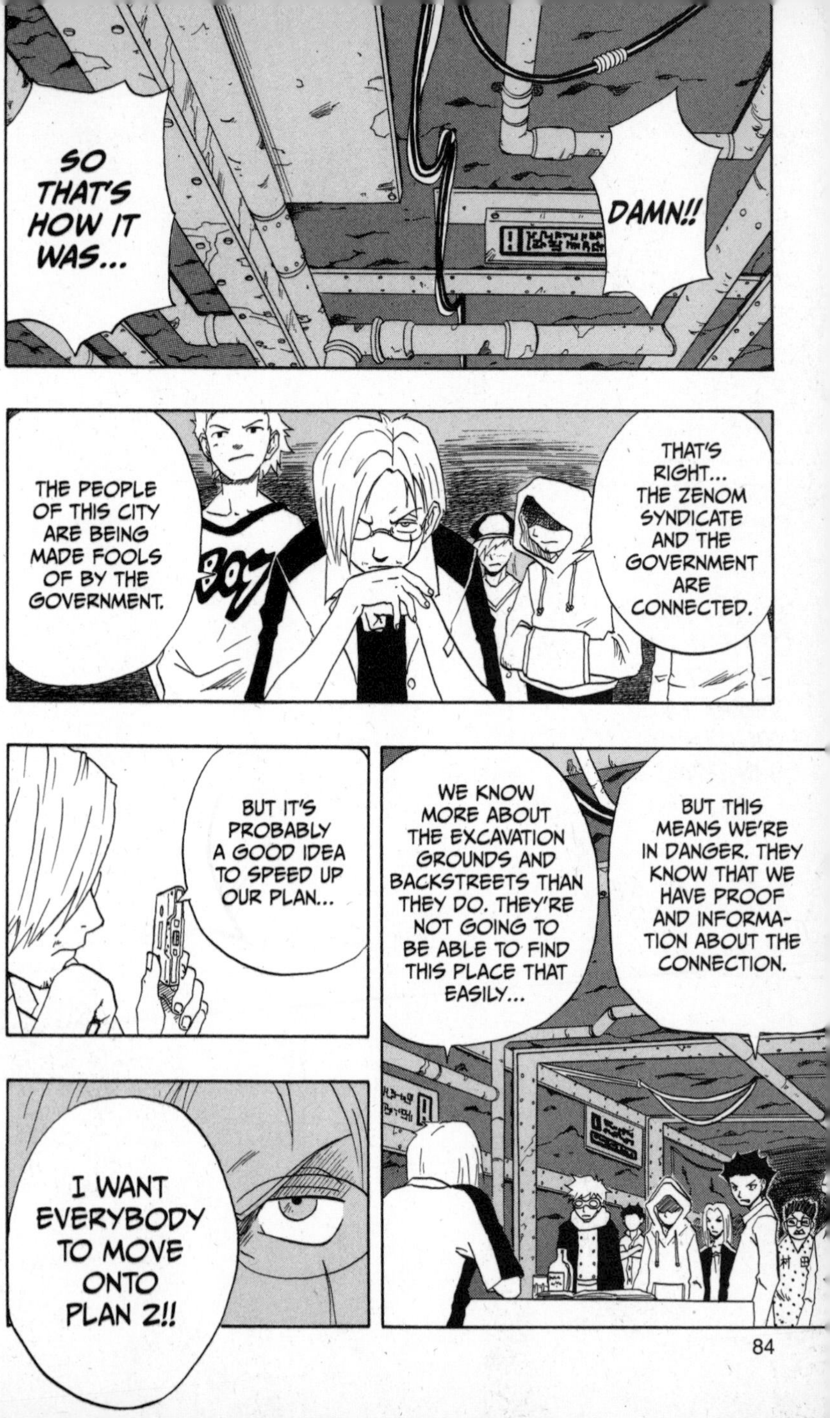
DAMN!!
SO THAT'S HOW IT WAS...
THAT'S RIGHT... THE ZENOM SYNDICATE AND THE GOVERNMENT ARE CONNECTED.
THE PEOPLE OF THIS CITY ARE BEING MADE FOOLS OF BY THE GOVERNMENT.
BUT THIS MEANS WE'RE IN DANGER. THEY KNOW THAT WE HAVE PROOF AND INFORMATION ABOUT THE CONNECTION.
WE KNOW MORE ABOUT THE EXCAVATION GROUNDS AND BACKSTREETS THAN THEY DO. THEY'RE NOT GOING TO BE ABLE TO FIND THIS PLACE THAT EASILY...
BUT IT'S PROBABLY A GOOD IDEA TO SPEED UP OUR PLAN...
I WANT EVERYBODY TO MOVE ONTO PLAN 2!!

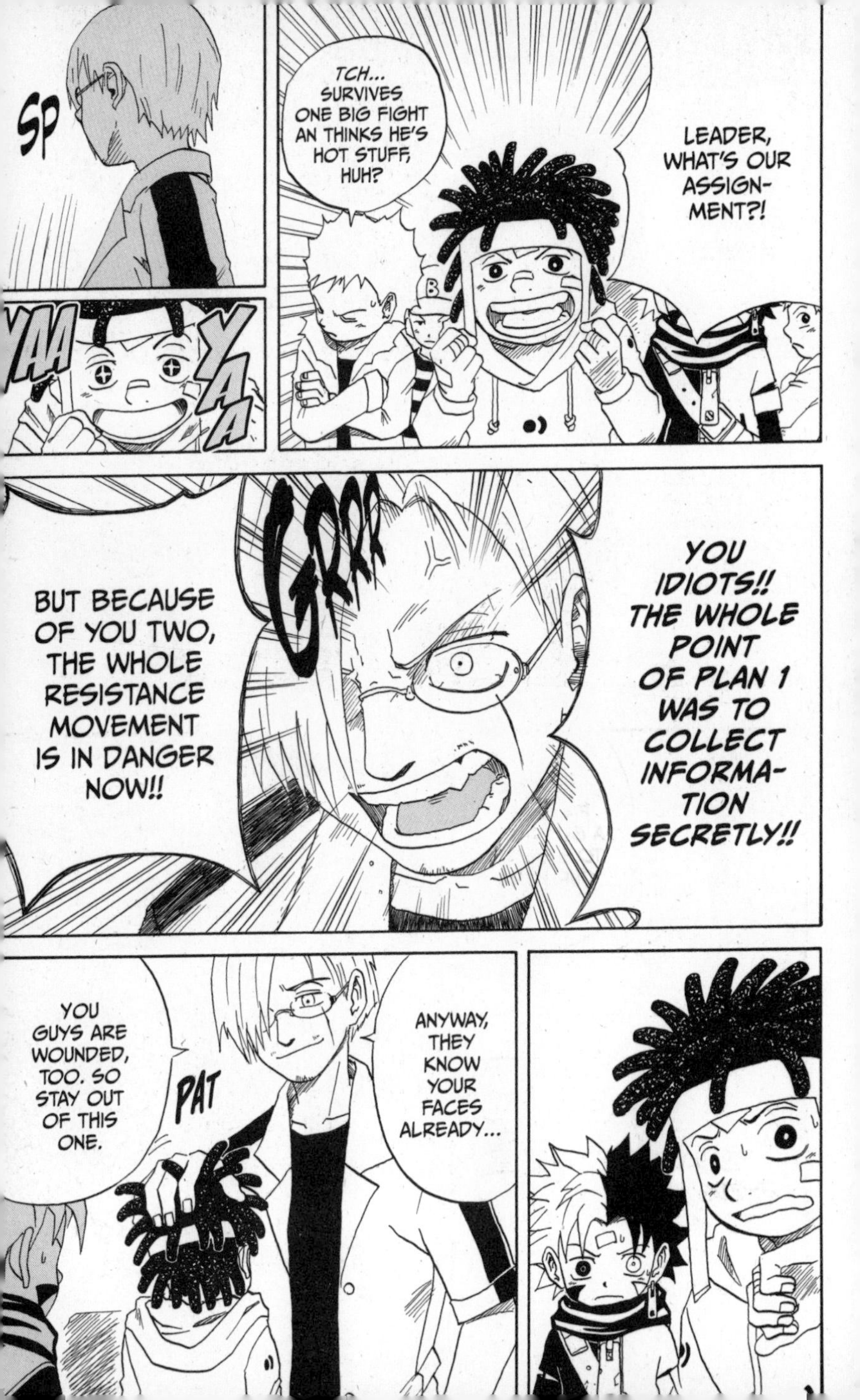

LEADER, WHAT'S OUR ASSIGNMENT?!
TCH... SURVIVES ONE BIG FIGHT AN THINKS HE'S HOT STUFF, HUH?
SP
YAA YAA
YOU IDIOTS!! THE WHOLE POINT OF PLAN 1 WAS TO COLLECT INFORMATION SECRETLY!!
GRRR
BUT BECAUSE OF YOU TWO, THE WHOLE RESISTANCE MOVEMENT IS IN DANGER NOW!!
ANYWAY, THEY KNOW YOUR FACES ALREADY...
PAT
YOU GUYS ARE WOUNDED, TOO. SO STAY OUT OF THIS ONE.

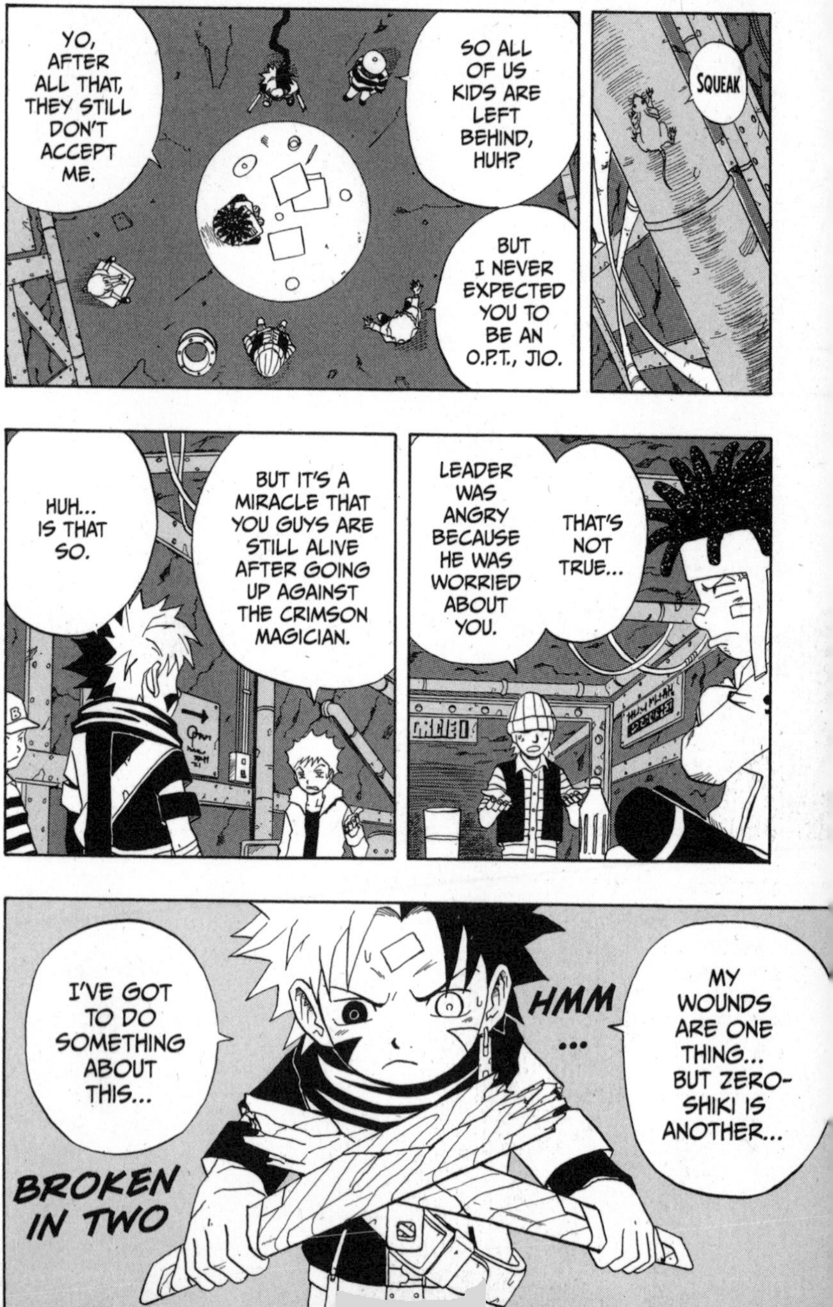
SQUEAK
SO ALL OF US KIDS ARE LEFT BEHIND, HUH?
YO, AFTER ALL THAT, THEY STILL DON'T ACCEPT ME.
BUT I NEVER EXPECTED YOU TO BE AN O.P.T., JIO.
THAT'S NOT TRUE...
LEADER WAS ANGRY BECAUSE HE WAS WORRIED ABOUT YOU.
BUT IT'S A MIRACLE THAT YOU GUYS ARE STILL ALIVE AFTER GOING UP AGAINST THE CRIMSON MAGICIAN.
HUH... IS THAT SO.
MY WOUNDS ARE ONE THING... BUT ZERO-SHIKI IS ANOTHER...
HMM...
I'VE GOT TO DO SOMETHING ABOUT THIS...
BROKEN IN TWO

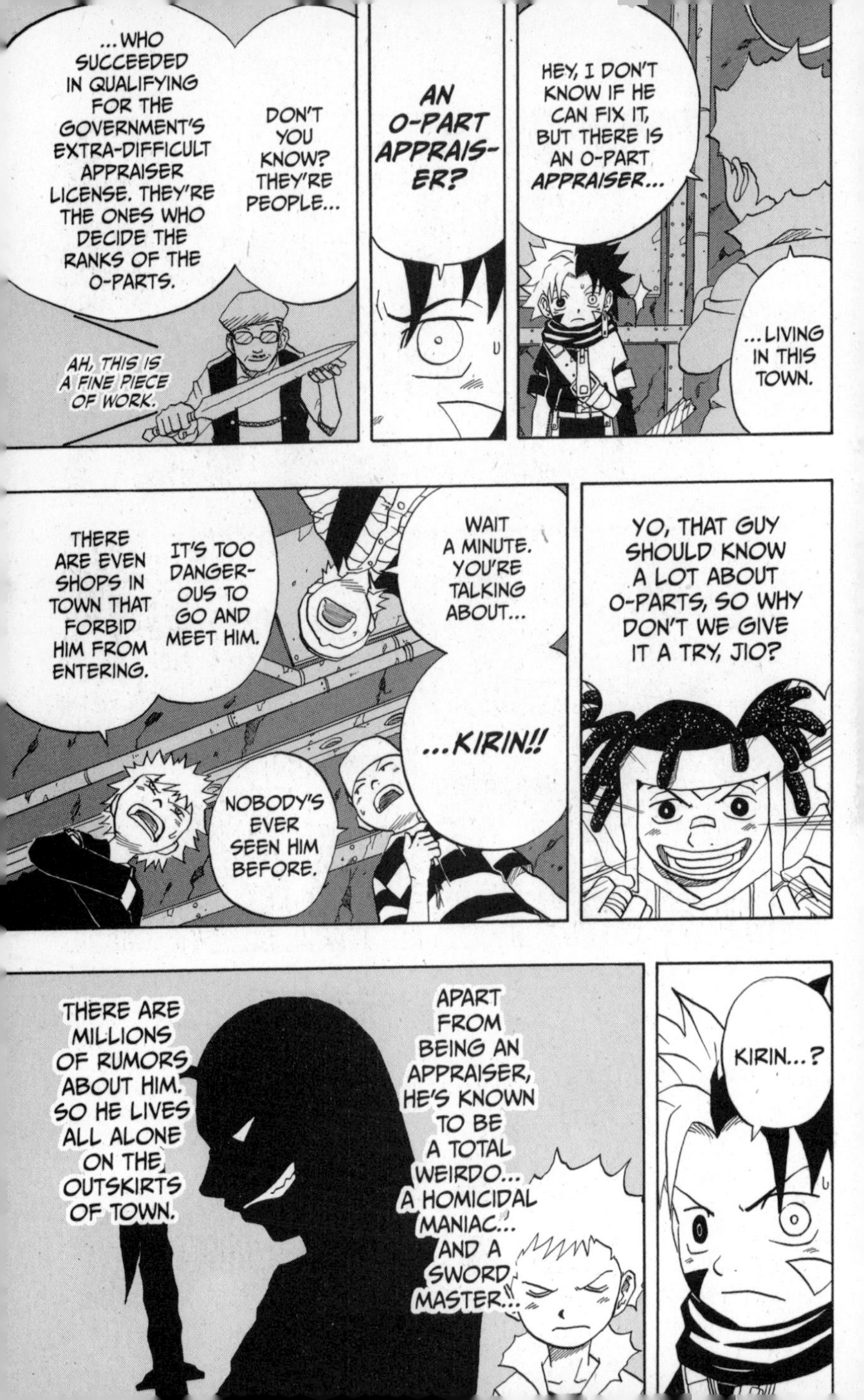
HEY, I DON'T KNOW IF HE CAN FIX IT, BUT THERE IS AN O-PART APPRAISER...
...LIVING IN THIS TOWN.
AN O-PART APPRAIS-ER?
DON'T YOU KNOW? THEY'RE PEOPLE...
...WHO SUCCEEDED IN QUALIFYING FOR THE GOVERNMENT'S EXTRA-DIFFICULT APPRAISER LICENSE. THEY'RE THE ONES WHO DECIDE THE RANKS OF THE O-PARTS.
AH, THIS IS A FINE PIECE OF WORK.
YO, THAT GUY SHOULD KNOW A LOT ABOUT O-PARTS, SO WHY DON'T WE GIVE IT A TRY, JIO?
WAIT A MINUTE. YOU'RE TALKING ABOUT...
...KIRIN!!
IT'S TOO DANGER-OUS TO GO AND MEET HIM.
THERE ARE EVEN SHOPS IN TOWN THAT FORBID HIM FROM ENTERING.
NOBODY'S EVER SEEN HIM BEFORE.
KIRIN...?
APART FROM BEING AN APPRAISER, HE'S KNOWN TO BE A TOTAL WEIRDO... A HOMICIDAL MANIAC... AND A SWORD MASTER...
THERE ARE MILLIONS OF RUMORS ABOUT HIM. SO HE LIVES ALL ALONE ON THE OUTSKIRTS OF TOWN.

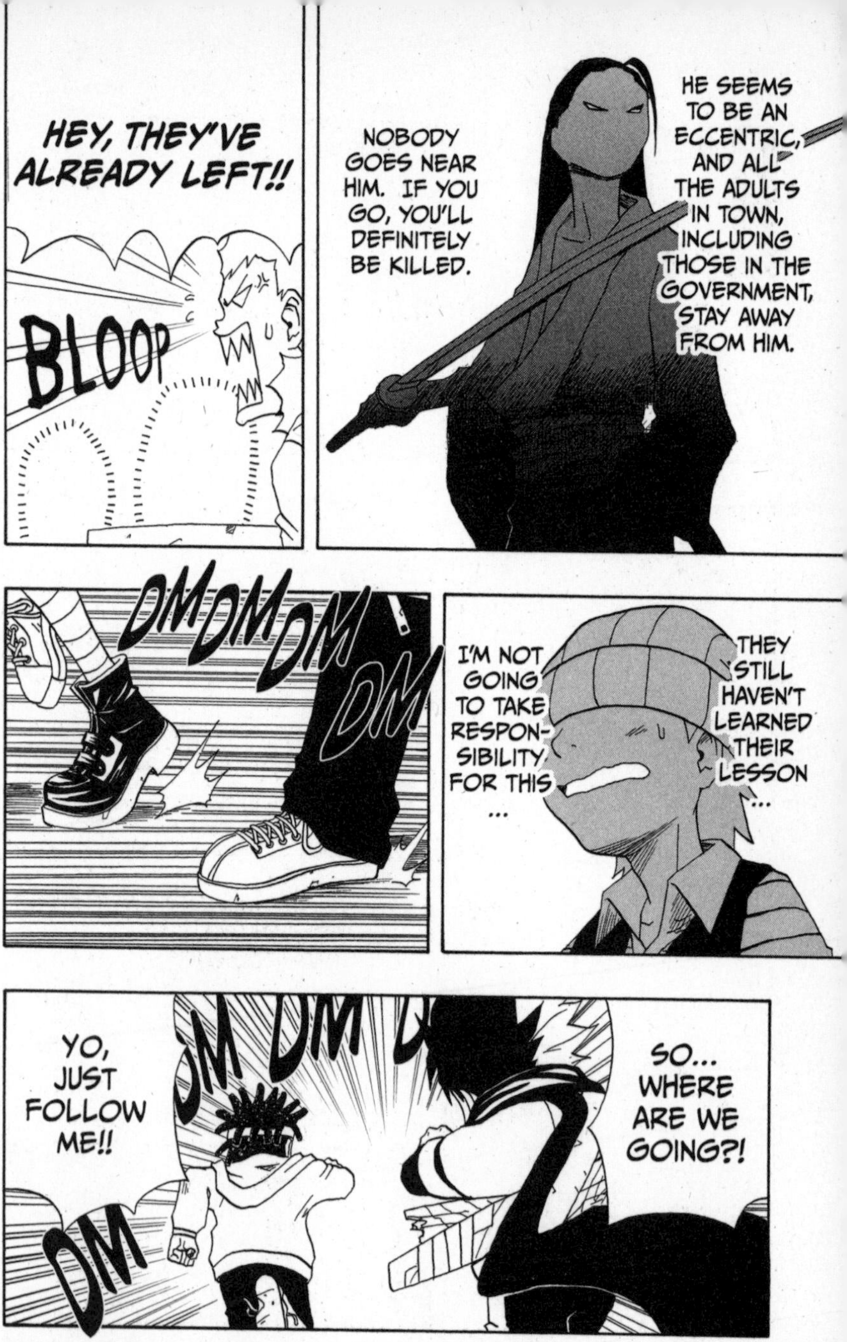
HE SEEMS TO BE AN ECCENTRIC, AND ALL THE ADULTS IN TOWN, INCLUDING THOSE IN THE GOVERNMENT, STAY AWAY FROM HIM.
NOBODY GOES NEAR HIM. IF YOU GO, YOU'LL DEFINITELY BE KILLED.
HEY, THEY'VE ALREADY LEFT!!
BLOOP
THEY STILL HAVEN'T LEARNED THEIR LESSON...
I'M NOT GOING TO TAKE RESPONSIBILITY FOR THIS...
DM DM DM DM DM
SO... WHERE ARE WE GOING?!
DM DM
YO, JUST FOLLOW ME!!
DM

BACK TO
ENTOTSU CITY

GOVERNMENT
BUILDING
DUNGEON

BUT BEFORE THAT...

!

SP

...LET ME INTRODUCE MYSELF.

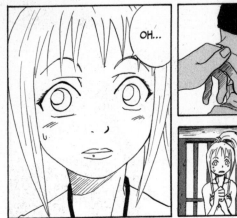

OH...

FLAP

89

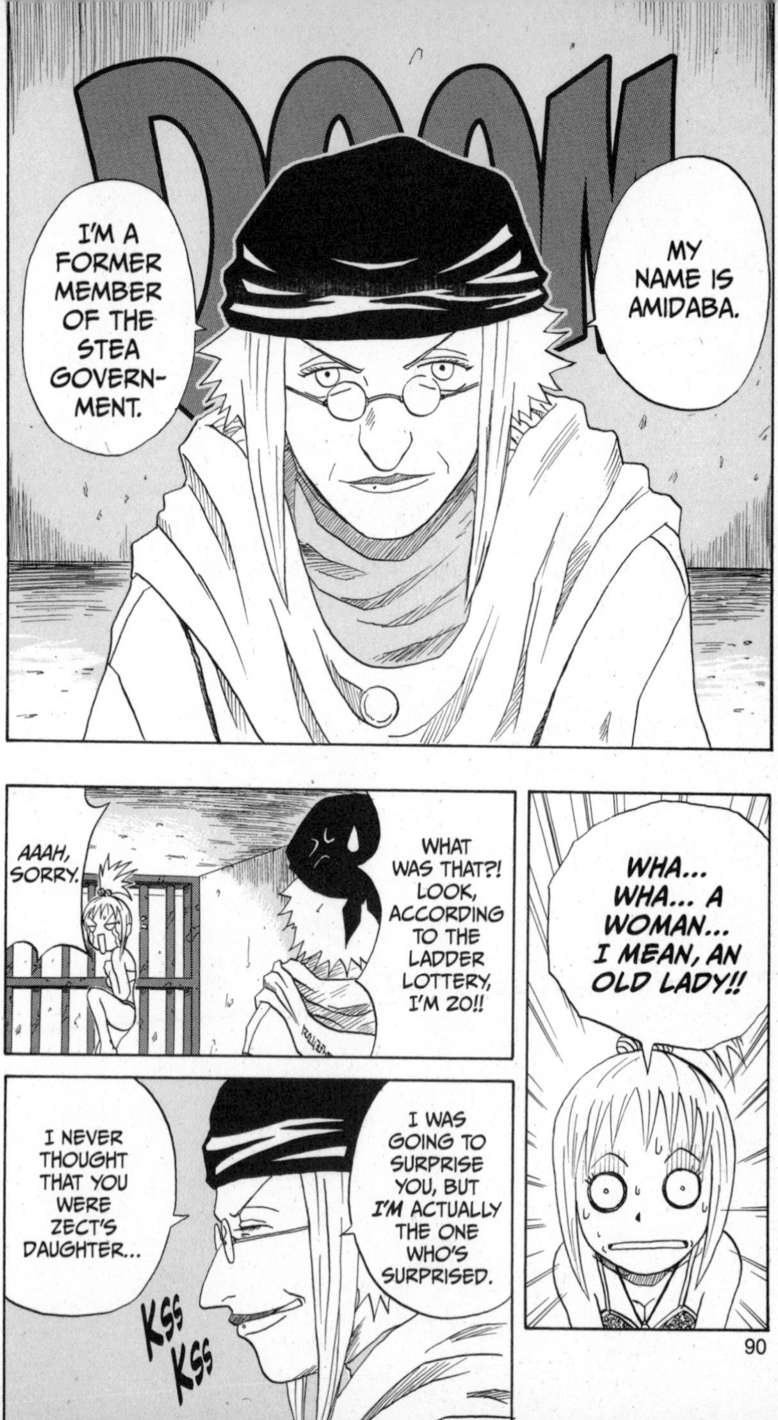
DOOM
MY NAME IS AMIDABA.
I'M A FORMER MEMBER OF THE STEA GOVERN-MENT.
WHA... WHA... A WOMAN... I MEAN, AN OLD LADY!!
WHAT WAS THAT?! LOOK, ACCORDING TO THE LADDER LOTTERY, I'M 20!!
AAAH, SORRY.
I WAS GOING TO SURPRISE YOU, BUT *I'M* ACTUALLY THE ONE WHO'S SURPRISED.
I NEVER THOUGHT THAT YOU WERE ZECT'S DAUGHTER...
KSS KSS

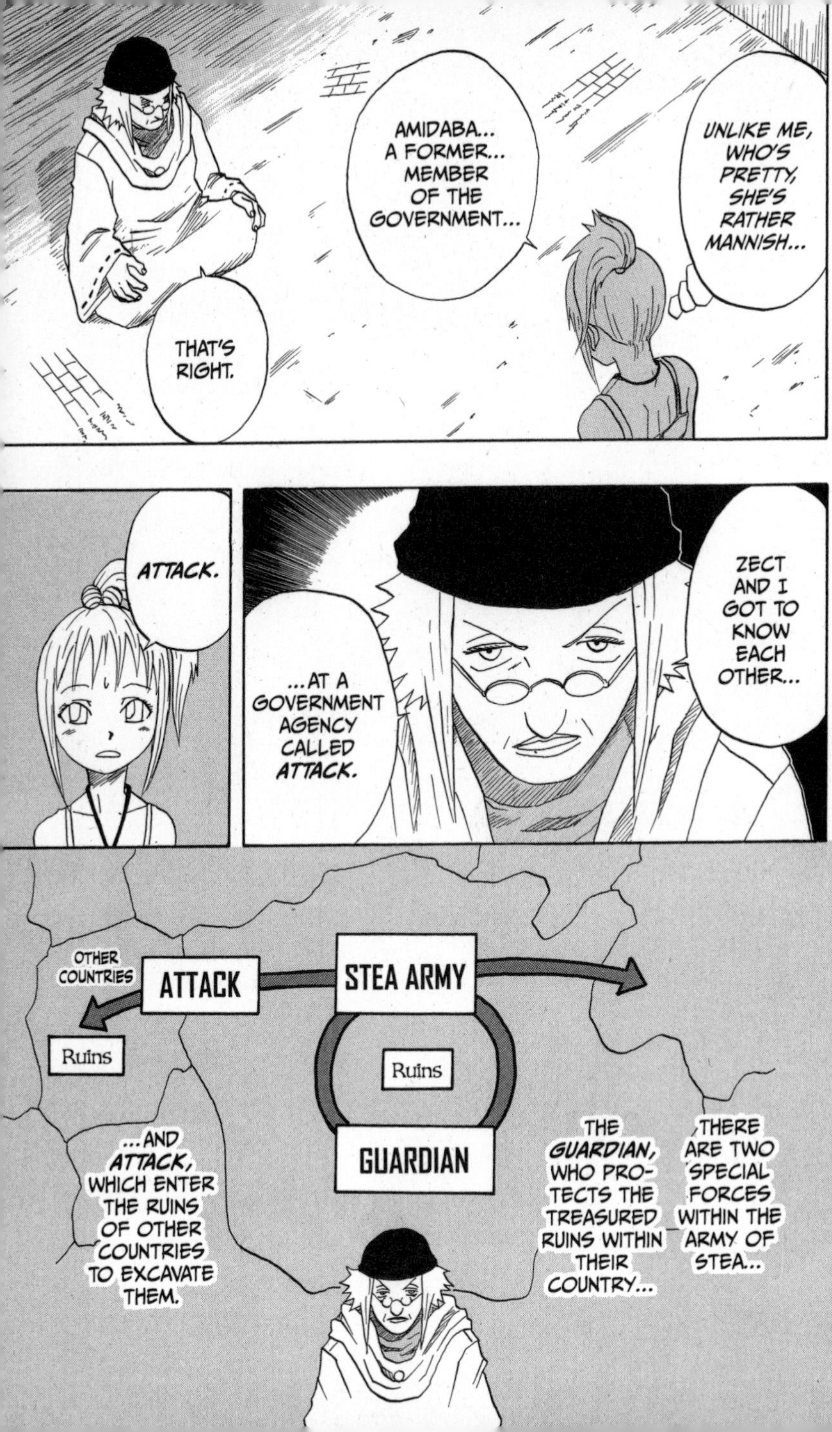
UNLIKE ME, WHO'S PRETTY, SHE'S RATHER MANNISH...
AMIDABA... A FORMER... MEMBER OF THE GOVERNMENT...
THAT'S RIGHT.
ZECT AND I GOT TO KNOW EACH OTHER...
...AT A GOVERNMENT AGENCY CALLED *ATTACK*.
ATTACK.
STEA ARMY
ATTACK
OTHER COUNTRIES
Ruins
Ruins
GUARDIAN
THERE ARE TWO SPECIAL FORCES WITHIN THE ARMY OF STEA...
THE *GUARDIAN*, WHO PRO-TECTS THE TREASURED RUINS WITHIN THEIR COUNTRY...
...AND *ATTACK*, WHICH ENTER THE RUINS OF OTHER COUNTRIES TO EXCAVATE THEM.

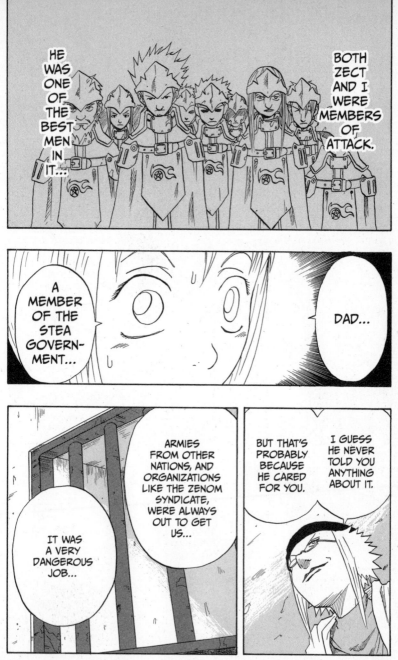

BOTH ZECT AND I WERE MEMBERS OF ATTACK.
HE WAS ONE OF THE BEST MEN IN IT...
DAD...
A MEMBER OF THE STEA GOVERN-MENT...
I GUESS HE NEVER TOLD YOU ANYTHING ABOUT IT.
BUT THAT'S PROBABLY BECAUSE HE CARED FOR YOU.
ARMIES FROM OTHER NATIONS, AND ORGANIZATIONS LIKE THE ZENOM SYNDICATE, WERE ALWAYS OUT TO GET US...
IT WAS A VERY DANGEROUS JOB...

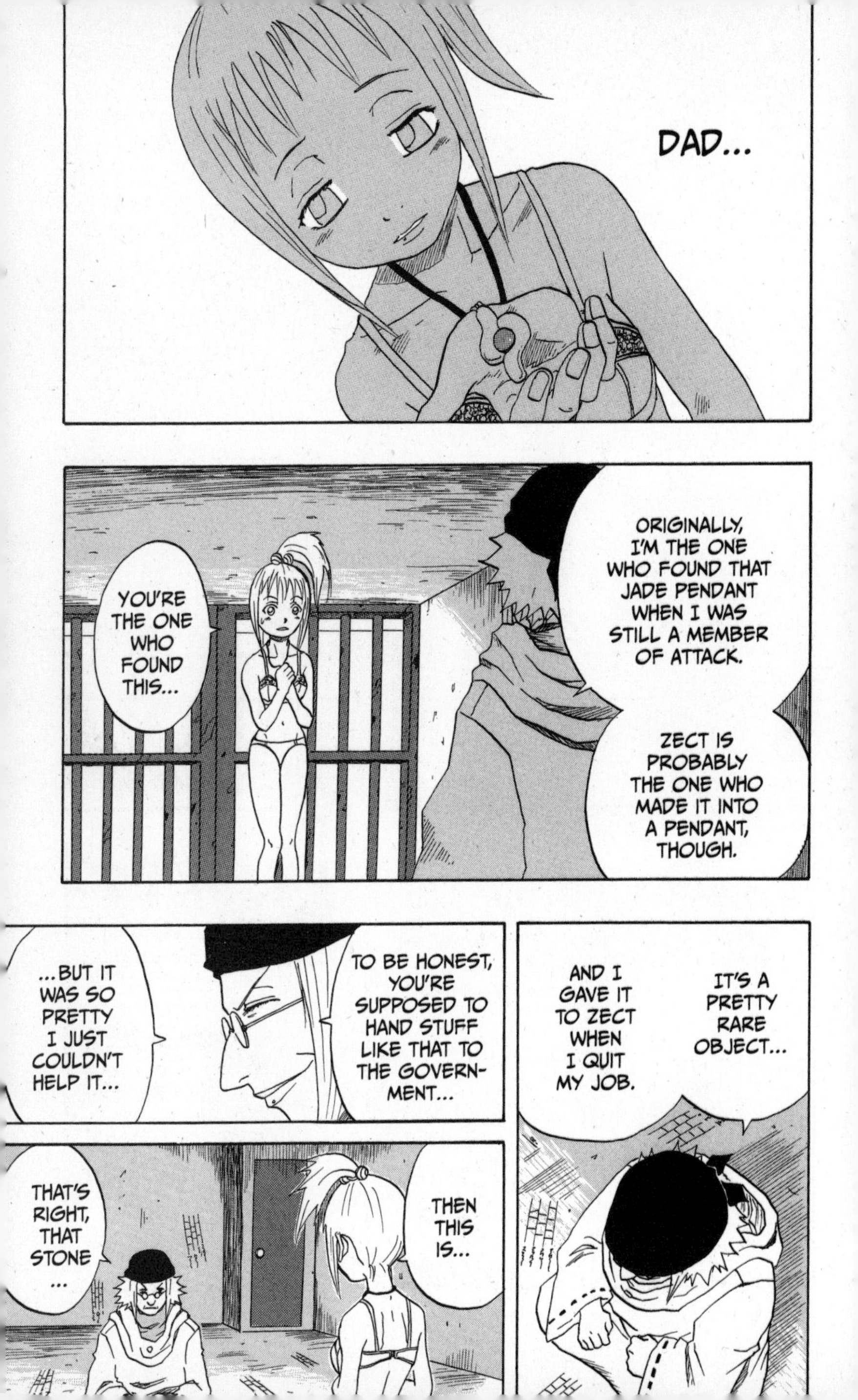
DAD...
ORIGINALLY, I'M THE ONE WHO FOUND THAT JADE PENDANT WHEN I WAS STILL A MEMBER OF ATTACK.
ZECT IS PROBABLY THE ONE WHO MADE IT INTO A PENDANT, THOUGH.
YOU'RE THE ONE WHO FOUND THIS...
IT'S A PRETTY RARE OBJECT...
AND I GAVE IT TO ZECT WHEN I QUIT MY JOB.
TO BE HONEST, YOU'RE SUPPOSED TO HAND STUFF LIKE THAT TO THE GOVERN-MENT...
...BUT IT WAS SO PRETTY I JUST COULDN'T HELP IT...
THEN THIS IS...
THAT'S RIGHT, THAT STONE ...

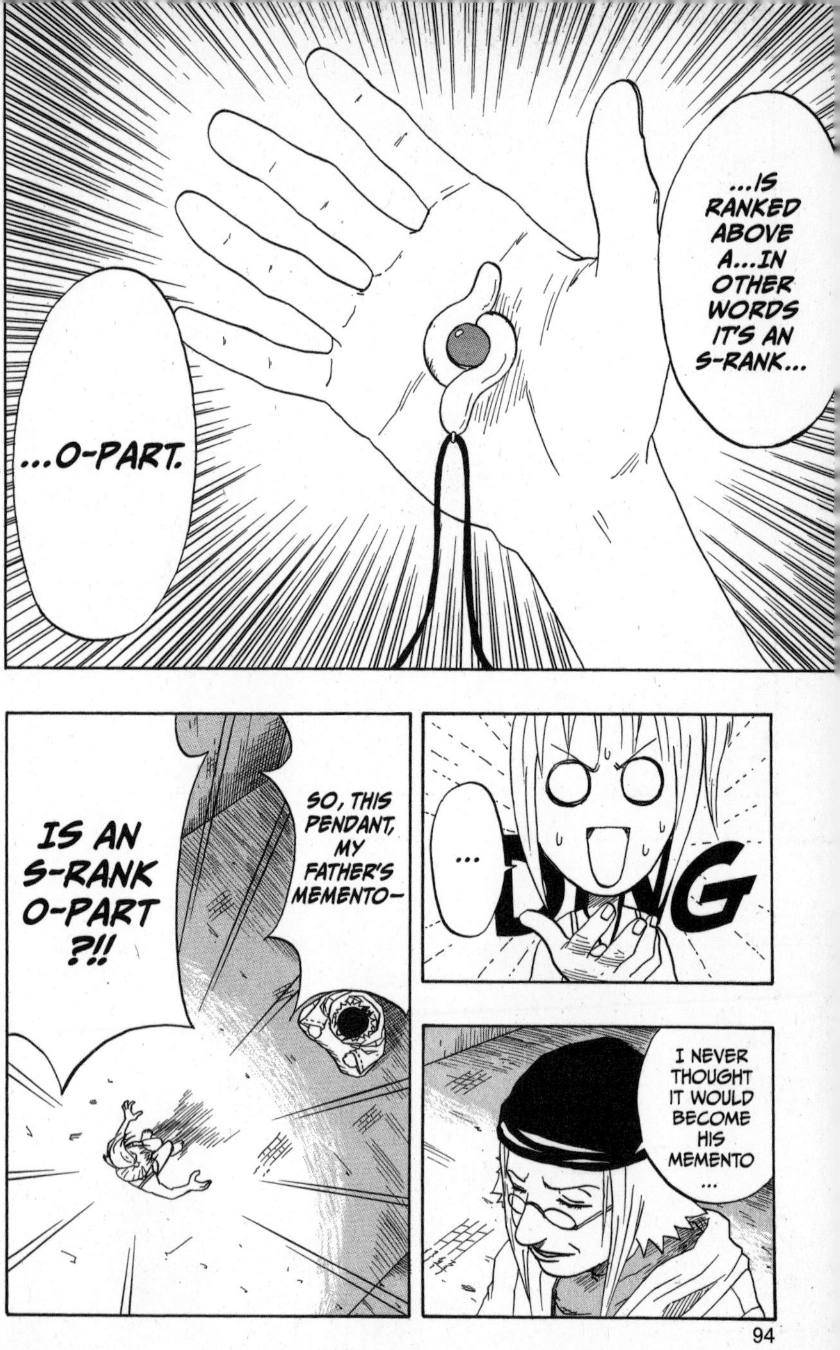
...IS RANKED ABOVE A...IN OTHER WORDS IT'S AN S-RANK...
...O-PART.
...
DING
I NEVER THOUGHT IT WOULD BECOME HIS MEMENTO ...
SO, THIS PENDANT, MY FATHER'S MEMENTO—
IS AN S-RANK O-PART ?!!

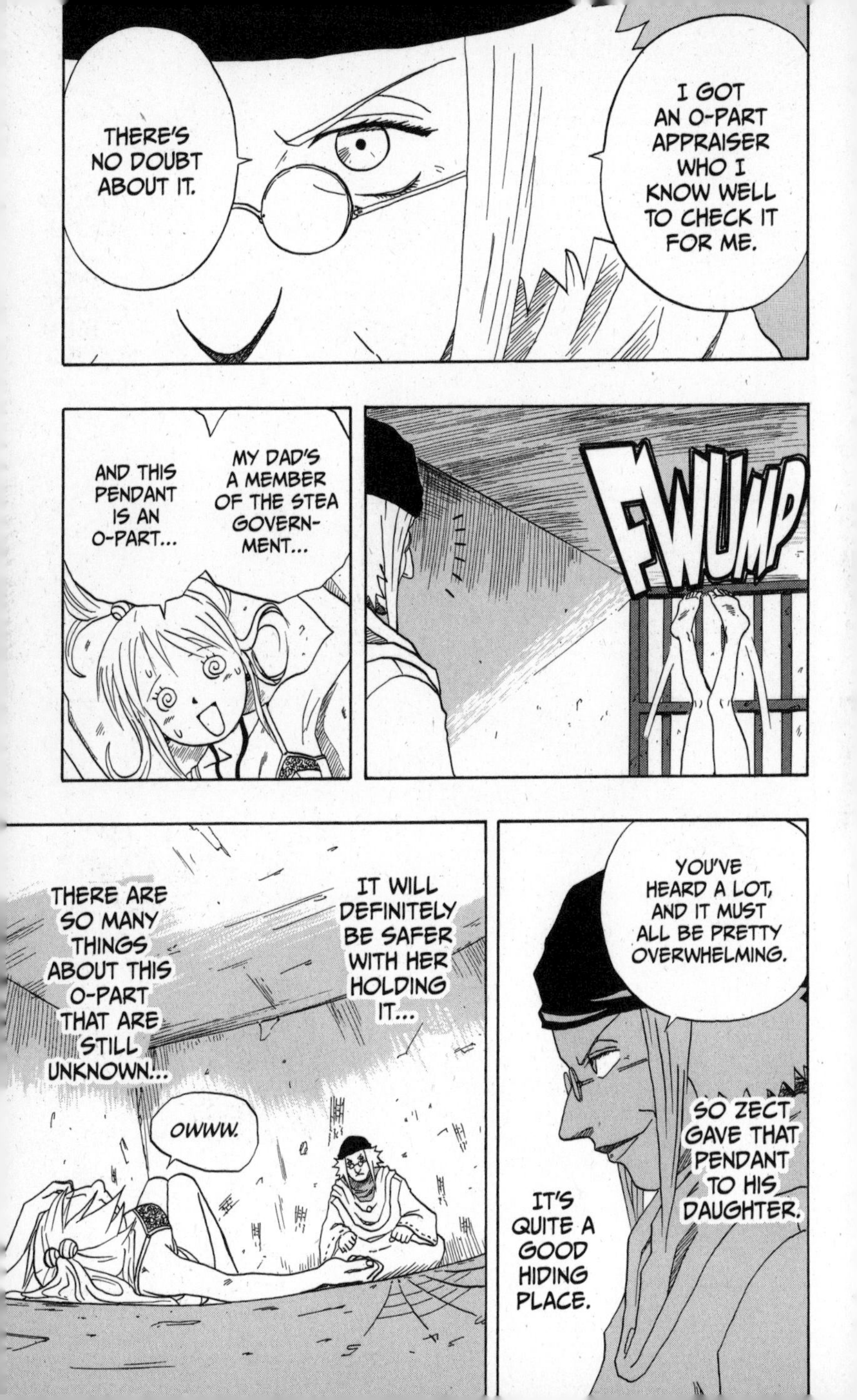
I GOT AN O-PART APPRAISER WHO I KNOW WELL TO CHECK IT FOR ME.
THERE'S NO DOUBT ABOUT IT.
FWUMP
MY DAD'S A MEMBER OF THE STEA GOVERN-MENT...
AND THIS PENDANT IS AN O-PART...
YOU'VE HEARD A LOT, AND IT MUST ALL BE PRETTY OVERWHELMING.
SO ZECT GAVE THAT PENDANT TO HIS DAUGHTER.
IT'S QUITE A GOOD HIDING PLACE.
IT WILL DEFINITELY BE SAFER WITH HER HOLDING IT...
THERE ARE SO MANY THINGS ABOUT THIS O-PART THAT ARE STILL UNKNOWN...
OWWW.

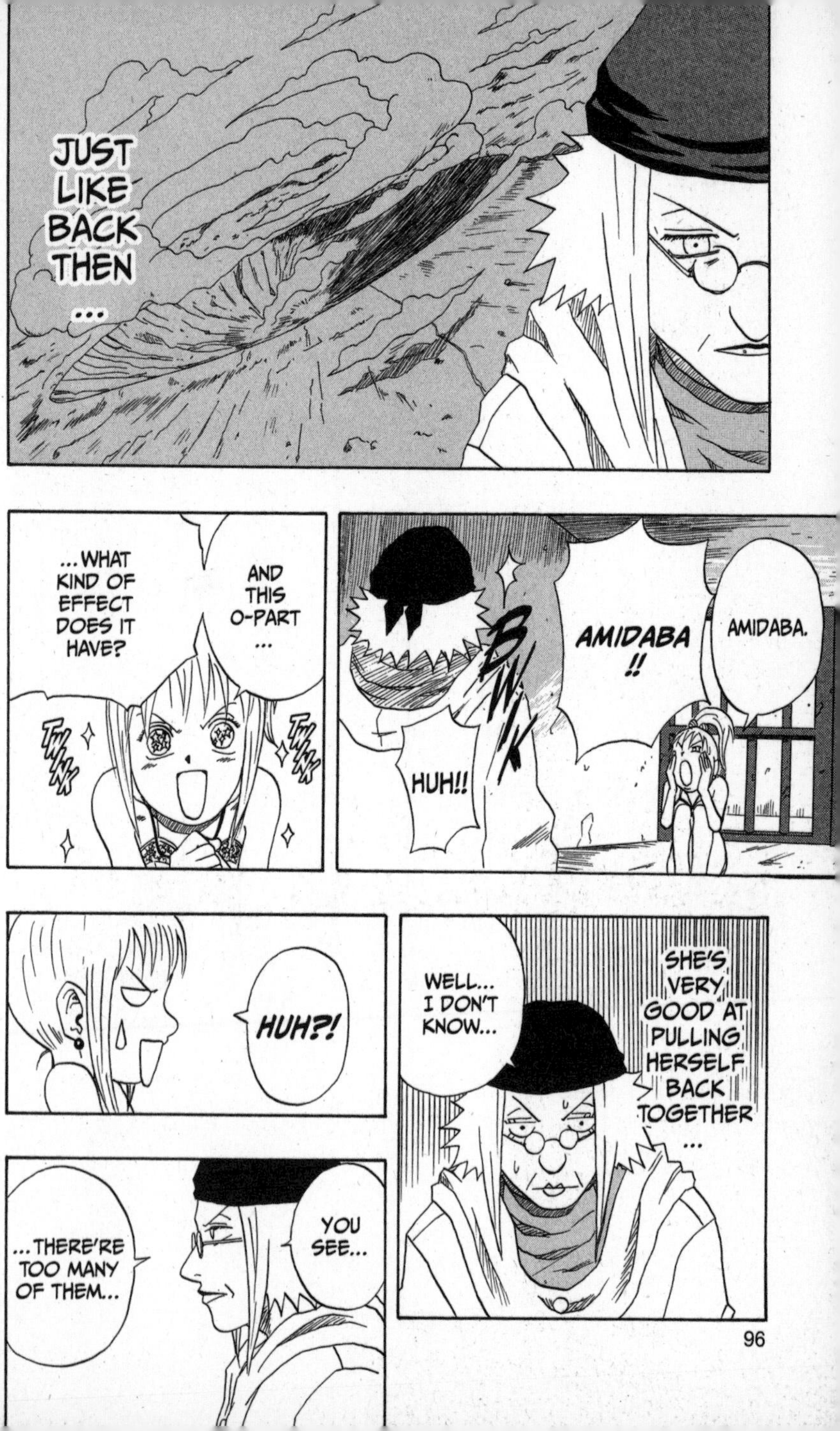
JUST LIKE BACK THEN ...
AMIDABA.
AMIDABA !!
BWIK
HUH!!
AND THIS O-PART ...
...WHAT KIND OF EFFECT DOES IT HAVE?
TWINK
TWINK
SHE'S VERY GOOD AT PULLING HERSELF BACK TOGETHER ...
WELL... I DON'T KNOW...
HUH?!
YOU SEE...
...THERE'RE TOO MANY OF THEM...

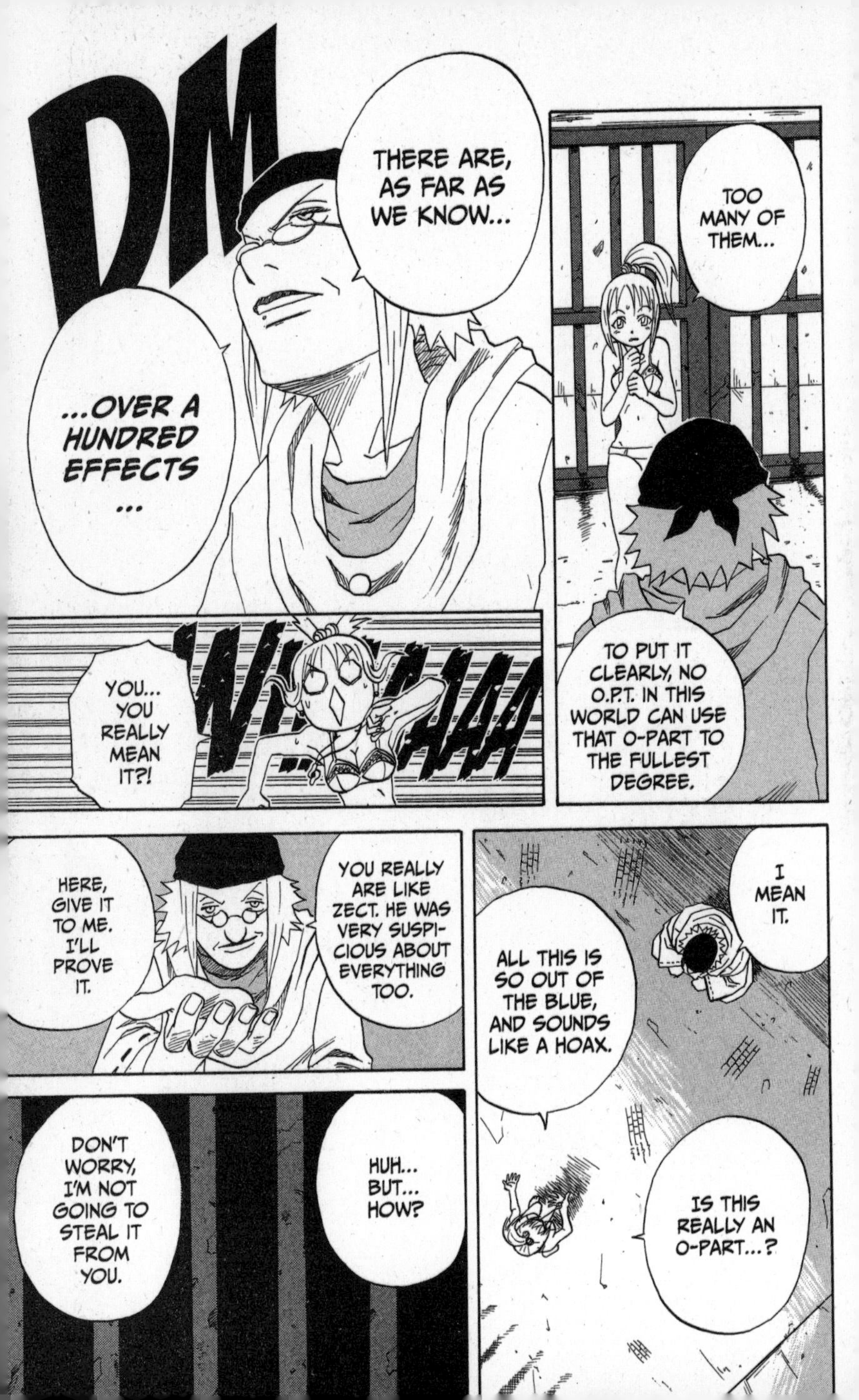
DM
THERE ARE, AS FAR AS WE KNOW...
...OVER A HUNDRED EFFECTS ...
TOO MANY OF THEM...
TO PUT IT CLEARLY, NO O.P.T. IN THIS WORLD CAN USE THAT O-PART TO THE FULLEST DEGREE.
YOU... YOU REALLY MEAN IT?!
I MEAN IT.
ALL THIS IS SO OUT OF THE BLUE, AND SOUNDS LIKE A HOAX.
IS THIS REALLY AN O-PART...?
YOU REALLY ARE LIKE ZECT. HE WAS VERY SUSPICIOUS ABOUT EVERYTHING TOO.
HERE, GIVE IT TO ME. I'LL PROVE IT.
HUH... BUT... HOW?
DON'T WORRY, I'M NOT GOING TO STEAL IT FROM YOU.

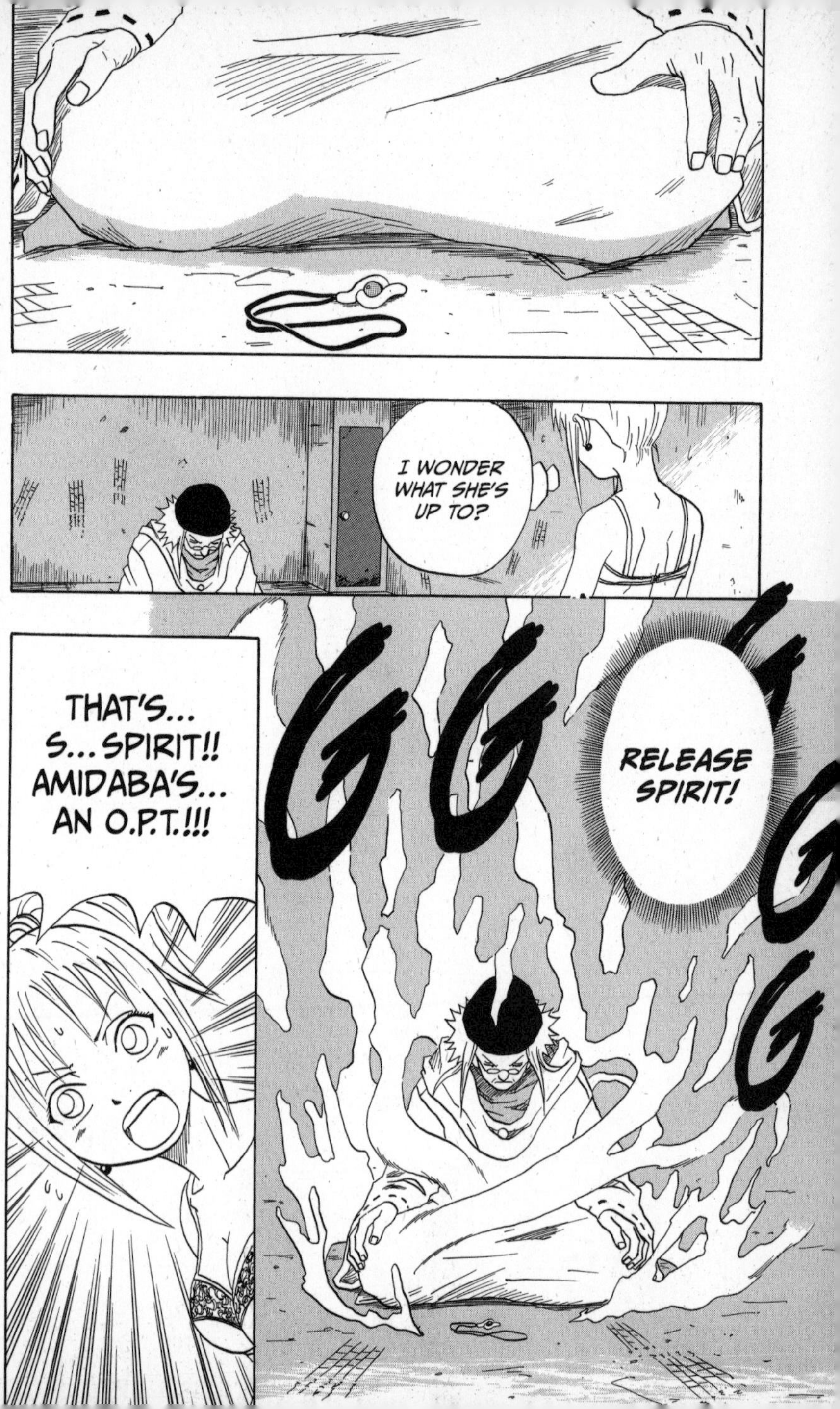
I WONDER WHAT SHE'S UP TO?
RELEASE SPIRIT!
GGGGG
THAT'S... S...SPIRIT!! AMIDABA'S... AN O.P.T.!!!

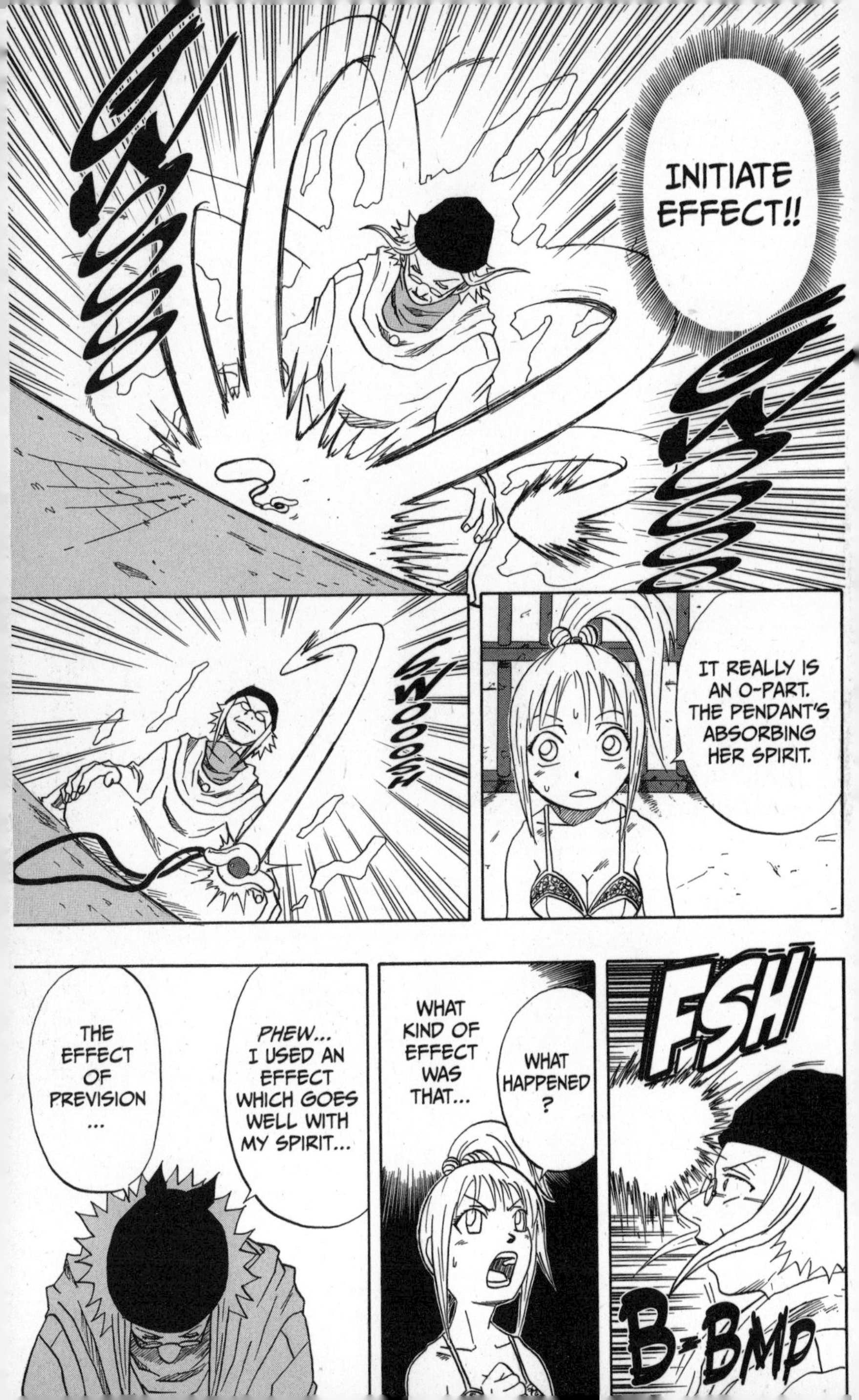
INITIATE EFFECT!!
IT REALLY IS AN O-PART. THE PENDANT'S ABSORBING HER SPIRIT.
FSH
B-BMP
WHAT HAPPENED?
WHAT KIND OF EFFECT WAS THAT...
PHEW... I USED AN EFFECT WHICH GOES WELL WITH MY SPIRIT...
THE EFFECT OF PREVISION...

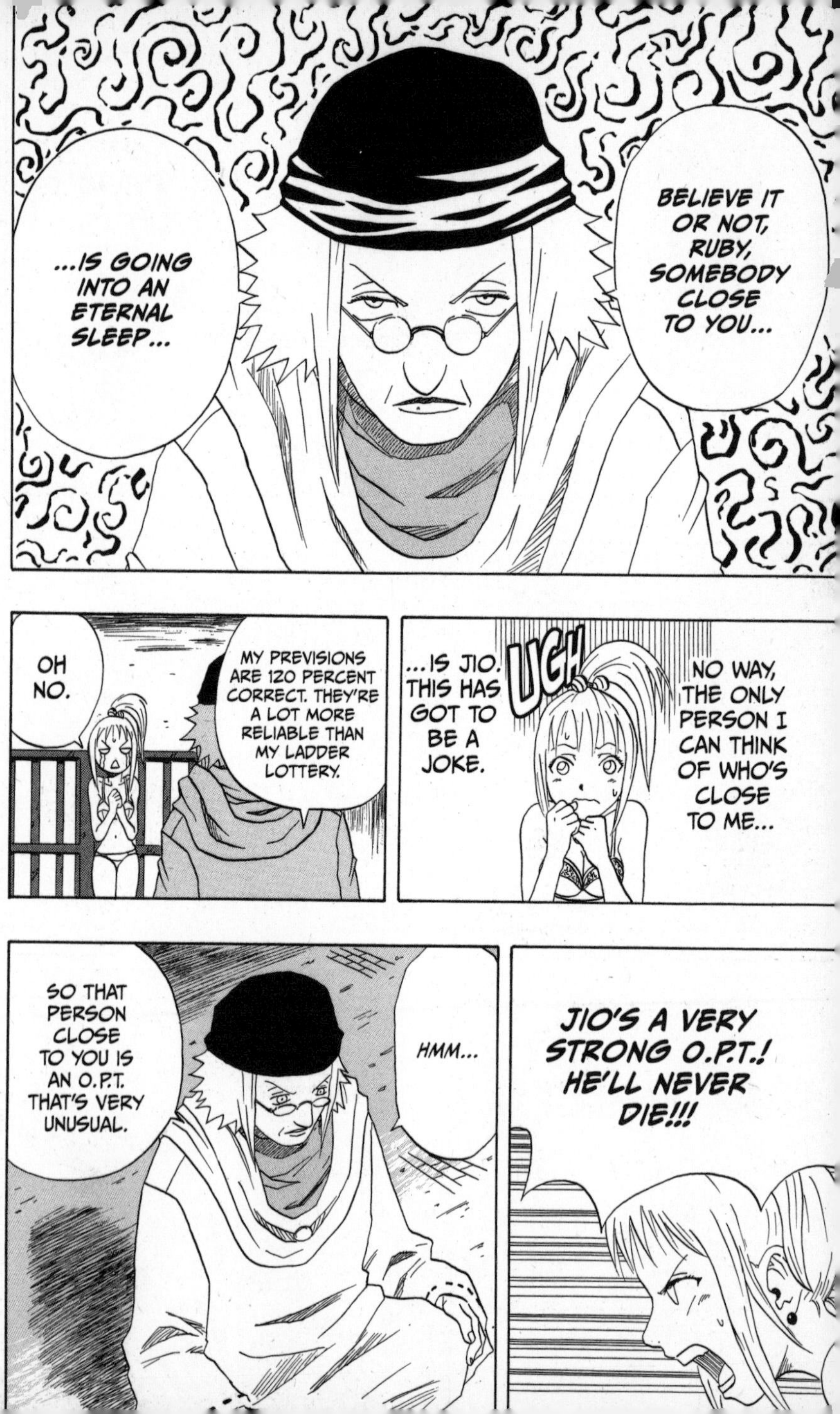
BELIEVE IT OR NOT, RUBY, SOMEBODY CLOSE TO YOU...
...IS GOING INTO AN ETERNAL SLEEP...
NO WAY, THE ONLY PERSON I CAN THINK OF WHO'S CLOSE TO ME...
UGH
...IS JIO. THIS HAS GOT TO BE A JOKE.
MY PREVISIONS ARE 120 PERCENT CORRECT. THEY'RE A LOT MORE RELIABLE THAN MY LADDER LOTTERY.
OH NO.
JIO'S A VERY STRONG O.P.T.! HE'LL NEVER DIE!!!
HMM...
SO THAT PERSON CLOSE TO YOU IS AN O.P.T. THAT'S VERY UNUSUAL.

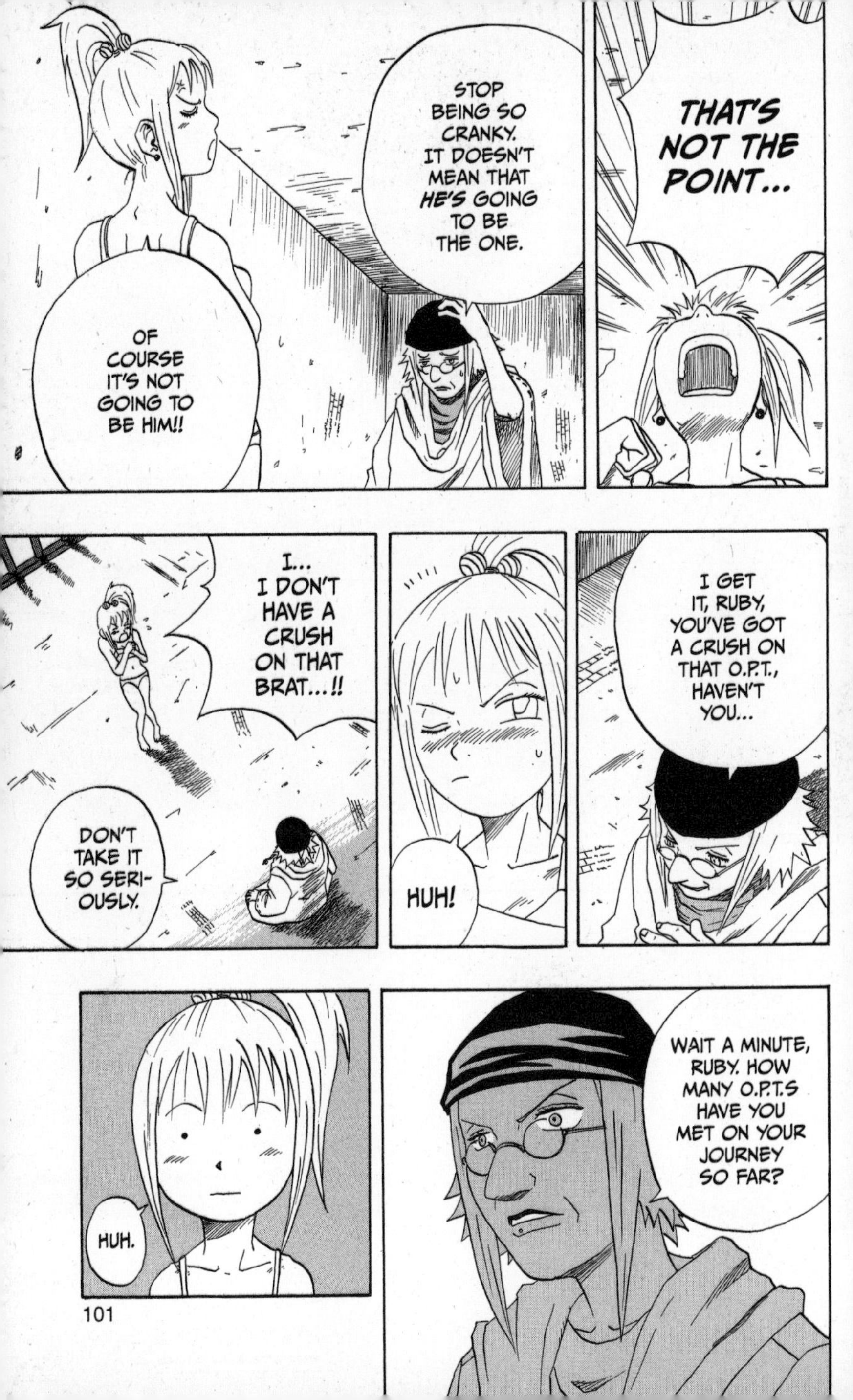
THAT'S NOT THE POINT...
STOP BEING SO CRANKY. IT DOESN'T MEAN THAT HE'S GOING TO BE THE ONE.
OF COURSE IT'S NOT GOING TO BE HIM!!
I GET IT, RUBY, YOU'VE GOT A CRUSH ON THAT O.P.T., HAVEN'T YOU...
HUH!
I... I DON'T HAVE A CRUSH ON THAT BRAT...!!
DON'T TAKE IT SO SERI-OUSLY.
WAIT A MINUTE, RUBY. HOW MANY O.P.T.S HAVE YOU MET ON YOUR JOURNEY SO FAR?
HUH.

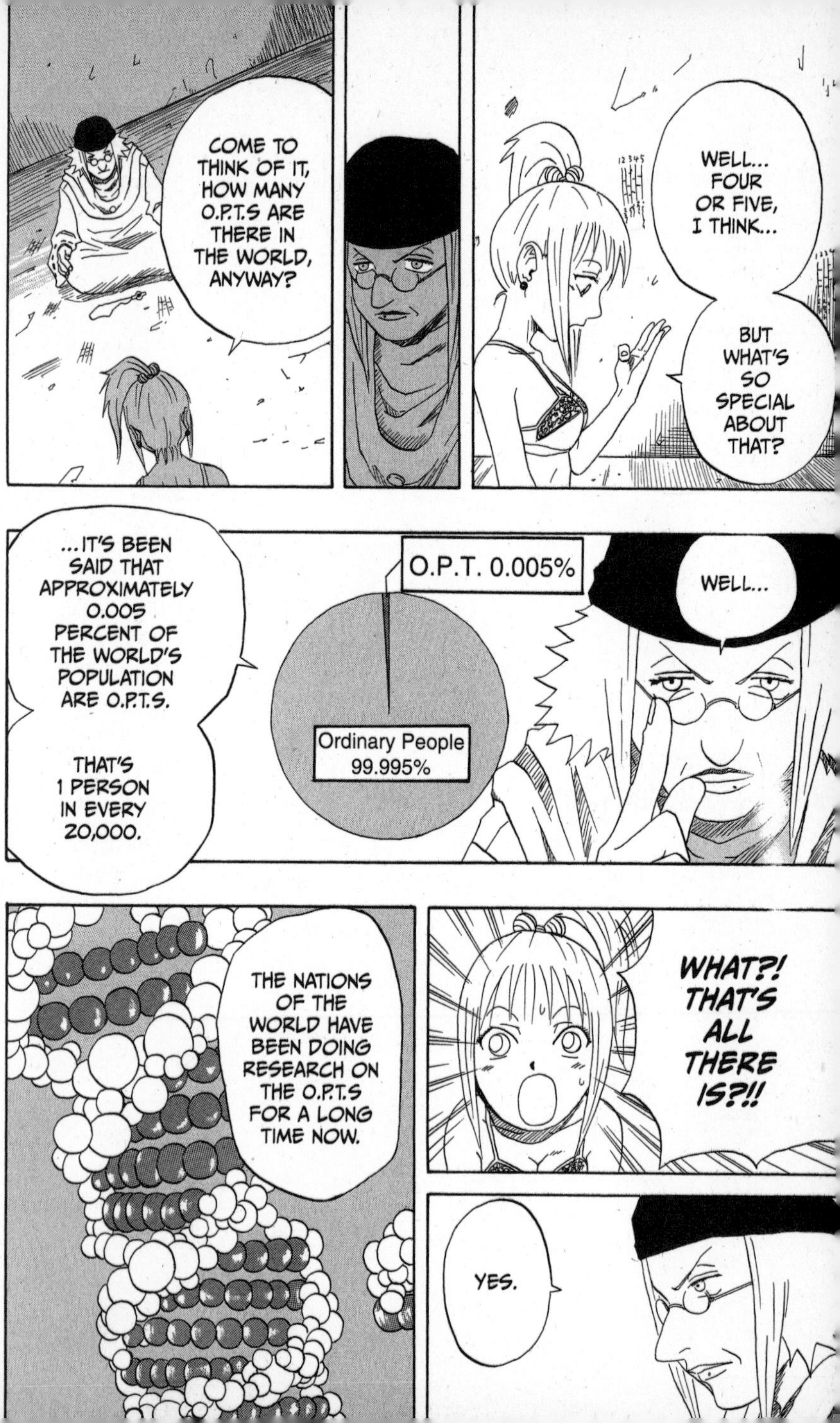
WELL... FOUR OR FIVE, I THINK...
BUT WHAT'S SO SPECIAL ABOUT THAT?
COME TO THINK OF IT, HOW MANY O.P.T.S ARE THERE IN THE WORLD, ANYWAY?
WELL...
O.P.T. 0.005%
Ordinary People 99.995%
...IT'S BEEN SAID THAT APPROXIMATELY 0.005 PERCENT OF THE WORLD'S POPULATION ARE O.P.T.S.
THAT'S 1 PERSON IN EVERY 20,000.
WHAT?! THAT'S ALL THERE IS?!!
YES.
THE NATIONS OF THE WORLD HAVE BEEN DOING RESEARCH ON THE O.P.T.S FOR A LONG TIME NOW.

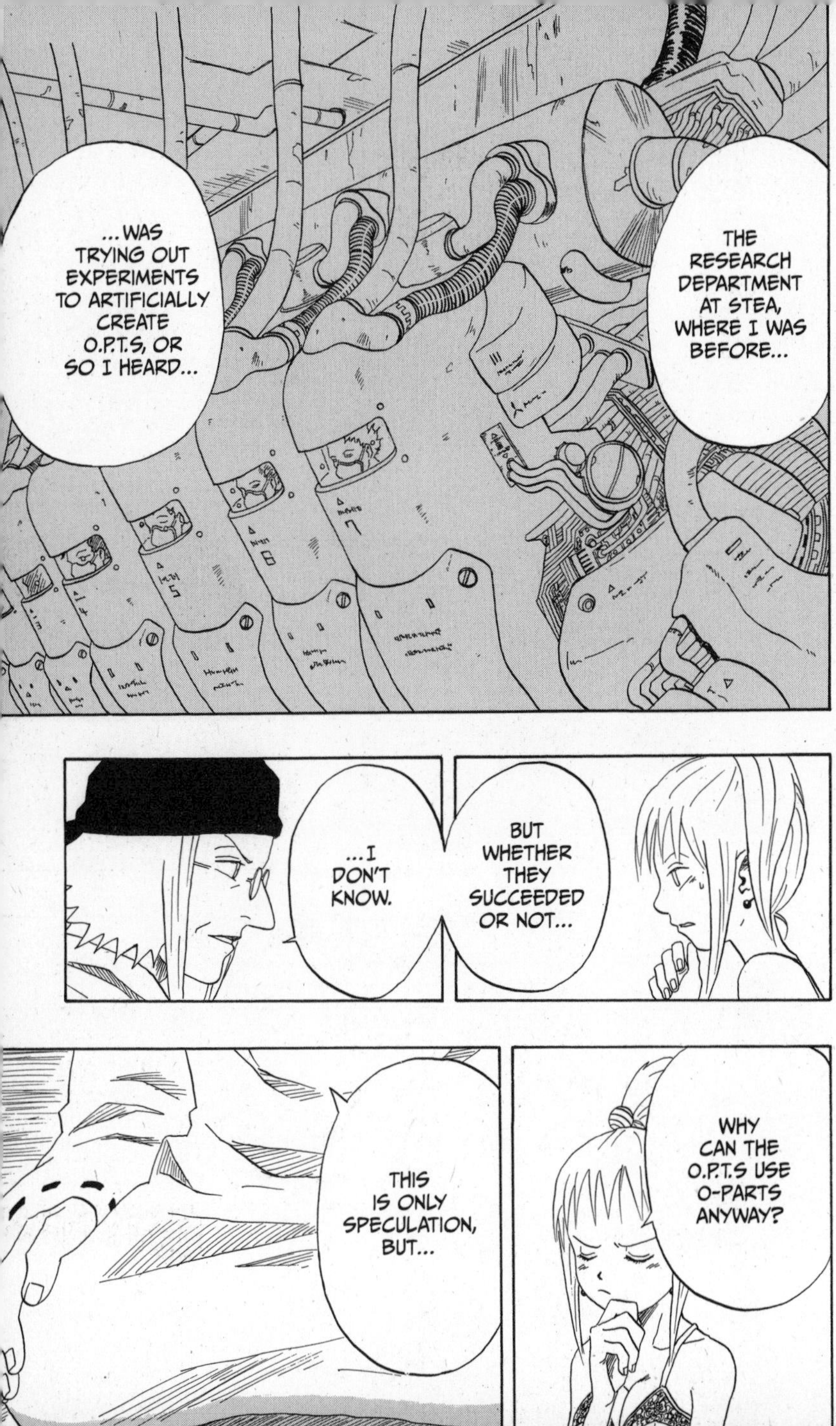
THE RESEARCH DEPARTMENT AT STEA, WHERE I WAS BEFORE...
...WAS TRYING OUT EXPERIMENTS TO ARTIFICIALLY CREATE O.P.T.S, OR SO I HEARD...
BUT WHETHER THEY SUCCEEDED OR NOT...
...I DON'T KNOW.
WHY CAN THE O.P.T.S USE O-PARTS ANYWAY?
THIS IS ONLY SPECULATION, BUT...

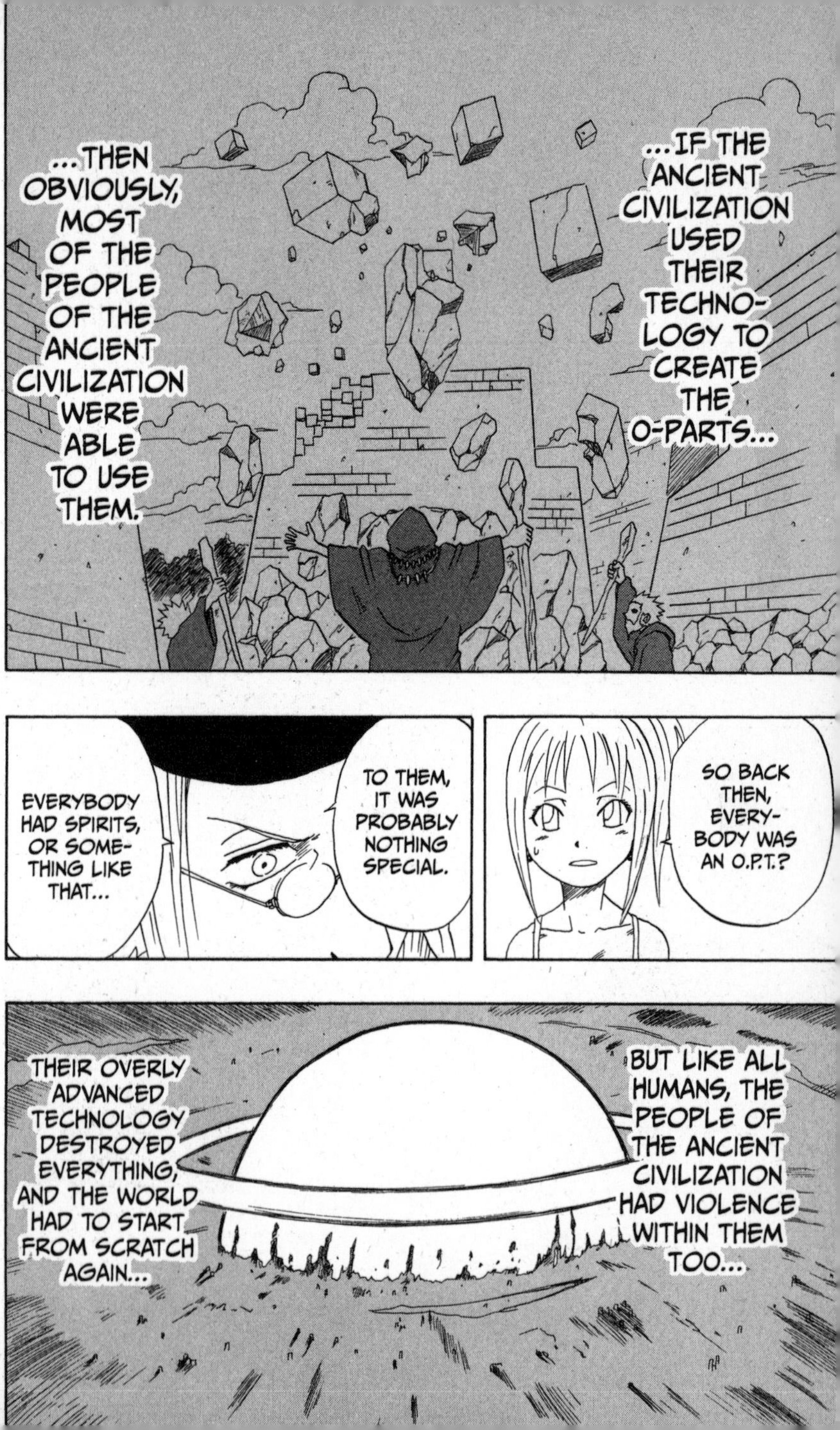
...IF THE ANCIENT CIVILIZATION USED THEIR TECHNO-LOGY TO CREATE THE O-PARTS...
...THEN OBVIOUSLY, MOST OF THE PEOPLE OF THE ANCIENT CIVILIZATION WERE ABLE TO USE THEM.
SO BACK THEN, EVERY-BODY WAS AN O.P.T.?
TO THEM, IT WAS PROBABLY NOTHING SPECIAL.
EVERYBODY HAD SPIRITS, OR SOME-THING LIKE THAT...
BUT LIKE ALL HUMANS, THE PEOPLE OF THE ANCIENT CIVILIZATION HAD VIOLENCE WITHIN THEM TOO...
THEIR OVERLY ADVANCED TECHNOLOGY DESTROYED EVERYTHING, AND THE WORLD HAD TO START FROM SCRATCH AGAIN...

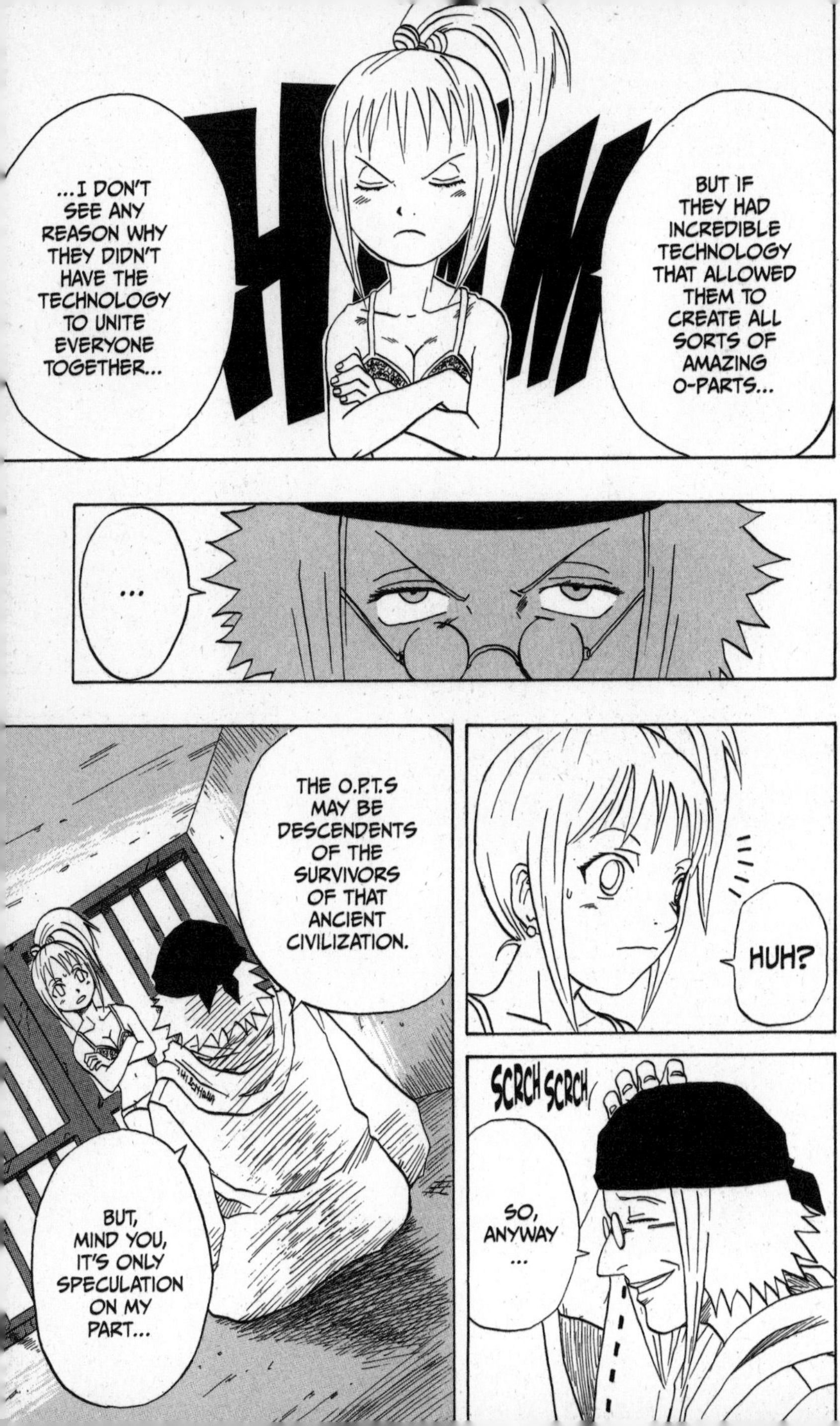
BUT IF THEY HAD INCREDIBLE TECHNOLOGY THAT ALLOWED THEM TO CREATE ALL SORTS OF AMAZING O-PARTS...
...I DON'T SEE ANY REASON WHY THEY DIDN'T HAVE THE TECHNOLOGY TO UNITE EVERYONE TOGETHER...
...
HUH?
SCRCH SCRCH
SO, ANYWAY ...
THE O.P.T.S MAY BE DESCENDENTS OF THE SURVIVORS OF THAT ANCIENT CIVILIZATION.
BUT, MIND YOU, IT'S ONLY SPECULATION ON MY PART...

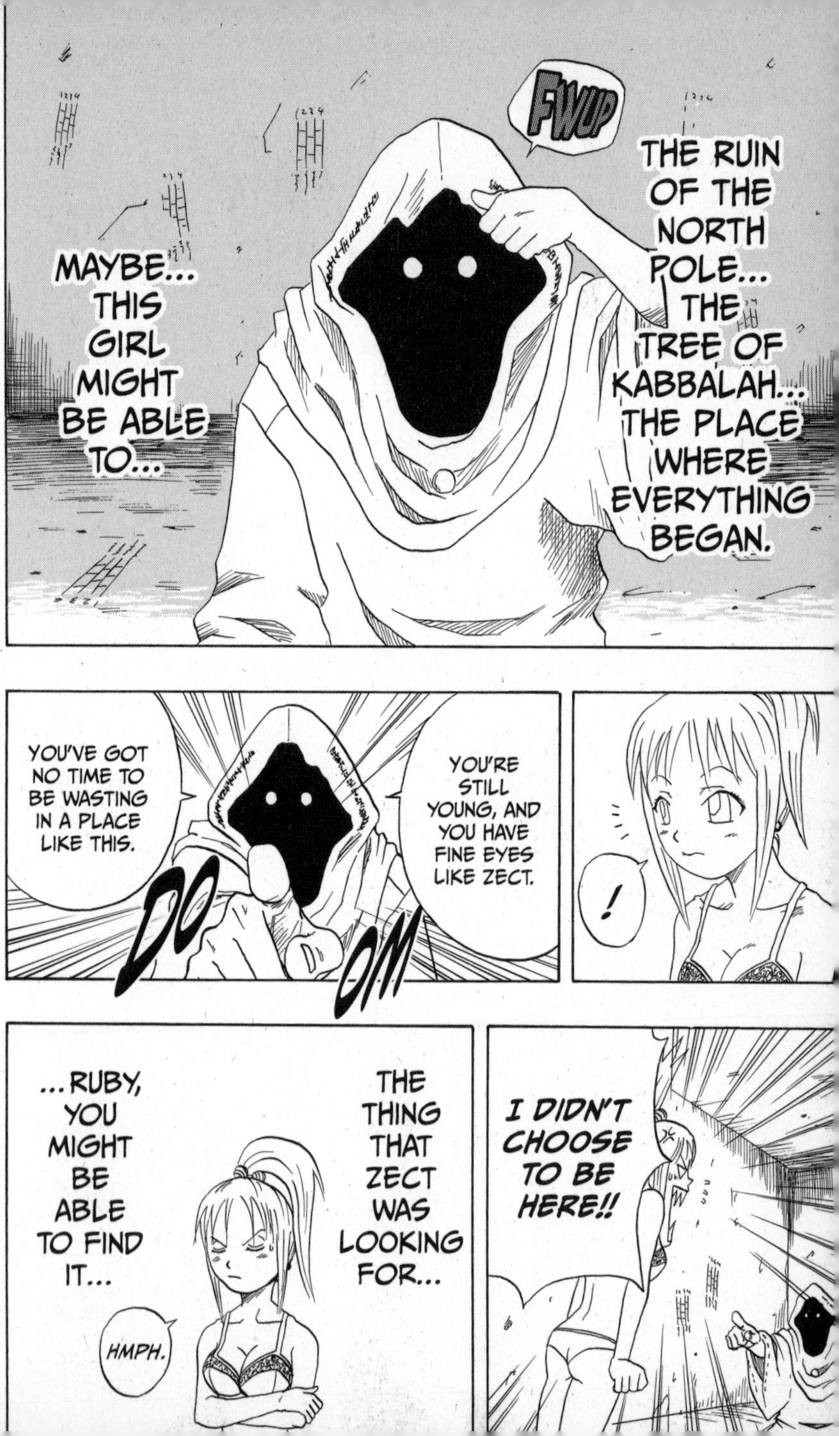
FWUP
THE RUIN OF THE NORTH POLE... THE TREE OF KABBALAH... THE PLACE WHERE EVERYTHING BEGAN.
MAYBE... THIS GIRL MIGHT BE ABLE TO...
!
YOU'RE STILL YOUNG, AND YOU HAVE FINE EYES LIKE ZECT.
YOU'VE GOT NO TIME TO BE WASTING IN A PLACE LIKE THIS.
DOOM
I DIDN'T CHOOSE TO BE HERE!!
THE THING THAT ZECT WAS LOOKING FOR...
...RUBY, YOU MIGHT BE ABLE TO FIND IT...
HMPH.

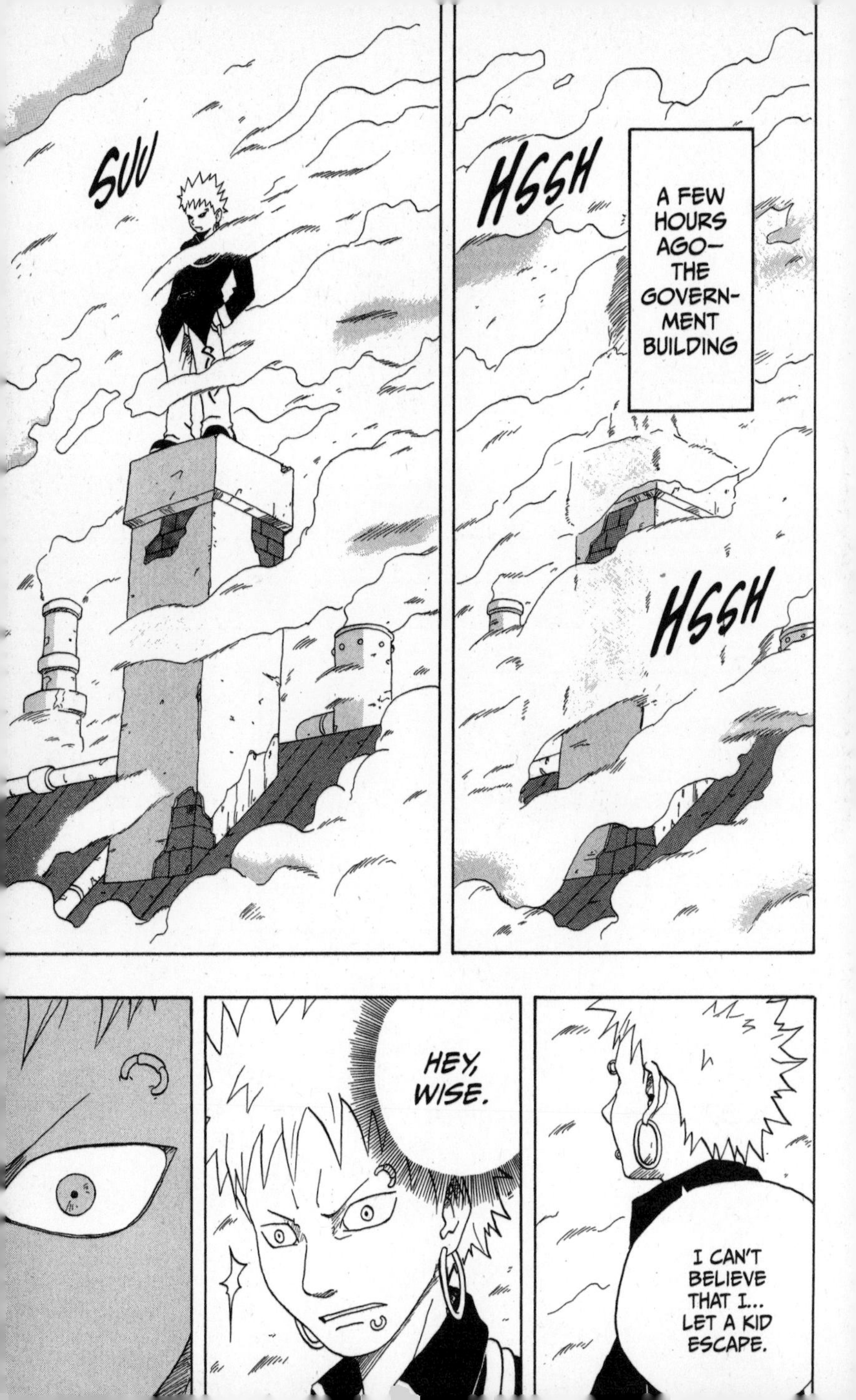
HSSH
A FEW HOURS AGO—THE GOVERNMENT BUILDING
HSSH
SUU
I CAN'T BELIEVE THAT I... LET A KID ESCAPE.
HEY, WISE.

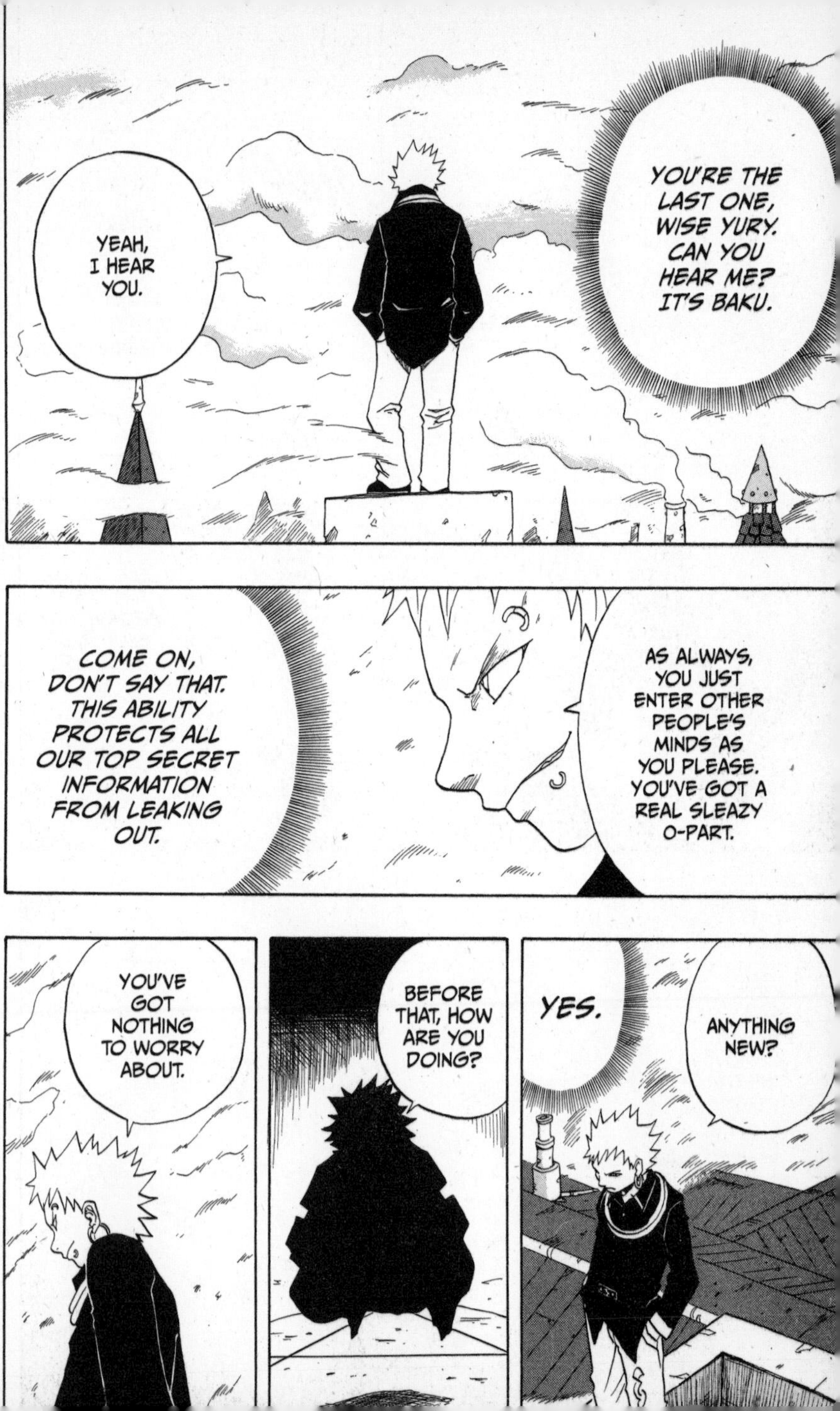
YOU'RE THE LAST ONE, WISE YURY. CAN YOU HEAR ME? IT'S BAKU.
YEAH, I HEAR YOU.
AS ALWAYS, YOU JUST ENTER OTHER PEOPLE'S MINDS AS YOU PLEASE. YOU'VE GOT A REAL SLEAZY O-PART.
COME ON, DON'T SAY THAT. THIS ABILITY PROTECTS ALL OUR TOP SECRET INFORMATION FROM LEAKING OUT.
YES.
ANYTHING NEW?
BEFORE THAT, HOW ARE YOU DOING?
YOU'VE GOT NOTHING TO WORRY ABOUT.

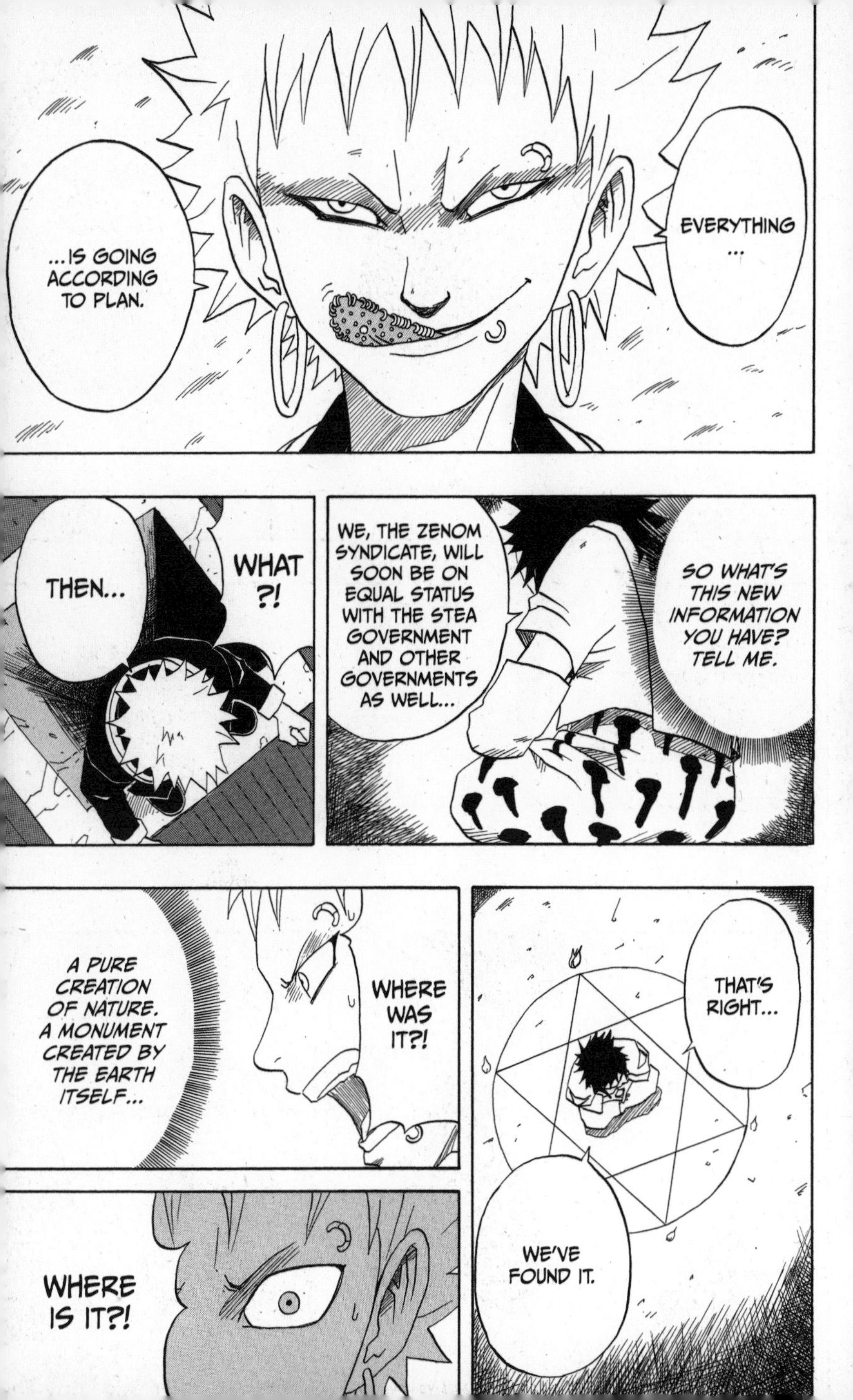
EVERYTHING ...
...IS GOING ACCORDING TO PLAN.
SO WHAT'S THIS NEW INFORMATION YOU HAVE? TELL ME.
WE, THE ZENOM SYNDICATE, WILL SOON BE ON EQUAL STATUS WITH THE STEA GOVERNMENT AND OTHER GOVERNMENTS AS WELL...
WHAT ?!
THEN...
THAT'S RIGHT...
WE'VE FOUND IT.
WHERE WAS IT?!
A PURE CREATION OF NATURE. A MONUMENT CREATED BY THE EARTH ITSELF...
WHERE IS IT?!

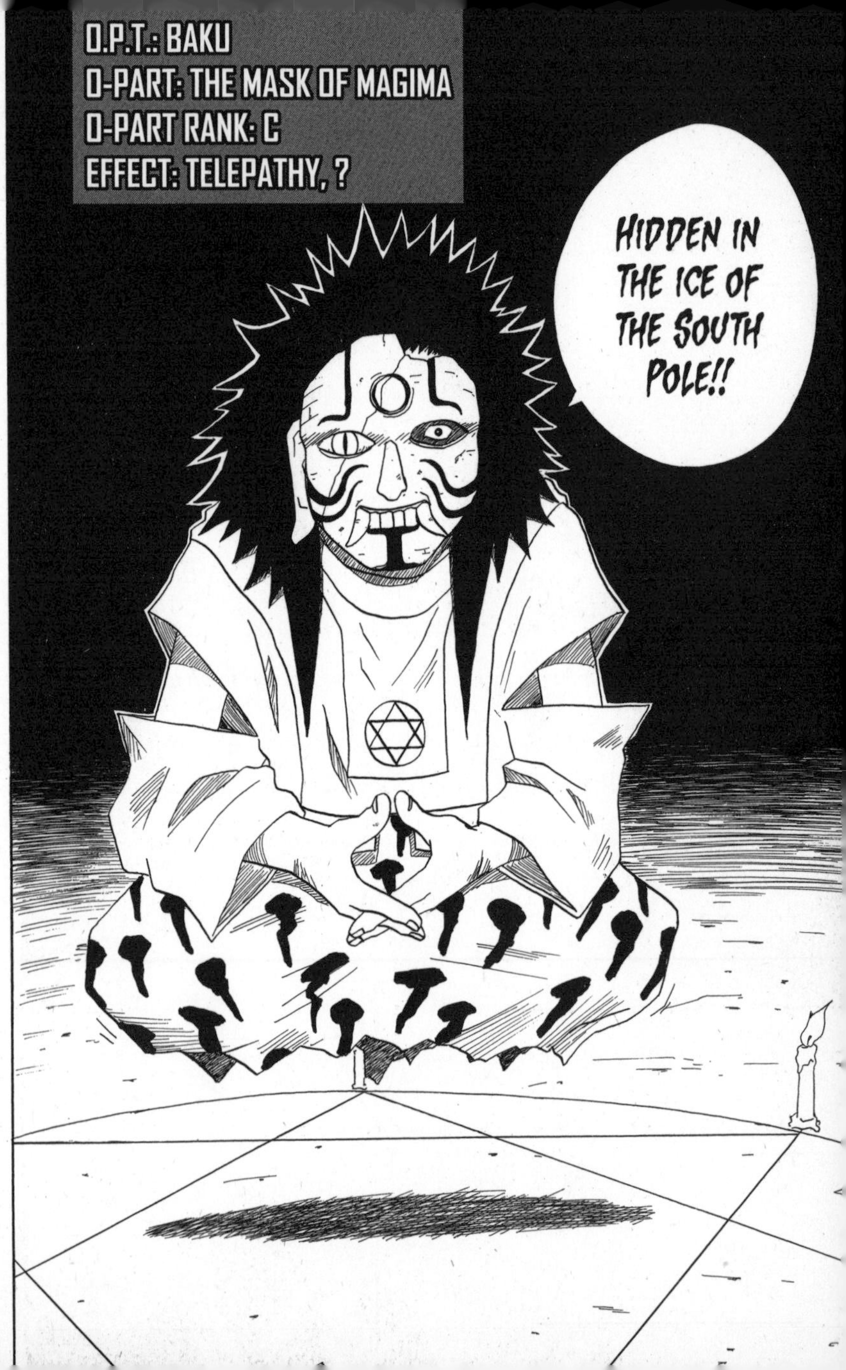
O.P.T.: BAKU
O-PART: THE MASK OF MAGIMA
O-PART RANK: C
EFFECT: TELEPATHY, ?
HIDDEN IN THE ICE OF THE SOUTH POLE!!

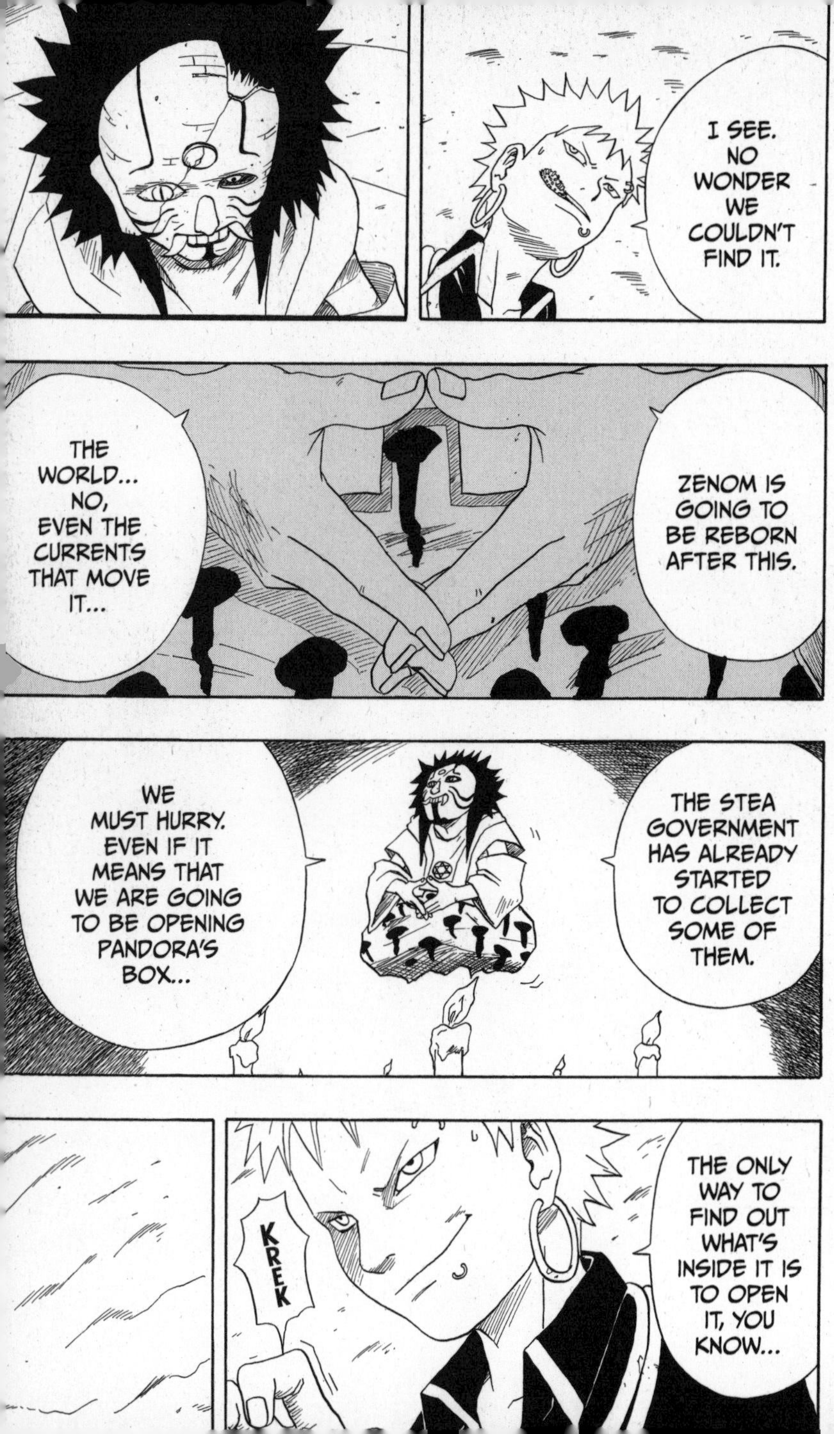
I SEE. NO WONDER WE COULDN'T FIND IT.
ZENOM IS GOING TO BE REBORN AFTER THIS.
THE WORLD... NO, EVEN THE CURRENTS THAT MOVE IT...
THE STEA GOVERNMENT HAS ALREADY STARTED TO COLLECT SOME OF THEM.
WE MUST HURRY. EVEN IF IT MEANS THAT WE ARE GOING TO BE OPENING PANDORA'S BOX...
THE ONLY WAY TO FIND OUT WHAT'S INSIDE IT IS TO OPEN IT, YOU KNOW...
KREK

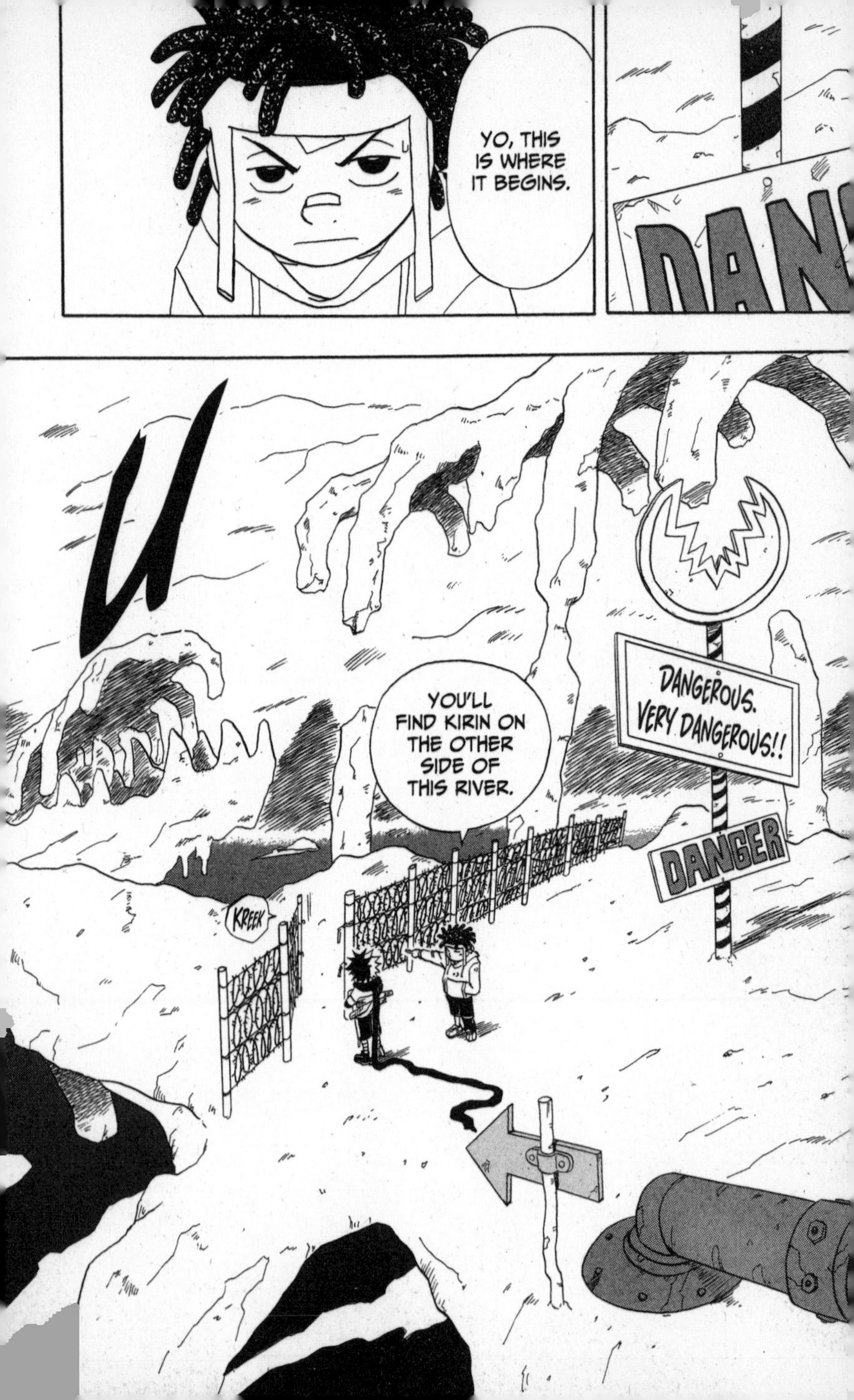
DAN
YO, THIS IS WHERE IT BEGINS.
U
DANGEROUS. VERY DANGEROUS!!
YOU'LL FIND KIRIN ON THE OTHER SIDE OF THIS RIVER.
DANGER
KREEK

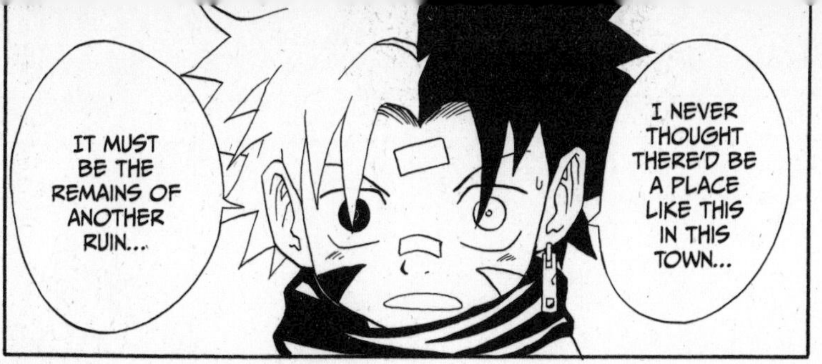
I NEVER THOUGHT THERE'D BE A PLACE LIKE THIS IN THIS TOWN...
IT MUST BE THE REMAINS OF ANOTHER RUIN...

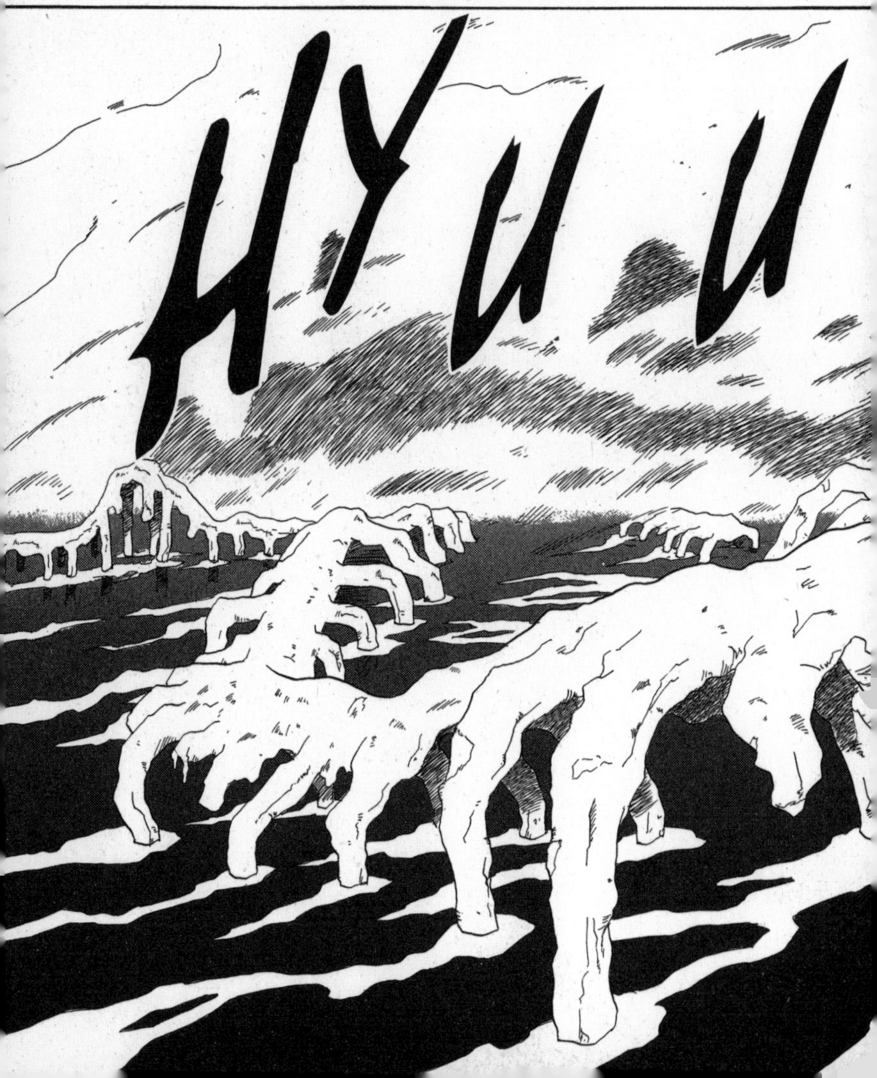
HYUU

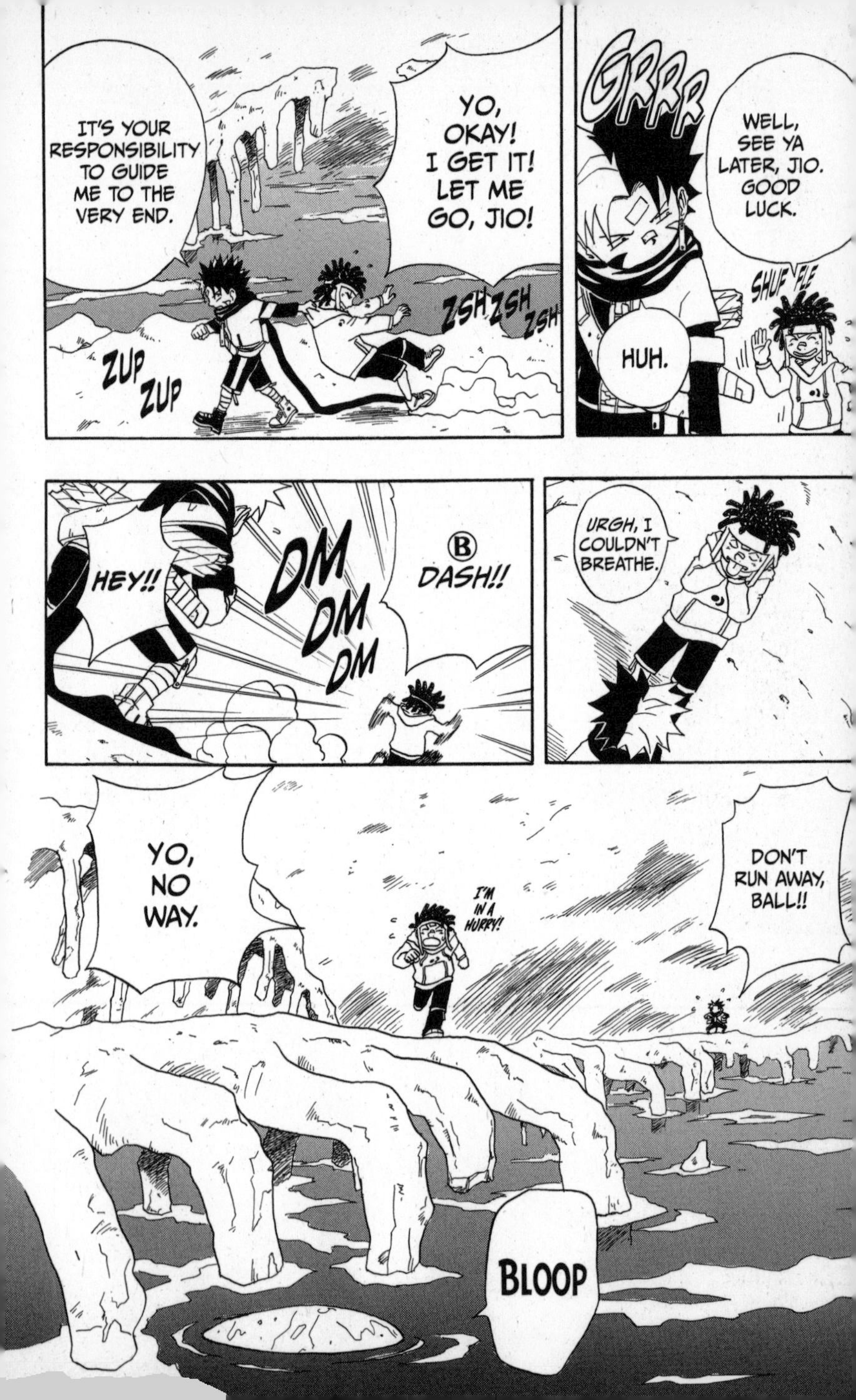
GRRR
WELL, SEE YA LATER, JIO. GOOD LUCK.
SHUFFLE
HUH.
YO, OKAY! I GET IT! LET ME GO, JIO!
IT'S YOUR RESPONSIBILITY TO GUIDE ME TO THE VERY END.
ZSH ZSH ZSH
ZUP ZUP
URGH, I COULDN'T BREATHE.
Ⓑ DASH!!
DM DM DM
HEY!!
DON'T RUN AWAY, BALL!!
I'M IN A HURRY!
YO, NO WAY.
BLOOP

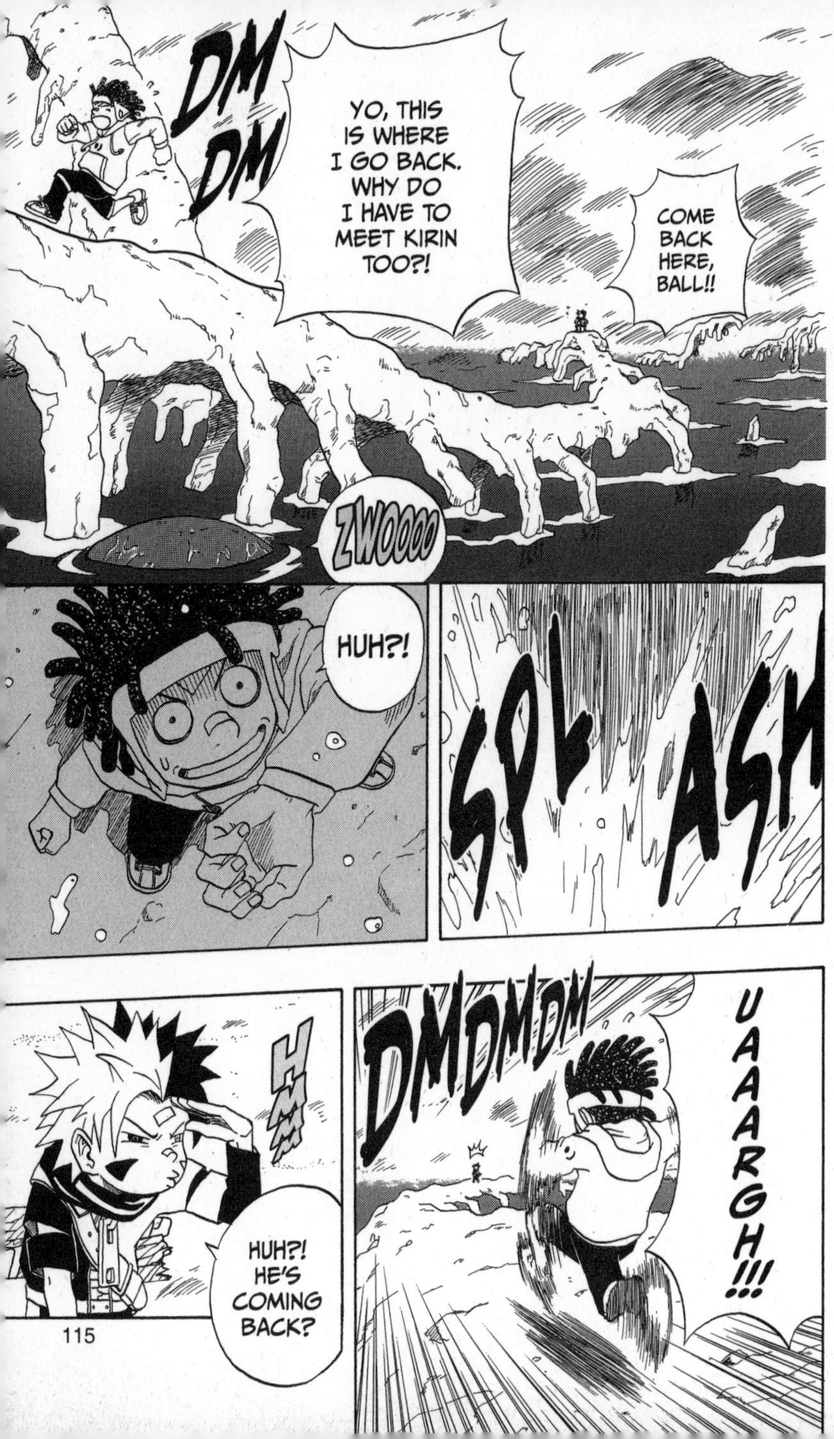
COME BACK HERE, BALL!!
YO, THIS IS WHERE I GO BACK. WHY DO I HAVE TO MEET KIRIN TOO?!
DM DM
ZWOOOO
SPLASH
HUH?!
UAAARGH!!!
DMDMDM
HMM
HUH?! HE'S COMING BACK?

CHAPTER 12: THE THREE ORDEALS

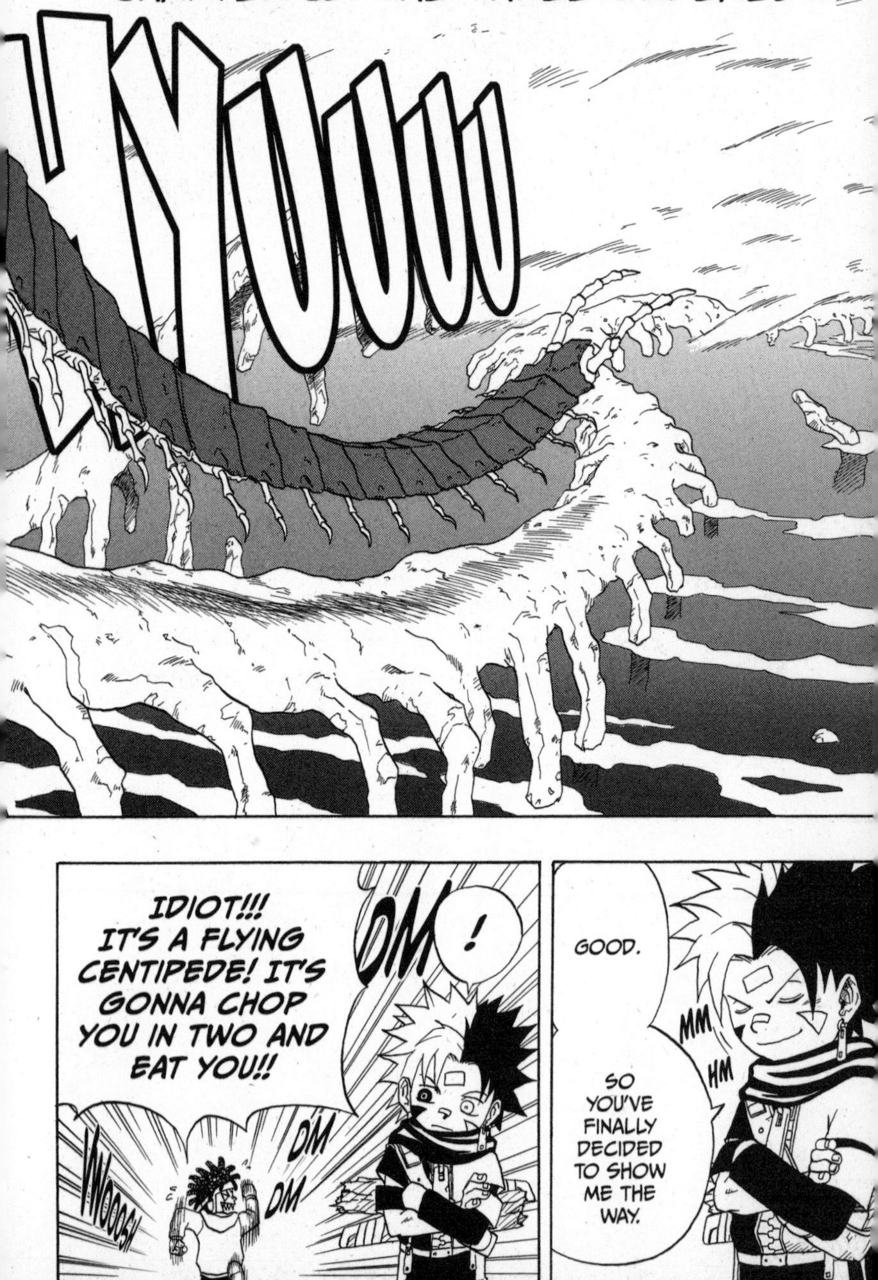

VYUUUU
GOOD.
MM HM
SO YOU'VE FINALLY DECIDED TO SHOW ME THE WAY.
OM
!
IDIOT!!! IT'S A FLYING CENTIPEDE! IT'S GONNA CHOP YOU IN TWO AND EAT YOU!!
DM DM
WOOOSH

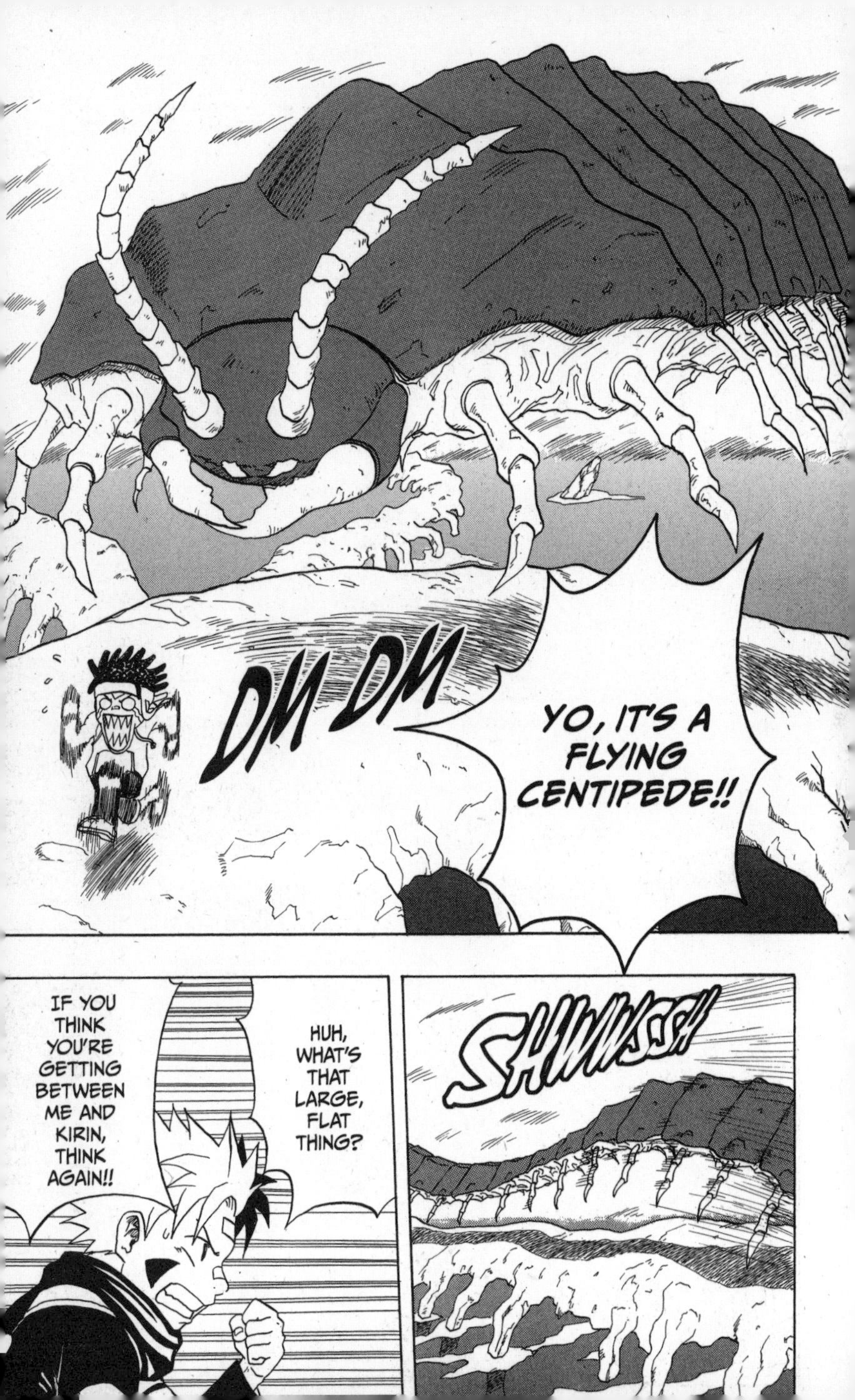
YO, IT'S A FLYING CENTIPEDE!!
DM DM
SHWISSH
HUH, WHAT'S THAT LARGE, FLAT THING?
IF YOU THINK YOU'RE GETTING BETWEEN ME AND KIRIN, THINK AGAIN!!

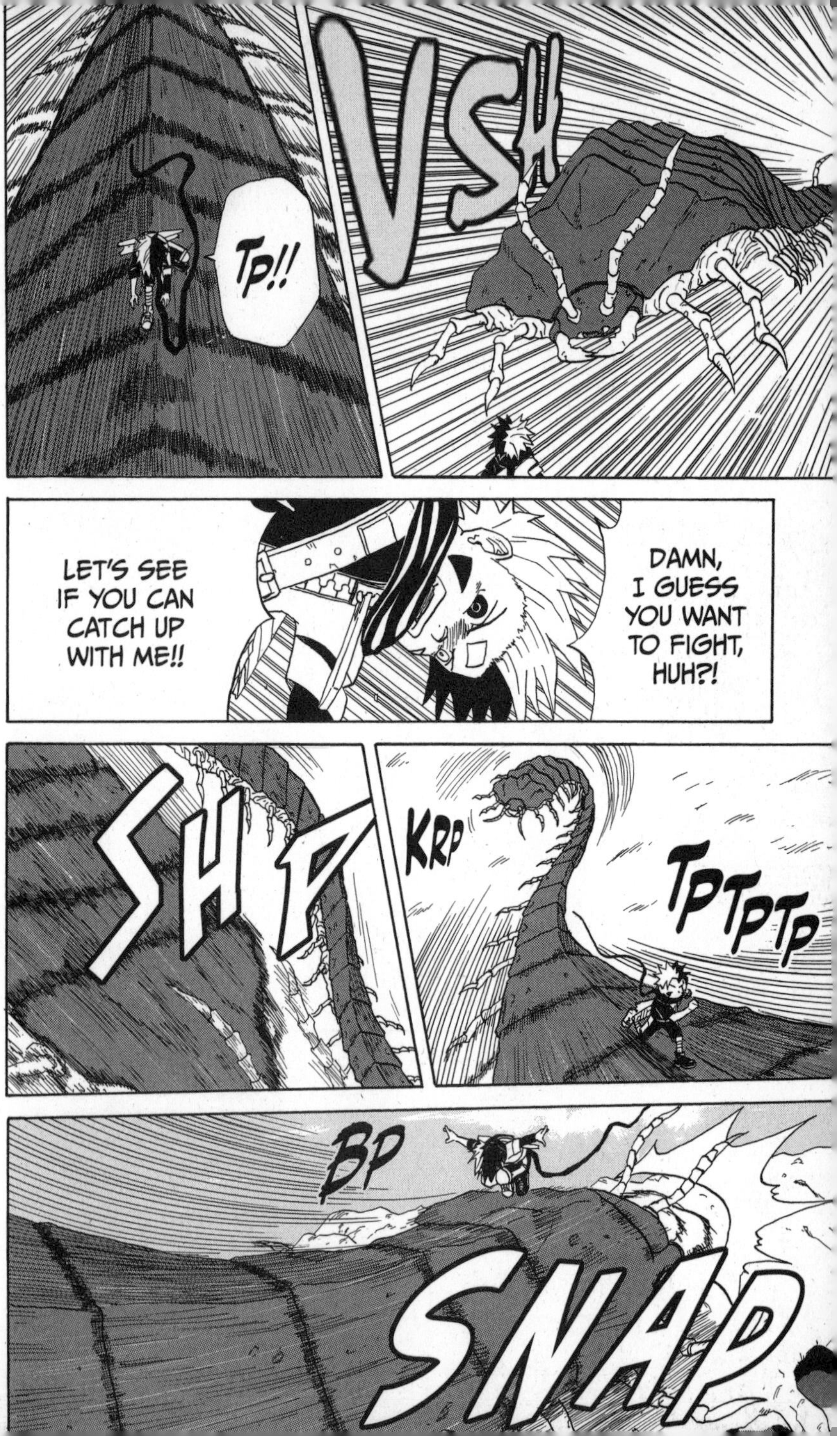
VSH
TP!!
DAMN, I GUESS YOU WANT TO FIGHT, HUH?!
LET'S SEE IF YOU CAN CATCH UP WITH ME!!
KRP
TPTPTP
SHP
BP
SNAP

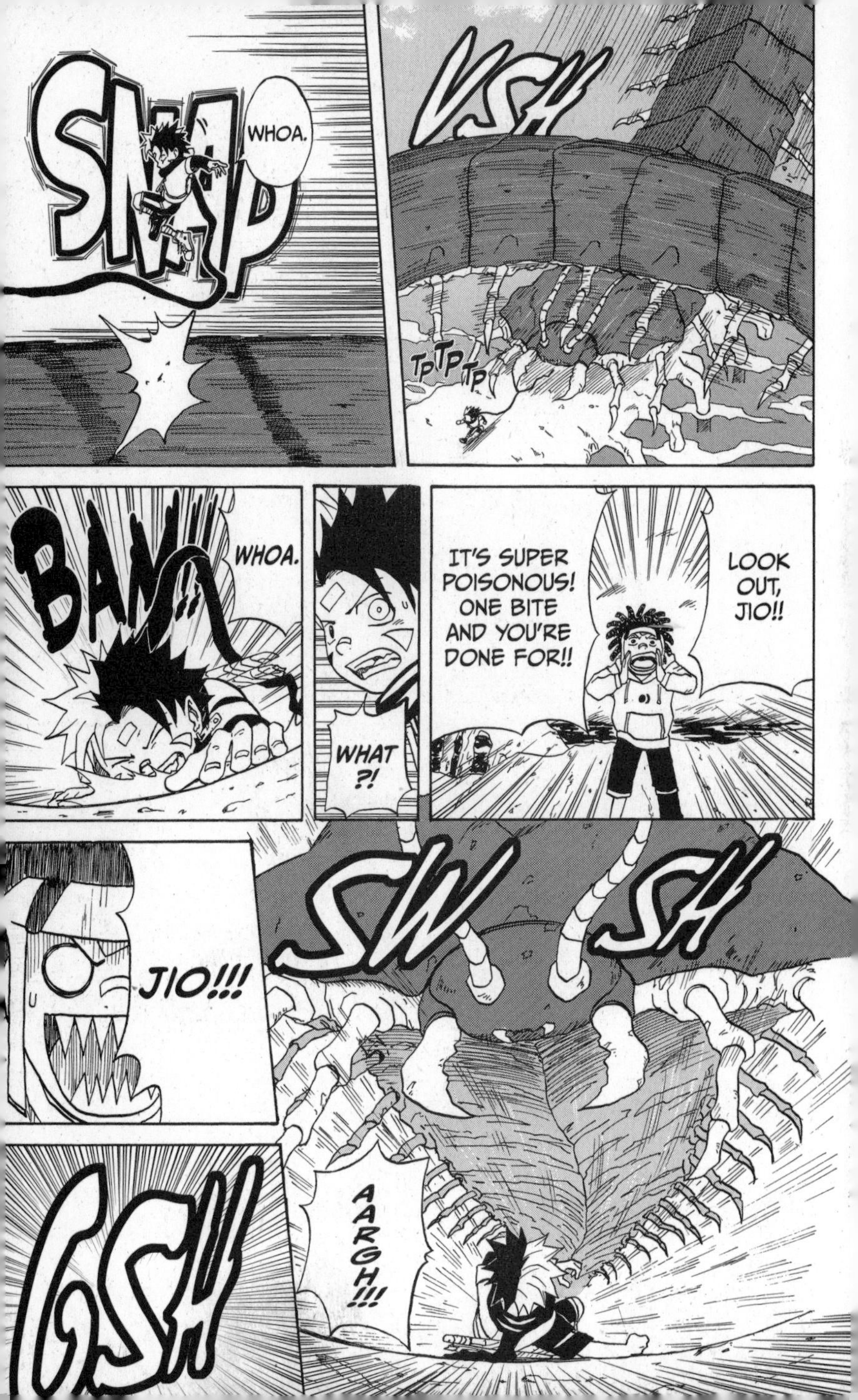
VSH
TP TP TP
SNAP
WHOA.
LOOK OUT, JIO!!
IT'S SUPER POISONOUS! ONE BITE AND YOU'RE DONE FOR!!
WHAT?!
BAM
WHOA.
SW SH
JIO!!!
GSH
AARGH!!!

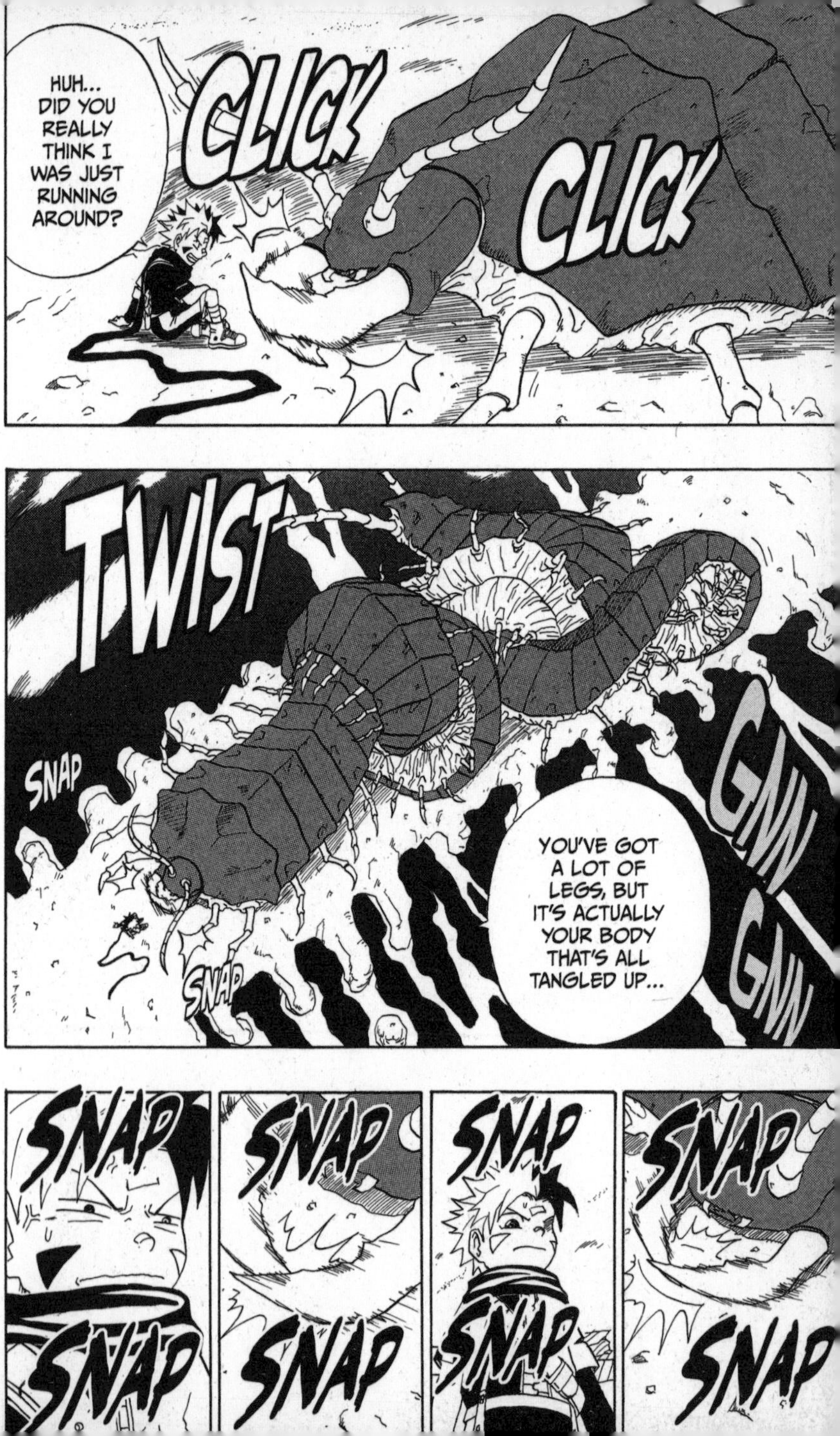
CLICK
CLICK
HUH... DID YOU REALLY THINK I WAS JUST RUNNING AROUND?
GNN
GNN
YOU'VE GOT A LOT OF LEGS, BUT IT'S ACTUALLY YOUR BODY THAT'S ALL TANGLED UP...
TWIST
SNAP
SNAP
SNAP
SNAP
SNAP
SNAP
SNAP
SNAP
SNAP
SNAP

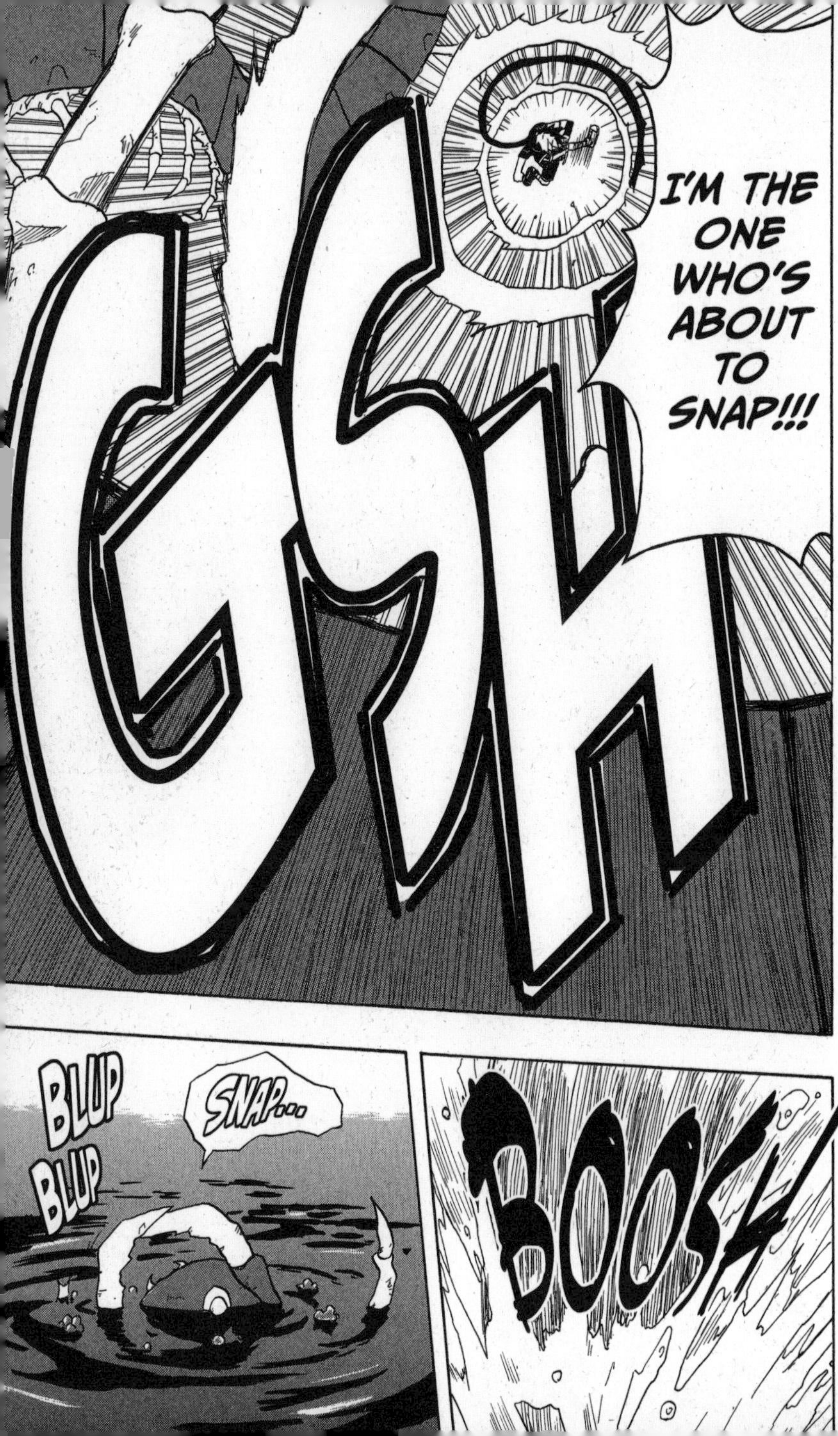

I'M THE ONE WHO'S ABOUT TO SNAP!!!
CSH
BOOSH
BLUP BLUP
SNAP...

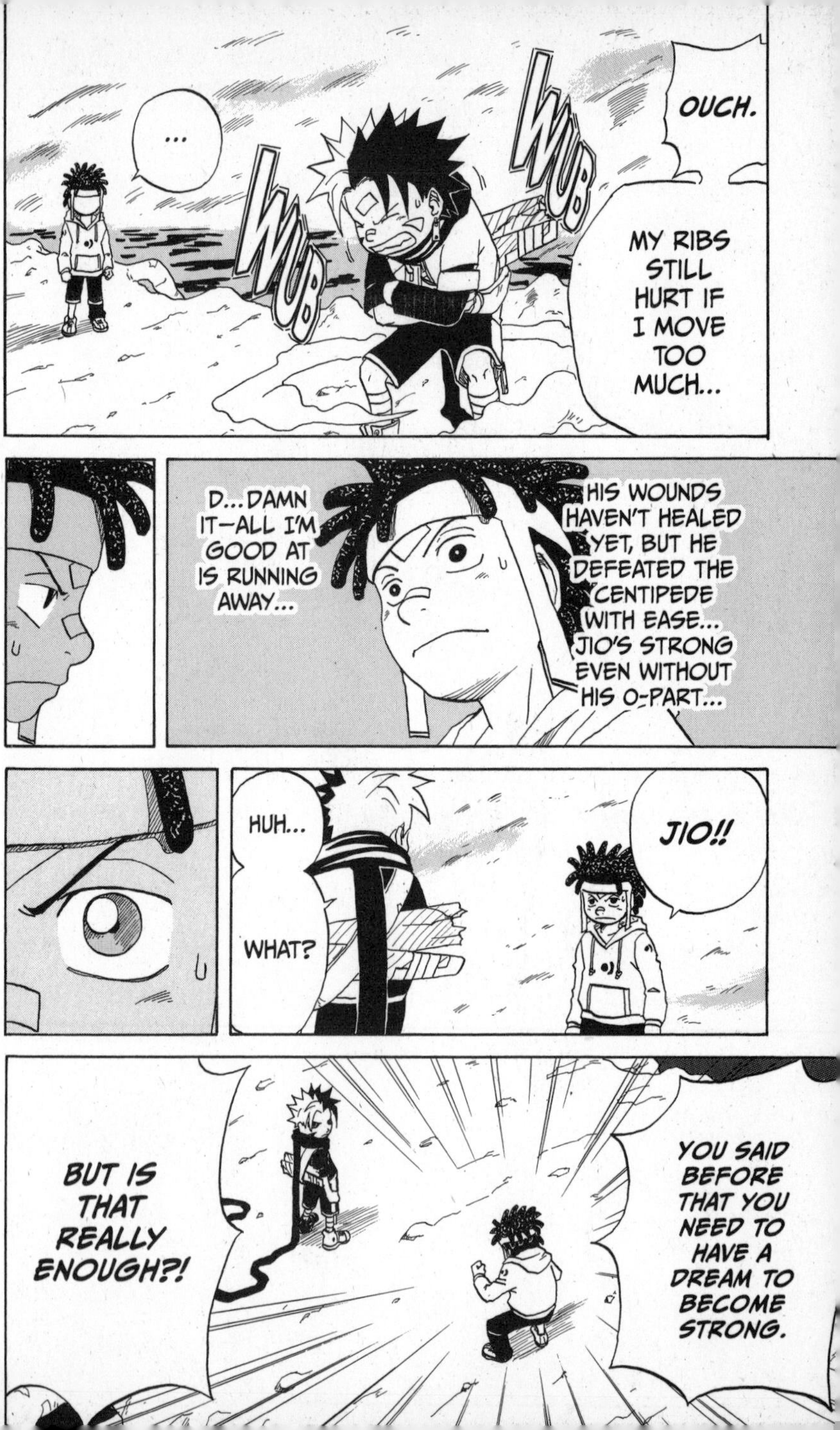
OUCH.
MY RIBS STILL HURT IF I MOVE TOO MUCH...
WUB
WUB
...
HIS WOUNDS HAVEN'T HEALED YET, BUT HE DEFEATED THE CENTIPEDE WITH EASE... JIO'S STRONG EVEN WITHOUT HIS O-PART...
D...DAMN IT—ALL I'M GOOD AT IS RUNNING AWAY...
JIO!!
HUH...
WHAT?
YOU SAID BEFORE THAT YOU NEED TO HAVE A DREAM TO BECOME STRONG.
BUT IS THAT REALLY ENOUGH?!

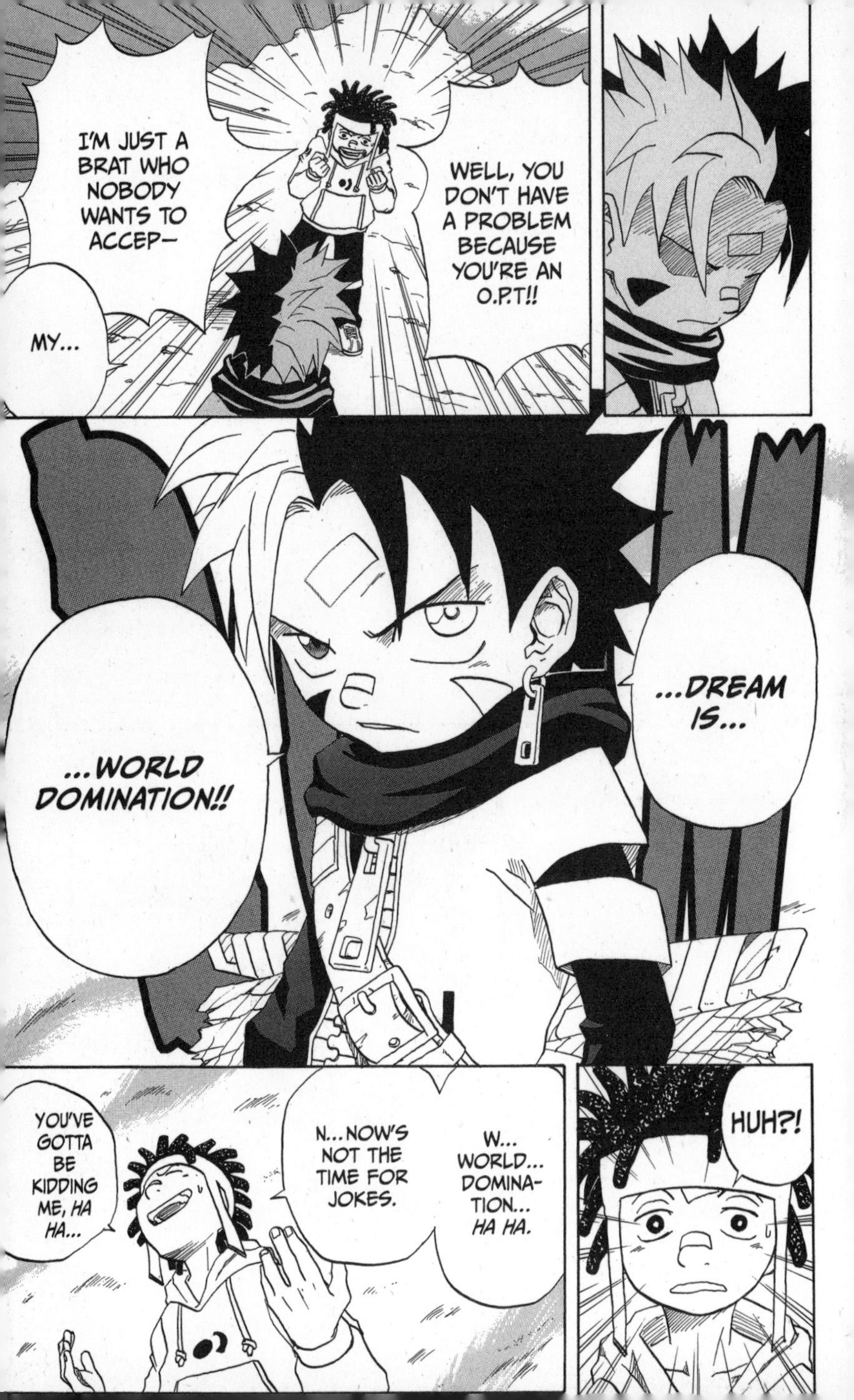
WELL, YOU DON'T HAVE A PROBLEM BECAUSE YOU'RE AN O.P.T!!
I'M JUST A BRAT WHO NOBODY WANTS TO ACCEP—
MY...
...DREAM IS...
...WORLD DOMINATION!!
HUH?!
W... WORLD... DOMINA-TION... HA HA.
N...NOW'S NOT THE TIME FOR JOKES.
YOU'VE GOTTA BE KIDDING ME, HA HA...

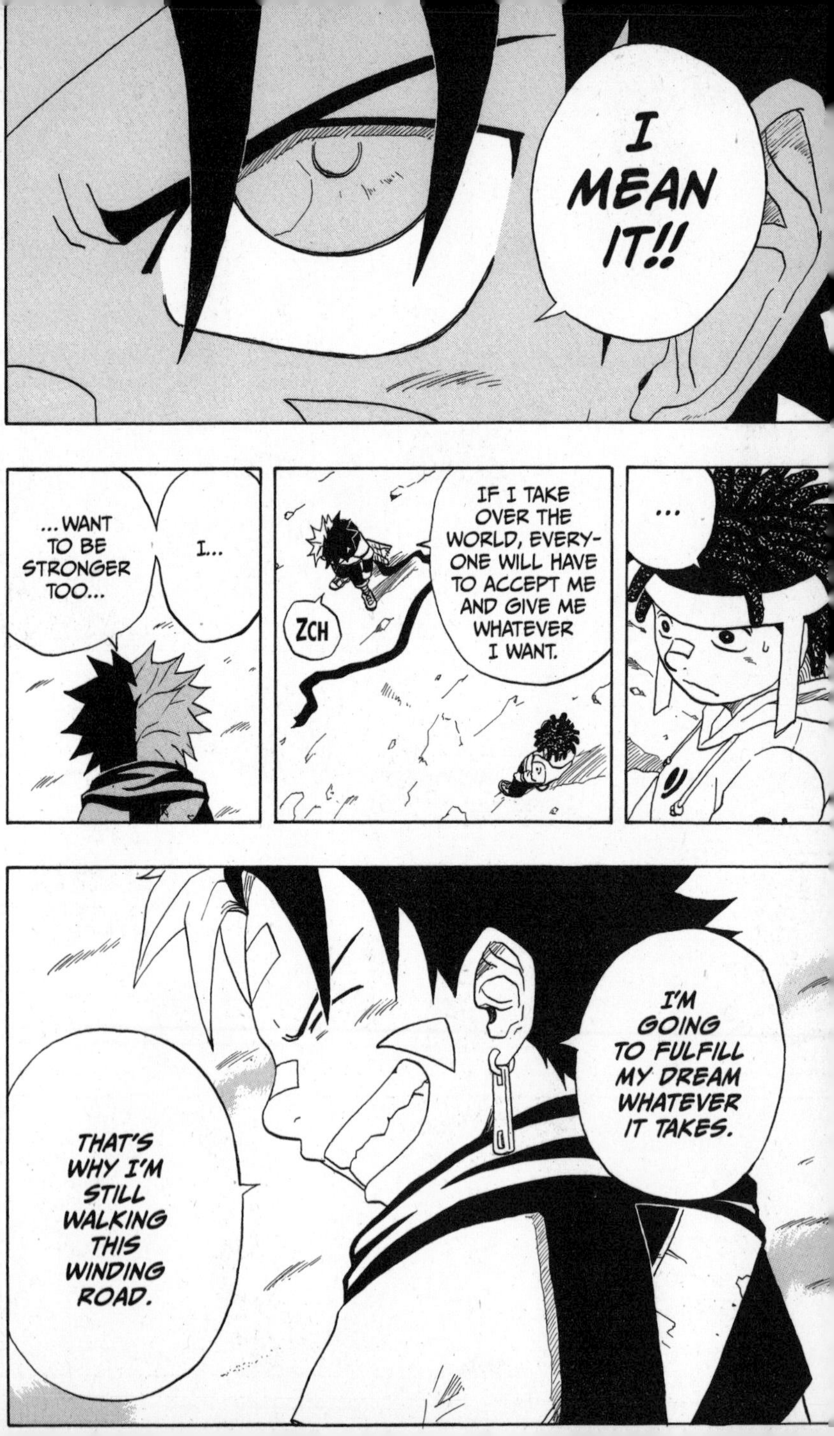
I MEAN IT!!
...
IF I TAKE OVER THE WORLD, EVERYONE WILL HAVE TO ACCEPT ME AND GIVE ME WHATEVER I WANT.
ZCH
I...
...WANT TO BE STRONGER TOO...
I'M GOING TO FULFILL MY DREAM WHATEVER IT TAKES.
THAT'S WHY I'M STILL WALKING THIS WINDING ROAD.

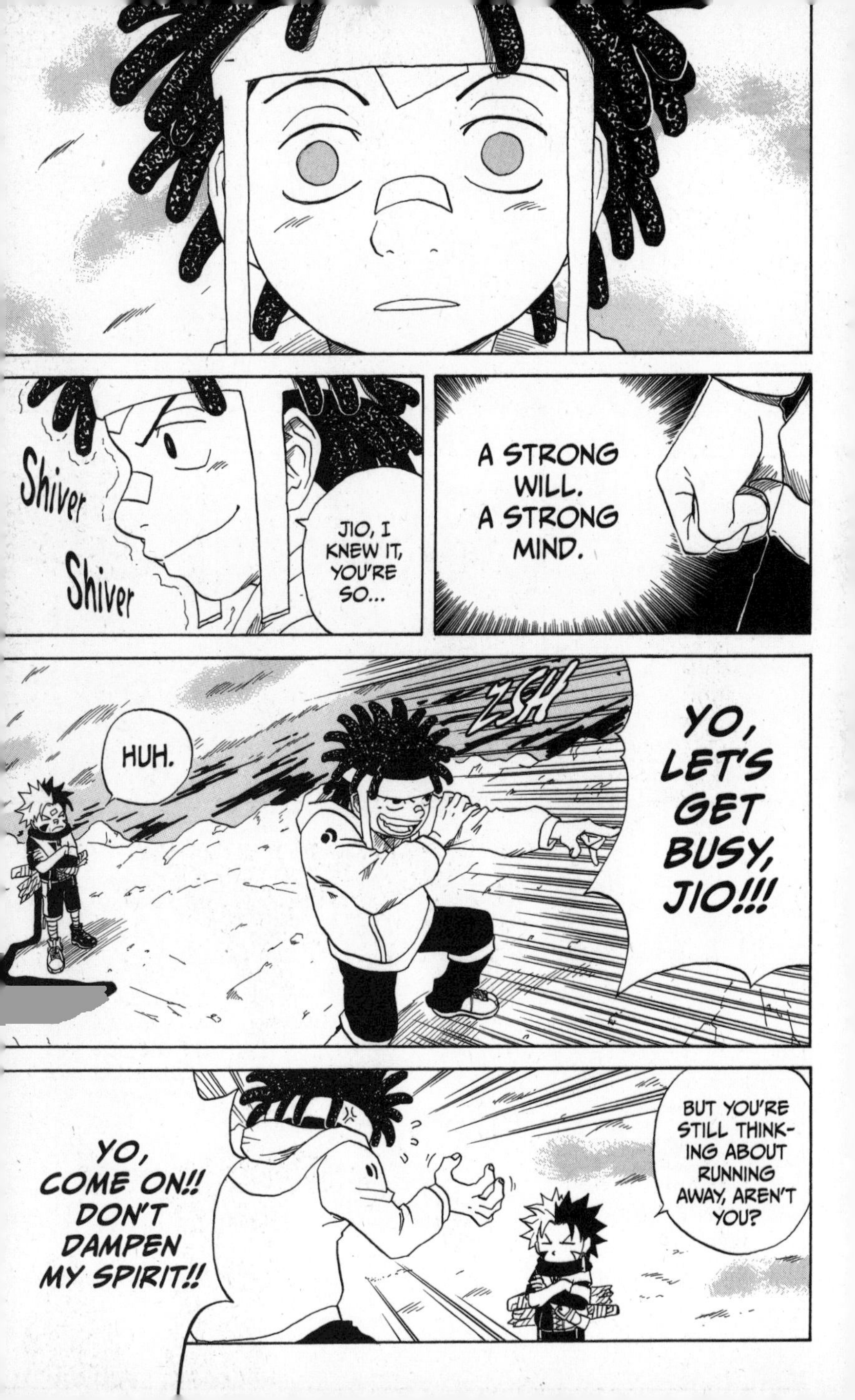
A STRONG WILL. A STRONG MIND.
JIO, I KNEW IT, YOU'RE SO...
Shiver
Shiver
YO, LET'S GET BUSY, JIO!!!
ZSH
HUH.
BUT YOU'RE STILL THINKING ABOUT RUNNING AWAY, AREN'T YOU?
YO, COME ON!! DON'T DAMPEN MY SPIRIT!!

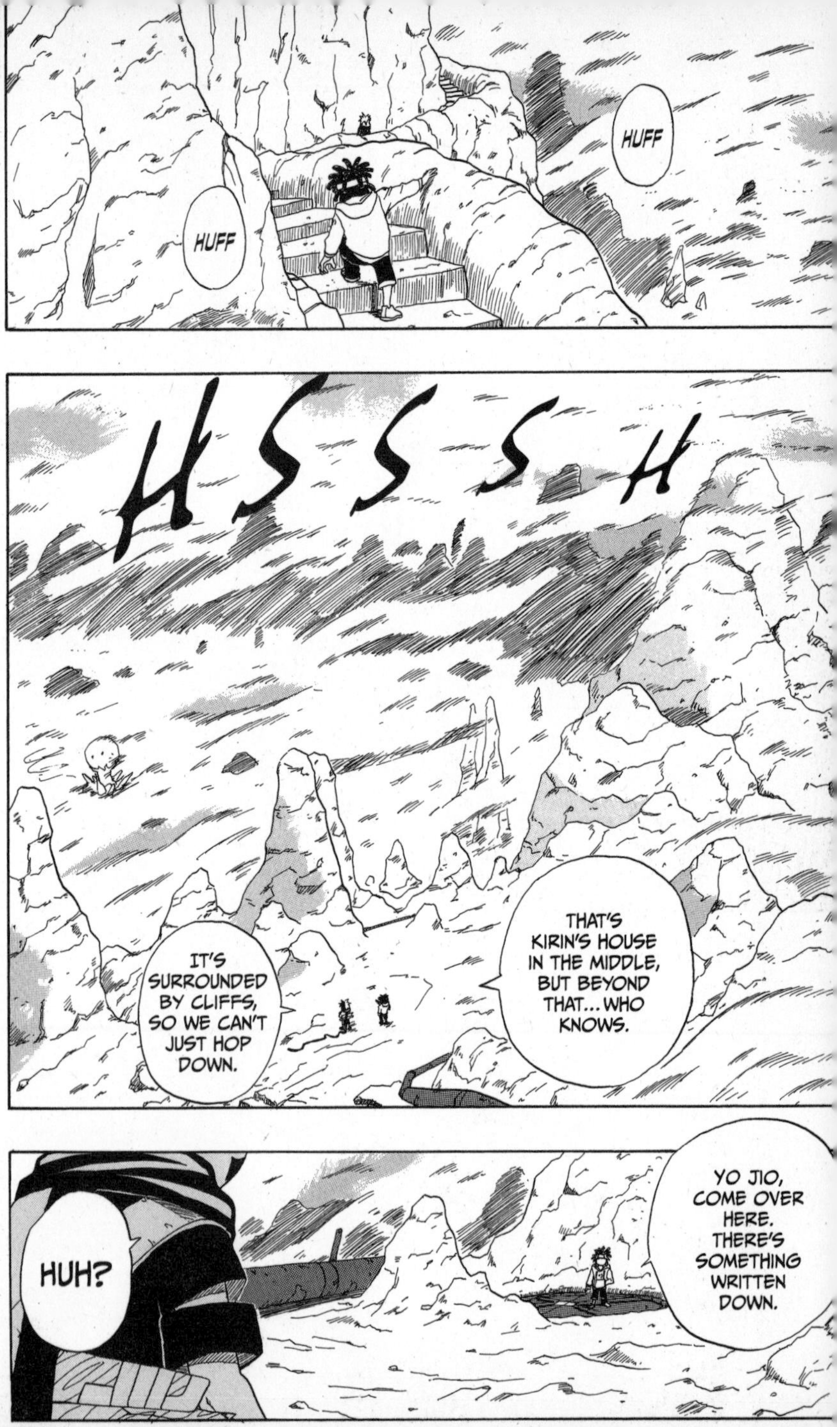
HUFF
HUFF
HSSSH
THAT'S KIRIN'S HOUSE IN THE MIDDLE, BUT BEYOND THAT... WHO KNOWS.
IT'S SURROUNDED BY CLIFFS, SO WE CAN'T JUST HOP DOWN.
YO JIO, COME OVER HERE. THERE'S SOMETHING WRITTEN DOWN.
HUH?

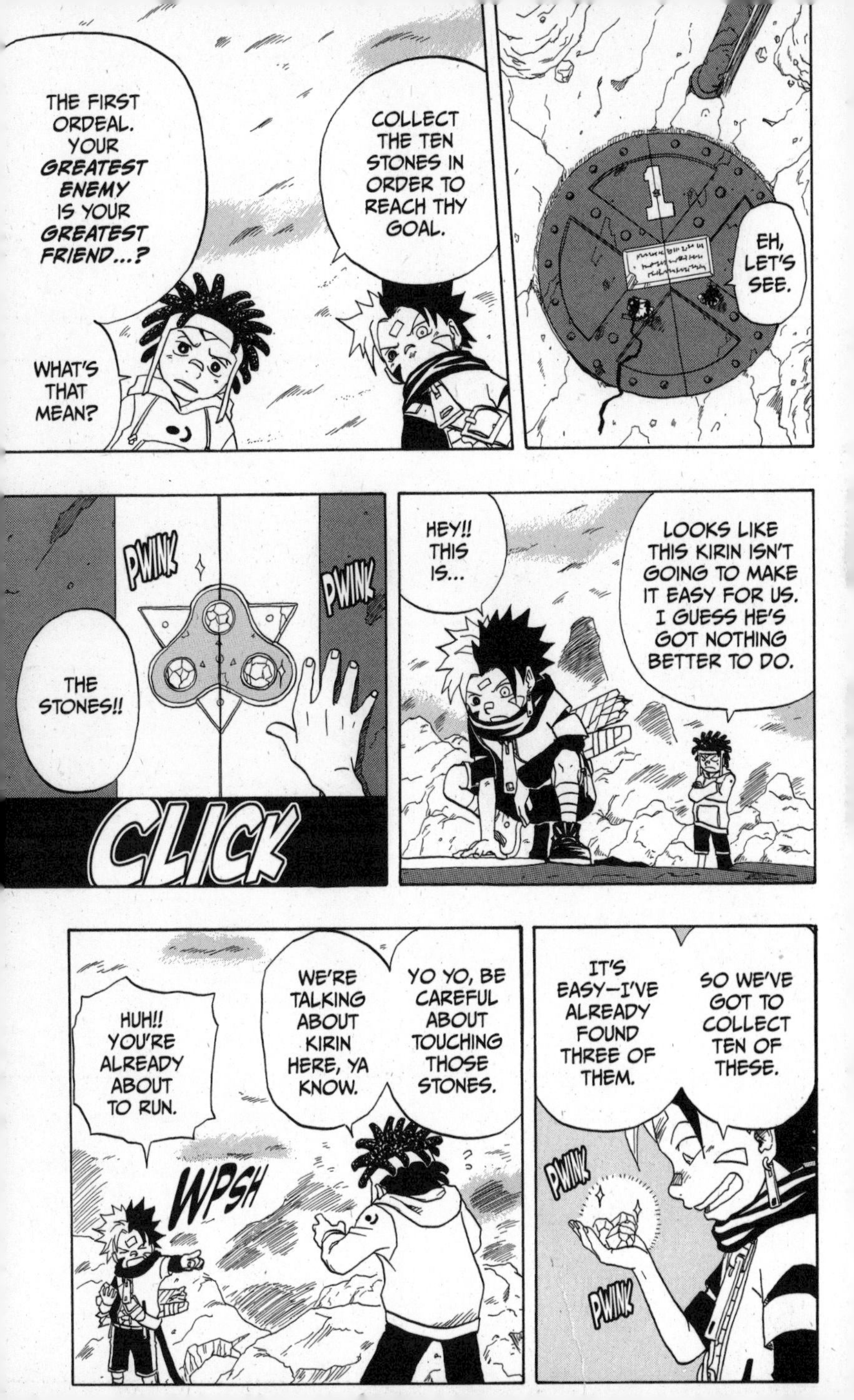
EH, LET'S SEE.
COLLECT THE TEN STONES IN ORDER TO REACH THY GOAL.
THE FIRST ORDEAL. YOUR GREATEST ENEMY IS YOUR GREATEST FRIEND...?
WHAT'S THAT MEAN?
LOOKS LIKE THIS KIRIN ISN'T GOING TO MAKE IT EASY FOR US. I GUESS HE'S GOT NOTHING BETTER TO DO.
HEY!! THIS IS...
PWINK
PWINK
THE STONES!!
CLICK
SO WE'VE GOT TO COLLECT TEN OF THESE.
IT'S EASY—I'VE ALREADY FOUND THREE OF THEM.
PWINK
PWINK
YO YO, BE CAREFUL ABOUT TOUCHING THOSE STONES.
WE'RE TALKING ABOUT KIRIN HERE, YA KNOW.
HUH!! YOU'RE ALREADY ABOUT TO RUN.
WPSH

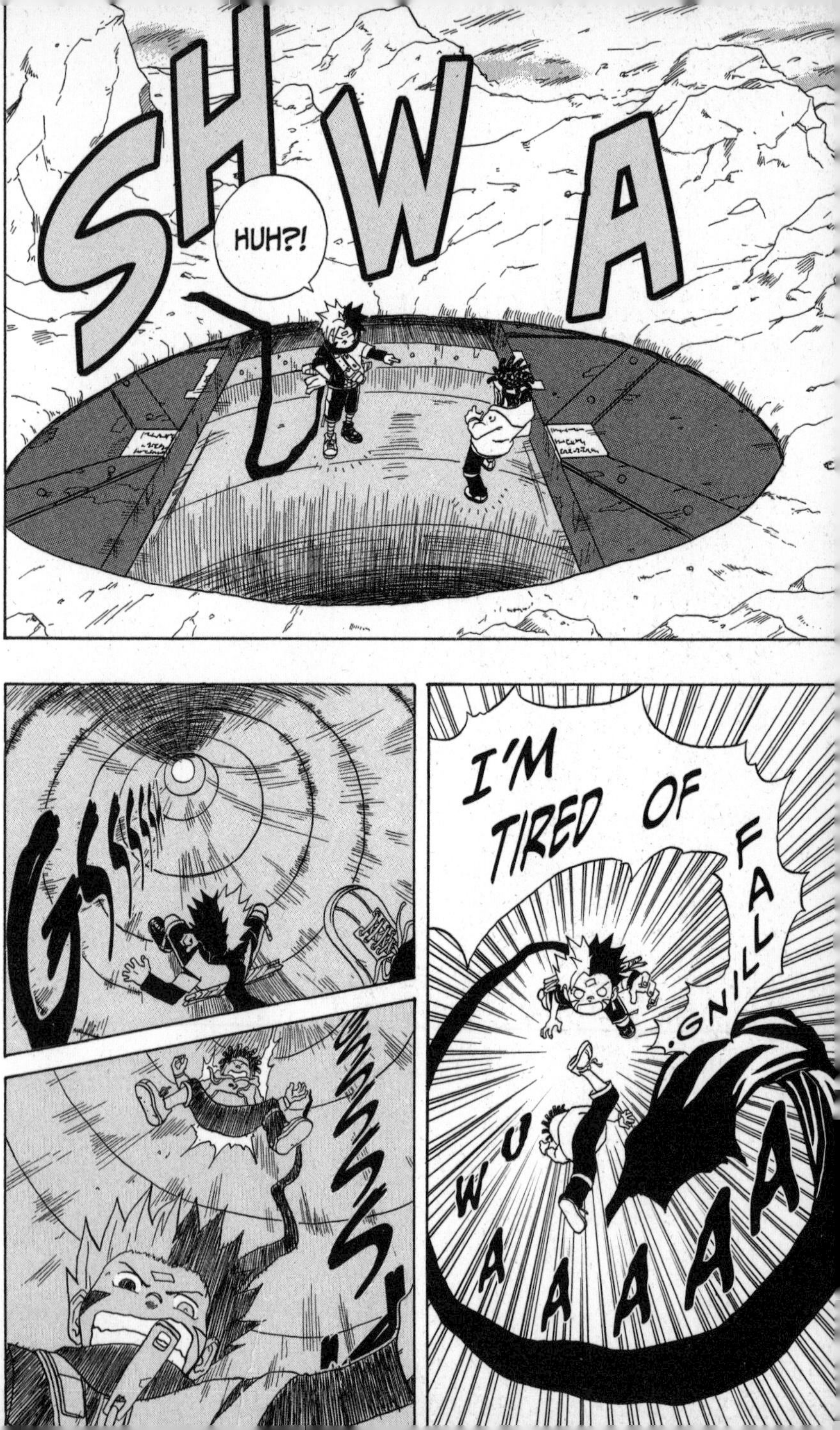
SHWA
HUH?!
I'M TIRED OF FALLING.
WUAAAAAA

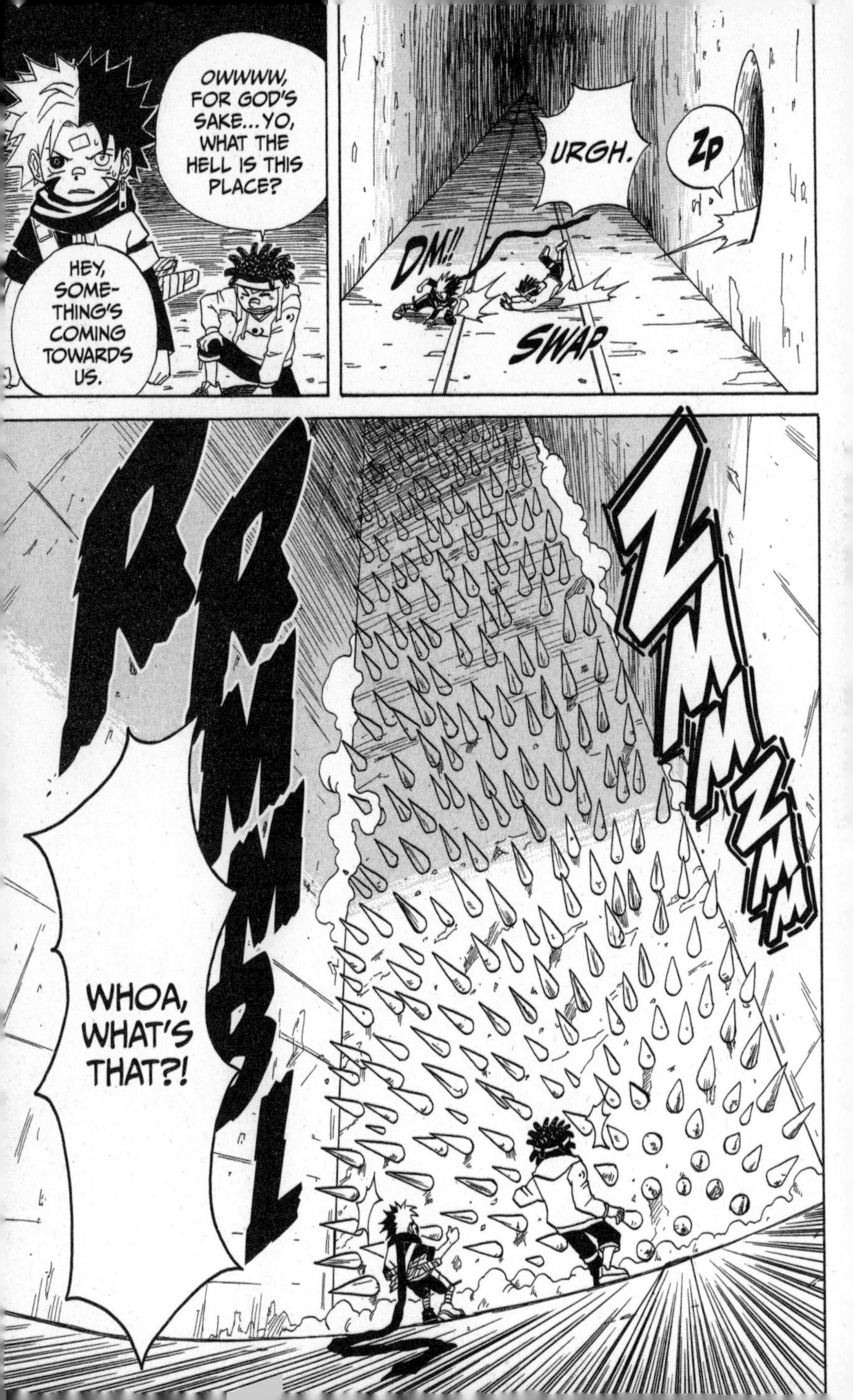
ZP
URGH.
DM!!
SWAP
OWWWW, FOR GOD'S SAKE...YO, WHAT THE HELL IS THIS PLACE?
HEY, SOME-THING'S COMING TOWARDS US.
WHOA, WHAT'S THAT?!

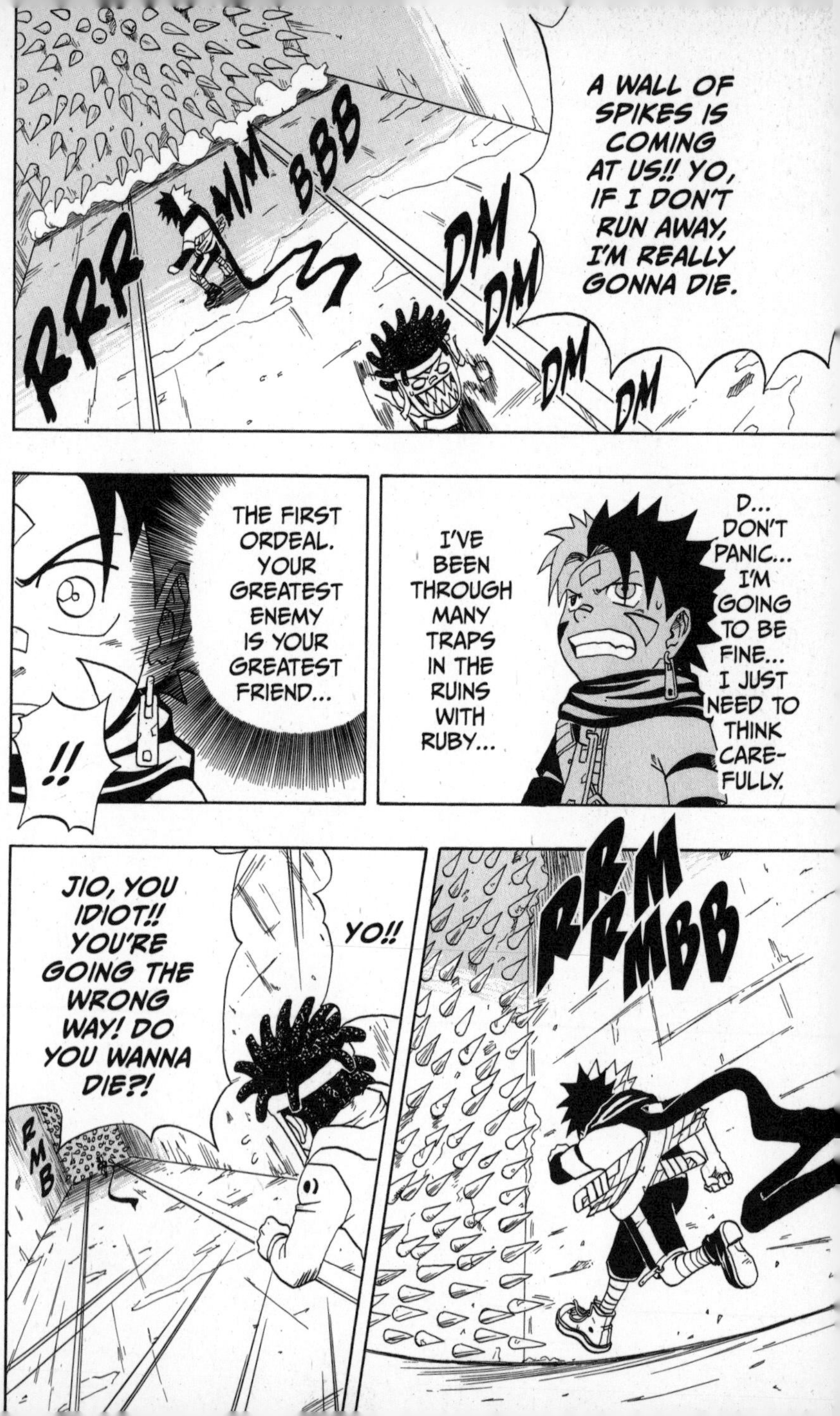
A WALL OF SPIKES IS COMING AT US!! YO, IF I DON'T RUN AWAY, I'M REALLY GONNA DIE.
RRR MMM BBB
DM DM DM DM
D... DON'T PANIC... I'M GOING TO BE FINE... I JUST NEED TO THINK CARE-FULLY.
I'VE BEEN THROUGH MANY TRAPS IN THE RUINS WITH RUBY...
THE FIRST ORDEAL. YOUR GREATEST ENEMY IS YOUR GREATEST FRIEND...
!!
RRM RMBB
YO!!
JIO, YOU IDIOT!! YOU'RE GOING THE WRONG WAY! DO YOU WANNA DIE?!
RMB

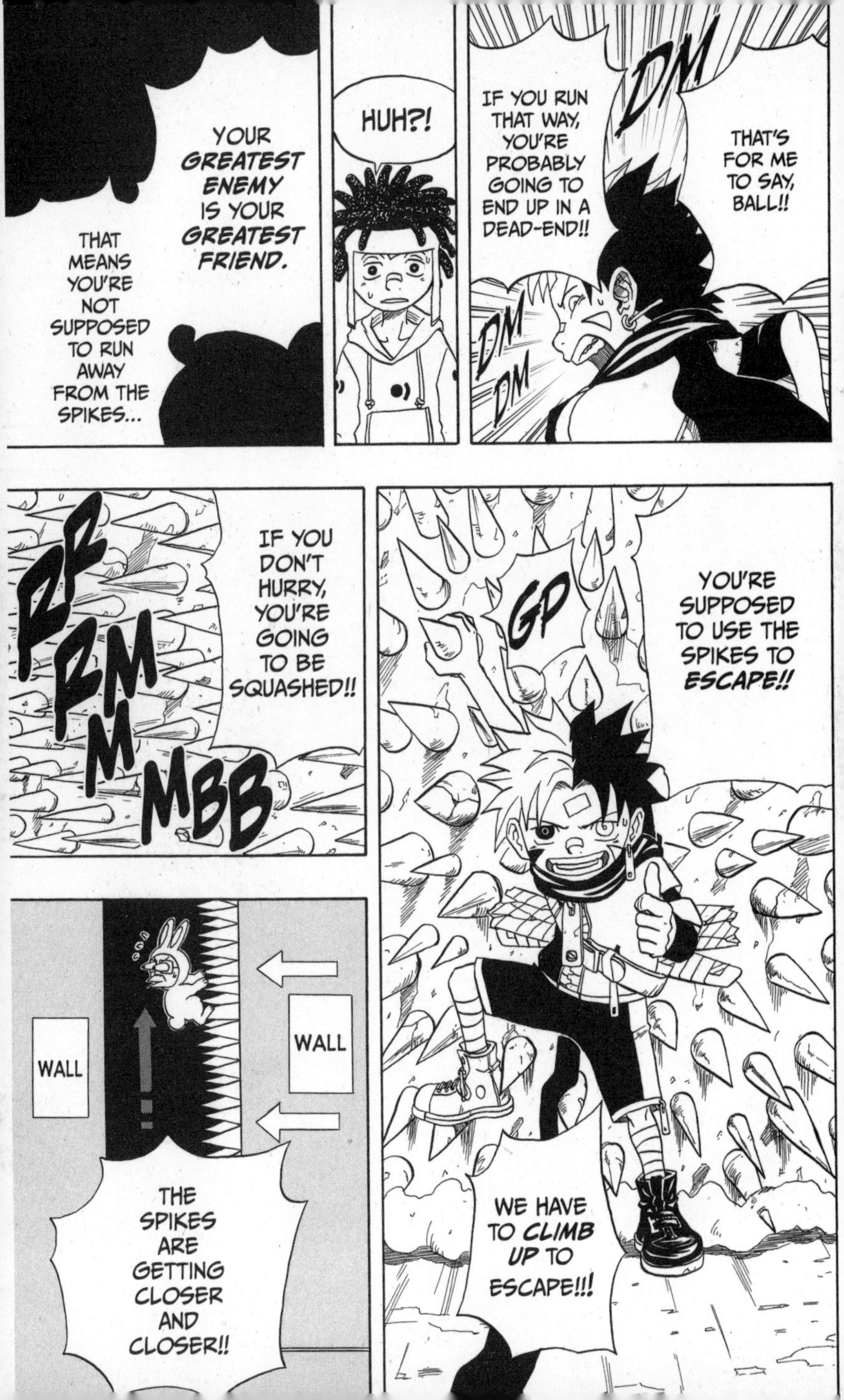
THAT'S FOR ME TO SAY, BALL!!
DM
IF YOU RUN THAT WAY, YOU'RE PROBABLY GOING TO END UP IN A DEAD-END!!
DM DM
HUH?!
YOUR GREATEST ENEMY IS YOUR GREATEST FRIEND.
THAT MEANS YOU'RE NOT SUPPOSED TO RUN AWAY FROM THE SPIKES...
YOU'RE SUPPOSED TO USE THE SPIKES TO ESCAPE!!
GP
WE HAVE TO CLIMB UP TO ESCAPE!!!
IF YOU DON'T HURRY, YOU'RE GOING TO BE SQUASHED!!
RRRMMMBB
WALL
WALL
THE SPIKES ARE GETTING CLOSER AND CLOSER!!

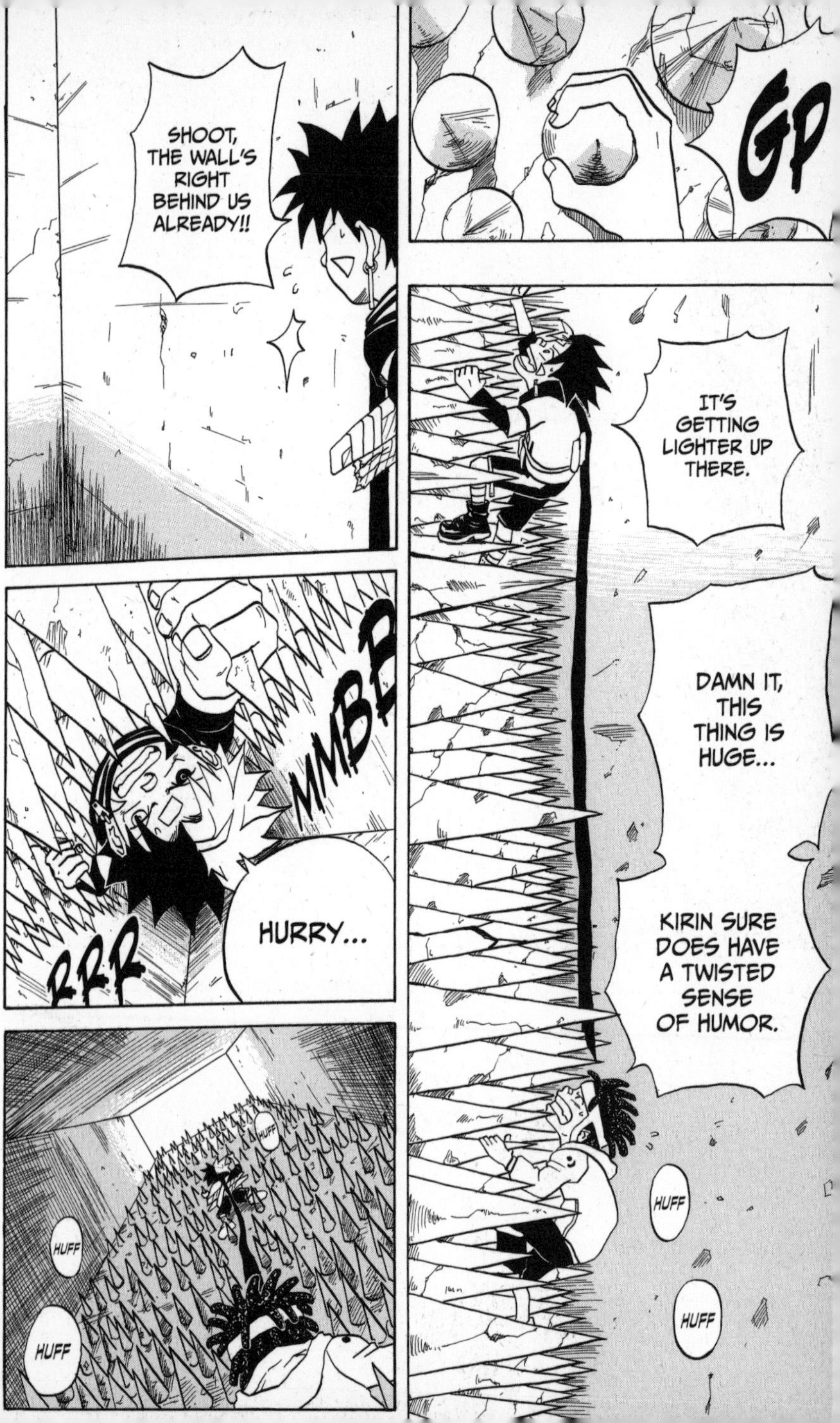
GP
SHOOT, THE WALL'S RIGHT BEHIND US ALREADY!!
IT'S GETTING LIGHTER UP THERE.
DAMN IT, THIS THING IS HUGE...
KIRIN SURE DOES HAVE A TWISTED SENSE OF HUMOR.
HUFF
HUFF
MMBB
HURRY...
RRR
HUFF
HUFF
HUFF

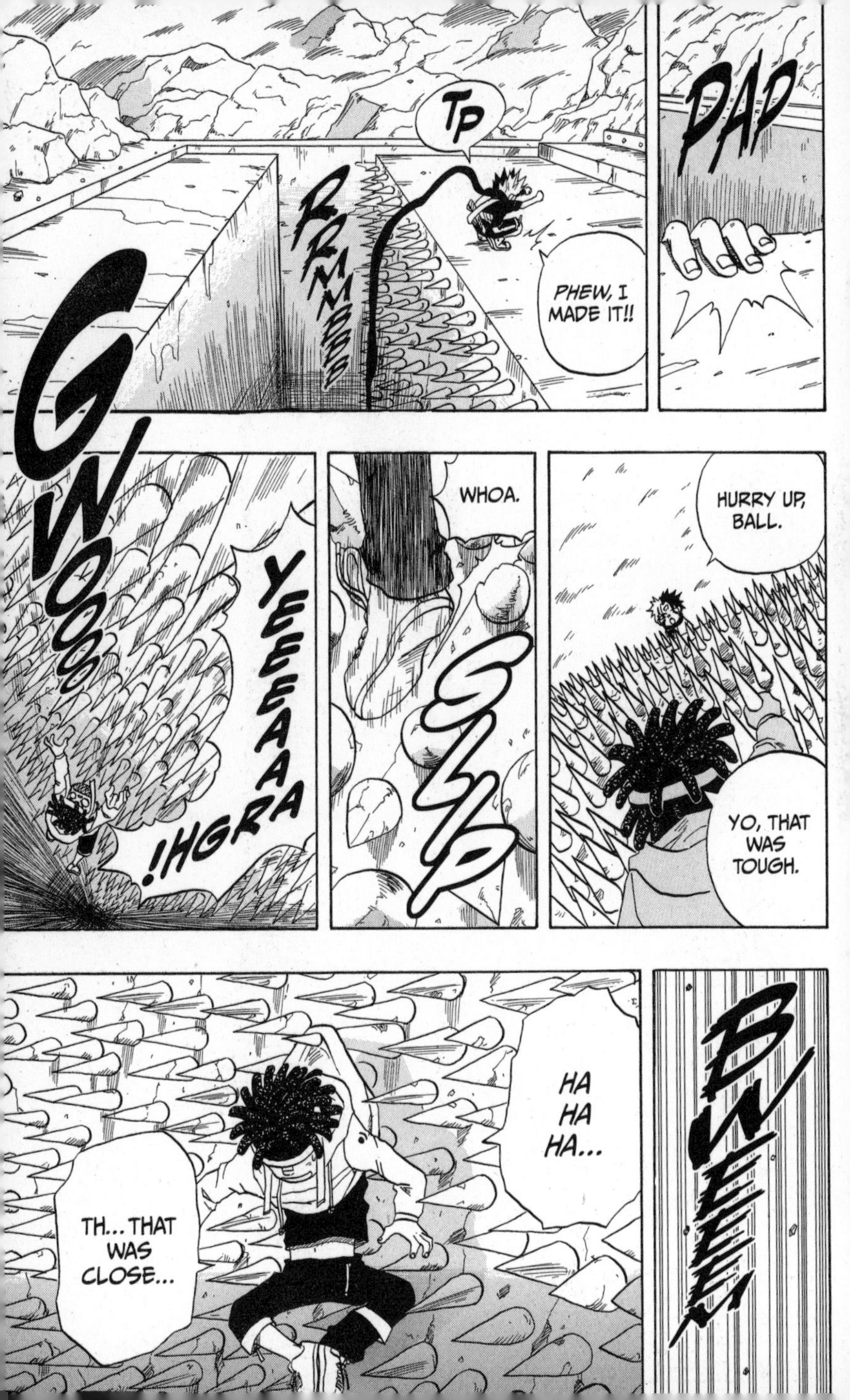
PAD
TP
PHEW, I MADE IT!!
HURRY UP, BALL.
YO, THAT WAS TOUGH.
WHOA.
SLIP
YEEEAAAA
!HGRA
HA HA HA...
TH... THAT WAS CLOSE...

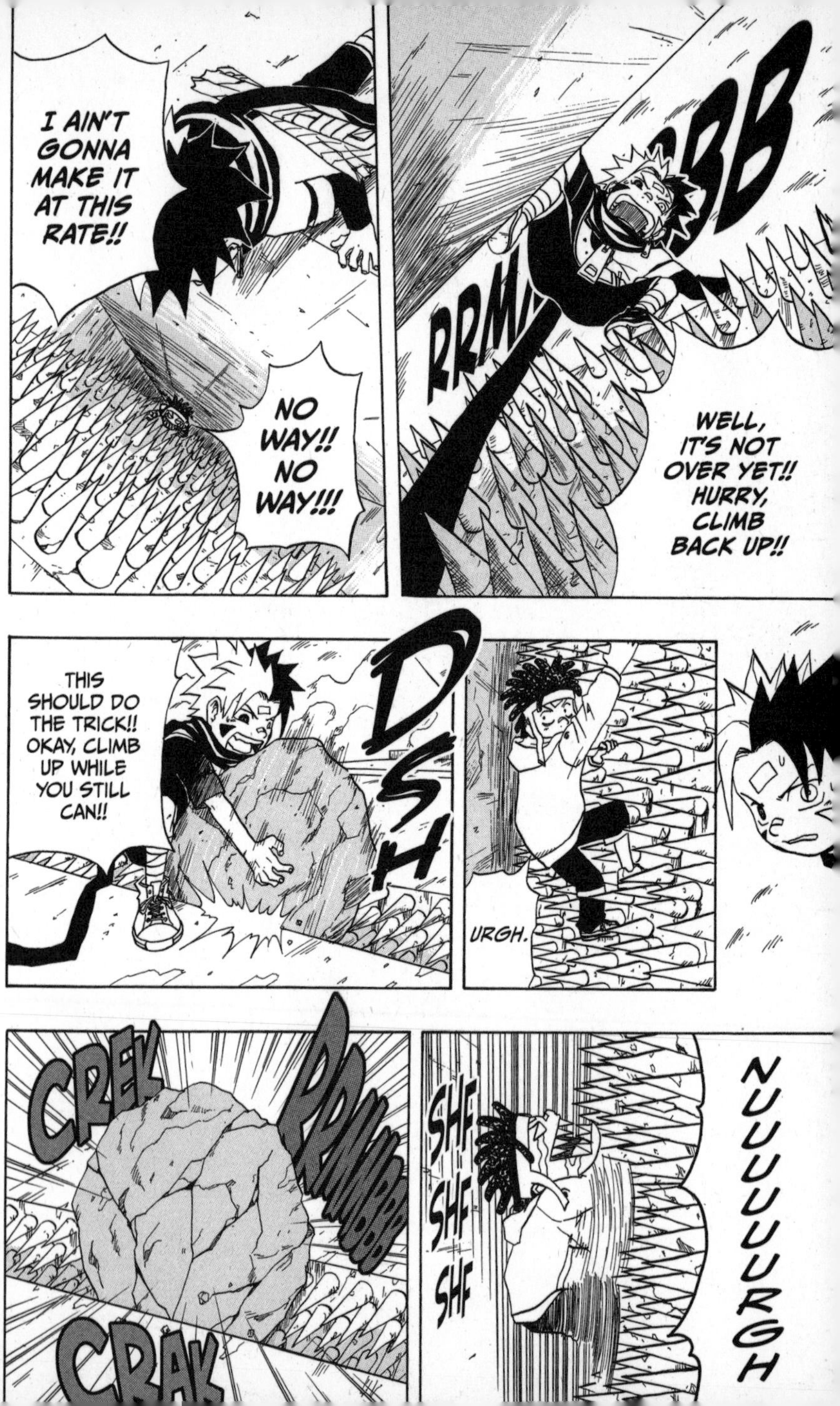
WELL, IT'S NOT OVER YET!! HURRY, CLIMB BACK UP!!
I AIN'T GONNA MAKE IT AT THIS RATE!!
NO WAY!! NO WAY!!!
URGH.
DSH
THIS SHOULD DO THE TRICK!! OKAY, CLIMB UP WHILE YOU STILL CAN!!
NUUUUUURGH
SHF SHF SHF SHF
CREK
CRAK

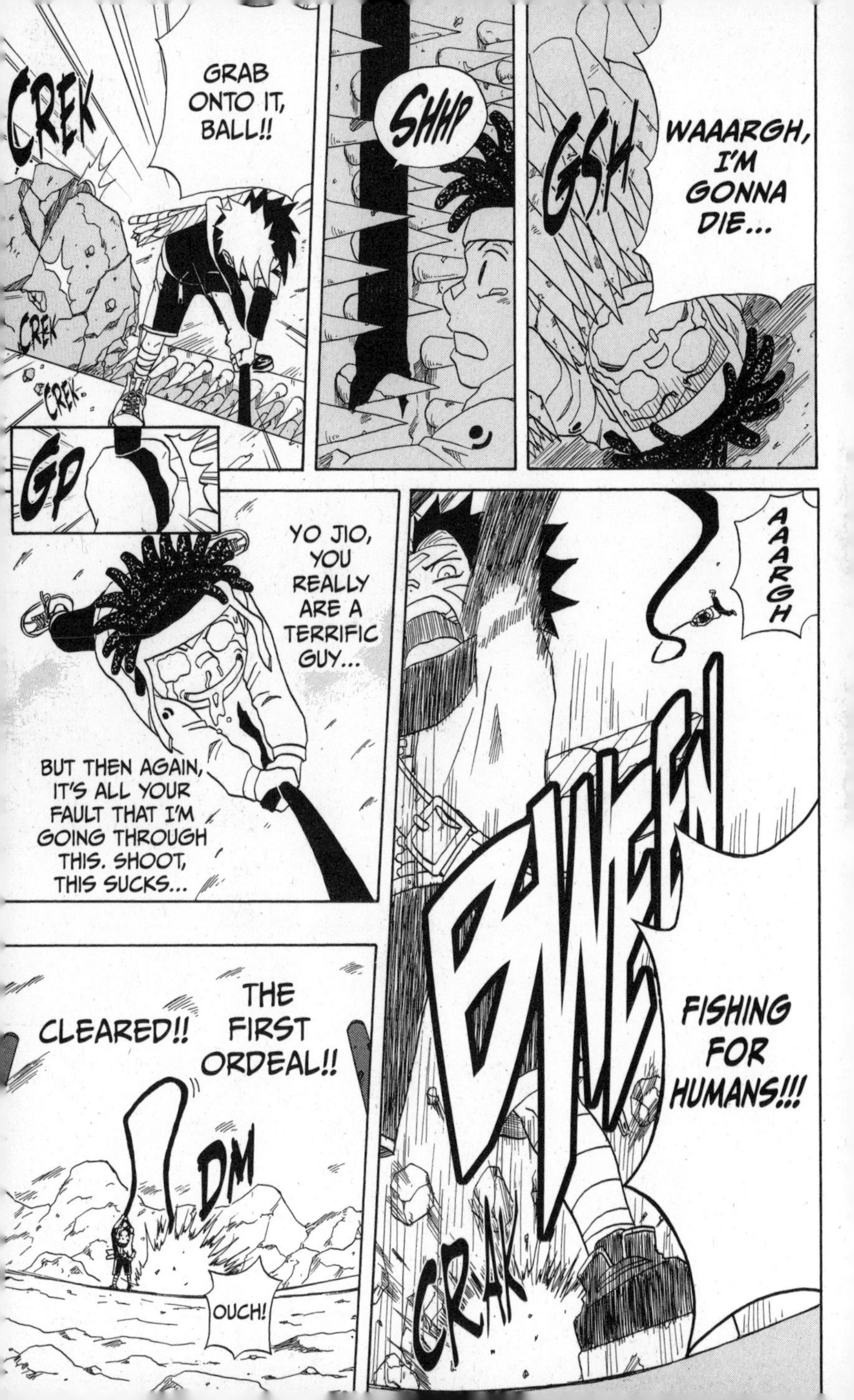
WAAARGH, I'M GONNA DIE...
GSH
SHHP
GRAB ONTO IT, BALL!!
CREK
CREK
CREK
GP
AAAARGH
FISHING FOR HUMANS!!!
CRAK
YO JIO, YOU REALLY ARE A TERRIFIC GUY...
BUT THEN AGAIN, IT'S ALL YOUR FAULT THAT I'M GOING THROUGH THIS. SHOOT, THIS SUCKS...
THE FIRST ORDEAL!!
CLEARED!!
DM
OUCH!

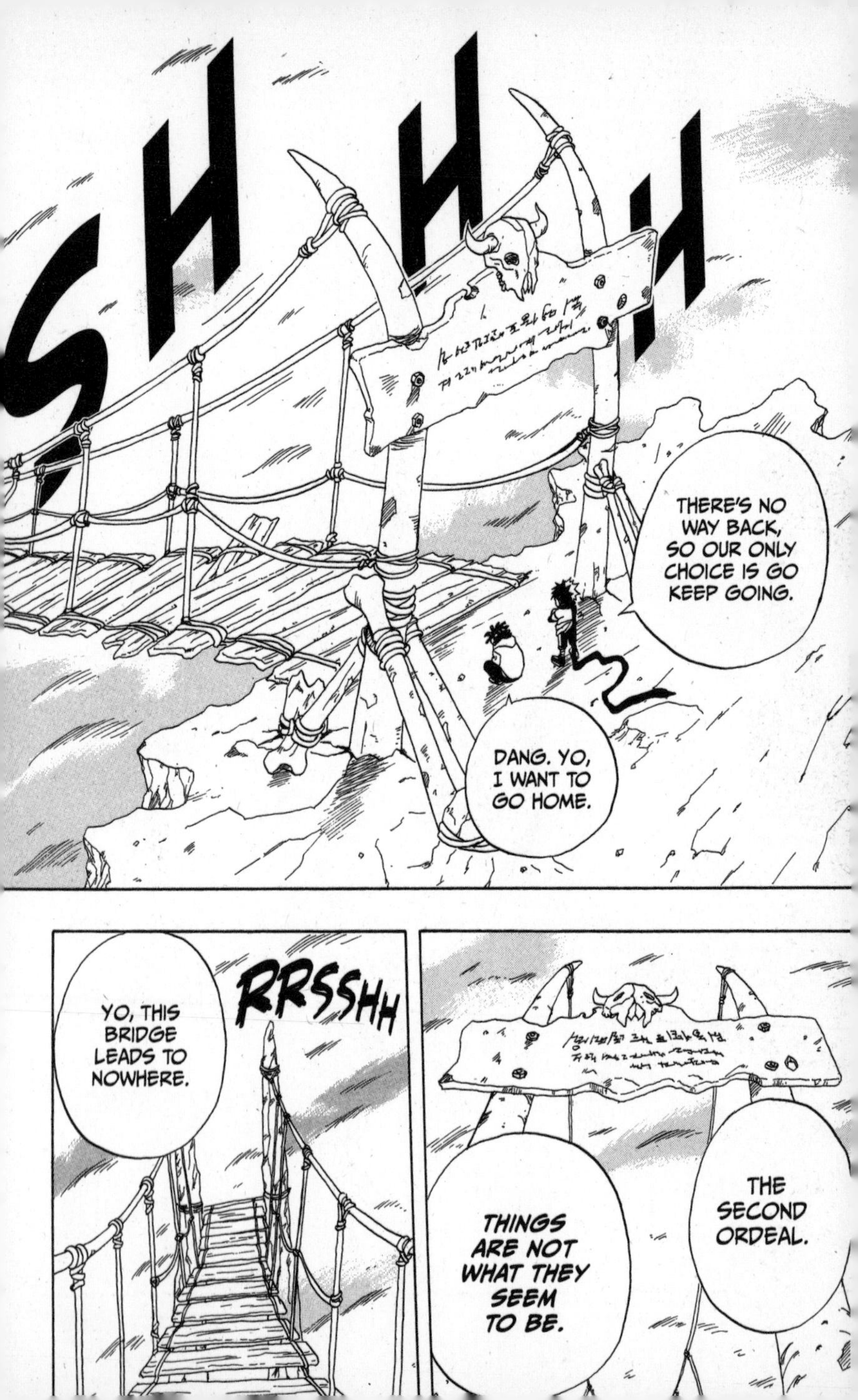
SHHH
THERE'S NO WAY BACK, SO OUR ONLY CHOICE IS GO KEEP GOING.
DANG. YO, I WANT TO GO HOME.
THE SECOND ORDEAL.
THINGS ARE NOT WHAT THEY SEEM TO BE.
RRSSHH
YO, THIS BRIDGE LEADS TO NOWHERE.

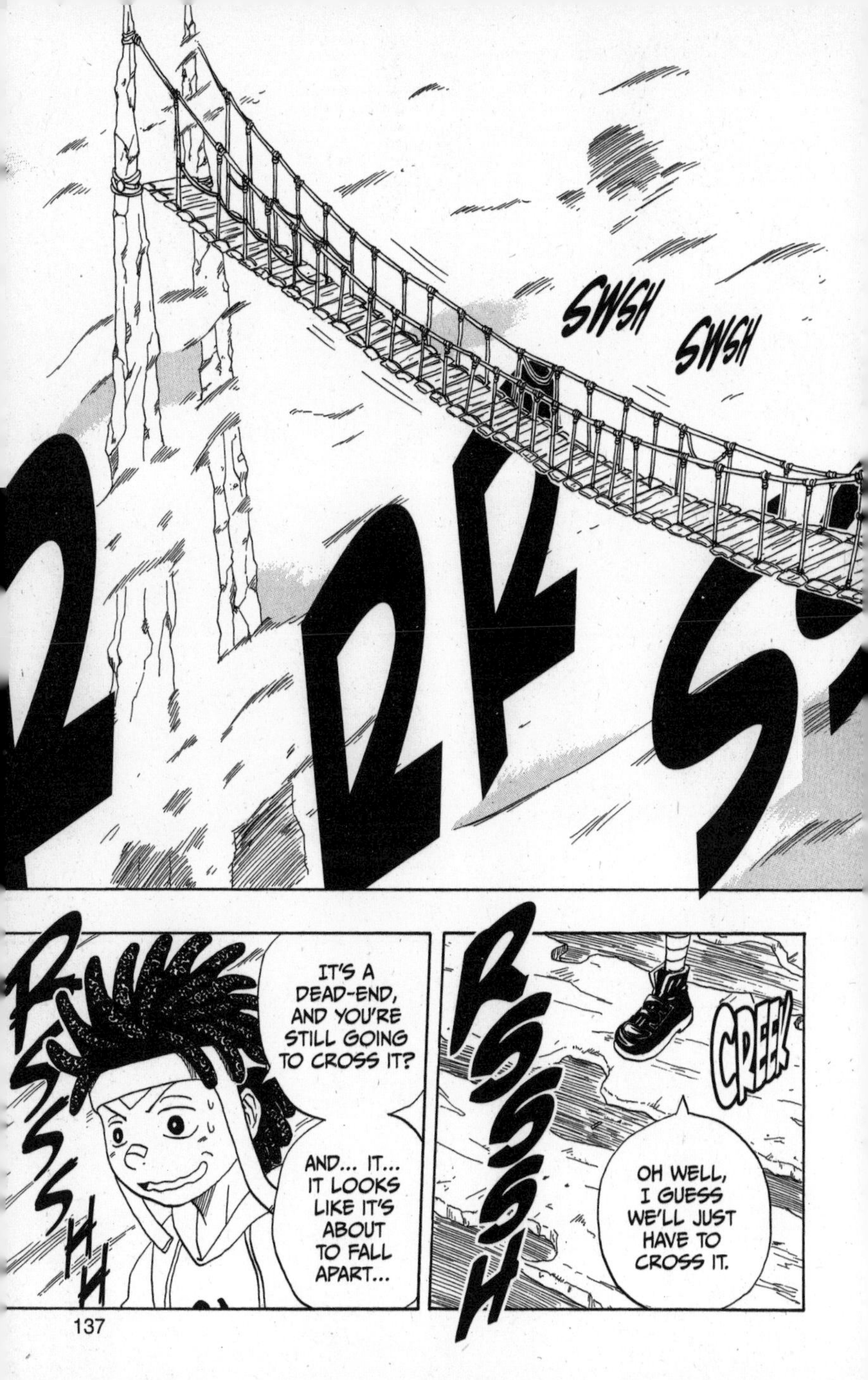
SWSH
SWSH
CREEK
OH WELL, I GUESS WE'LL JUST HAVE TO CROSS IT.
IT'S A DEAD-END, AND YOU'RE STILL GOING TO CROSS IT?
AND... IT... IT LOOKS LIKE IT'S ABOUT TO FALL APART...

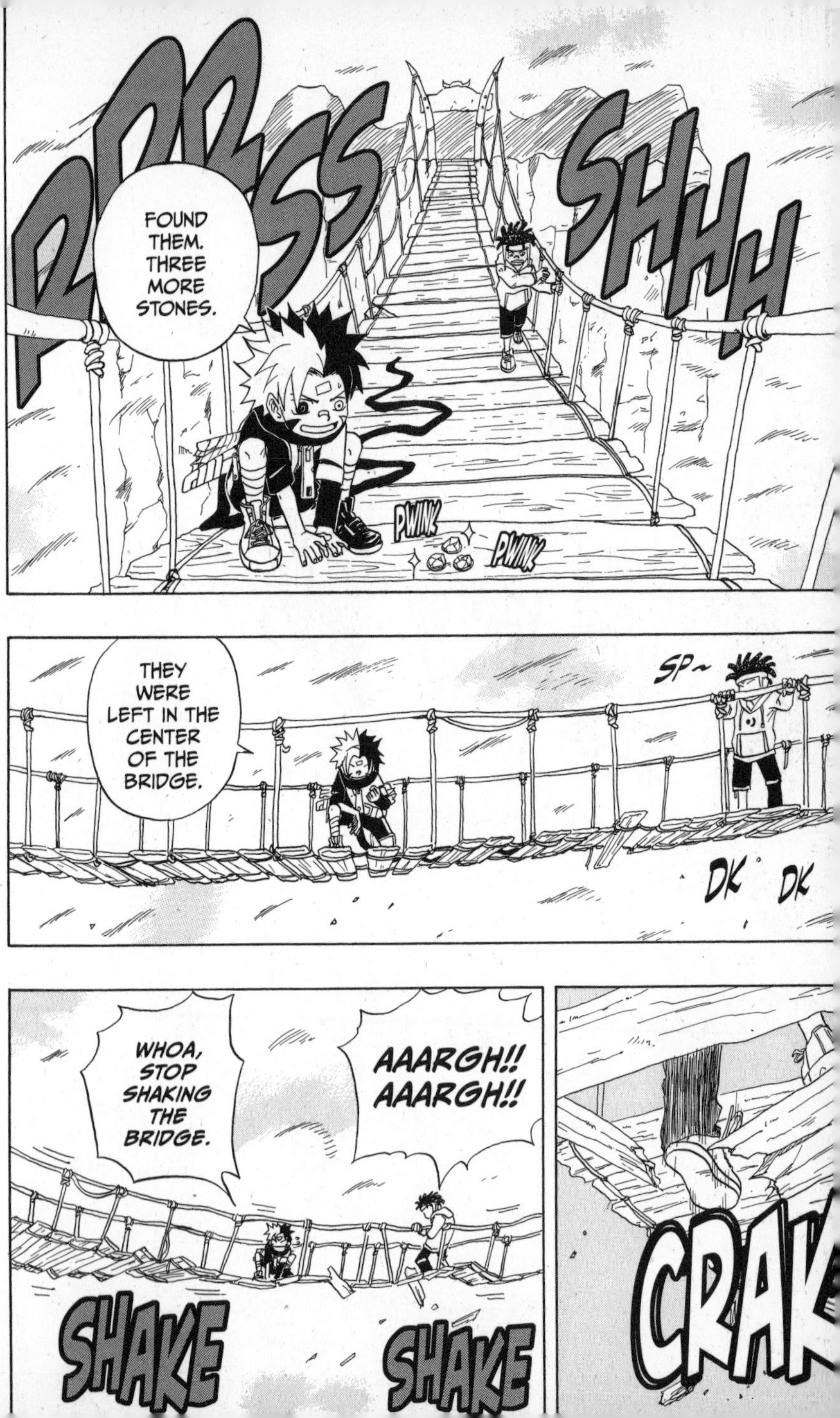
SHHH
RRRSS
FOUND THEM. THREE MORE STONES.
PWINK
PWINK
SP~
THEY WERE LEFT IN THE CENTER OF THE BRIDGE.
DK DK
CRAK
AAARGH!! AAARGH!!
WHOA, STOP SHAKING THE BRIDGE.
SHAKE
SHAKE

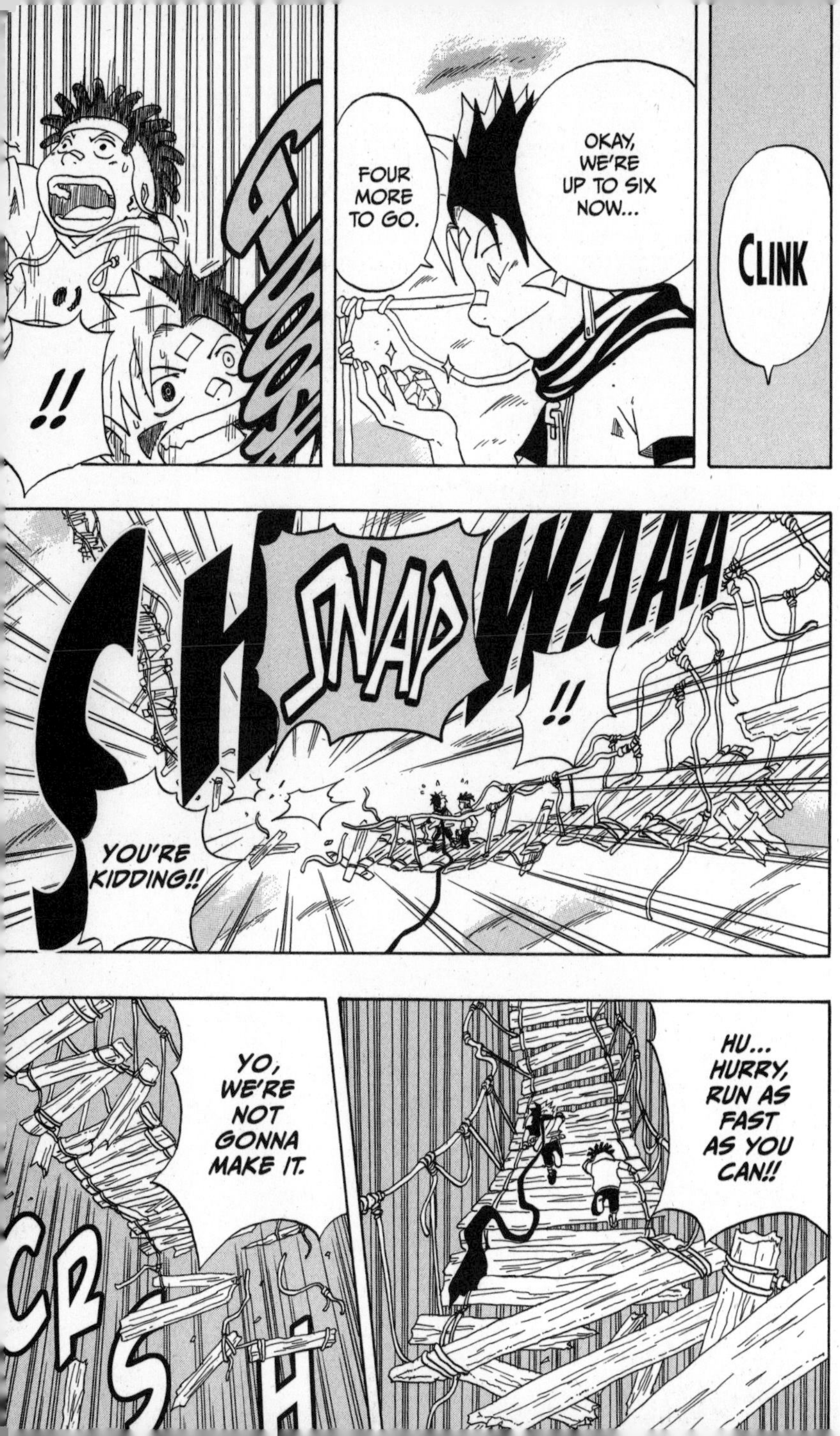
CLINK
OKAY, WE'RE UP TO SIX NOW...
FOUR MORE TO GO.
!!
WAAAH
!!
SNAP
YOU'RE KIDDING!!
HU... HURRY, RUN AS FAST AS YOU CAN!!
YO, WE'RE NOT GONNA MAKE IT.

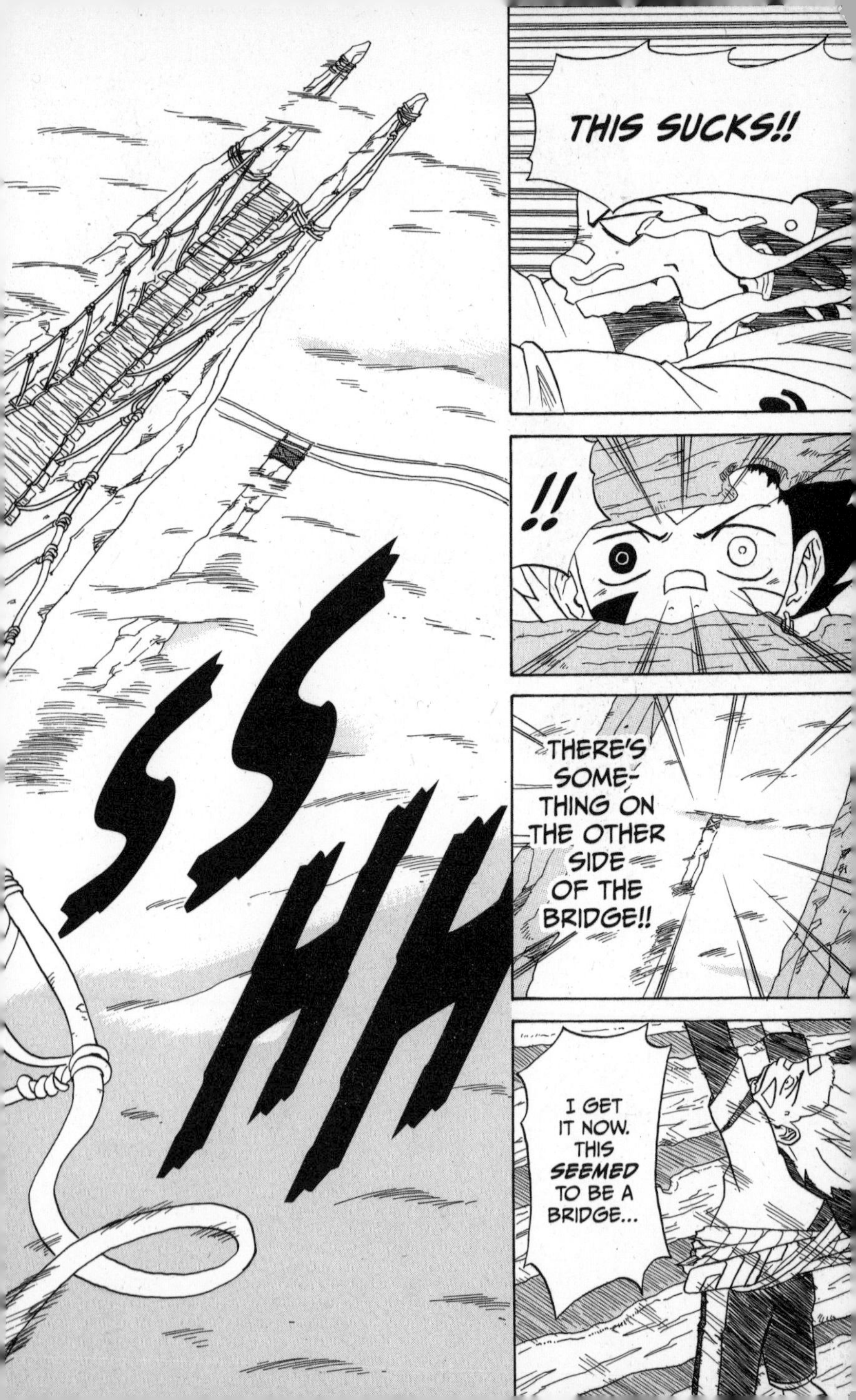
THIS SUCKS!!
!!
THERE'S SOME-THING ON THE OTHER SIDE OF THE BRIDGE!!
I GET IT NOW. THIS *SEEMED* TO BE A BRIDGE...
SSHH

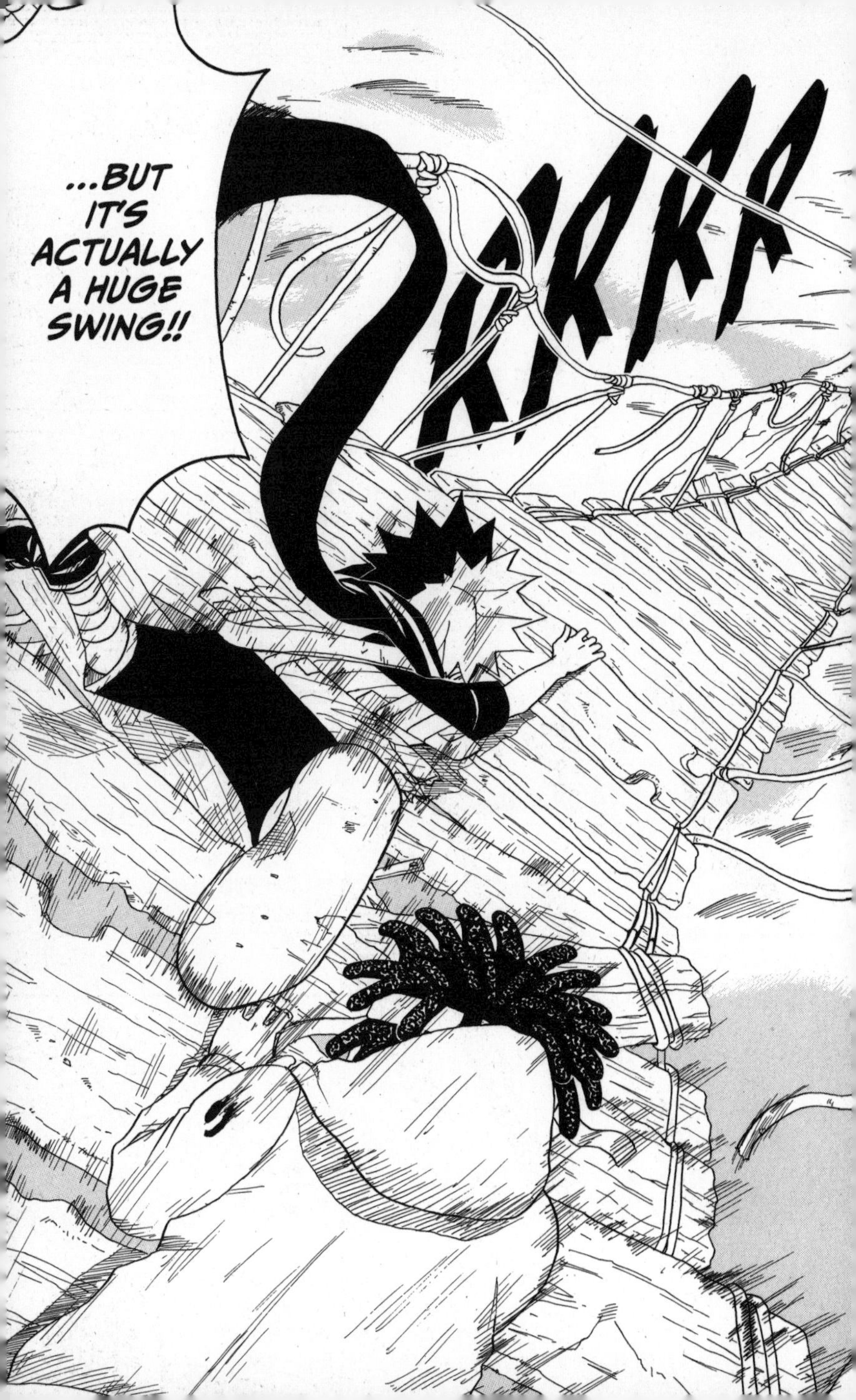
...BUT IT'S ACTUALLY A HUGE SWING!!
ZRRRRR

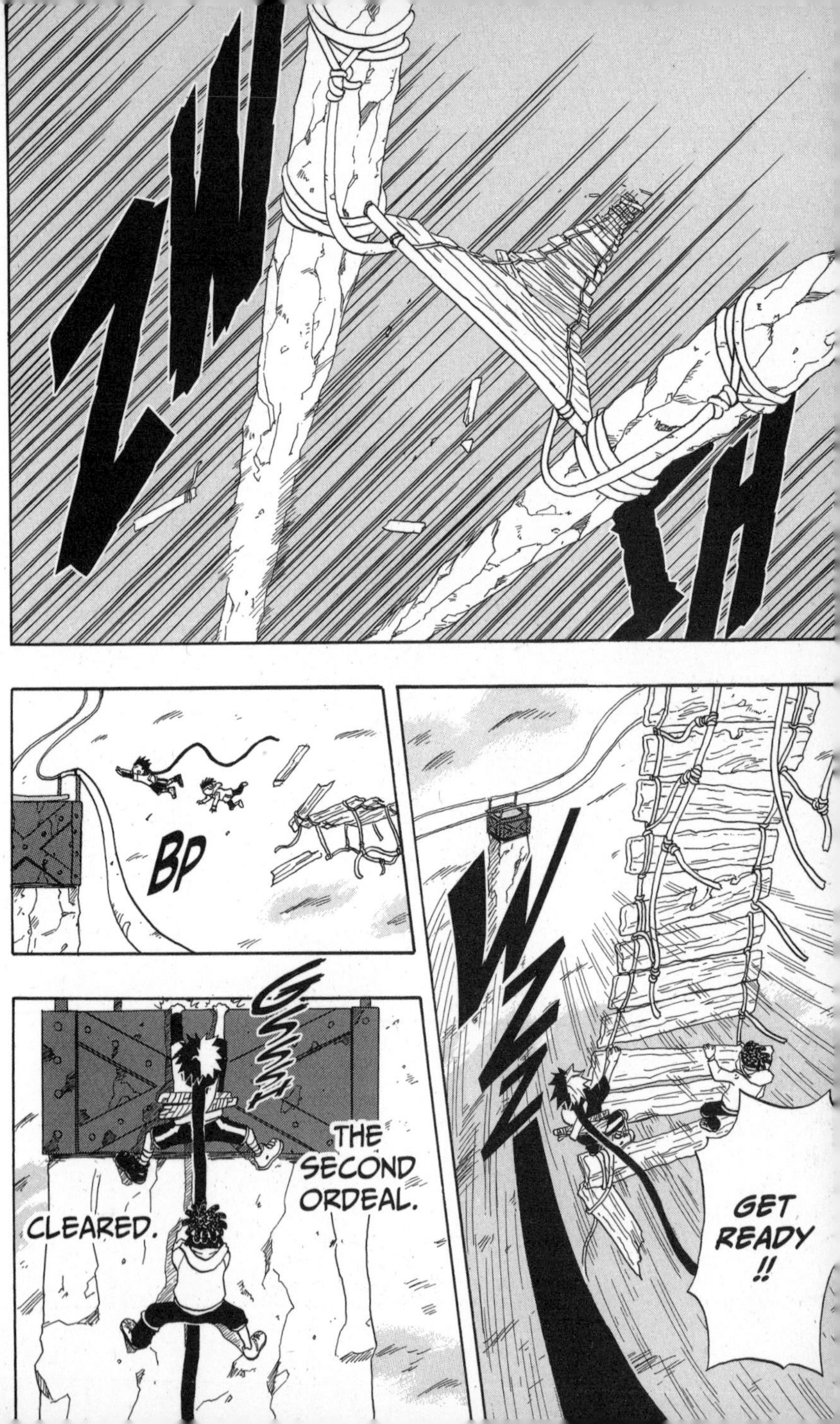
ZWI
SH
GET READY!!
BP
THE SECOND ORDEAL.
CLEARED.

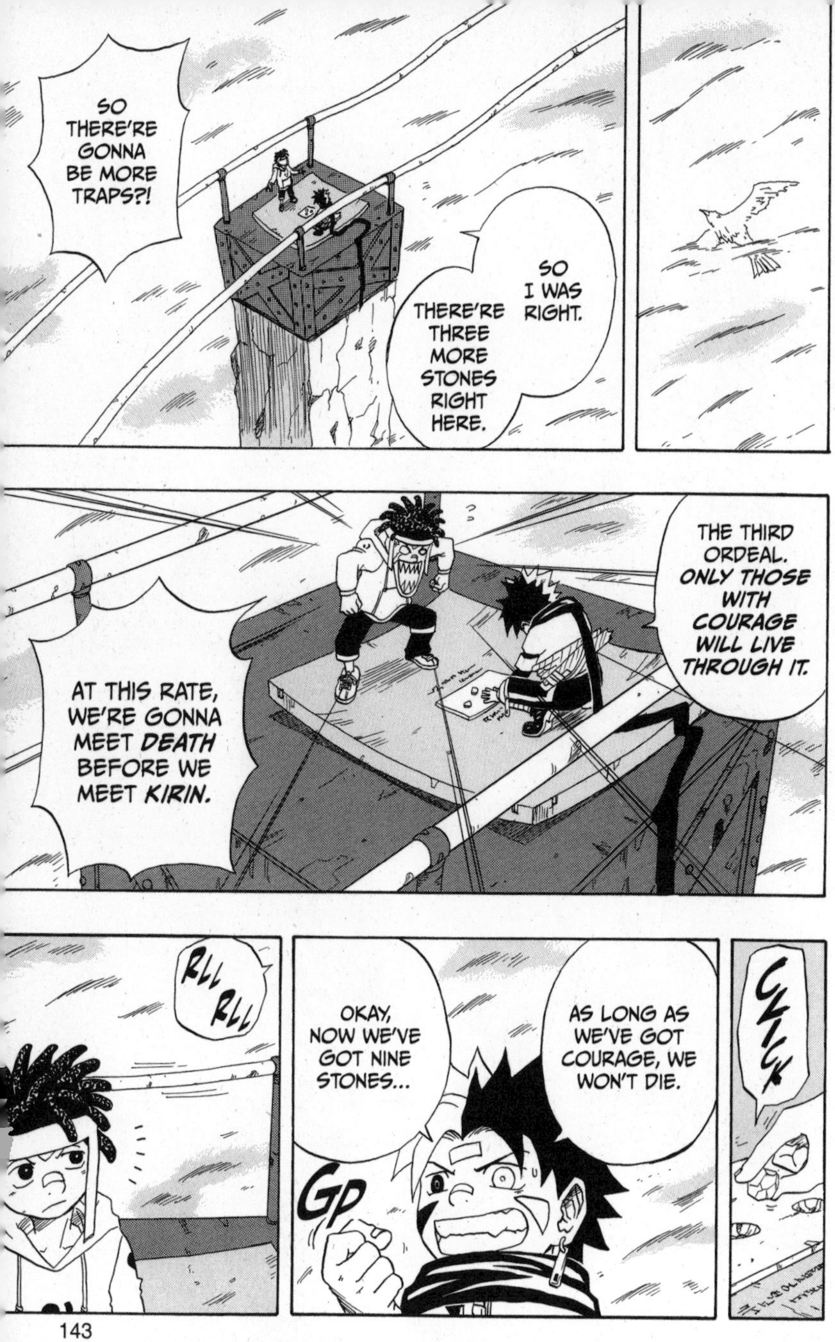
SO I WAS RIGHT.
THERE'RE THREE MORE STONES RIGHT HERE.
SO THERE'RE GONNA BE MORE TRAPS?!
THE THIRD ORDEAL. ONLY THOSE WITH COURAGE WILL LIVE THROUGH IT.
AT THIS RATE, WE'RE GONNA MEET DEATH BEFORE WE MEET KIRIN.
CLICK
AS LONG AS WE'VE GOT COURAGE, WE WON'T DIE.
OKAY, NOW WE'VE GOT NINE STONES...
GP
RLL RLL

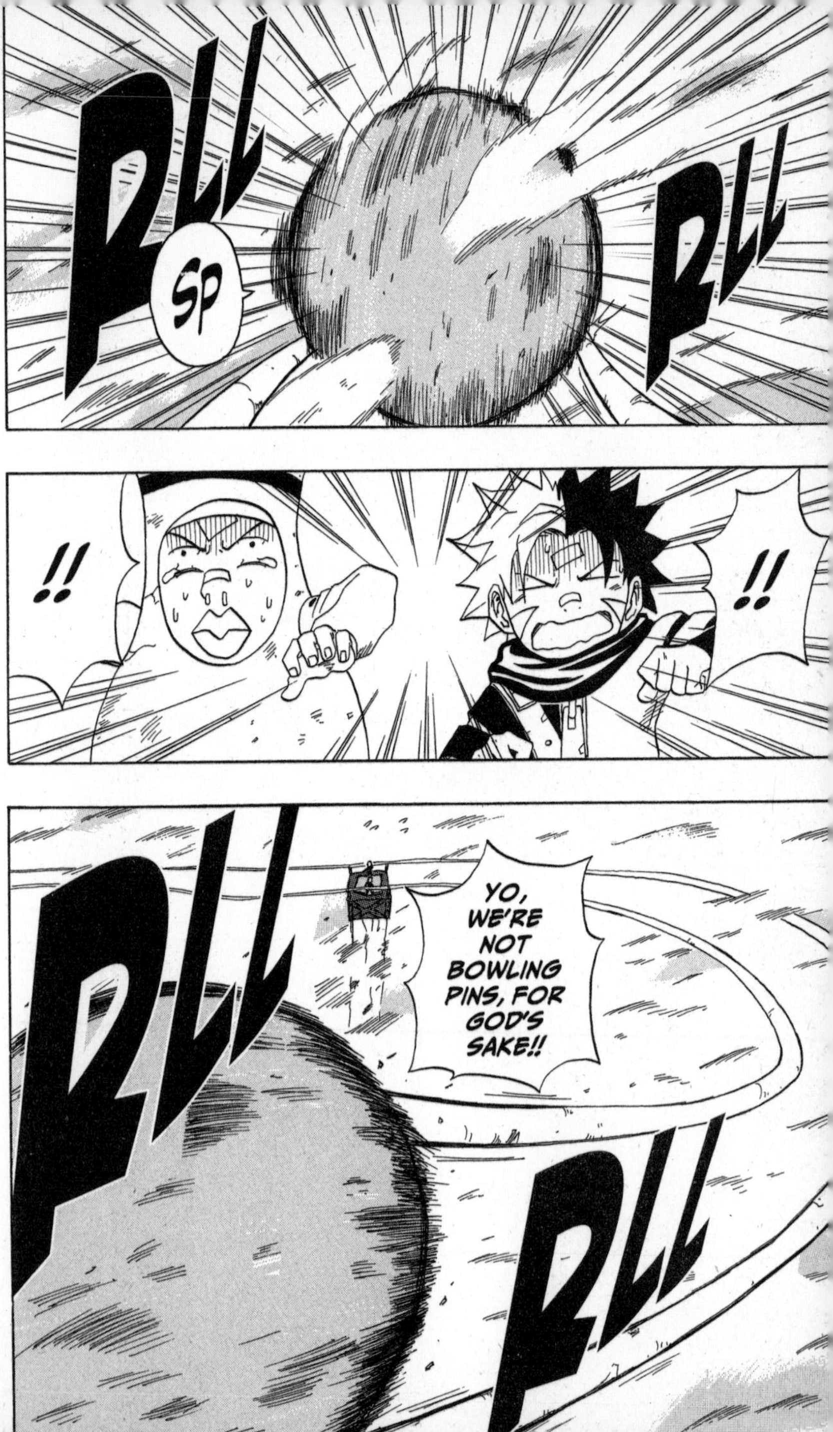
BLL
SP
BLL
!!
!!
YO, WE'RE NOT BOWLING PINS, FOR GOD'S SAKE!!
BLL
BLL

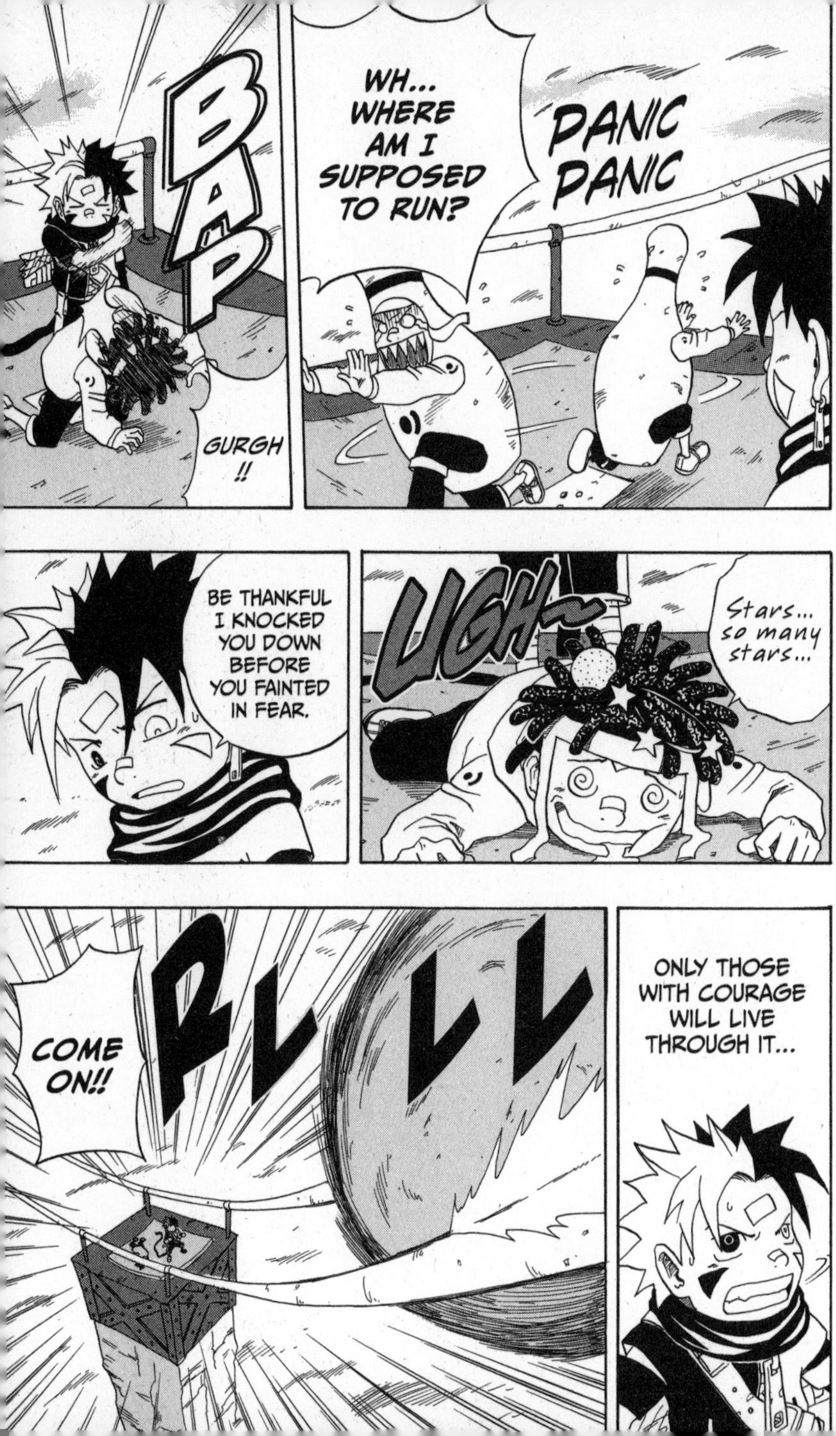
PANIC PANIC
WH... WHERE AM I SUPPOSED TO RUN?
BAP
GURGH!!
Stars... so many stars...
UGH~
BE THANKFUL I KNOCKED YOU DOWN BEFORE YOU FAINTED IN FEAR.
ONLY THOSE WITH COURAGE WILL LIVE THROUGH IT...
RLLL
COME ON!!

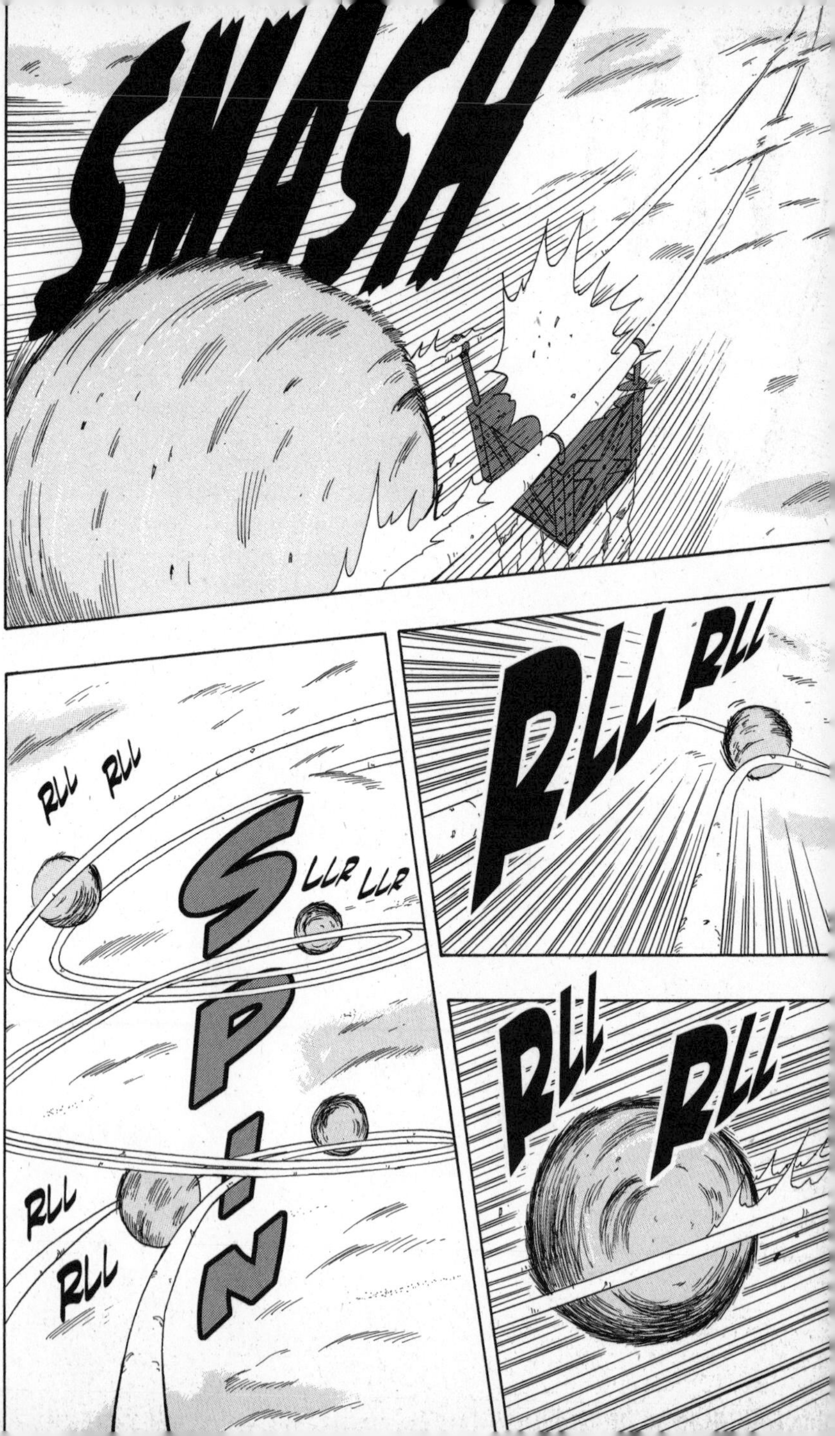
SMASH
RLL
RLL
RLL
RLL
SLLR LLR
RLL RLL
SPIN
RLL
RLL

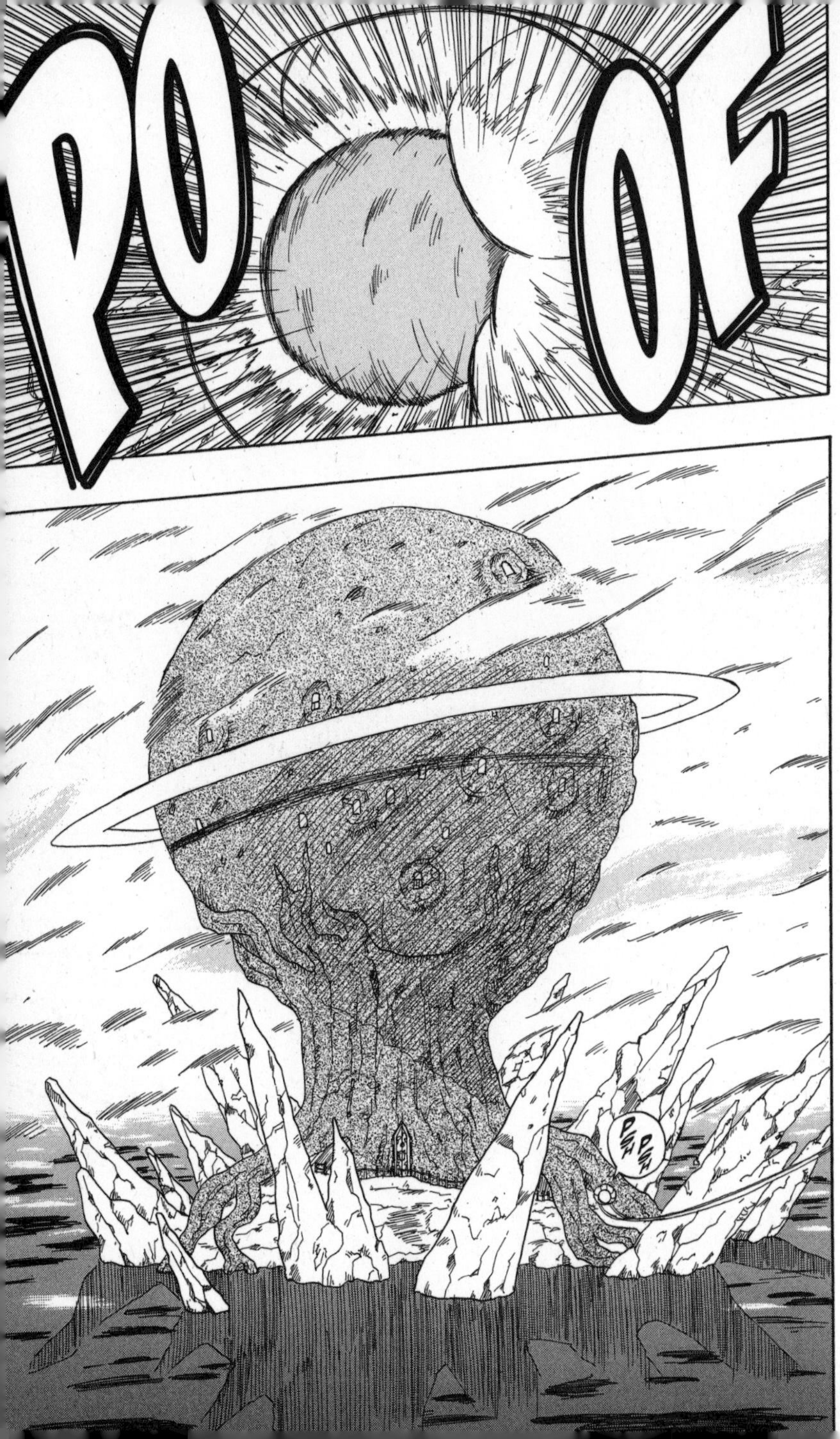
POOF
PSH PSH

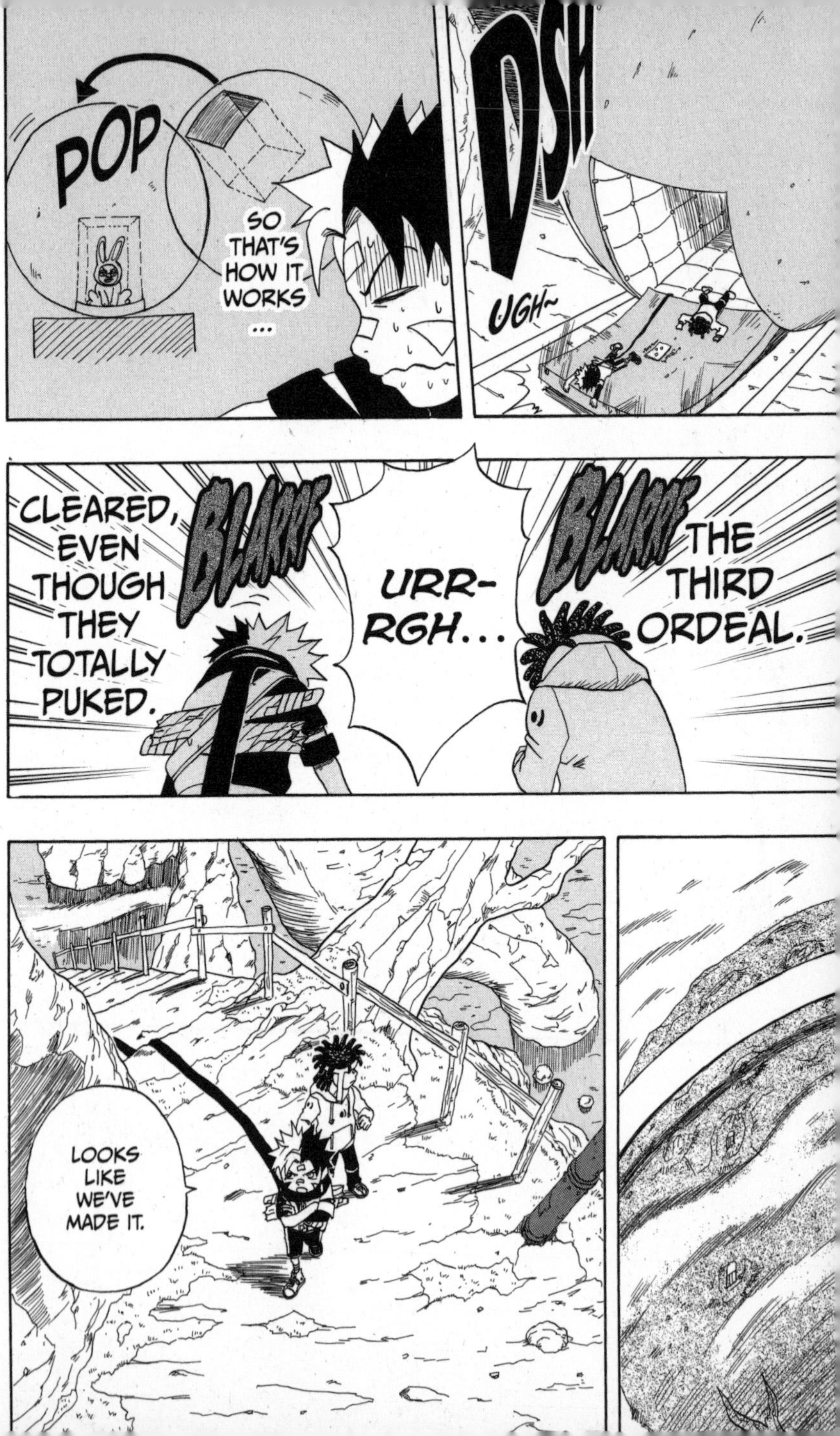
DSH
UGH~
POP
SO THAT'S HOW IT WORKS ...
THE THIRD ORDEAL.
BLARF
URR-RGH...
BLARF
CLEARED, EVEN THOUGH THEY TOTALLY PUKED.
LOOKS LIKE WE'VE MADE IT.

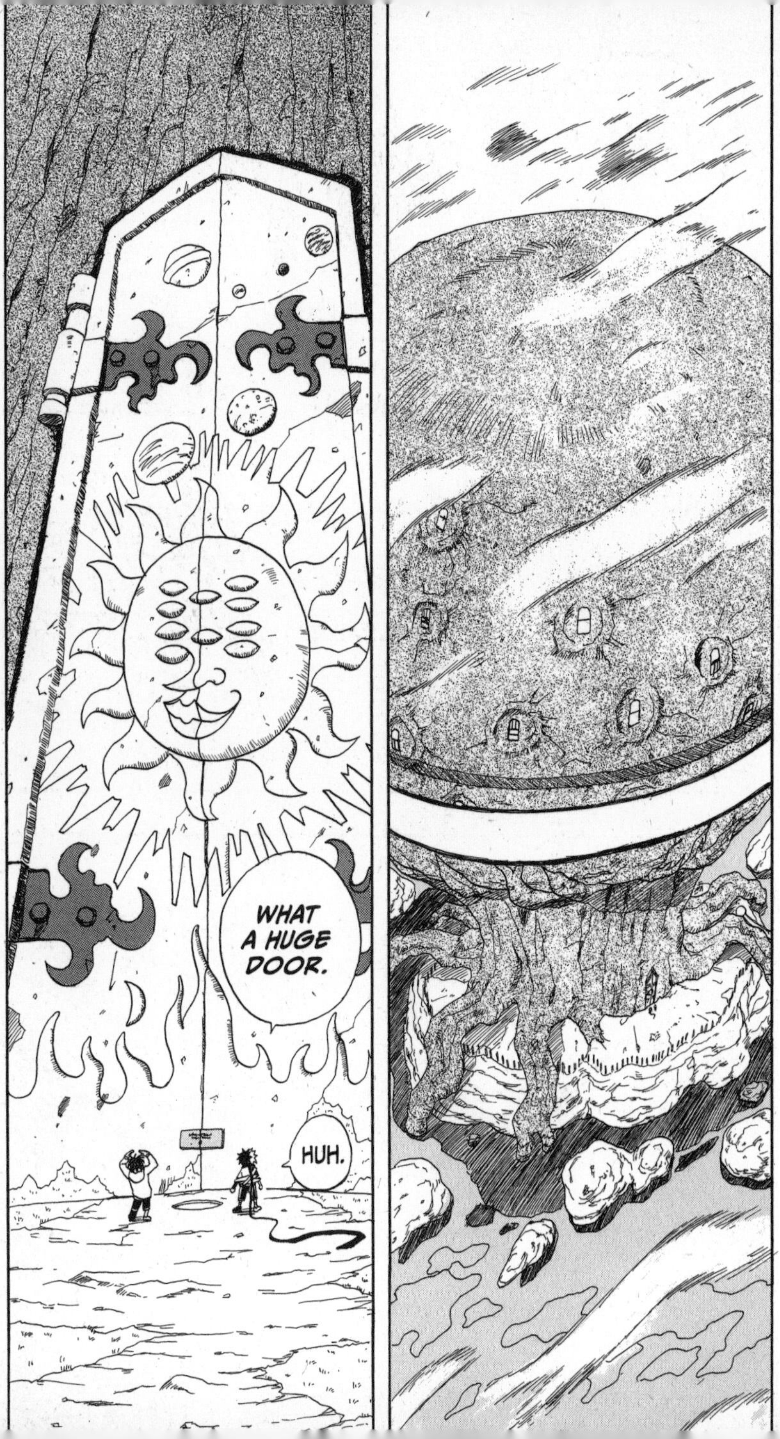
WHAT A HUGE DOOR.
HUH.

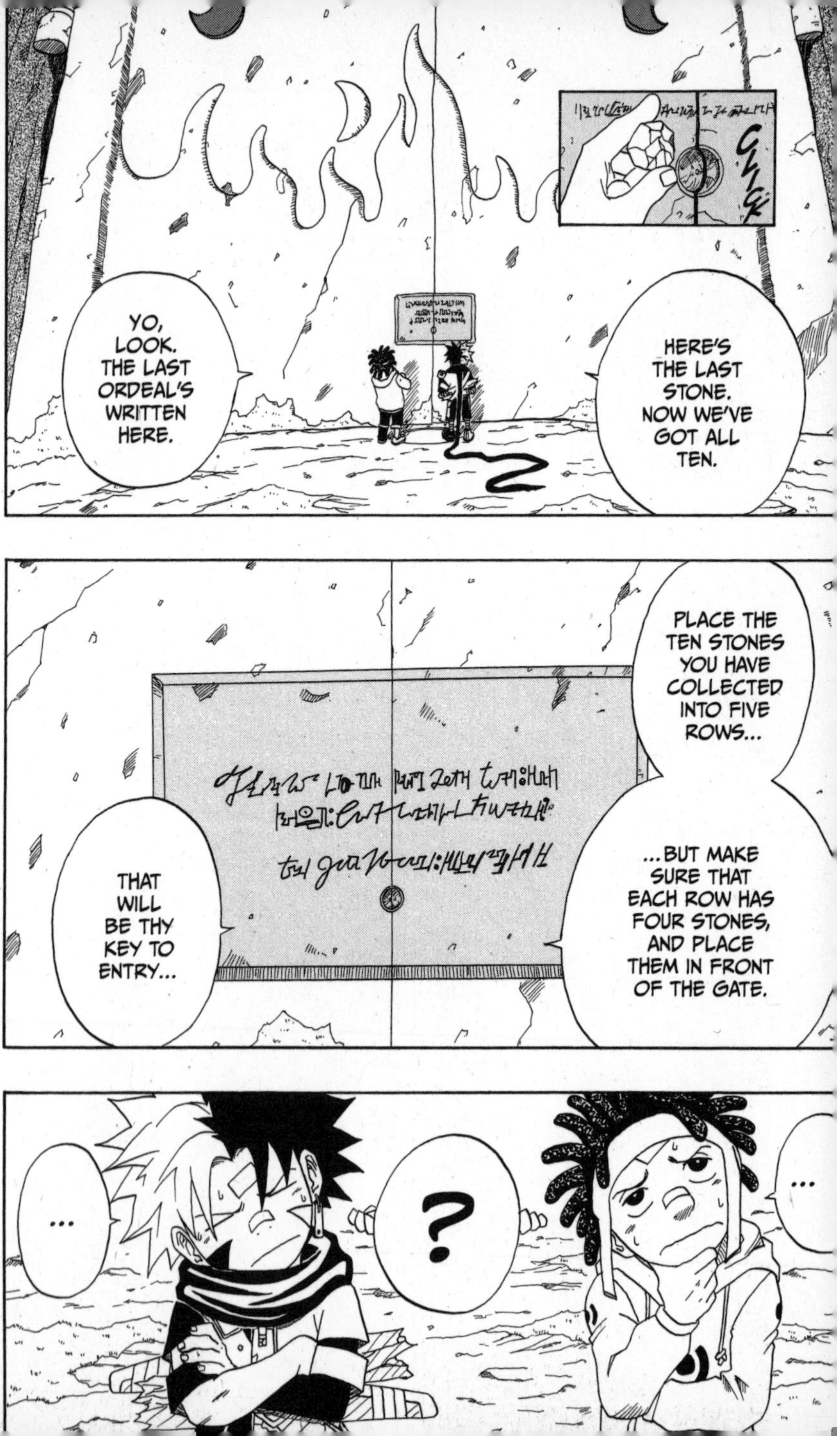
CLICK
HERE'S THE LAST STONE. NOW WE'VE GOT ALL TEN.
YO, LOOK. THE LAST ORDEAL'S WRITTEN HERE.
PLACE THE TEN STONES YOU HAVE COLLECTED INTO FIVE ROWS...
...BUT MAKE SURE THAT EACH ROW HAS FOUR STONES, AND PLACE THEM IN FRONT OF THE GATE.
THAT WILL BE THY KEY TO ENTRY...
...
?
...

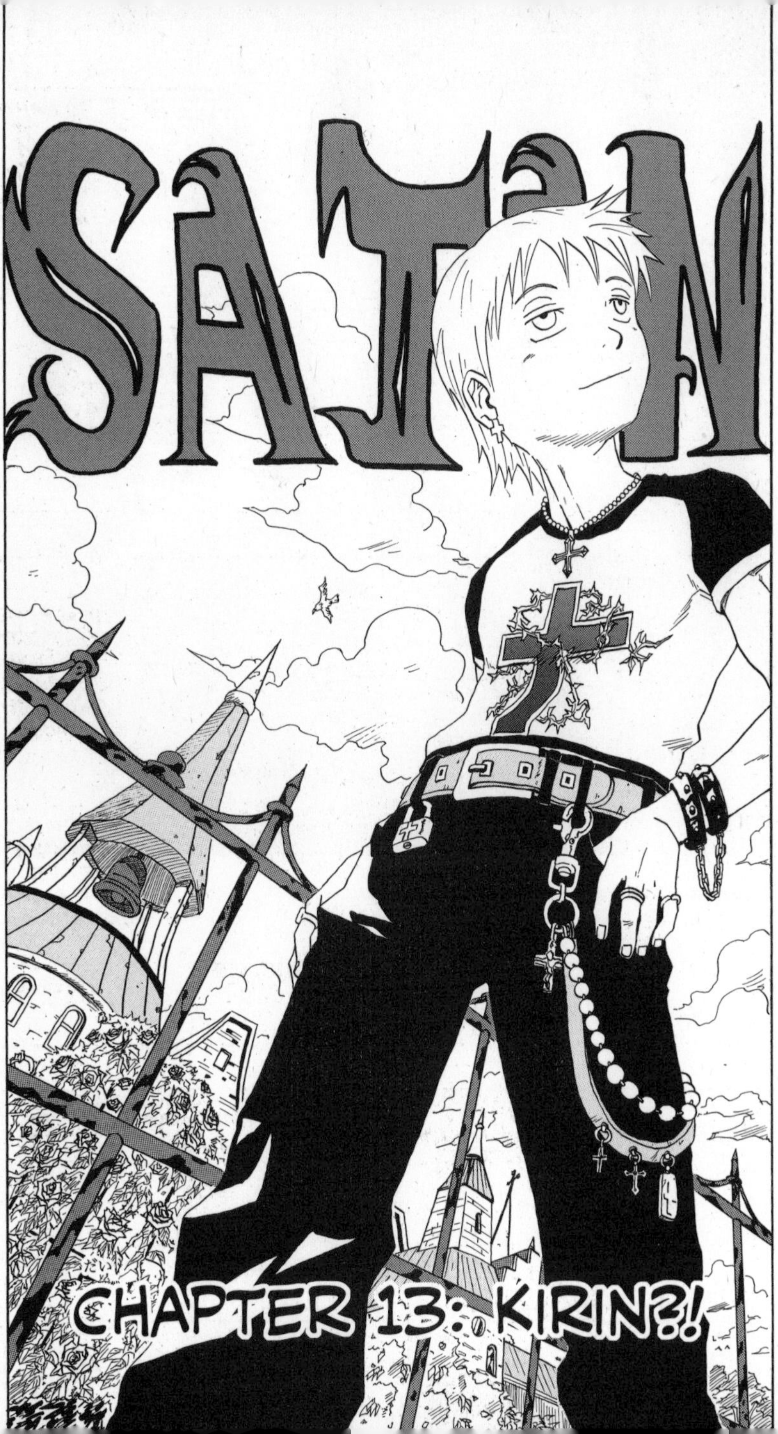
SATAN
CHAPTER 13: KIRIN?!

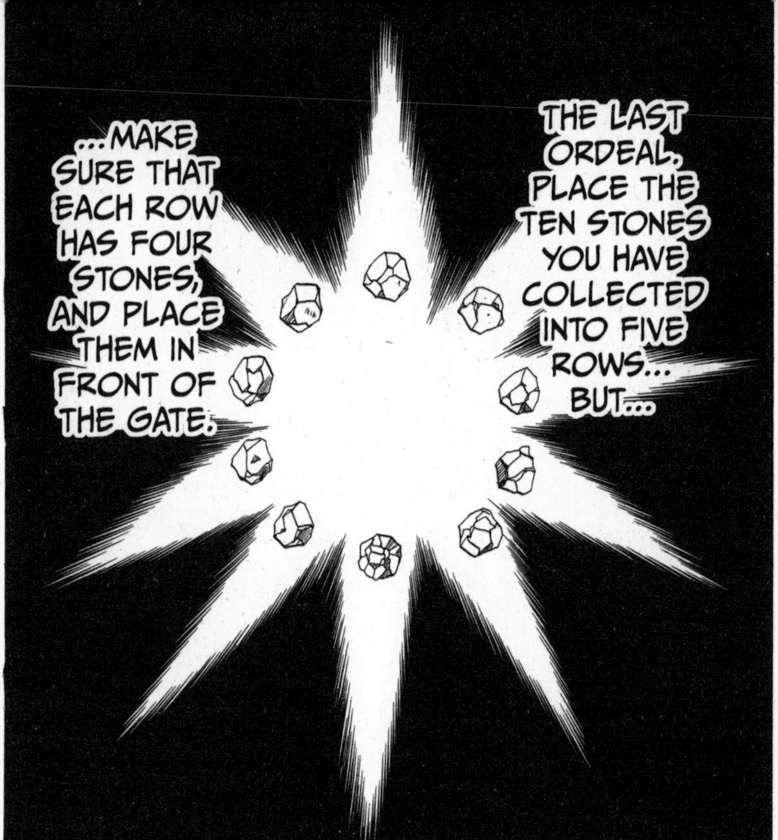
THE LAST ORDEAL. PLACE THE TEN STONES YOU HAVE COLLECTED INTO FIVE ROWS... BUT...
...MAKE SURE THAT EACH ROW HAS FOUR STONES, AND PLACE THEM IN FRONT OF THE GATE.

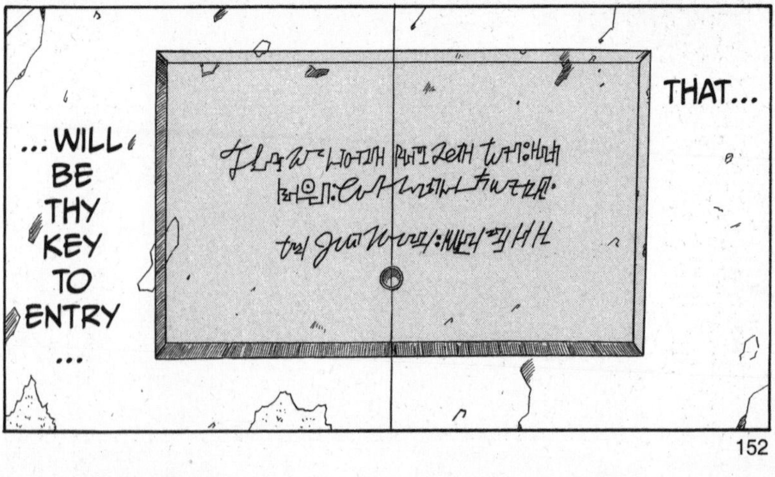
THAT...
...WILL BE THY KEY TO ENTRY...

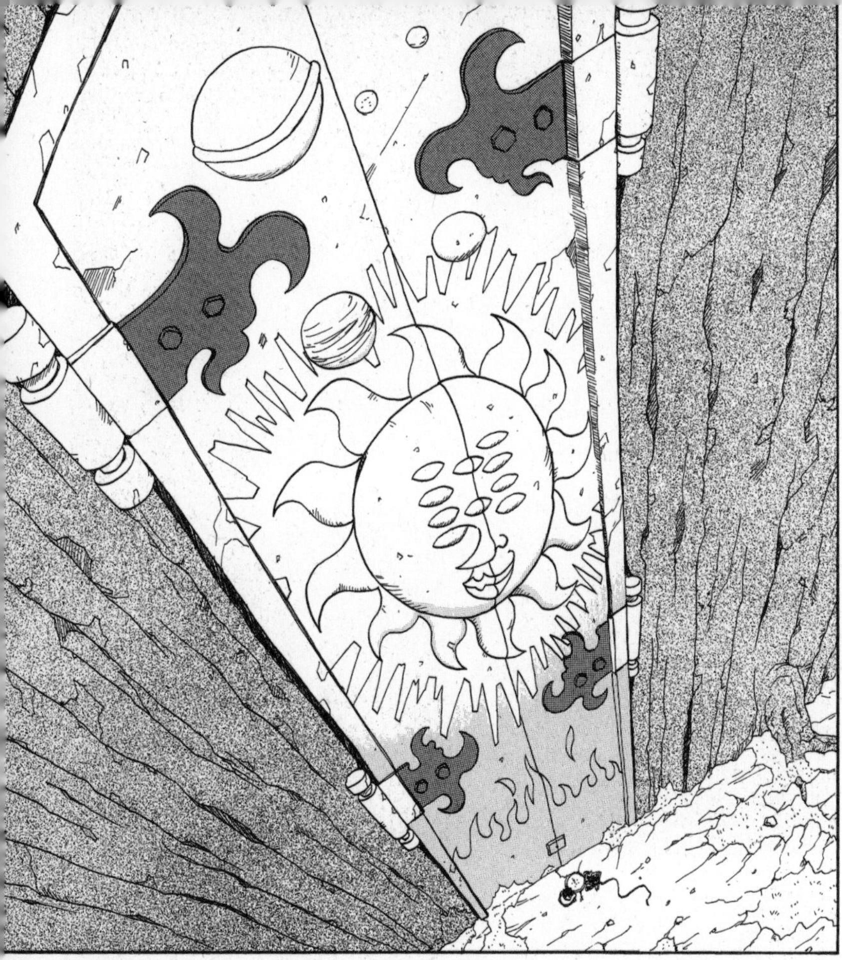

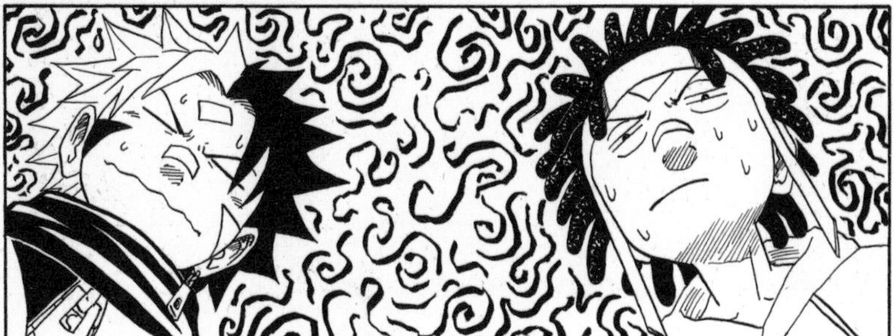

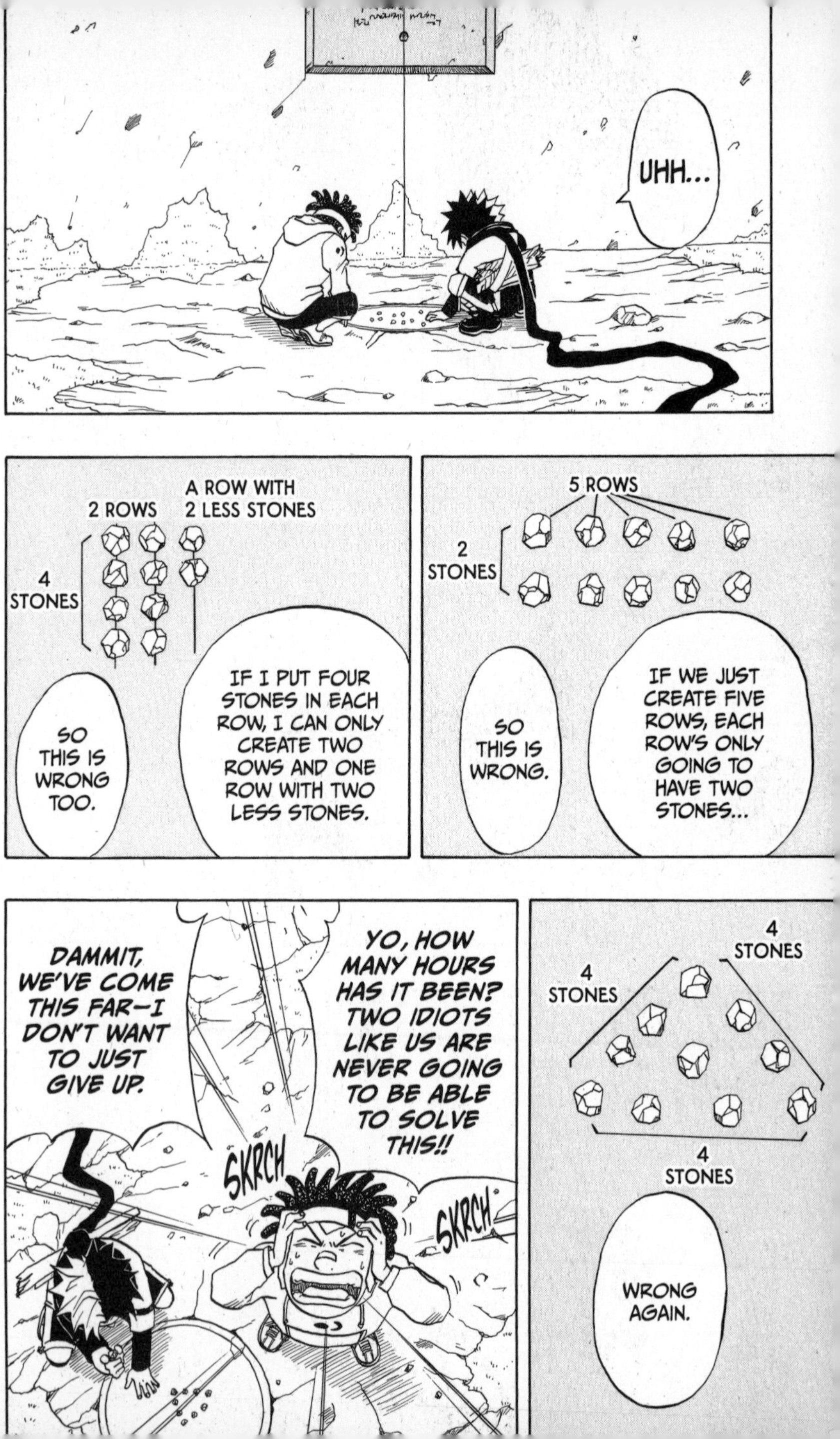
UHH...
5 ROWS
2 STONES
IF WE JUST CREATE FIVE ROWS, EACH ROW'S ONLY GOING TO HAVE TWO STONES...
SO THIS IS WRONG.
A ROW WITH 2 LESS STONES
2 ROWS
4 STONES
IF I PUT FOUR STONES IN EACH ROW, I CAN ONLY CREATE TWO ROWS AND ONE ROW WITH TWO LESS STONES.
SO THIS IS WRONG TOO.
4 STONES
4 STONES
4 STONES
WRONG AGAIN.
YO, HOW MANY HOURS HAS IT BEEN? TWO IDIOTS LIKE US ARE NEVER GOING TO BE ABLE TO SOLVE THIS!!
SKRCH
SKRCH
DAMMIT, WE'VE COME THIS FAR—I DON'T WANT TO JUST GIVE UP.

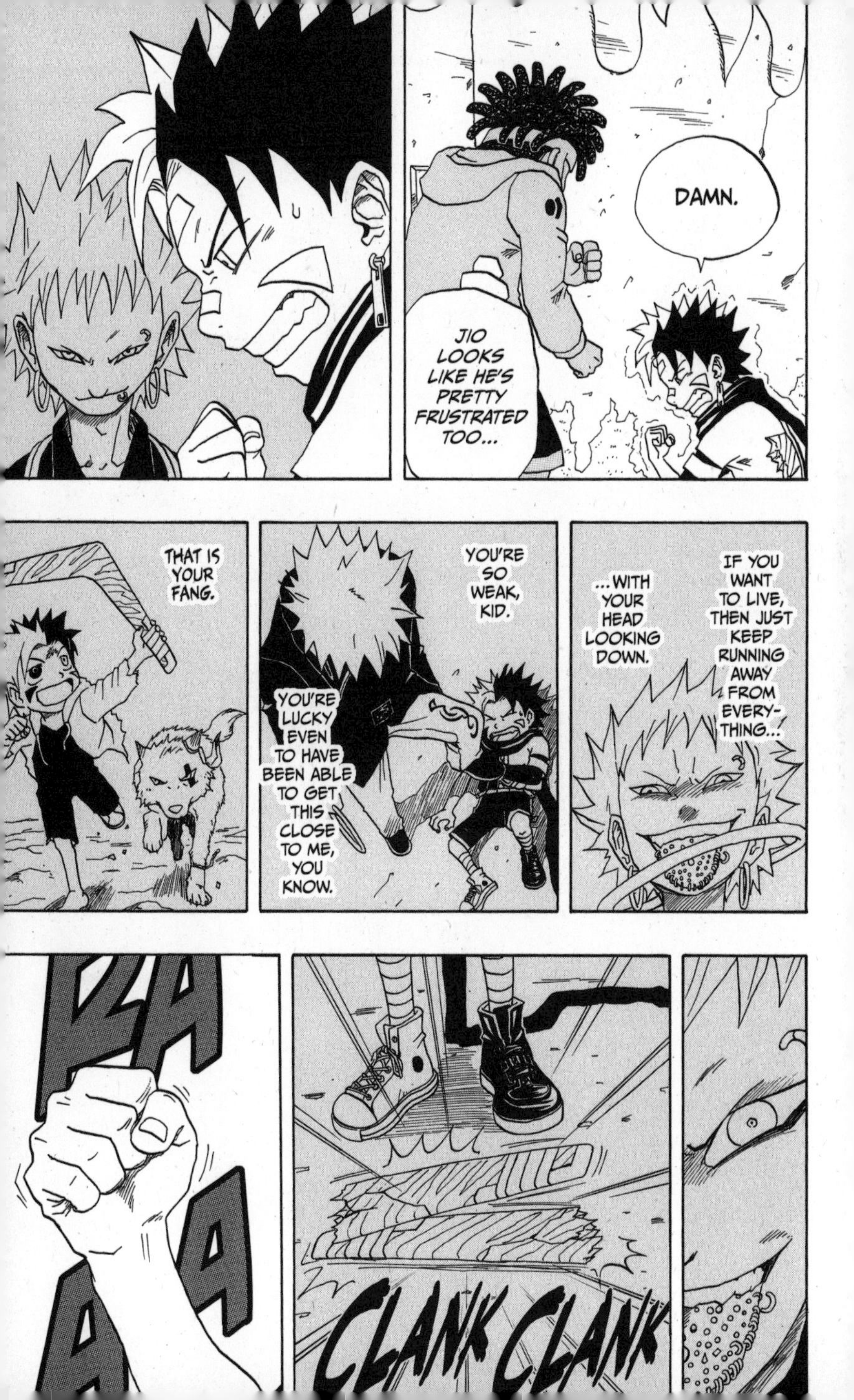
DAMN.
JIO LOOKS LIKE HE'S PRETTY FRUSTRATED TOO...
IF YOU WANT TO LIVE, THEN JUST KEEP RUNNING AWAY FROM EVERY-THING...
...WITH YOUR HEAD LOOKING DOWN.
YOU'RE SO WEAK, KID.
YOU'RE LUCKY EVEN TO HAVE BEEN ABLE TO GET THIS CLOSE TO ME, YOU KNOW.
THAT IS YOUR FANG.
CLANK CLANK
ZAAA

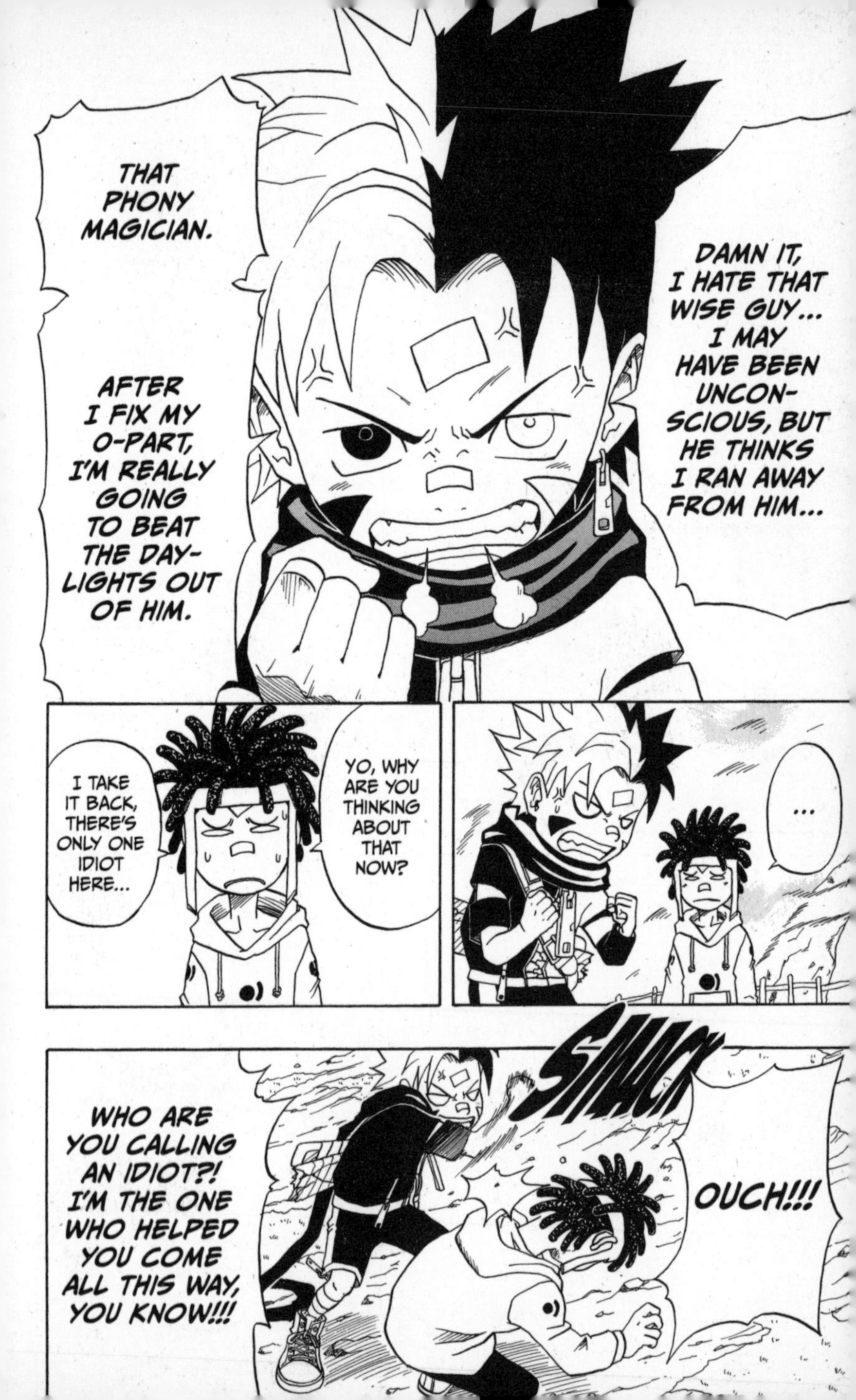

DAMN IT, I HATE THAT WISE GUY... I MAY HAVE BEEN UNCONSCIOUS, BUT HE THINKS I RAN AWAY FROM HIM...
THAT PHONY MAGICIAN.
AFTER I FIX MY O-PART, I'M REALLY GOING TO BEAT THE DAYLIGHTS OUT OF HIM.
...
YO, WHY ARE YOU THINKING ABOUT THAT NOW?
I TAKE IT BACK, THERE'S ONLY ONE IDIOT HERE...
SMACK
OUCH!!!
WHO ARE YOU CALLING AN IDIOT?! I'M THE ONE WHO HELPED YOU COME ALL THIS WAY, YOU KNOW!!!

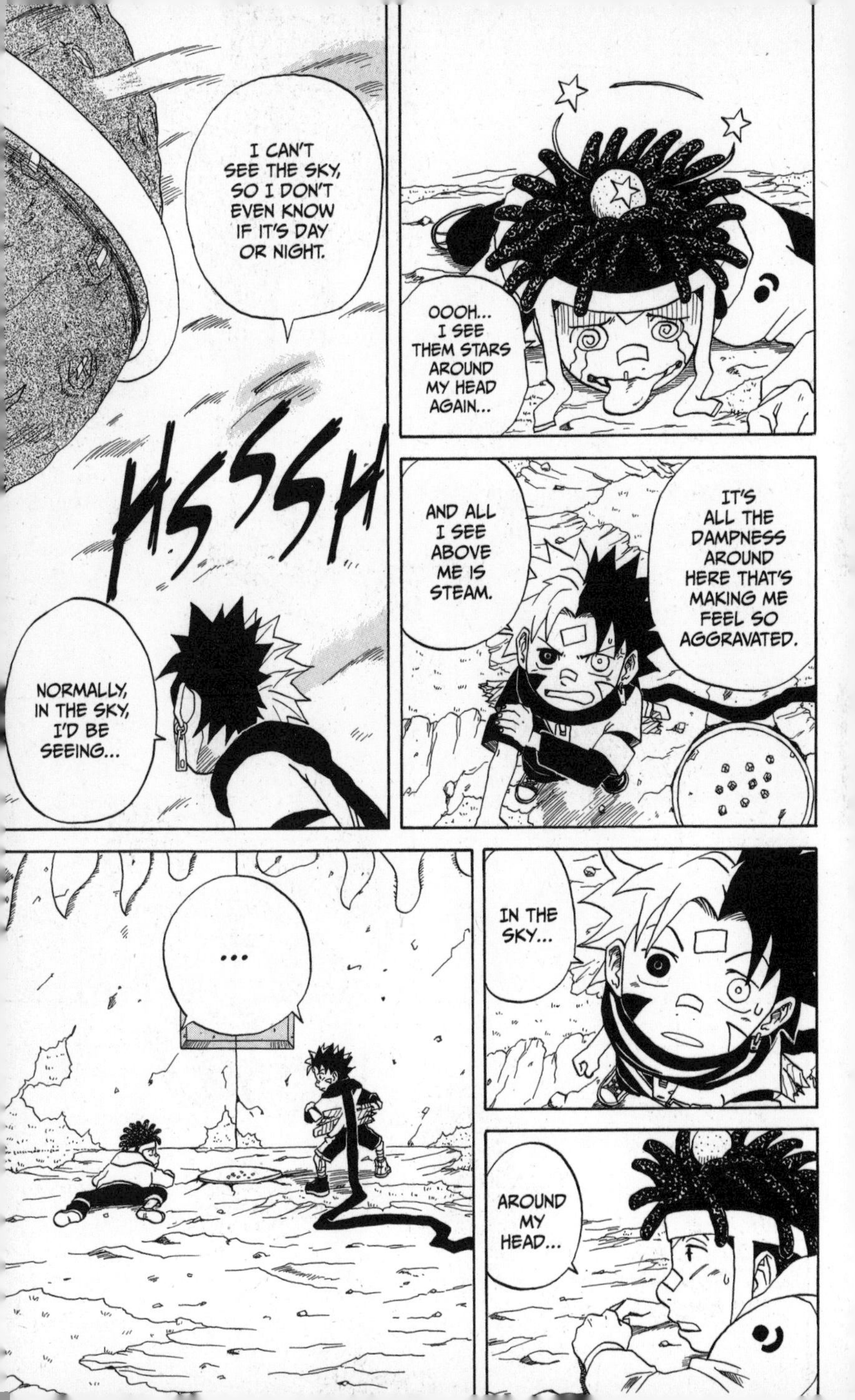
OOOH... I SEE THEM STARS AROUND MY HEAD AGAIN...
IT'S ALL THE DAMPNESS AROUND HERE THAT'S MAKING ME FEEL SO AGGRAVATED.
AND ALL I SEE ABOVE ME IS STEAM.
I CAN'T SEE THE SKY, SO I DON'T EVEN KNOW IF IT'S DAY OR NIGHT.
HSSSH
NORMALLY, IN THE SKY, I'D BE SEEING...
IN THE SKY...
AROUND MY HEAD...
...

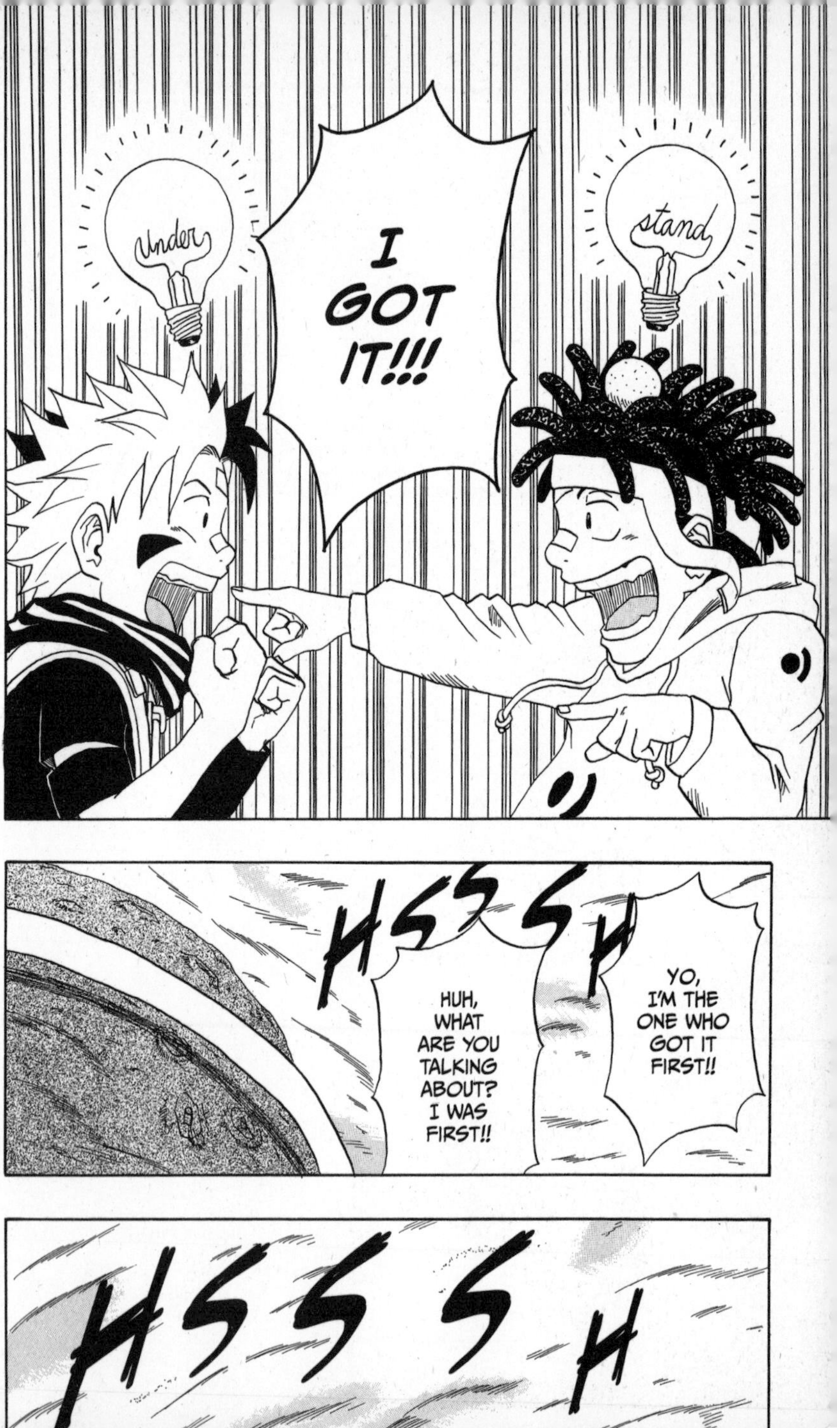
I GOT IT!!!
under
stand
HSSSH
YO, I'M THE ONE WHO GOT IT FIRST!!
HUH, WHAT ARE YOU TALKING ABOUT? I WAS FIRST!!
HSSSH

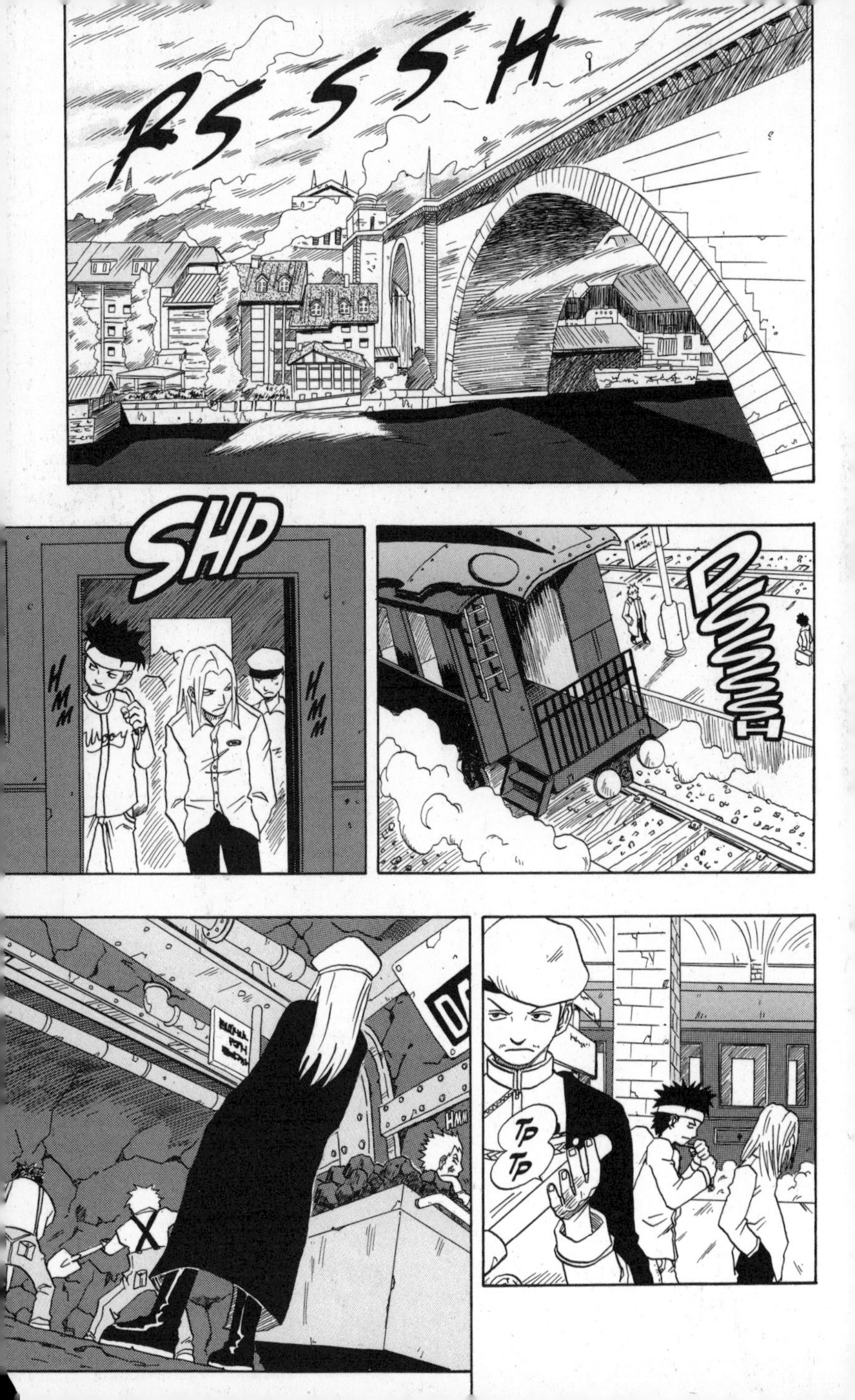
RSSSH
DSSSSH
SHP
HMM
HMM
TP TP
HMM

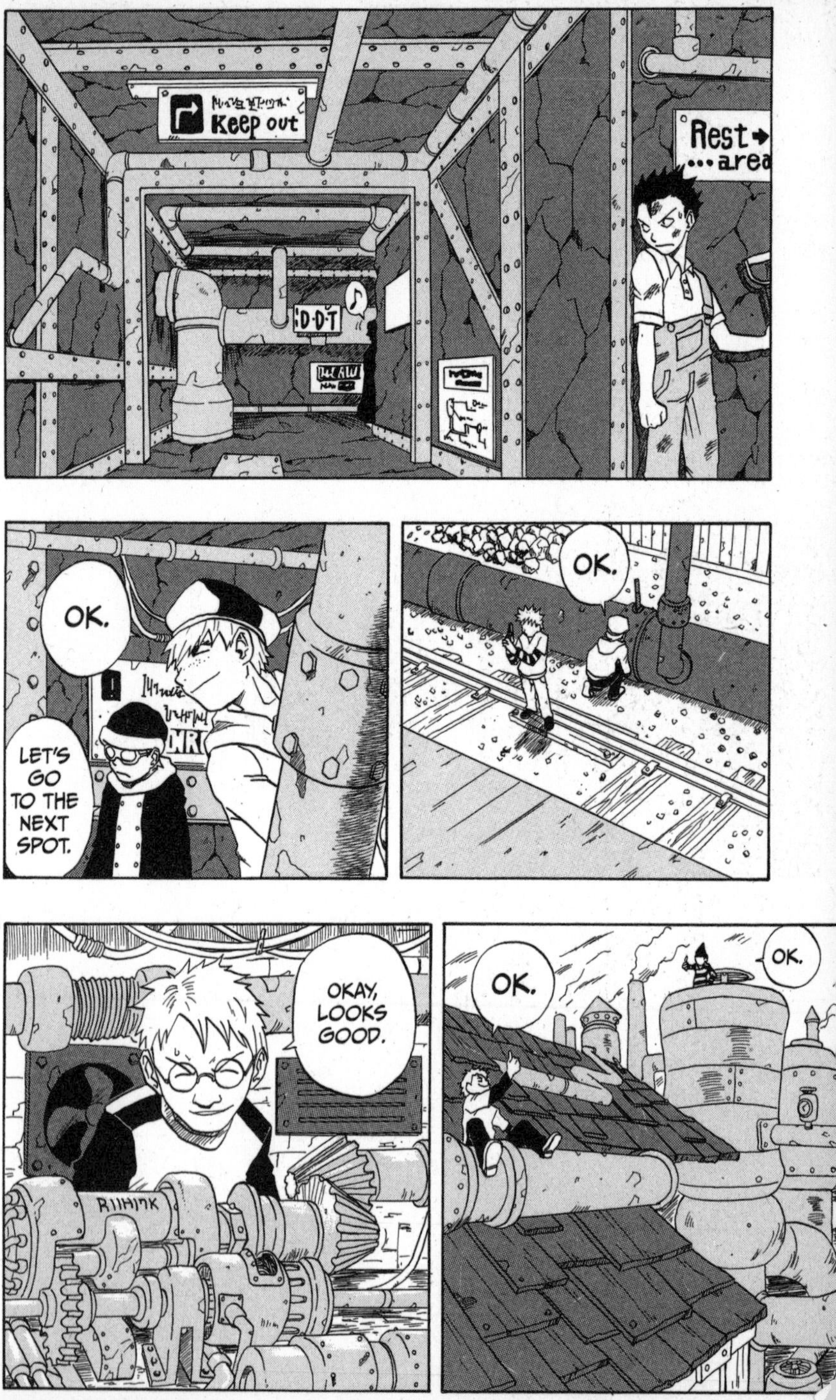
Keep out
Rest
area
D·D·T
OK.
OK.
LET'S GO TO THE NEXT SPOT.
OK.
OK.
OKAY, LOOKS GOOD.

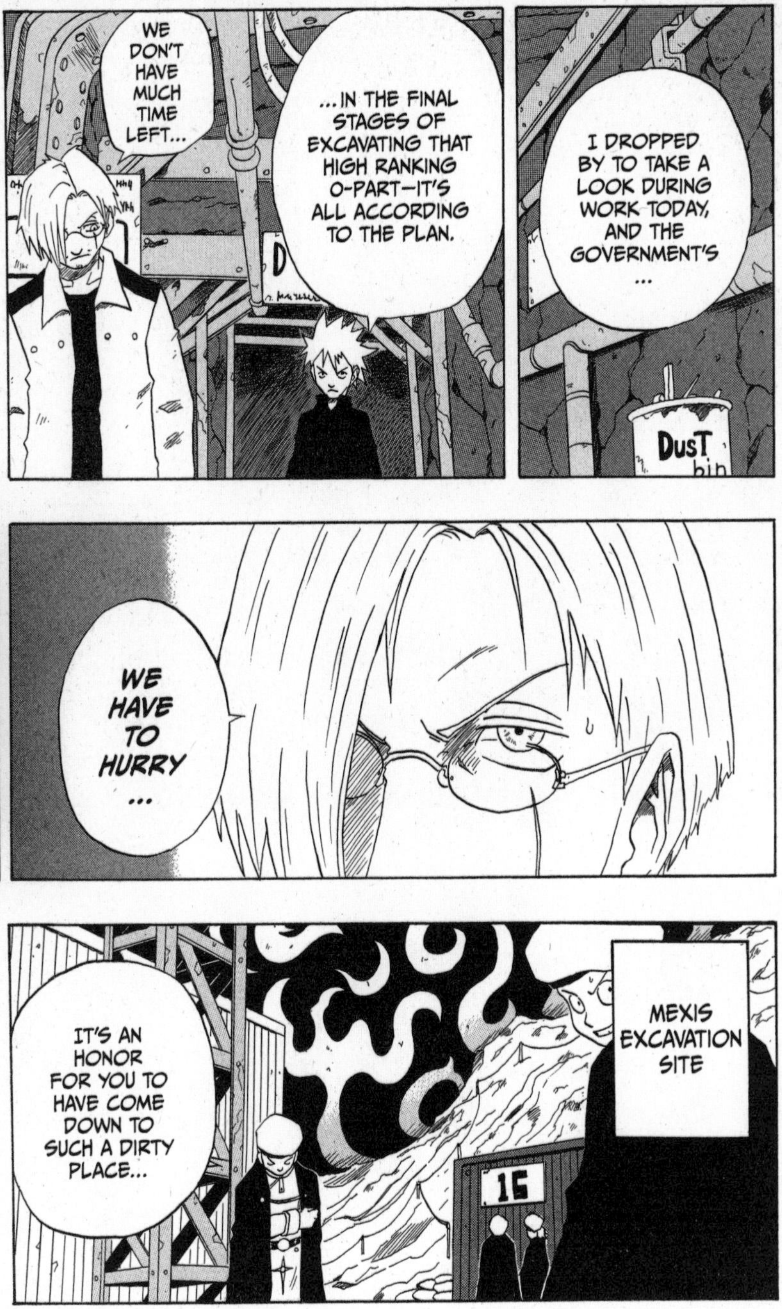
I DROPPED BY TO TAKE A LOOK DURING WORK TODAY, AND THE GOVERNMENT'S ...
DusT bin
...IN THE FINAL STAGES OF EXCAVATING THAT HIGH RANKING O-PART—IT'S ALL ACCORDING TO THE PLAN.
WE DON'T HAVE MUCH TIME LEFT...
WE HAVE TO HURRY ...
MEXIS EXCAVATION SITE
15
IT'S AN HONOR FOR YOU TO HAVE COME DOWN TO SUCH A DIRTY PLACE...

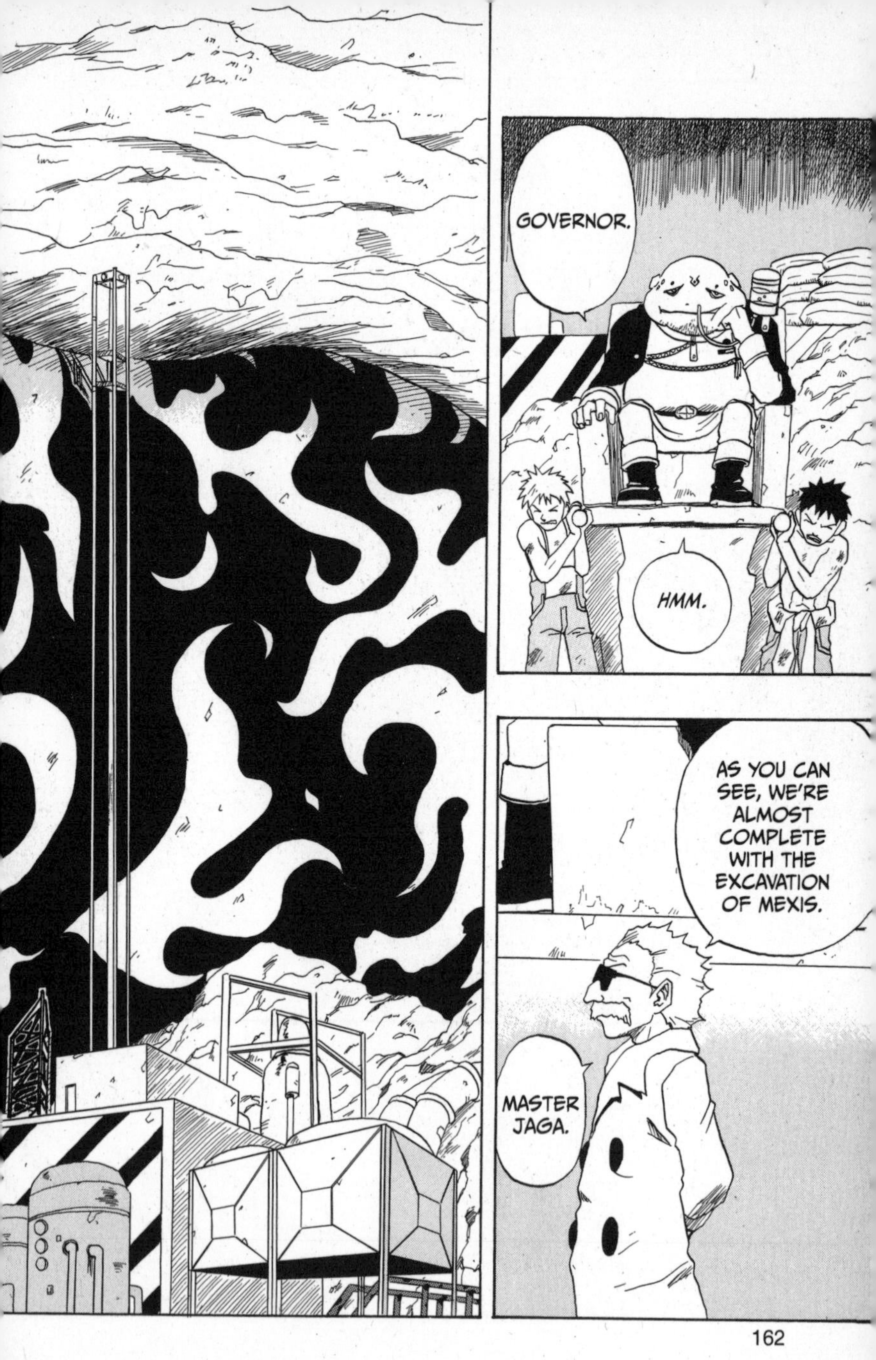
GOVERNOR.
HMM.
AS YOU CAN SEE, WE'RE ALMOST COMPLETE WITH THE EXCAVATION OF MEXIS.
MASTER JAGA.

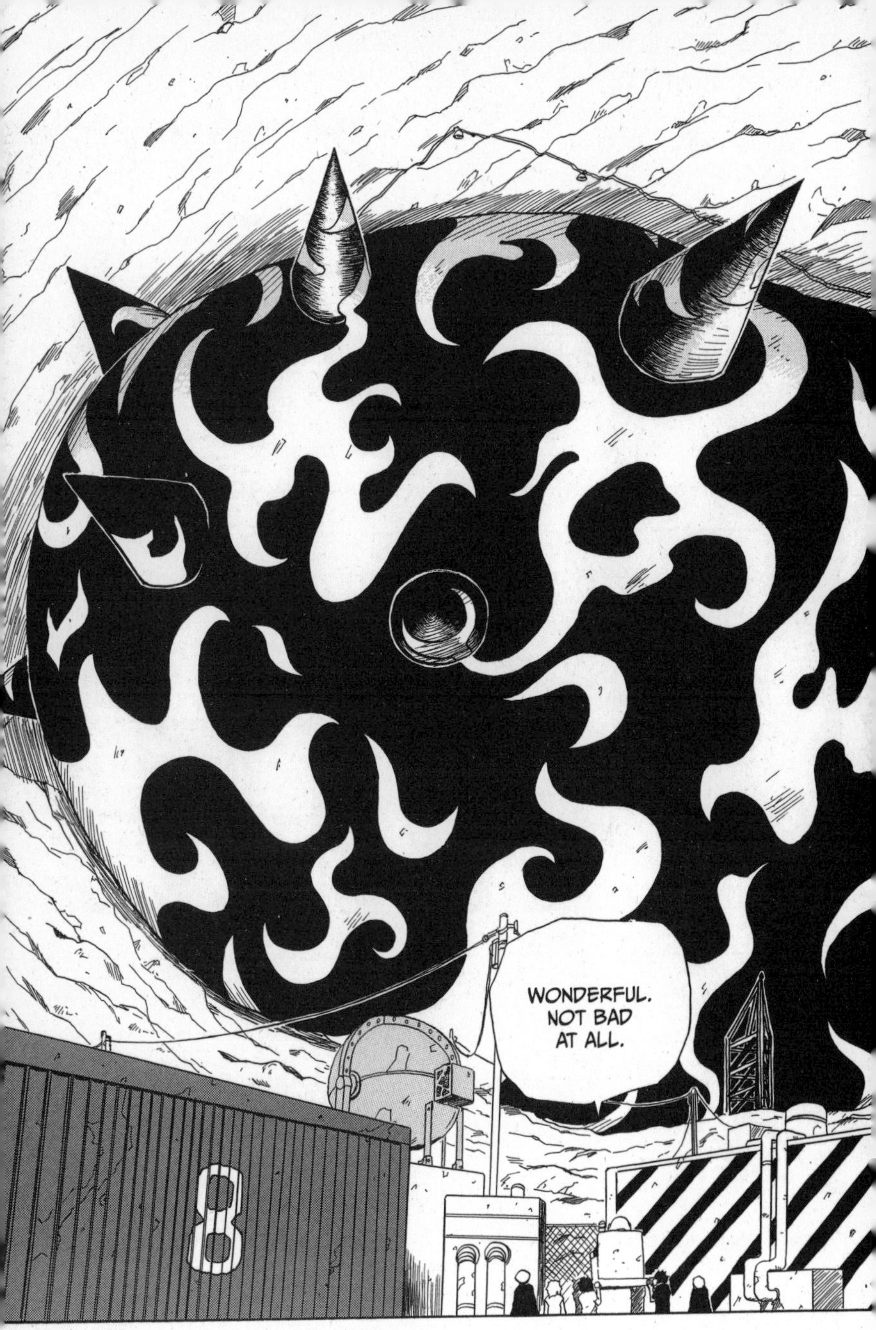
WONDERFUL. NOT BAD AT ALL.

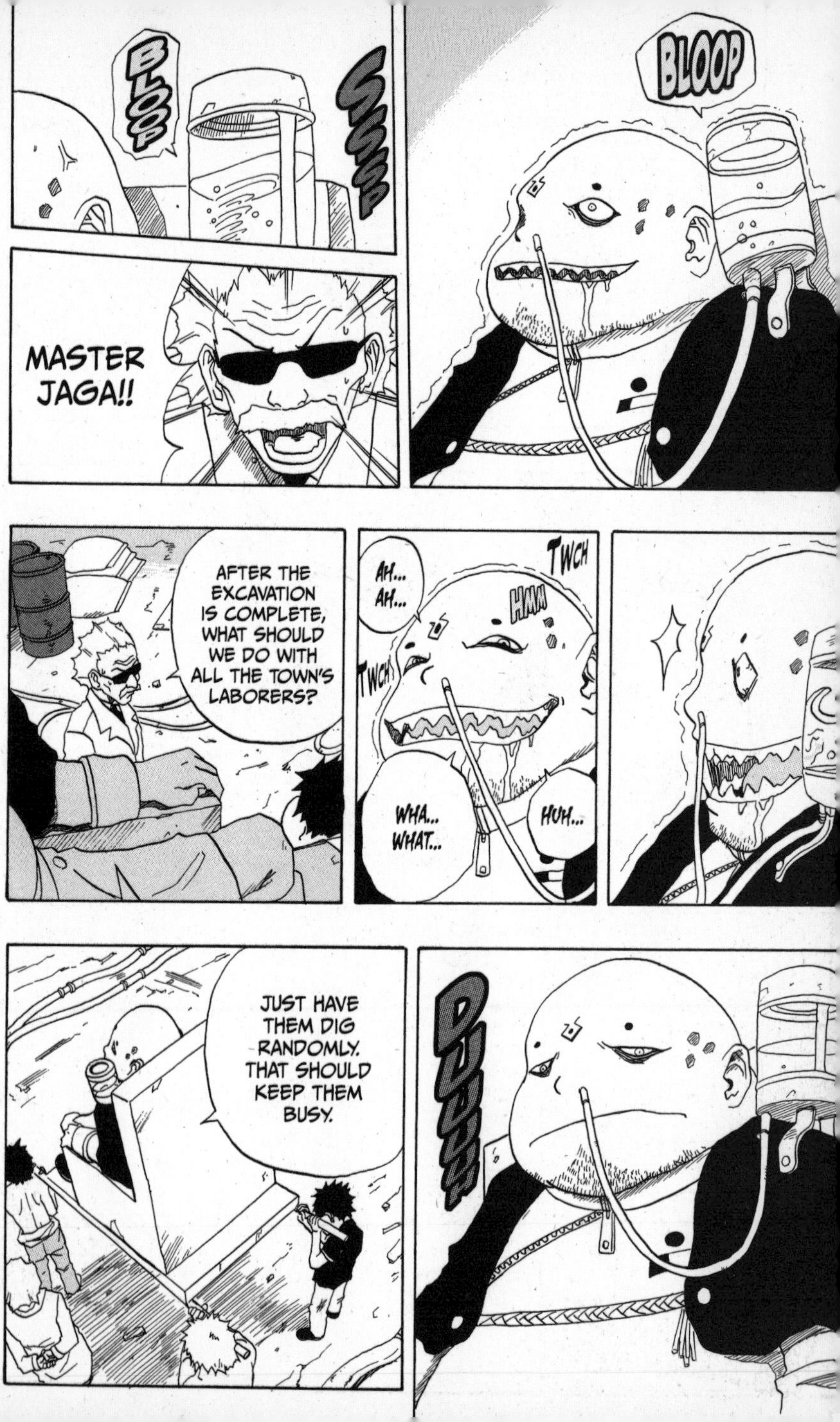
BLOOP
BLOOP
MASTER JAGA!!
TWCH
AH... AH...
HMM
TWCH
HUH...
WHA... WHAT...
AFTER THE EXCAVATION IS COMPLETE, WHAT SHOULD WE DO WITH ALL THE TOWN'S LABORERS?
JUST HAVE THEM DIG RANDOMLY. THAT SHOULD KEEP THEM BUSY.

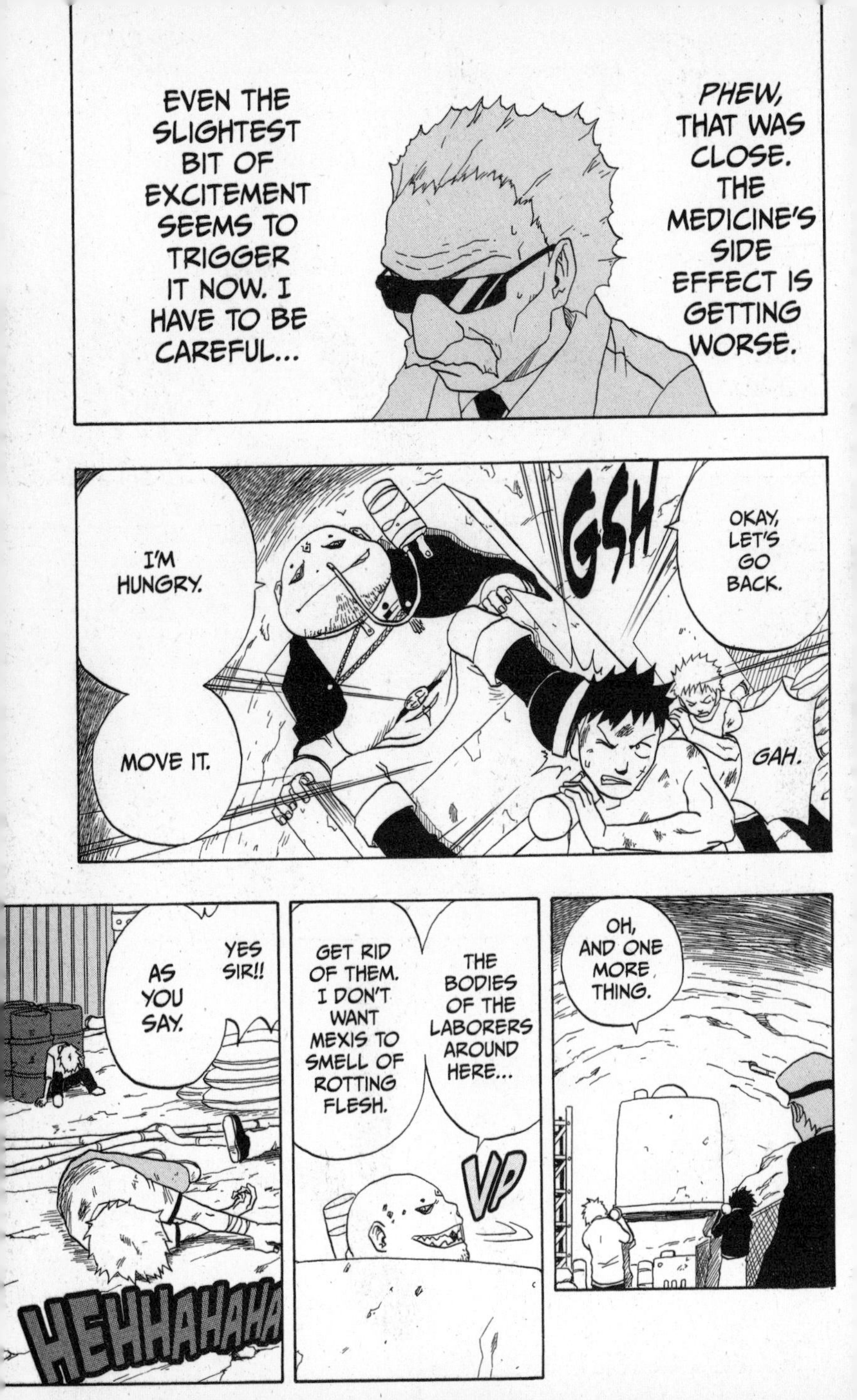
PHEW, THAT WAS CLOSE. THE MEDICINE'S SIDE EFFECT IS GETTING WORSE.
EVEN THE SLIGHTEST BIT OF EXCITEMENT SEEMS TO TRIGGER IT NOW. I HAVE TO BE CAREFUL...
OKAY, LET'S GO BACK.
GSH
GAH.
I'M HUNGRY.
MOVE IT.
OH, AND ONE MORE THING.
THE BODIES OF THE LABORERS AROUND HERE...
GET RID OF THEM. I DON'T WANT MEXIS TO SMELL OF ROTTING FLESH.
VP
YES SIR!!
AS YOU SAY.
HEHHAHAHA

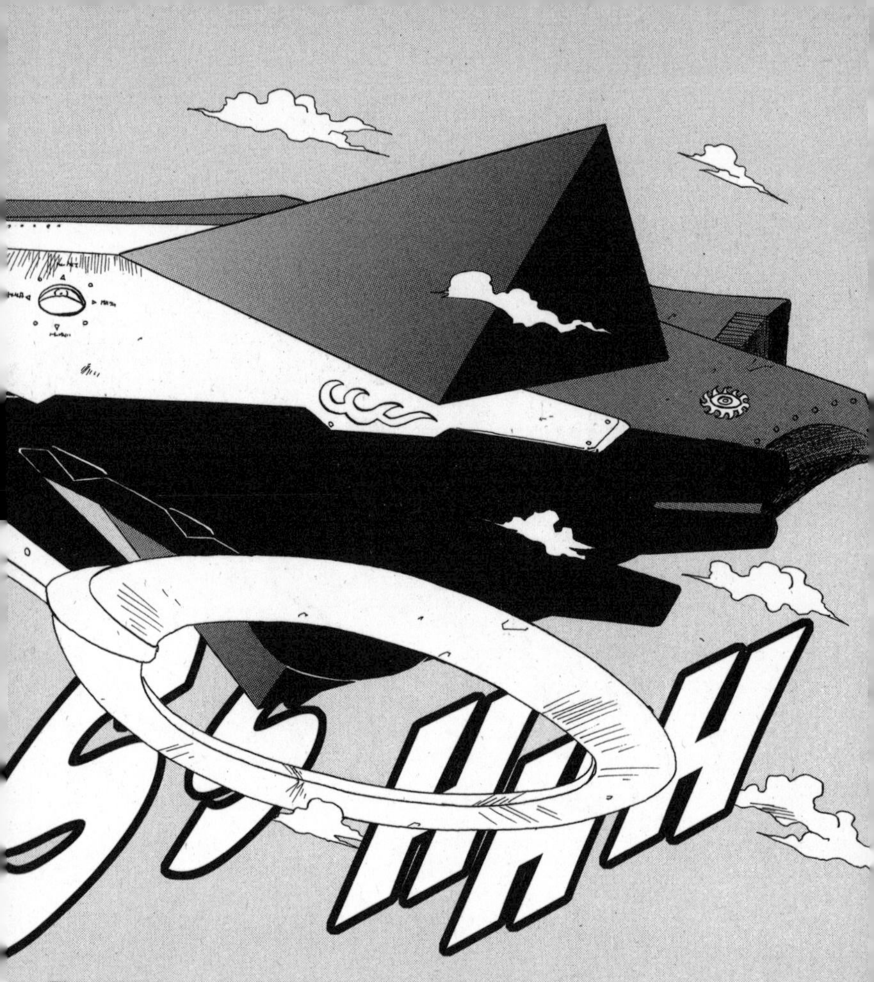

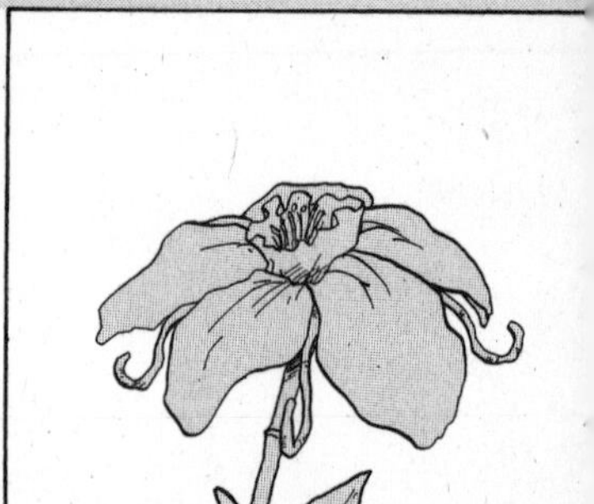

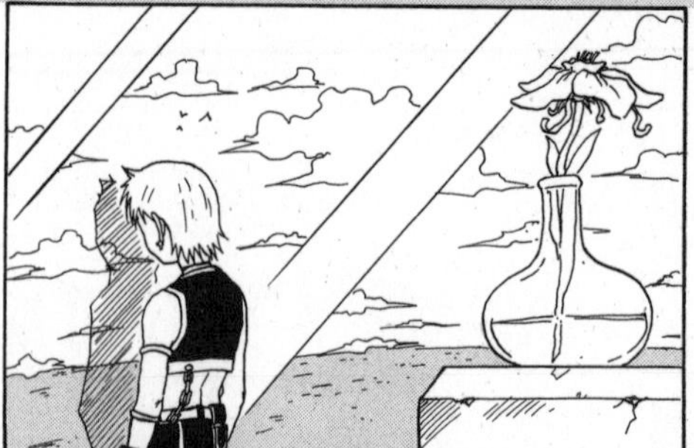

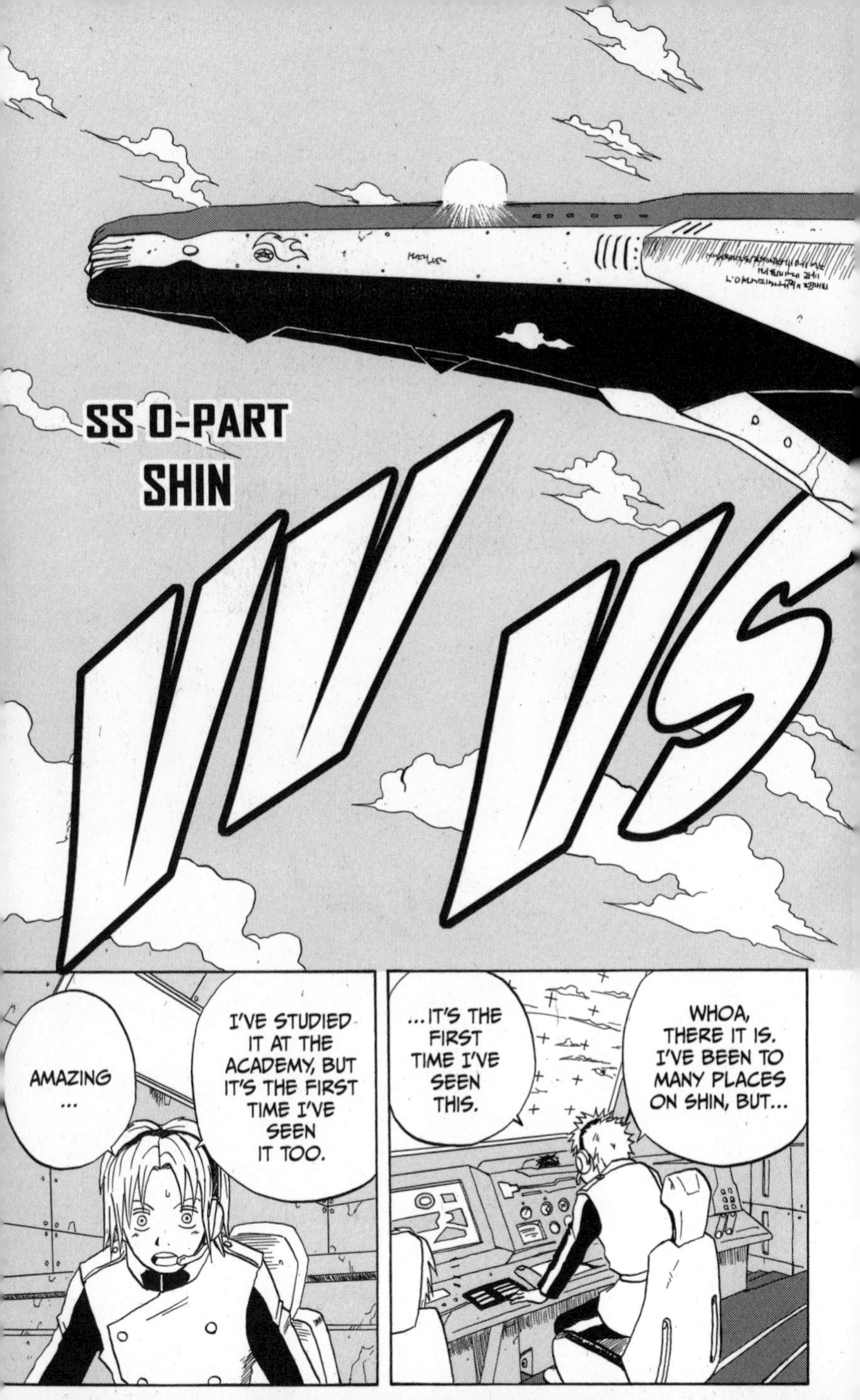
SS O-PART SHIN
WHOA, THERE IT IS. I'VE BEEN TO MANY PLACES ON SHIN, BUT...
...IT'S THE FIRST TIME I'VE SEEN THIS.
I'VE STUDIED IT AT THE ACADEMY, BUT IT'S THE FIRST TIME I'VE SEEN IT TOO.
AMAZING ...

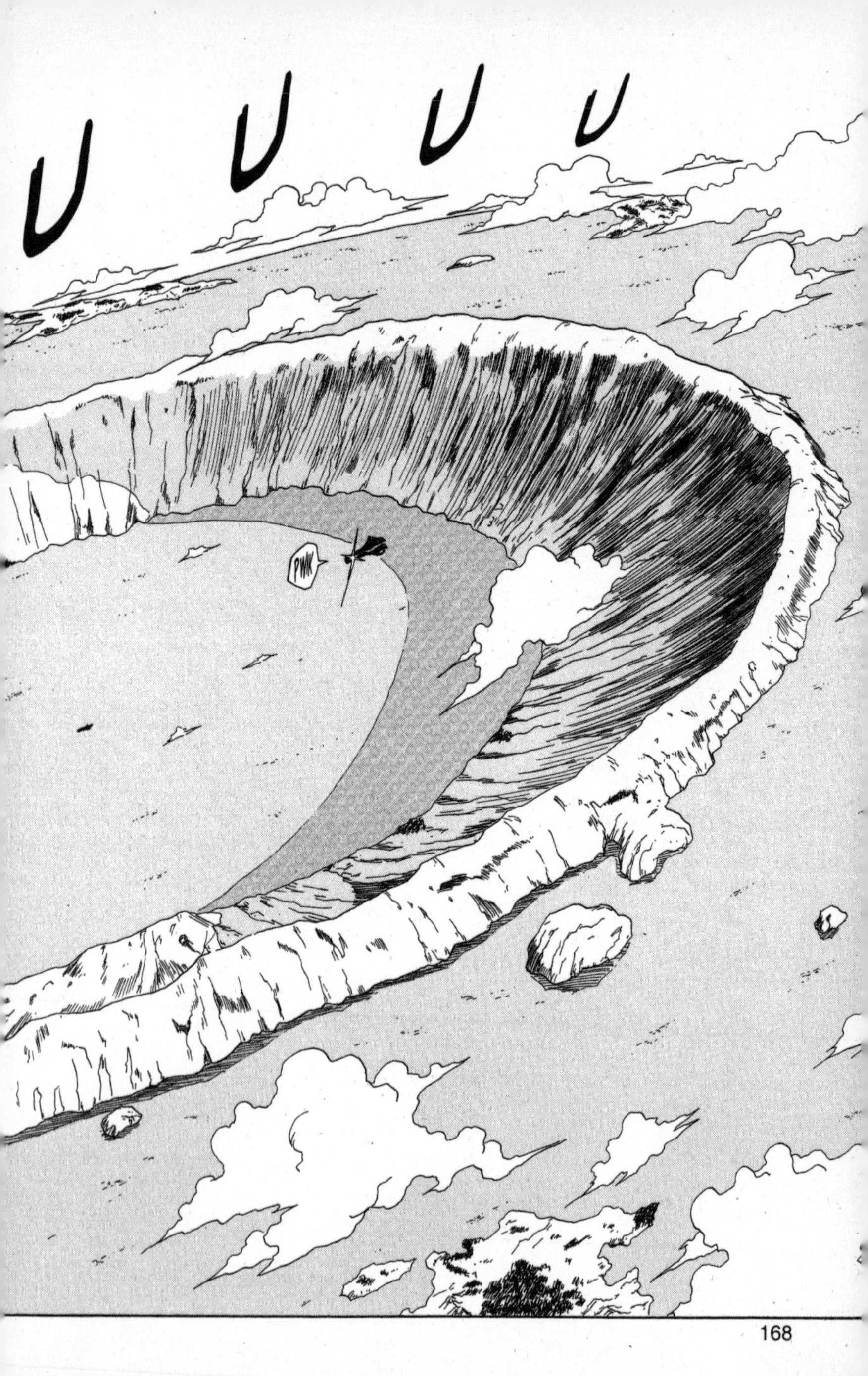
PWIK

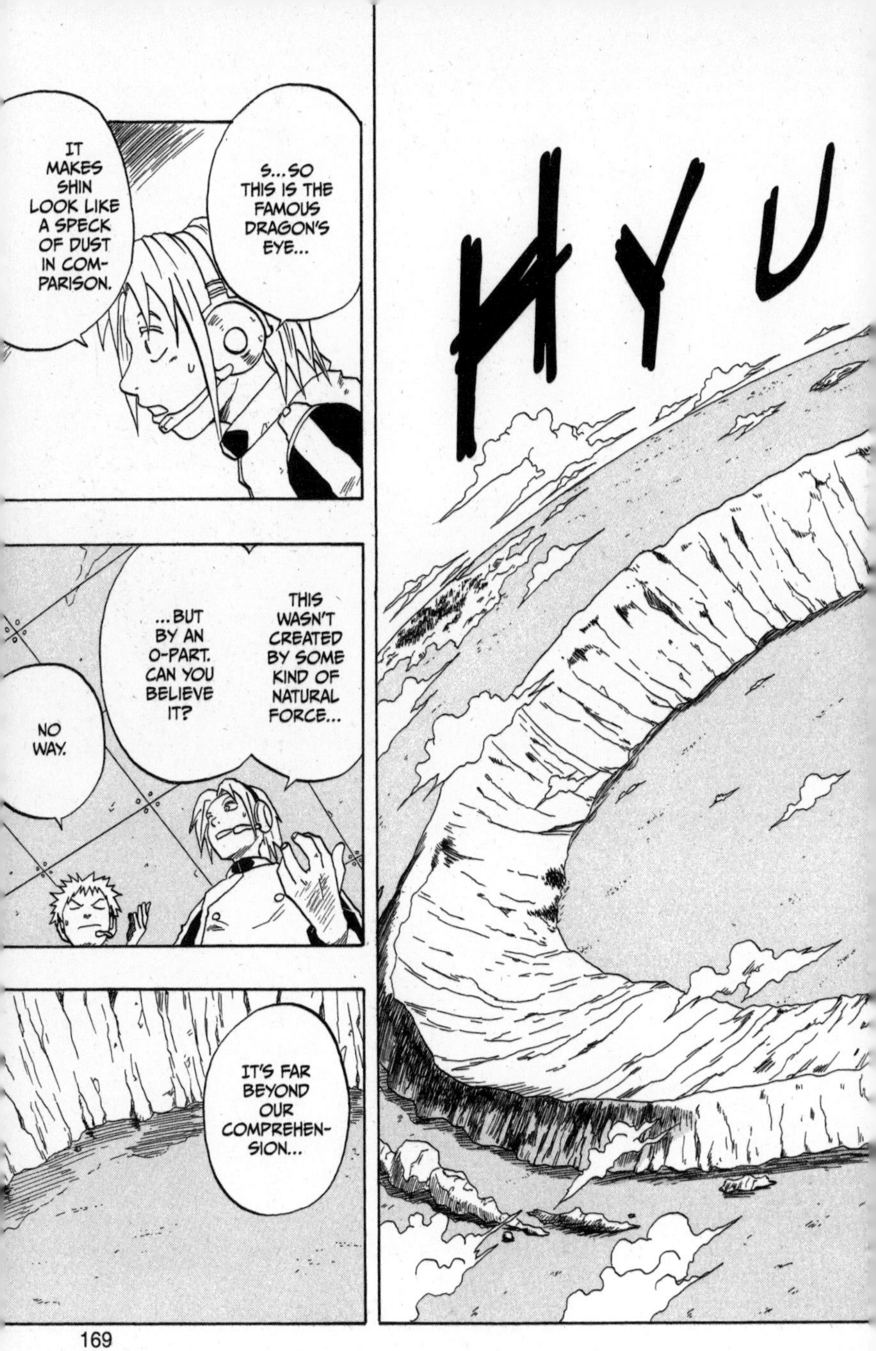
HYU
S...SO THIS IS THE FAMOUS DRAGON'S EYE...
IT MAKES SHIN LOOK LIKE A SPECK OF DUST IN COMPARISON.
THIS WASN'T CREATED BY SOME KIND OF NATURAL FORCE...
...BUT BY AN O-PART. CAN YOU BELIEVE IT?
NO WAY.
IT'S FAR BEYOND OUR COMPREHENSION...

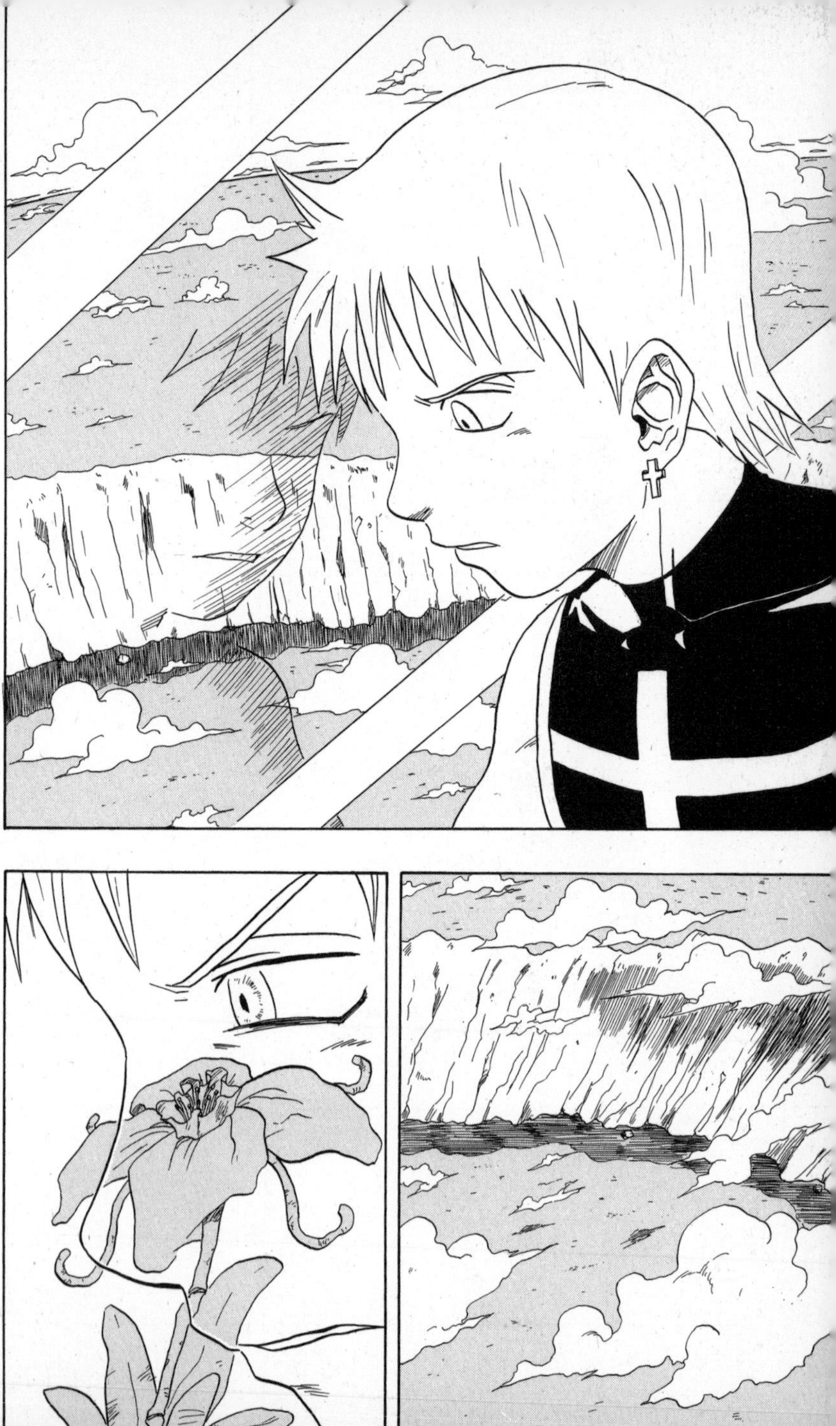

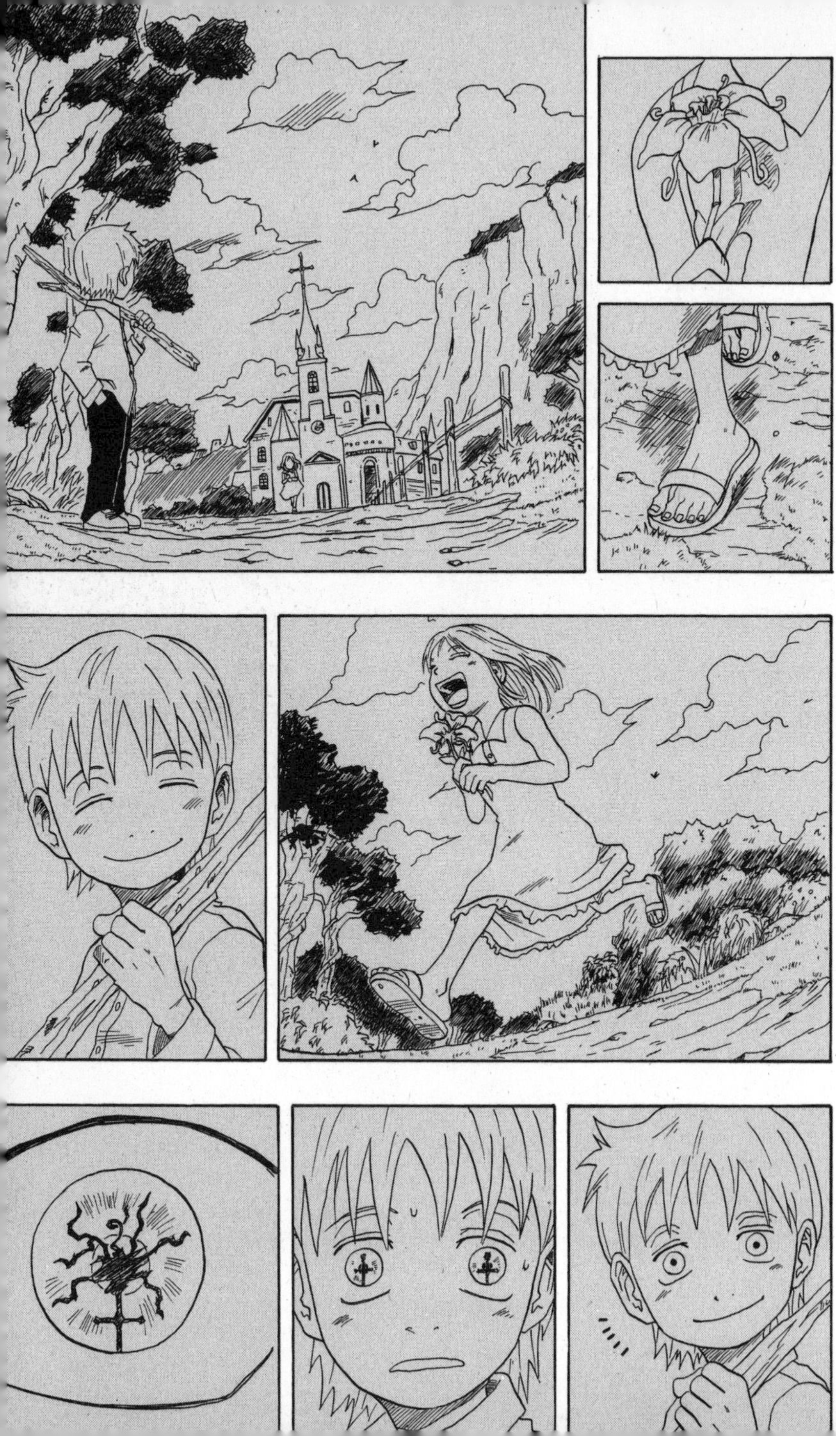
……

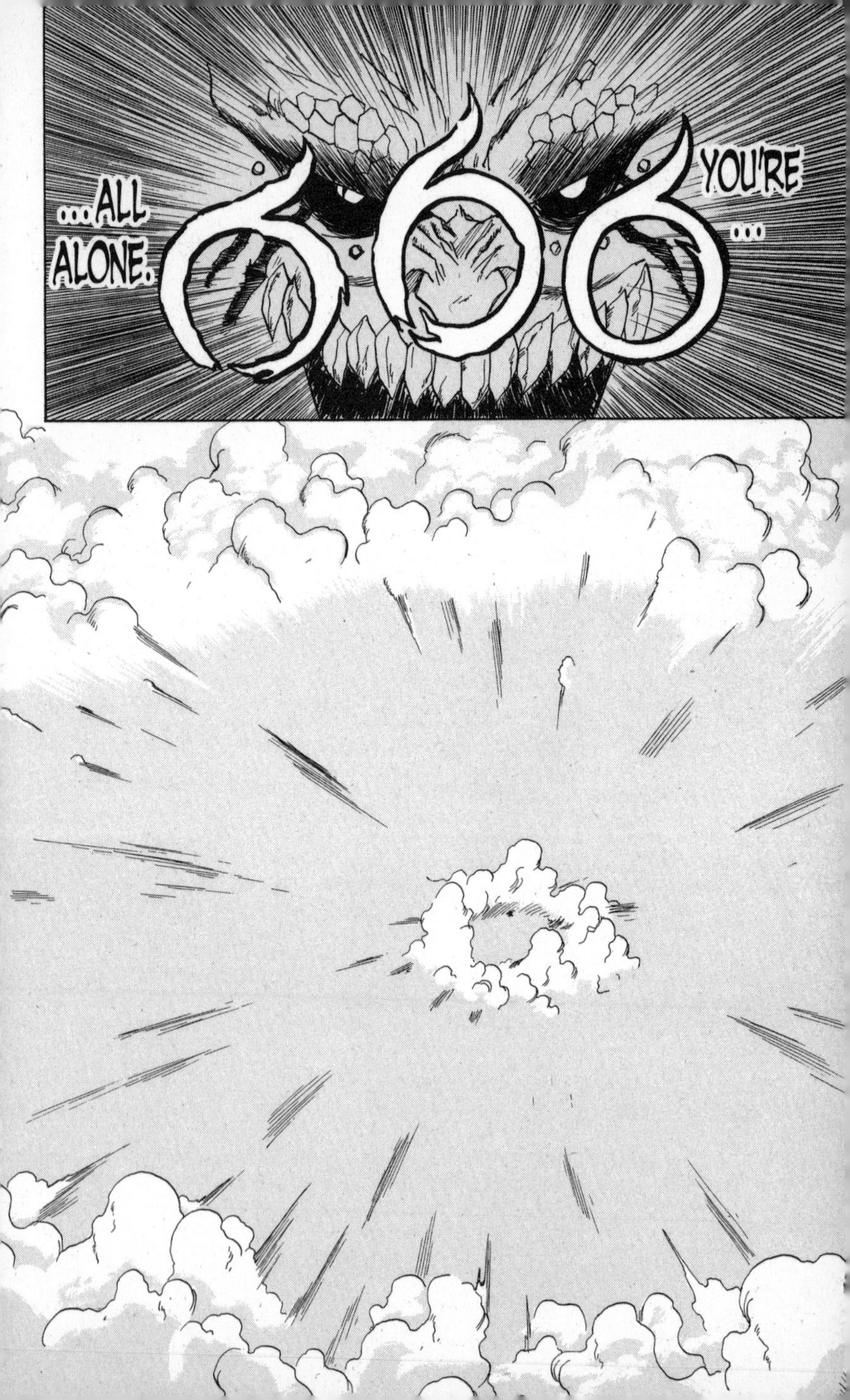
YOU'RE...
...ALL ALONE.

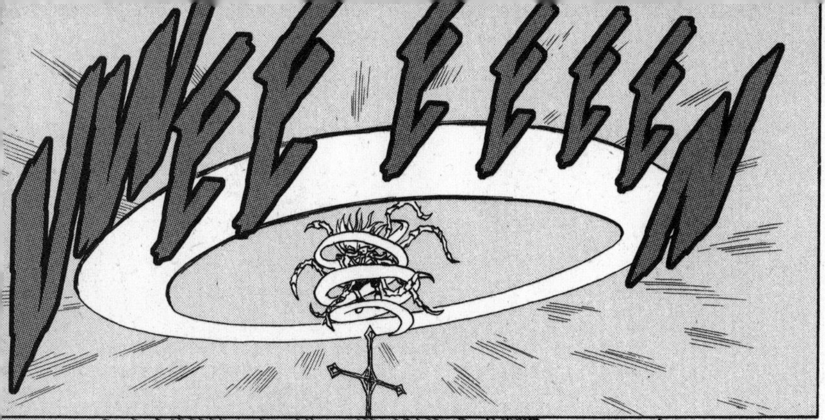
JWEEEEEEN
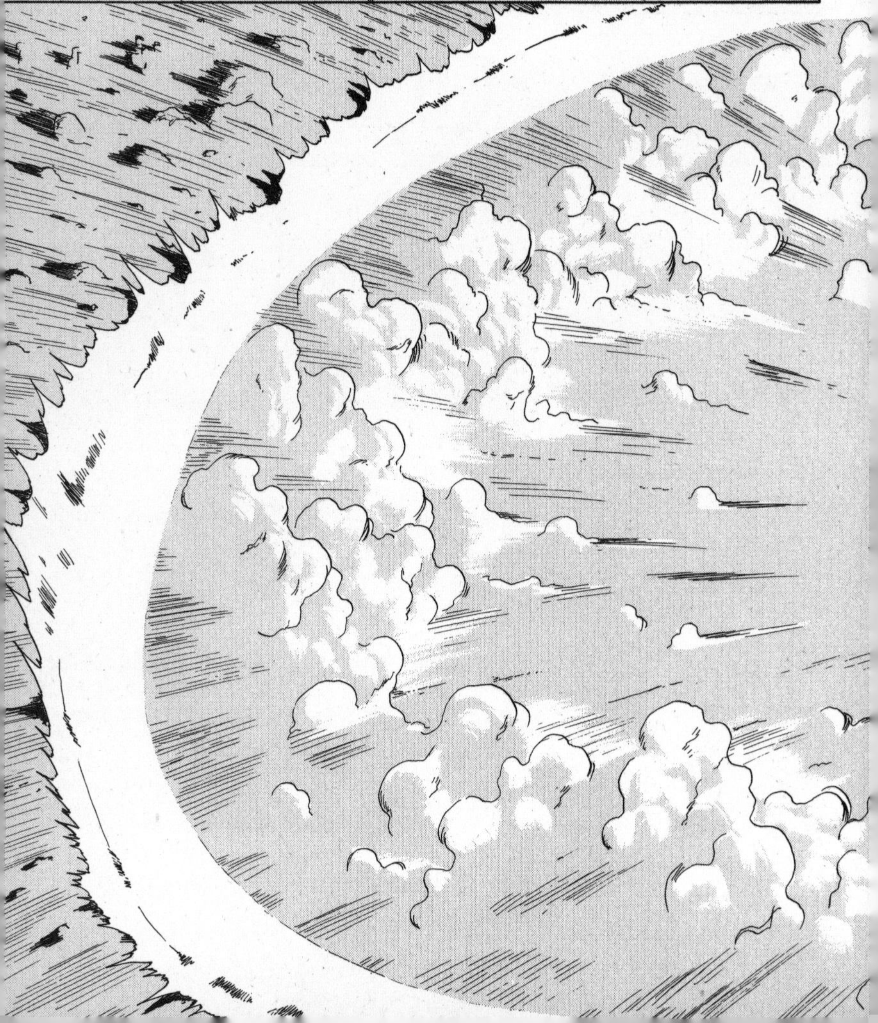

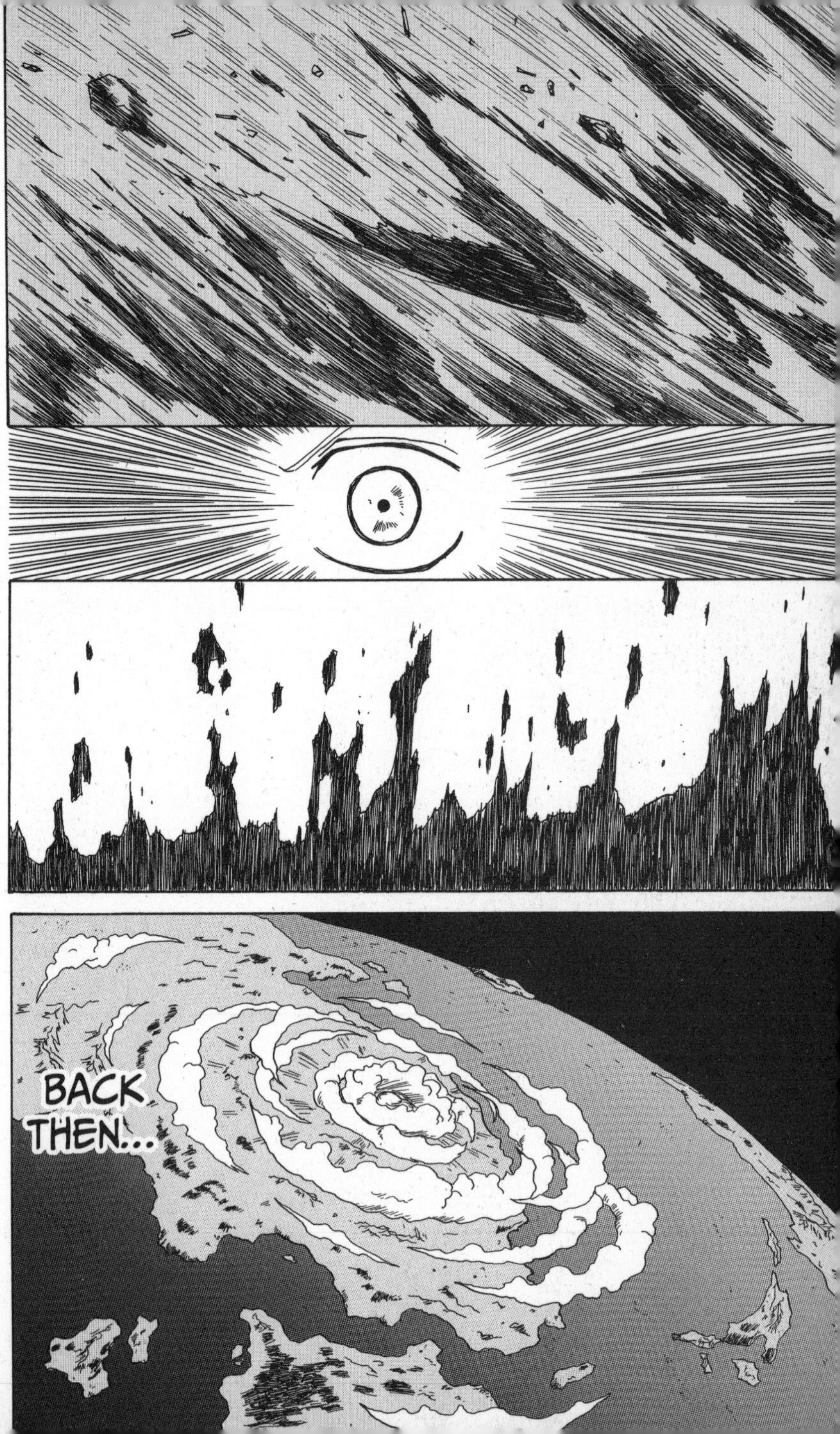
BACK THEN...

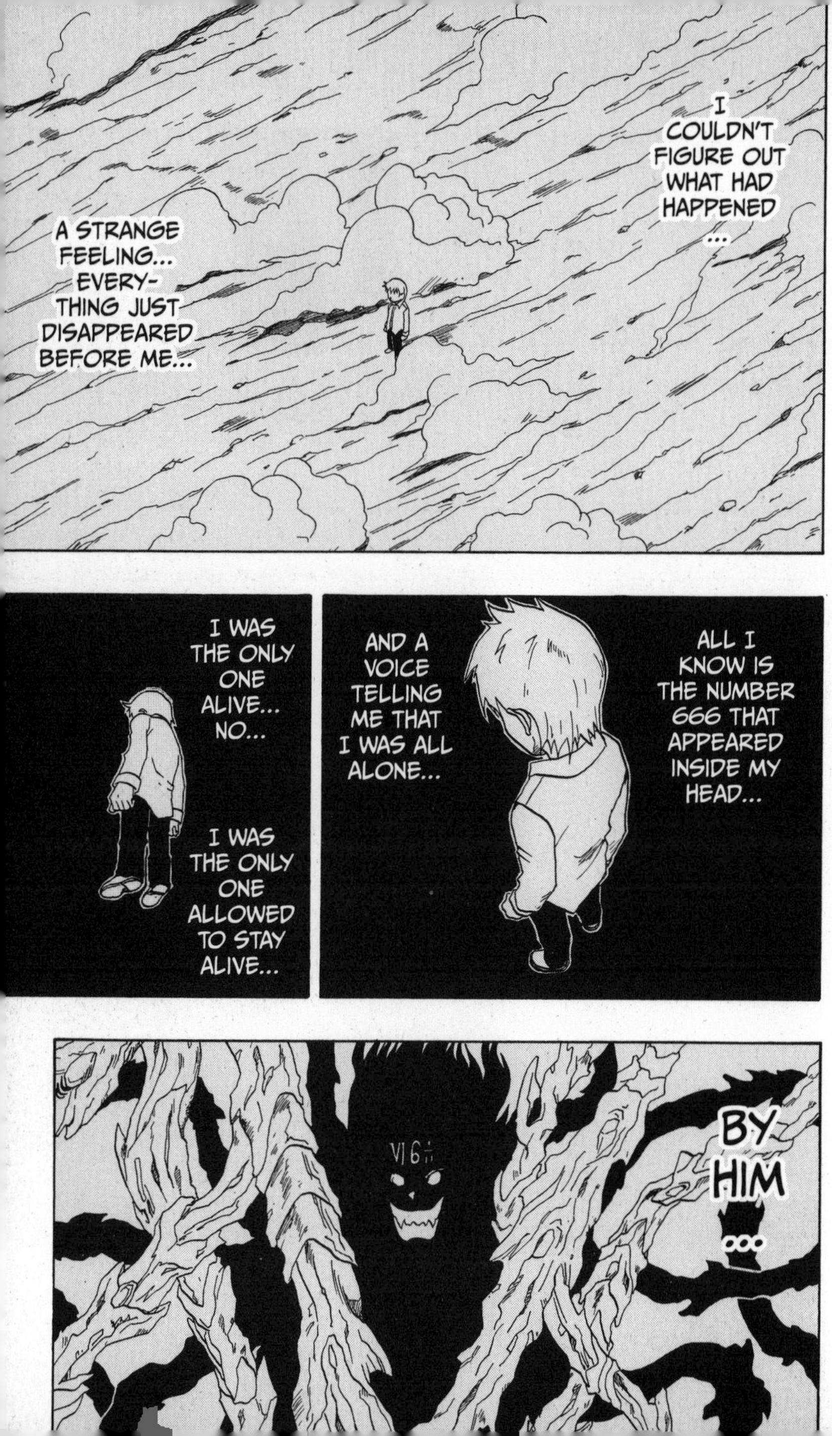
I COULDN'T FIGURE OUT WHAT HAD HAPPENED...
A STRANGE FEELING... EVERY-THING JUST DISAPPEARED BEFORE ME...
ALL I KNOW IS THE NUMBER 666 THAT APPEARED INSIDE MY HEAD...
AND A VOICE TELLING ME THAT I WAS ALL ALONE...
I WAS THE ONLY ONE ALIVE... NO...
I WAS THE ONLY ONE ALLOWED TO STAY ALIVE...
BY HIM...

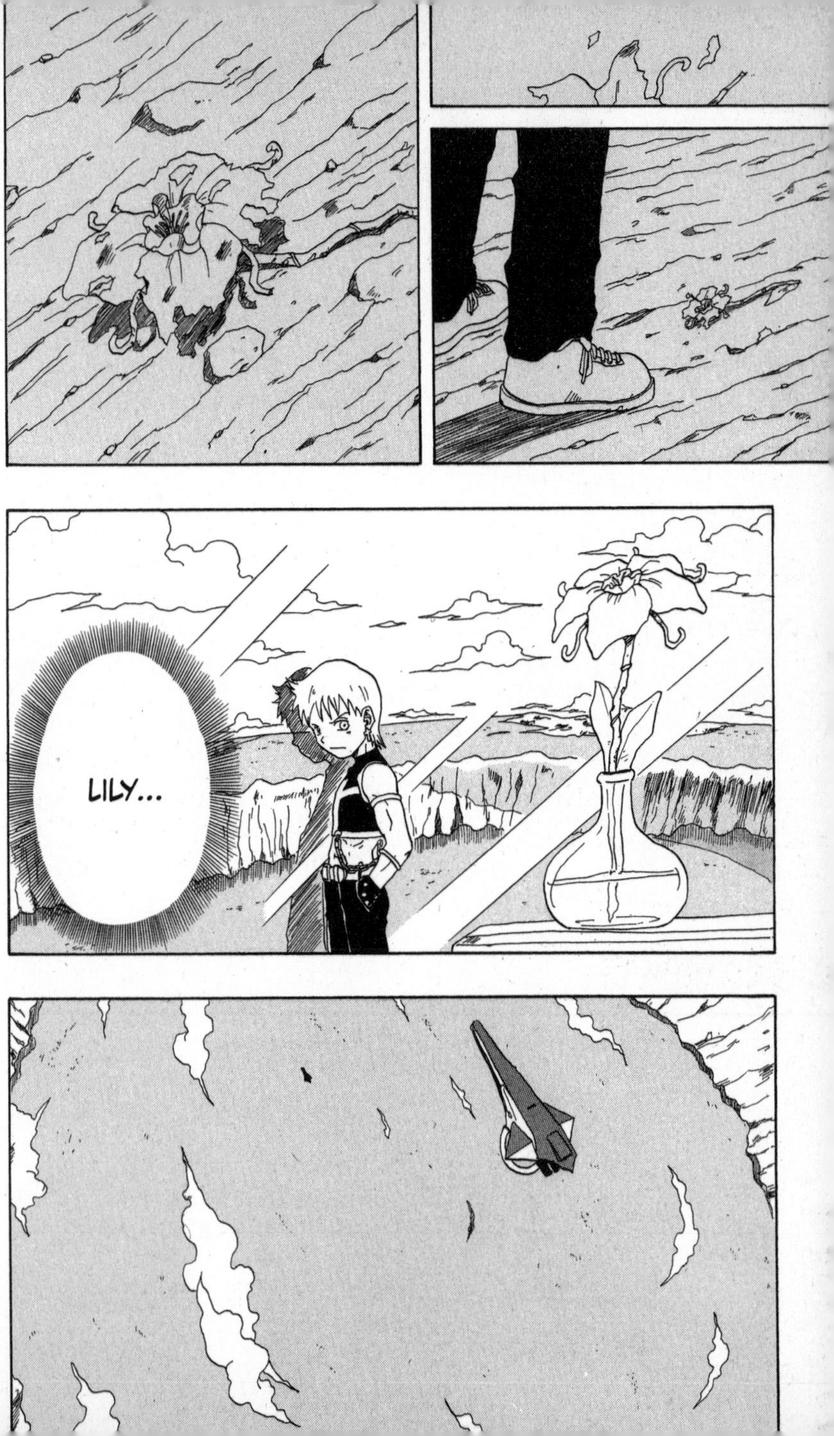
LILY...

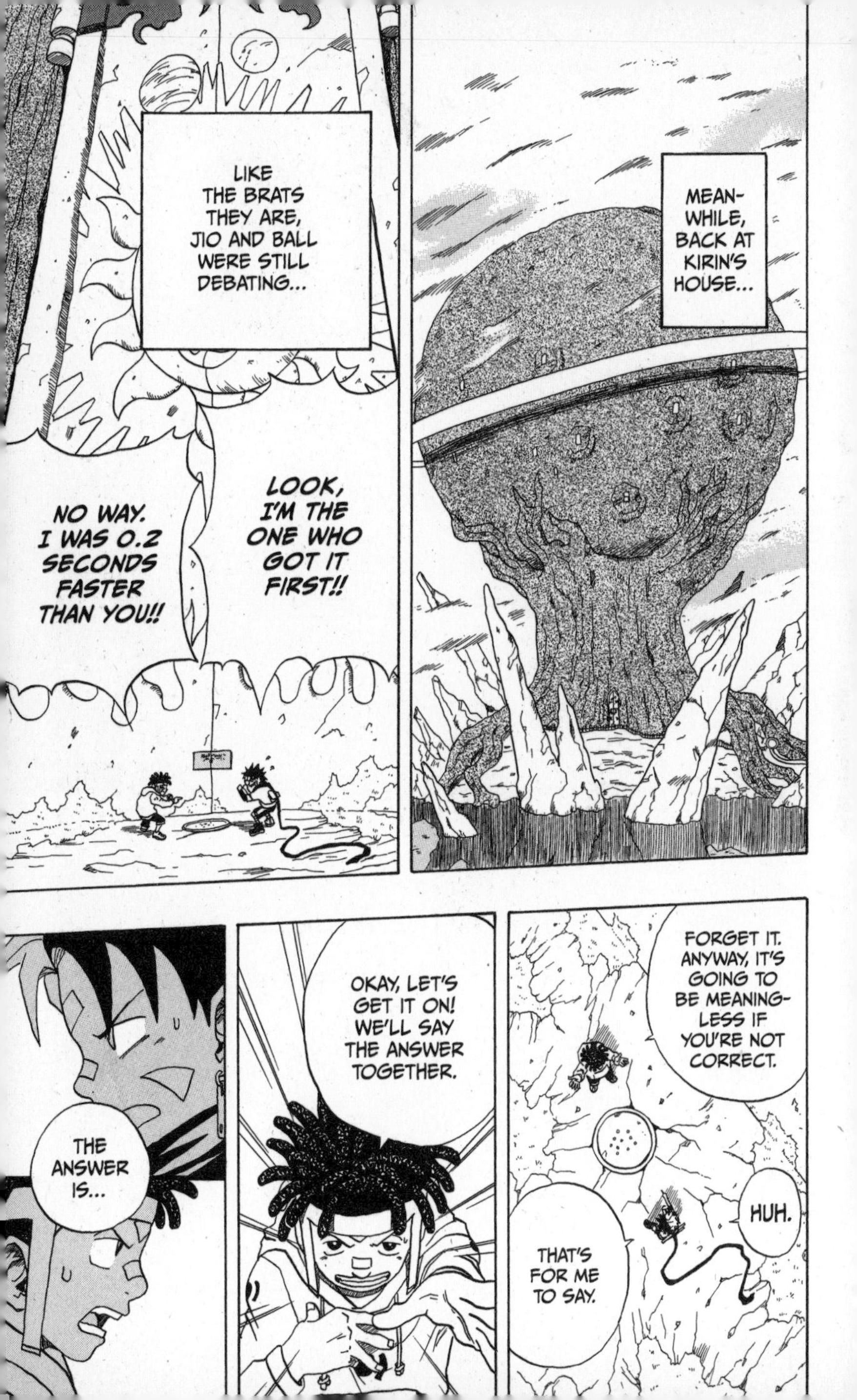
MEAN-WHILE, BACK AT KIRIN'S HOUSE...
LIKE THE BRATS THEY ARE, JIO AND BALL WERE STILL DEBATING...
LOOK, I'M THE ONE WHO GOT IT FIRST!!
NO WAY. I WAS 0.2 SECONDS FASTER THAN YOU!!
FORGET IT. ANYWAY, IT'S GOING TO BE MEANING-LESS IF YOU'RE NOT CORRECT.
HUH.
THAT'S FOR ME TO SAY.
OKAY, LET'S GET IT ON! WE'LL SAY THE ANSWER TOGETHER.
THE ANSWER IS...

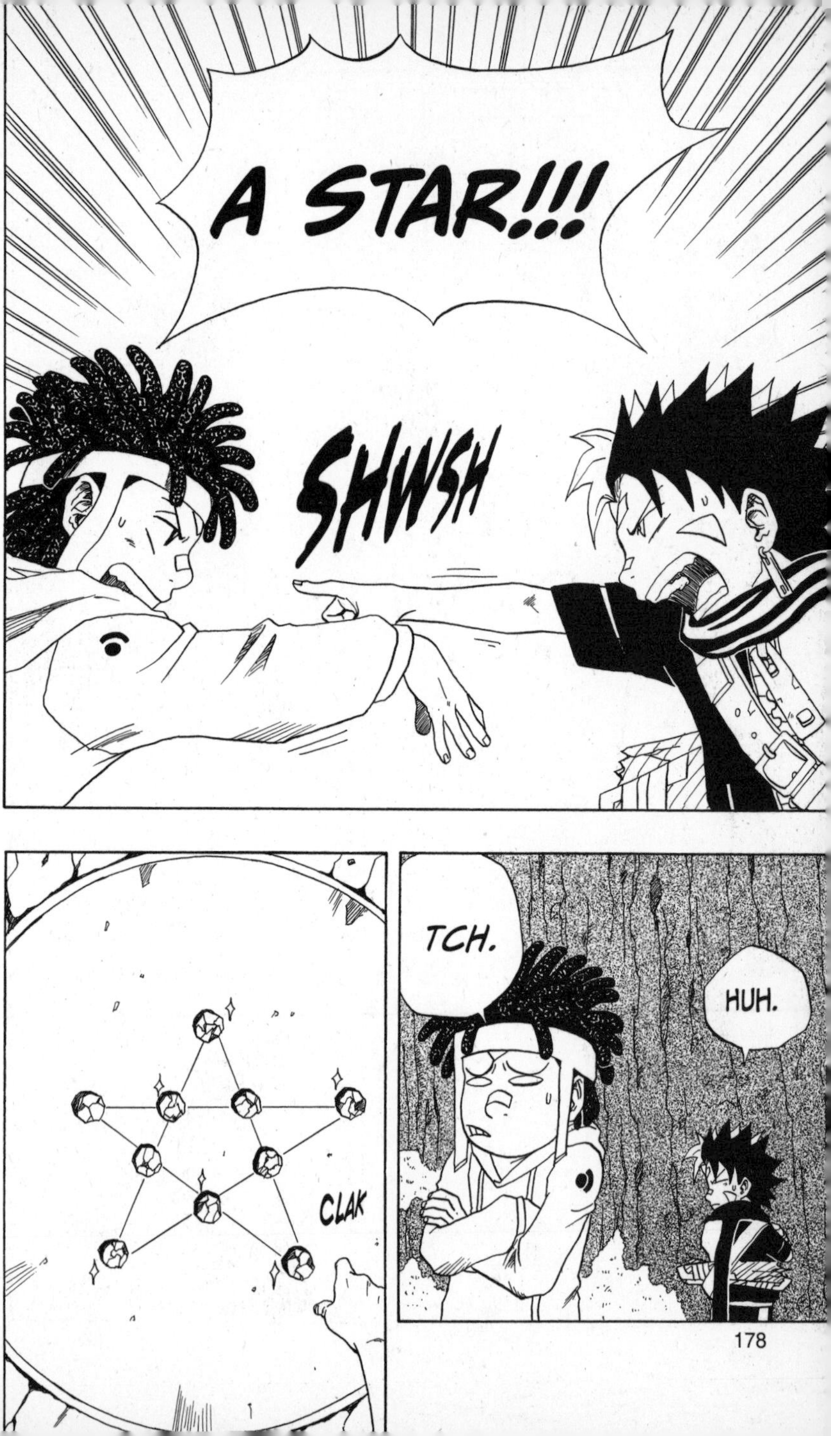
A STAR!!!
SHWSH
TCH.
HUH.
CLAK

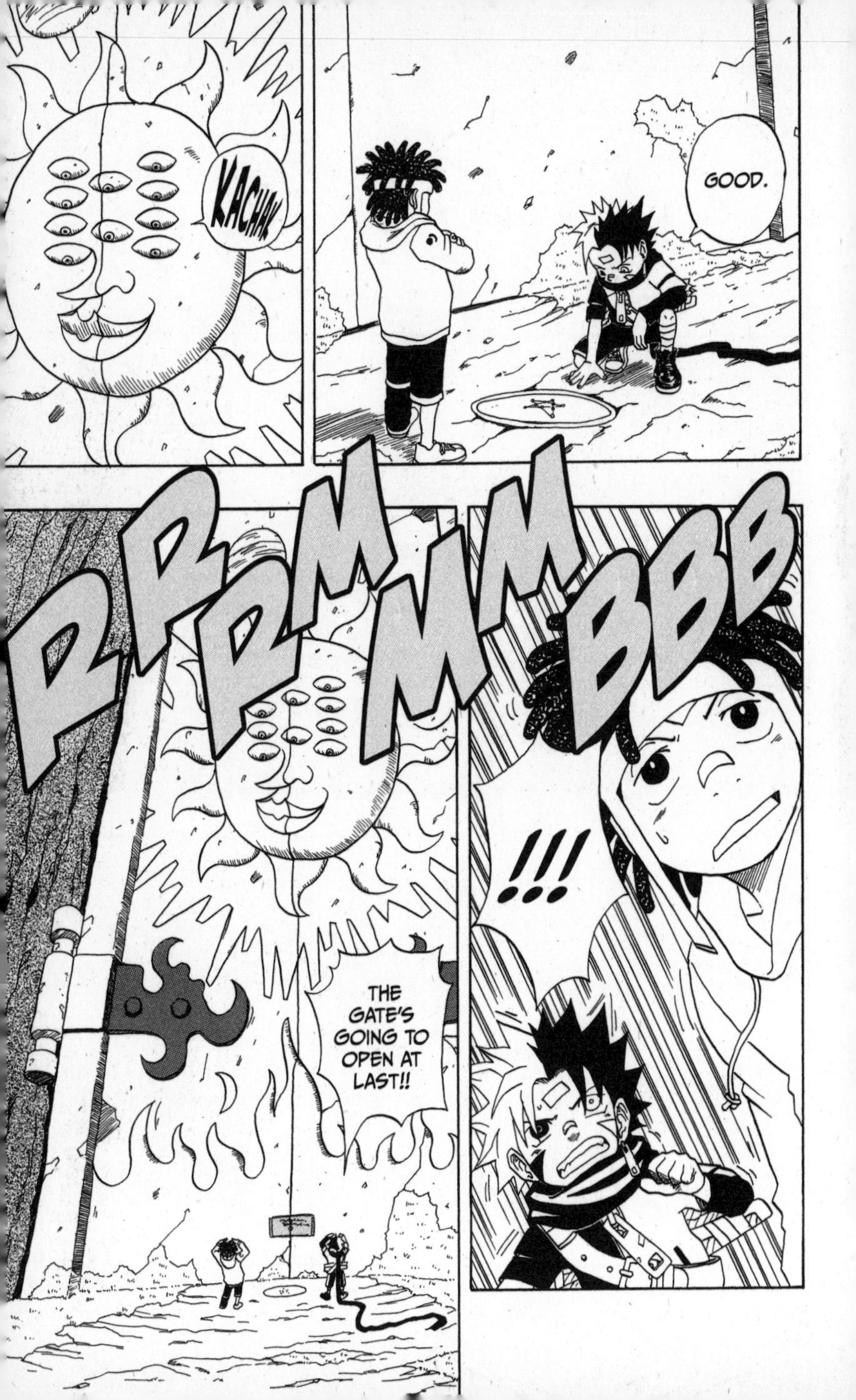
GOOD.
KACHAK
RRRMMMMBBB
!!!
THE GATE'S GOING TO OPEN AT LAST!!

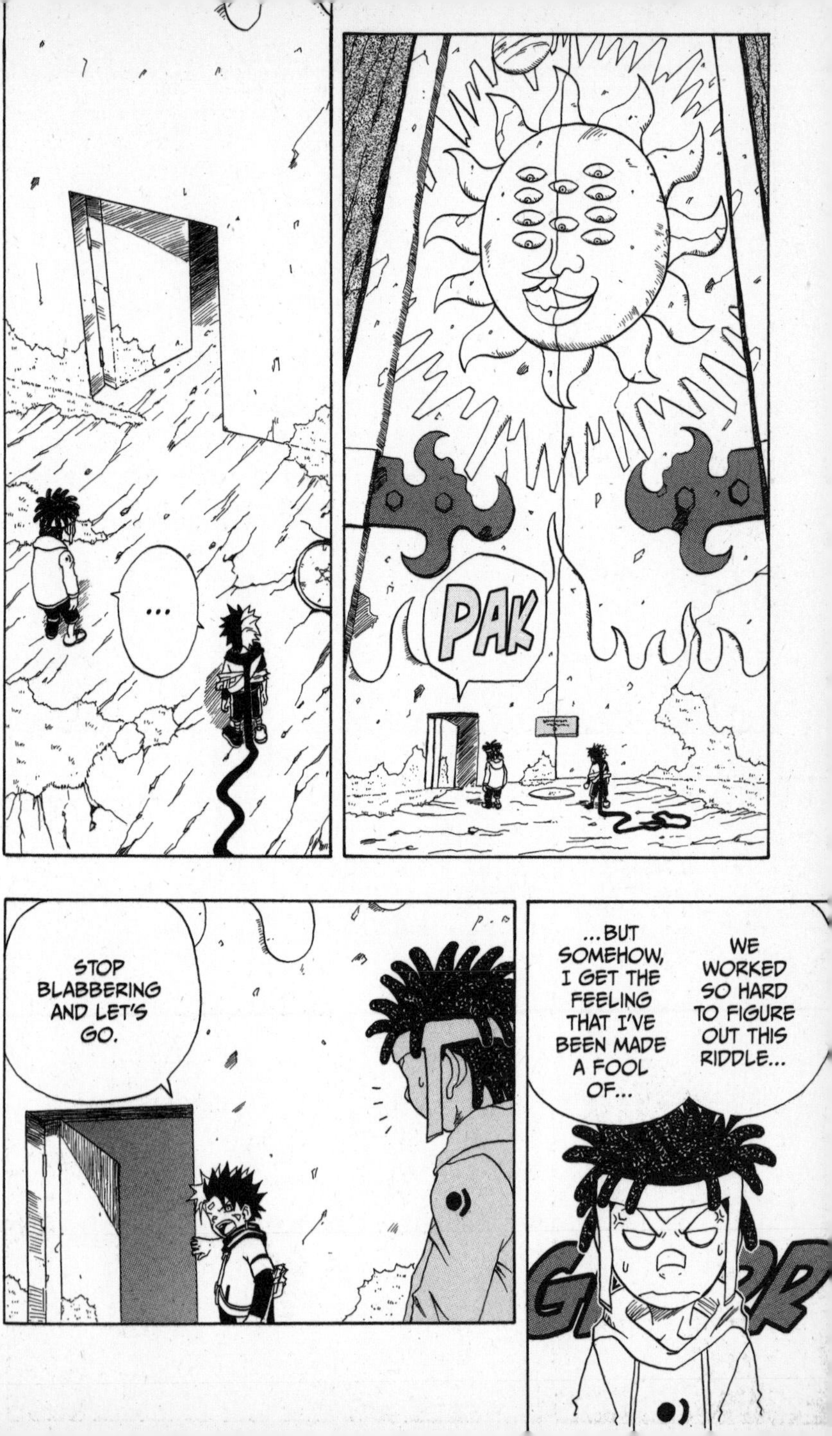
PAK
...
WE WORKED SO HARD TO FIGURE OUT THIS RIDDLE...
...BUT SOMEHOW, I GET THE FEELING THAT I'VE BEEN MADE A FOOL OF...
STOP BLABBERING AND LET'S GO.

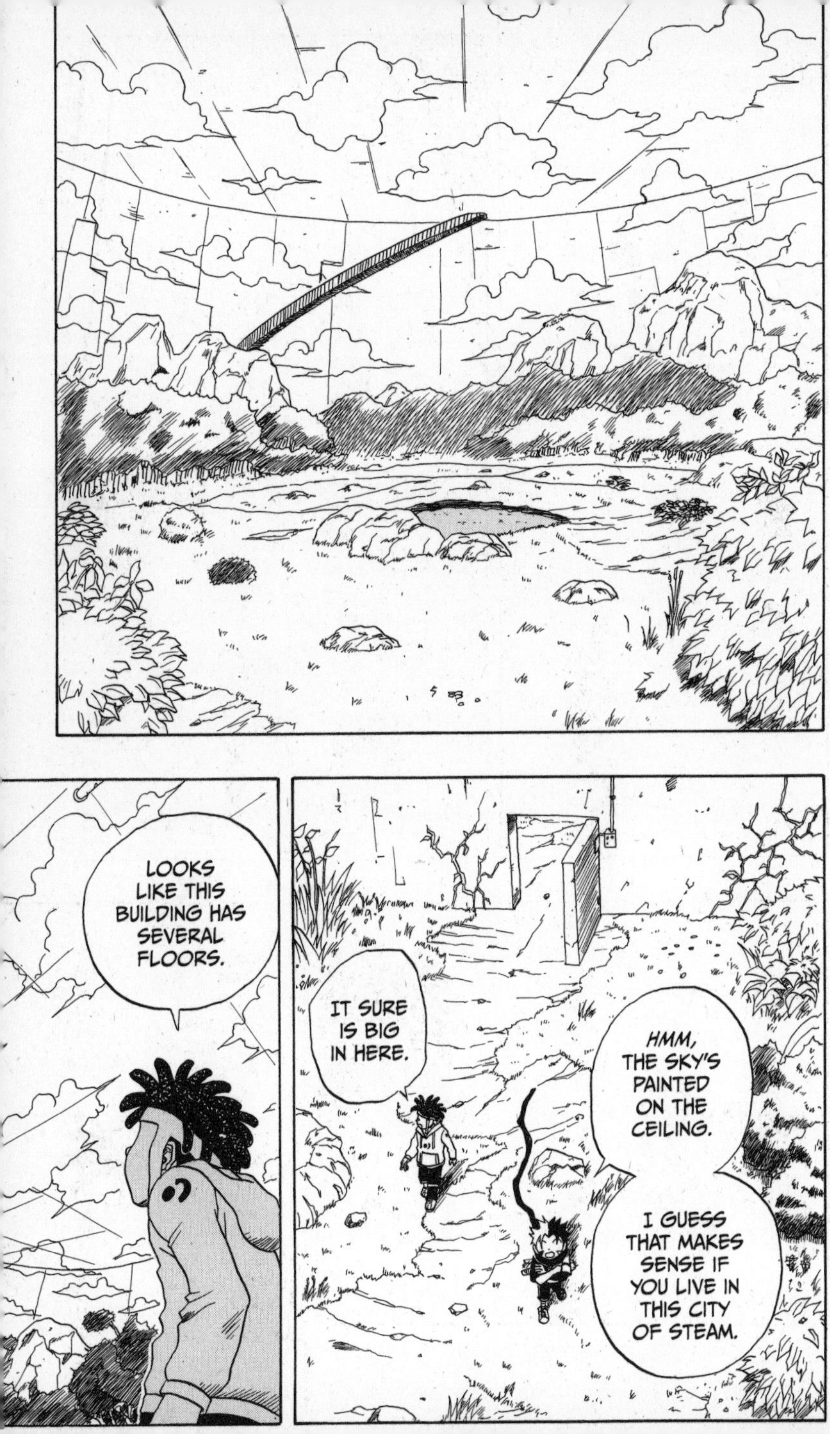
HMM, THE SKY'S PAINTED ON THE CEILING.
I GUESS THAT MAKES SENSE IF YOU LIVE IN THIS CITY OF STEAM.
IT SURE IS BIG IN HERE.
LOOKS LIKE THIS BUILDING HAS SEVERAL FLOORS.

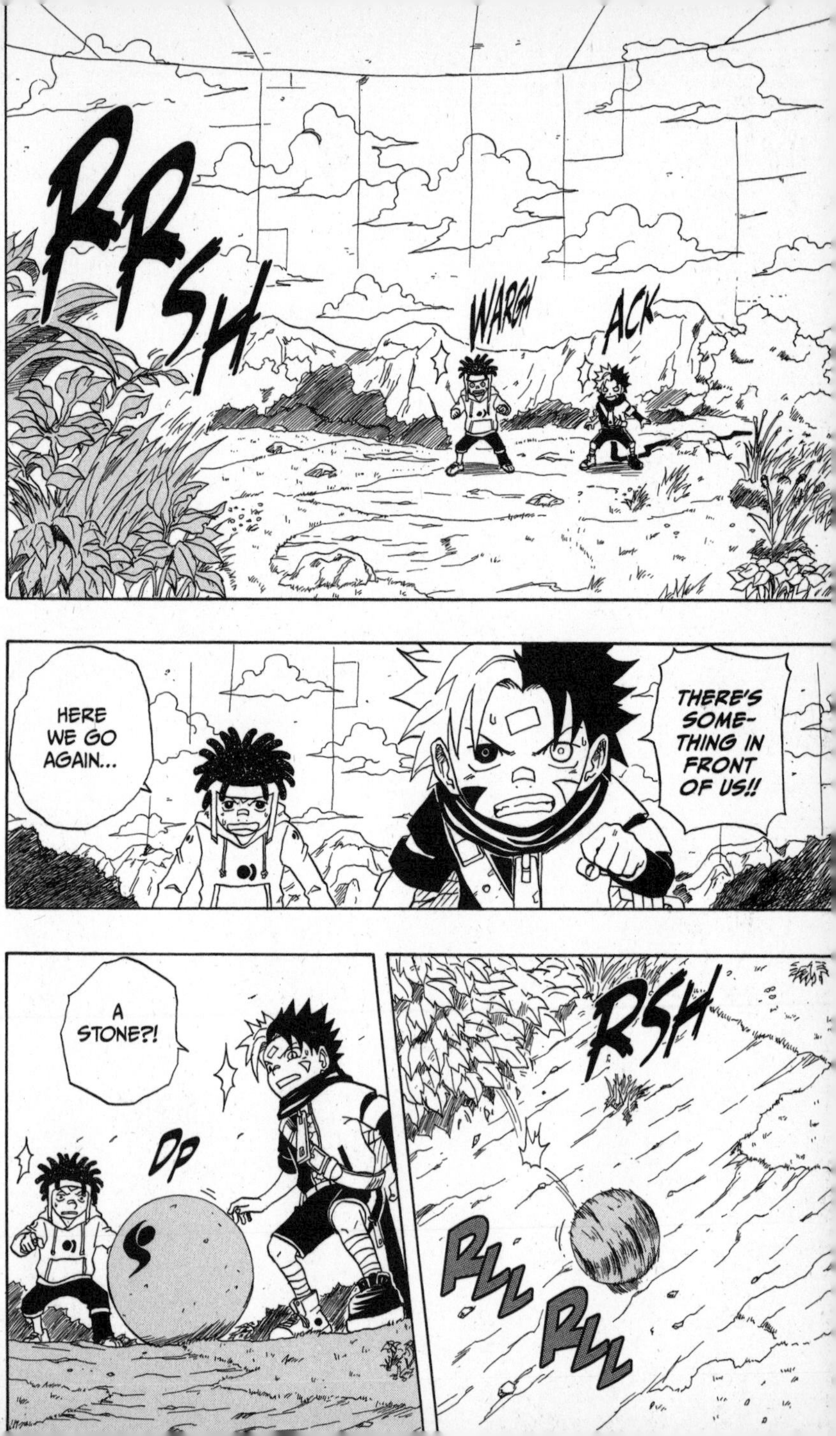
ACK
WARGH
RRSH
THERE'S SOME-THING IN FRONT OF US!!
HERE WE GO AGAIN...
RSH
RLL
RLL
A STONE?!
DP

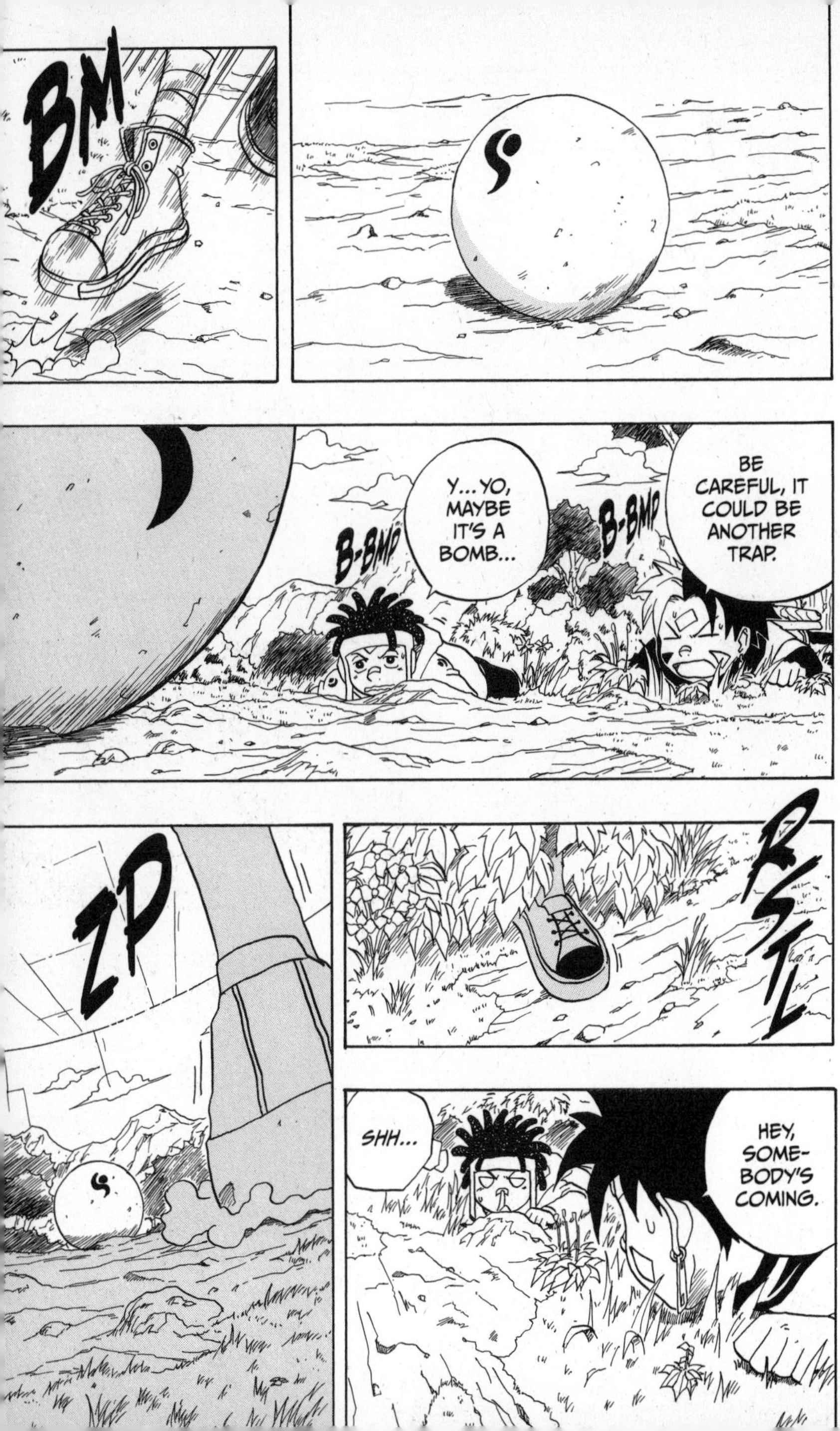
BM
BE CAREFUL, IT COULD BE ANOTHER TRAP.
B-BMP
Y...YO, MAYBE IT'S A BOMB...
B-BMP
RSTL
HEY, SOME-BODY'S COMING.
SHH...
ZP

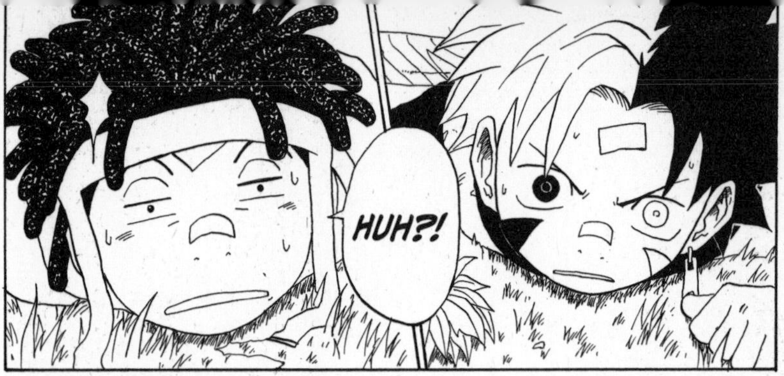
HUH?!
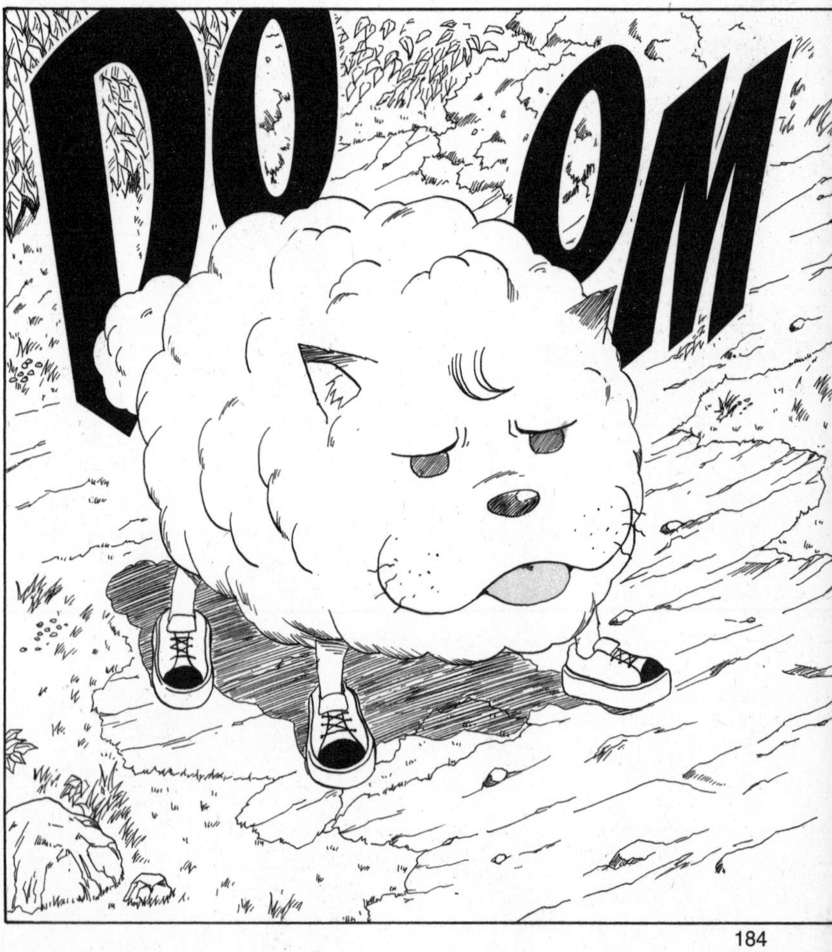
DOOM

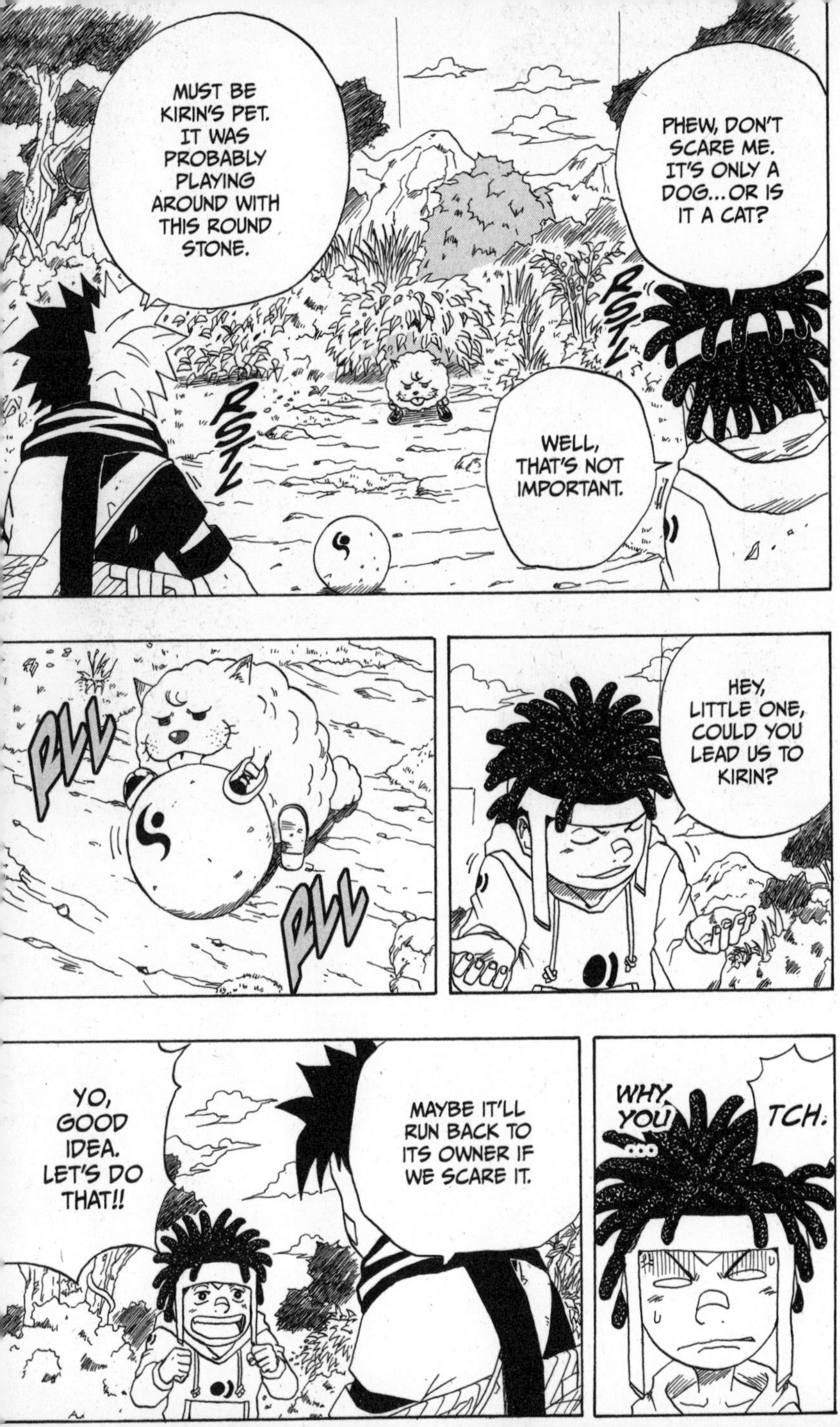
PHEW, DON'T SCARE ME. IT'S ONLY A DOG...OR IS IT A CAT?
RSTL
MUST BE KIRIN'S PET. IT WAS PROBABLY PLAYING AROUND WITH THIS ROUND STONE.
RSTL
WELL, THAT'S NOT IMPORTANT.
HEY, LITTLE ONE, COULD YOU LEAD US TO KIRIN?
RLL
RLL
TCH.
WHY, YOU...
MAYBE IT'LL RUN BACK TO ITS OWNER IF WE SCARE IT.
YO, GOOD IDEA. LET'S DO THAT!!

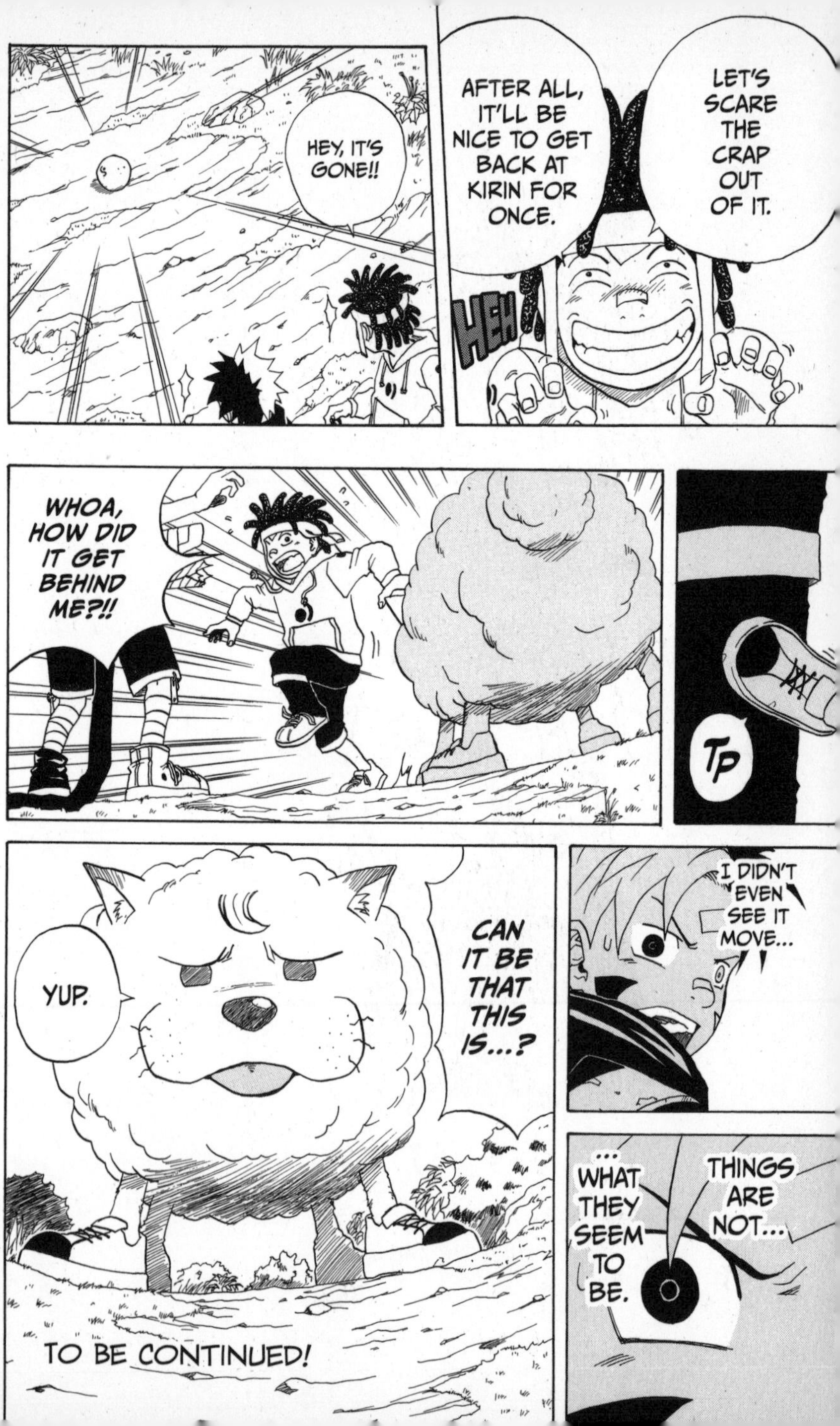
LET'S SCARE THE CRAP OUT OF IT.
AFTER ALL, IT'LL BE NICE TO GET BACK AT KIRIN FOR ONCE.
HEH
HEY, IT'S GONE!!
TP
WHOA, HOW DID IT GET BEHIND ME?!!
I DIDN'T EVEN SEE IT MOVE...
THINGS ARE NOT...
...WHAT THEY SEEM TO BE.
CAN IT BE THAT THIS IS...?
YUP.
TO BE CONTINUED!

◄BALL

THIS IS WHAT BALL INITIALLY LOOKED LIKE. UNLIKE NOW, HIS FACE IS NOT THAT ROUND, AND HIS HAIR IS LONGER. NOW THAT I SEE IT AGAIN, THIS ONE SEEMS BETTER, DOESN'T IT?!
.....

SEISHI AND CENTIPEDES

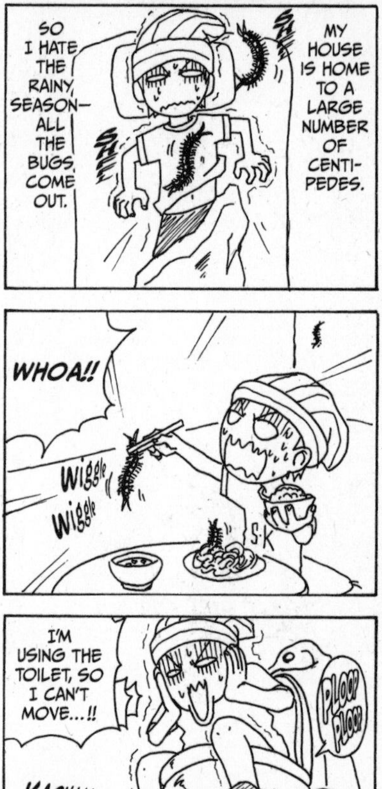
MY HOUSE IS HOME TO A LARGE NUMBER OF CENTIPEDES.
SO I HATE THE RAINY SEASON— ALL THE BUGS COME OUT.
WHOA!!
wiggle
wiggle
I'M USING THE TOILET, SO I CAN'T MOVE...!!
PLOOP PLOOP
KASHAAA
I WAS SO IRRITATED WITH THEM...
GRRR
GRR
...THAT I DREW A CENTIPEDE IN MY MANGA, AND HAD JIO KICK THE CRAP OUT OF IT.
SKRCH
SKRCH

SEISHI AND HIS TAILBONE

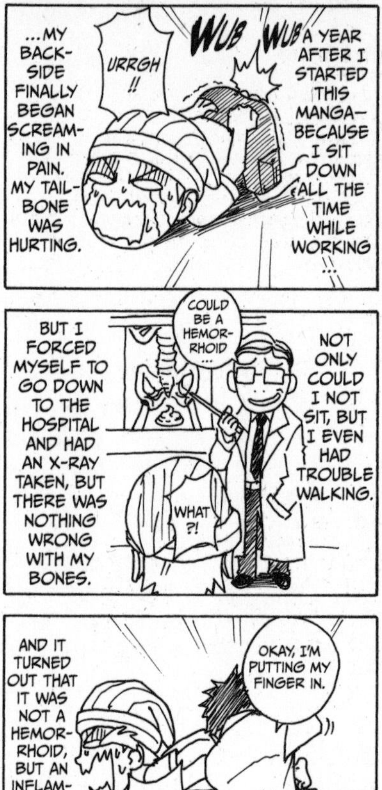
A YEAR AFTER I STARTED THIS MANGA— BECAUSE I SIT DOWN ALL THE TIME WHILE WORKING...
WUB WUB
URRGH!!
...MY BACKSIDE FINALLY BEGAN SCREAMING IN PAIN. MY TAILBONE WAS HURTING.
NOT ONLY COULD I NOT SIT, BUT I EVEN HAD TROUBLE WALKING.
COULD BE A HEMORRHOID...
WHAT?!
BUT I FORCED MYSELF TO GO DOWN TO THE HOSPITAL AND HAD AN X-RAY TAKEN, BUT THERE WAS NOTHING WRONG WITH MY BONES.
OKAY, I'M PUTTING MY FINGER IN.
SO, WITH TEARS IN MY EYES, I WENT TO A HEMORRHOID SPECIALIST.
AAAA-ARGH!!
AND IT TURNED OUT THAT IT WAS NOT A HEMORRHOID, BUT AN INFLAMMATION AROUND MY TAILBONE.
Phew
NOW, I'M GETTING ELECTROTHERAPY ON IT. IT'S SO WARM...

O-Parts CATALOGUE③

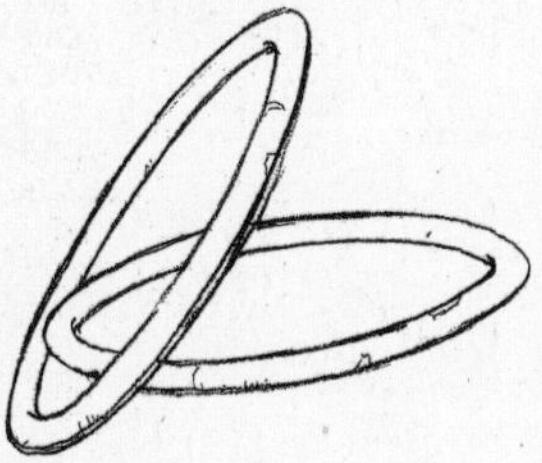

O-PART: BROTHER
O-PART RANK: B
EFFECT: HANDLING (MANIPULATION), TRANSPORTATION OF MATTER
EACH RING HAS ITS OWN EFFECT AND RESONATES WITH ITS TWIN. THIS O-PART IS LIKE TWO BROTHERS. IT IS THOUGHT THAT IT WAS USED IN THE ANCIENT TIMES TO MOVE THINGS BETWEEN TWO FARAWAY AREAS, AS WELL AS TO TAKE OR STASH OBJECTS ON HIGH PLACES.

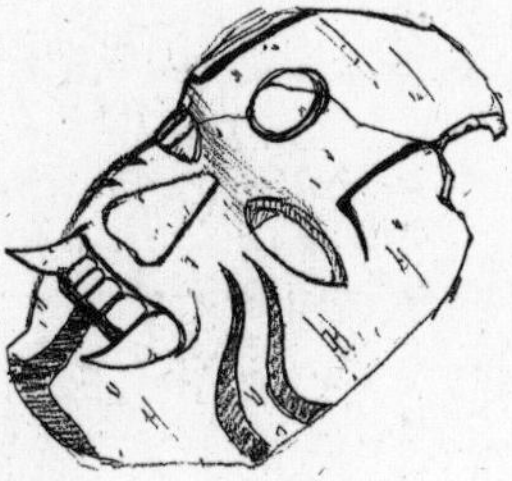

O-PART: MASK OF MAGIMA
O-PART RANK: C
EFFECT: TELEPATHY, ?
AN O-PART USED BY THE CONTACT MAN OF THE ZENOM SYNDICATE. ITS EFFECT IS PRETTY AMAZING, BUT IT'S ALSO SUPPOSED TO FEEL REALLY COMFORTABLE WHEN YOU WEAR IT.

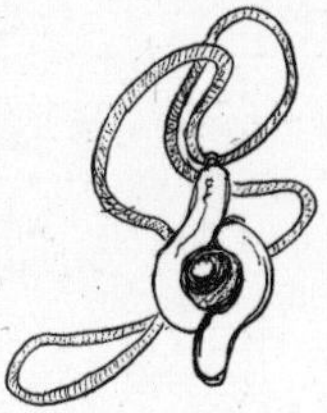

O-PART: THE JADE PENDANT(?)
O-PART RANK: S
EFFECT: MORE THAN 100 KNOWN AT THIS POINT
A MEMENTO OF RUBY'S FATHER, TO HER SURPRISE, IT'S ALSO AN S-RANK O-PART. JUST TO HAVE IT WITH YOU IS CONSIDERED A CRIME. IF THE GOVERNMENT FINDS OUT, RUBY WILL BE CHARGED WITH ILLEGAL POSSESSION, WHICH IS A SERIOUS OFFENSE.

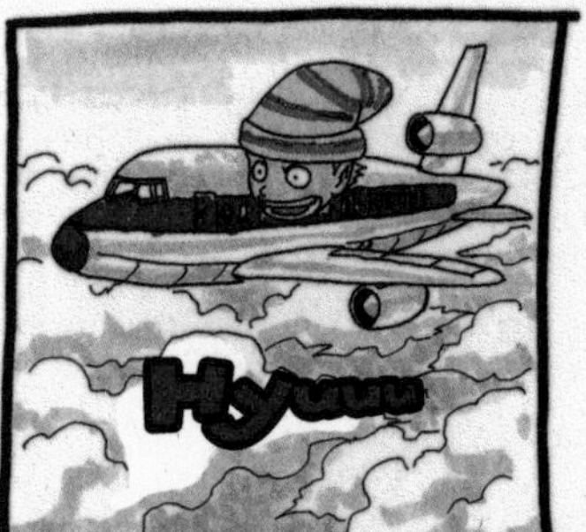
Hyuuu

SEISHI KISHIMOTO

I'm the only one in my whole family who has never ridden a plane before. Since I've come this far already, maybe I'll never bother riding one...

O-Parts HUNTER™ 3

VIZ Media Edition
STORY AND ART BY SEISHI KISHIMOTO

English Adaptation/Tetsuichiro Miyaki
Touch-up Art & Lettering/Gia Cam Luc
Design/Amy Martin
Editor/Kit Fox

Managing Editor/Annette Roman
Editorial Director/Elizabeth Kawasaki
Editor in Chief/Alvin Lu
Sr. Director of Acquisitions/Rika Inouye
Sr. VP of Marketing/Liza Coppola
Exec. VP of Sales & Marketing/John Easum
Publisher/Hyoe Narita

Printed in the U.S.A.

Published by VIZ Media, LLC
P.O. Box 77010
San Francisco, CA 94107

10 9 8 7 6 5 4 3 2 1
First printing, April 2007

www.viz.com   store.viz.com

LOVE MANGA?
LET US KNOW WHAT YOU THINK!